Also by Joan Nathan

Jewish Cooking in America,
Expanded Edition

The Jewish Holiday Baker

Jewish Cooking in America

The Jewish Holiday Kitchen

The Children's Jewish Holiday Kitchen

An American Folklife Cookbook

The Flavor of Jerusalem
(with Judy Stacey Goldman)

The Foods of Israel Today

The Foods of
Israel Today

Joan Nathan

Alfred A. Knopf

New York

2001

THIS IS A BORZOI BOOK
PUBLISHED BY ALFRED A. KNOPF

Copyright © 2001 by Joan Nathan
Color photographs copyright © 2001 by Nelli Sheffer

Library of Congress Cataloging-in-Publication Data

Nathan, Joan.
    The foods of Israel today / by Joan Nathan.
       p.   cm.
    Includes bibliographical references and index.
    ISBN 0-679-45107-2
    1. Cookery, Israeli.   I. Title.
TX724 .N3674 2001
641.595694—dc21   00-044354

Manufactured in the United States of America

FIRST EDITION

To Allan, Daniela, David, and Merissa,

who have shared so much of Israel with me

Contents

Acknowledgments

Books like mine are a collaboration between the writer and many generous human beings. First of all I want to thank my family, Allan, David, Merissa, and Daniela, who on so many trips to Israel visited people with me, often enduring my endless interviews when they might have preferred tubing on the Jordan River. Allan patiently and beautifully photographed some of these cooks in their kitchens and, as he always does, went over much of the manuscript. My mother, Pearl Nathan, and my daughter Daniela Gerson also edited the manuscript at various stages.

My Jerusalem friend Pamela Loval treated this book as a personal challenge. Using e-mail she played Sherlock Holmes with me, searching for recipes and people throughout Israel. Historian Meron Benvenisti and Professor Pamela Nadell, director of the Jewish Studies Program at American University, read the entire manuscript, constructively critiquing me every step of the way. Peggy Pearlstein of the Hebraic Section of the Library of Congress not only accompanied me on one of my many research trips but continued to assist me in obtaining the correct sources for much of my information. This is the second book that I have had the privilege to write with Judith Jones as my editor. Not only did she come to Israel with me, with Bronwyn Dunne, but in her brilliant way she carefully guided and encouraged me in this mammoth project. Together we had the good fortune to work with Israel's preeminent food photographer, Nelli Sheffer, who is a delight. Seth Lipsky and Ira Stoll, formerly of the *Forward,* Michalene Busico, Rick Flaste, and Trish Hall of the *New York Times,* Alan Tigay of *Hadassah Magazine,* Hershell Shanks and Suzanne Singer of *Moment* magazine, and Dana Cowin of *Food and Wine* magazine all encouraged me to write articles on Israel, some of which are incorporated in this book. John Potthast of Maryland Public Television and Charlie Pinsky of Frappe Inc., who collaborated with me on the documentary *Passover: Traditions of Freedom,* gave me the opportunity to observe customs in Israel I otherwise might not have seen, and as always Dalia Carmel was there when I needed her. My friend Celia Regev and assistants Deb Sagaloff, Jennifer Herman, Eve Lindenblatt, and Susie Kramer tested and retested the recipes. In addition, Susan Barocas, Betsy Garside, Ann Henings, Joan Michel, Sophie Oberfeld, and Knopf's Ken Schneider and Kevin Bourke all helped with the manuscript at crucial points. Knopf's designers Carol Devine Carson and Ralph Fowler produced a beautiful book. My agent, Susan Lescher, spiritually supported me throughout this long period. And thank you Colette Avital, Dottie and David Harman, Liz and Rafi Magnes, and Zvika and Nitza Stauber, who housed and hosted me during my trips to Israel.

In Israel, many people generously shared their expertise with me: Israel Aharoni, Sherri Ansky, Gideon Avrami, Jihad Babai, Clinton and Maya Bailey, Hanoch Bar Shalom, Yoel Benesh, Michael Ben Dror, Zachi Buchester, Dan Cohen, David Eitam, Zev Friedman, Daniel and Naomi Furman, Rosa Goldberg, Judy Stacey Goldman, Ruthie Golan, Murray and Hana Greenfield, Zena Harman, Jill Indyk, Ruth Kark, Yaron Kestenboum, Dalia Lamdani, Benjamin and Hannah Levy, Pini Levy, Tziona Levy, Ya'akov Lishansky, Adam Montefiore, Dov Noy, Gila and Eitan Raz, Daniel Rogov, Nira Rousso, Ruthie and Robbie Sabel, Meir Shalev, Valentine Vester, and Maurice Zemach. The many others who let me peek into their kitchens are mentioned throughout the book.

In the United States, Avi Granott, Rachel Marani, Jacob Sagiv, and Nadav Tamir of the Israeli embassy fielded my many questions. The Israeli ambassadors and their wives—Zalman and Kena Shoval and the late Eli and Nitza Ben Elissar—helped me with queries, sometimes at ungodly hours. Mona Riklis Ackerman, Nicole Amsellem, Wendy Bernstein, Jay Buchsbaum, Robert Eschman, Marcie Cohen Ferris, Michael Ginor, Debbie Goldberg, Nora Hessen, Jessica Hirsch, Avraham Holtz, Aviva Kempner, Shirley King, Sleiman and Leila Kysia, Pnina Lahav, Robert Lenzner, Dalya Luttwak, Shoshanna Marcus, Charles Perry, Yael Raviv, Janet Kaplan Rodgers, Elizabeth Schneider, Molly Schuchat, Gail Shirazi, Sheryl Stein, Linda Sterling, Adam Tihany, Hava Volman, Geoffrey Weill, Rabbi Jeff and Judy Wohlberg, Susan Woodland, and Uzzi Zucker willingly shared their knowledge with me in so many ways. I thank them all.

The Foods of Israel Today

Introduction

The night of November 4, 1995, when I learned of the assassination of Israel's prime minister, Itzhak Rabin, I felt compelled to write a book about the foods of modern Israel. Rabin was to me an emblem of the vibrant, dynamic spirit of Israel, a blending of many cultures and ethnic and religious diversity. I wanted to capture that spirit through the medium I knew best— food and culinary traditions. I wanted to show the richness of Israel's past and present through its many cuisines.

I am not an Israeli, but I have had a long and intimate association with the country. At the impressionable age of twenty-six, I went to Israel, curious to discover whether the myths and stories I had grown up with were in fact true. It was my good fortune to land a job as the foreign press attaché to Teddy Kollek, then the mayor of Jerusalem. My task was to learn everything about the city and to translate that knowledge to visiting foreign journalists. Today, Teddy (as everyone calls the former mayor) jokes that I learned through him about the power of food as a bridge to people—and I truly did. During that two-and-a-half-year period with the Jerusalem municipality, I wrote (with Judy Stacey Goldman) my first cookbook, *The Flavor of Jerusalem.*

On many occasions, Teddy introduced me to the diverse peoples and foods of the city by taking me with him on visits to his constituents. Jews,

Right: Romanian Zionist poster from the 1930s

Christians, and Moslems alike often opened their kitchens to us. Food became a means of breaking down political and ethnic barriers.

One afternoon stands out in my memory. We were visiting an Arab *mukhtar* (leader) in a village near Jerusalem. The villagers wanted a paved road and were  upset with the municipality for its failure to act. When we arrived, the tension in the air was palpable. Sitting down with the mayor over Turkish coffee was, for the villagers, the first step in easing the tension that for so long had caused a standstill. The *mukhtar*'s wife served us a feast with a centerpiece of *mousakhan,* a tantalizing chicken dish spiced with sumac, cloves, sautéed onions, and pine nuts and baked on a large pita bread. Suddenly, the conversation began to run smoothly, as mayor and villagers alike savored the good food. Eventually the village got its road.

Another evening, after a terrorist attack at Ben-Gurion Airport, the mayor and I had just been to the hospital to visit some pilgrims from Puerto Rico who had been shot. Teddy was angry, and also hungry. So we went to a place where he could relax and wind down—a tiny, family-run Moroccan Jewish restaurant where we had a delicious meal of stuffed vegetables and cooked salads for six shekels (about a dollar) per person. Teddy kept saying it was a pity that American tourists spent fortunes at hotel restaurants for taste-less food. Ever since, I have sought out family-run holes-in-the-wall

Teddy Kollek with one of his constituents

like that one. I am happy to say that they still exist throughout the country: in the Hatikva market, in Tel Aviv; in and around the Mahane Yehudah marketplace, in Jerusalem; inside the Old City's markets. I am also happy to say that most upscale restaurants are, these days, finally worth the prices they charge.

Although I eventually moved back to the United States, I have returned to Israel often throughout the years. In 1992 I went with a Maryland Public Television crew to film segments for my documentary, *Passover: Traditions of Freedom.* I returned from this trip with a determination to tell more of the stories that make Israeli culture and cuisine so compelling. Over the years, from the clear perspective of an affectionate outsider, I have been able to observe the changes Israel has undergone, with a clarity that only distance can provide.

Someone once told me that even if you don't live in Israel, Israel can teach you how to live. It's true: the intensity of the political atmosphere reminds us of the preciousness of life and the importance of seizing the moment. This extreme sense of the present interacts with the rich ancient history of the land, the biblical birth-place of the Western world, to bring a certain energy and dynamism to every aspect of life there, whether religious or secular.

But an Israeli cuisine? A cuisine is usually defined as cooking which derives from a particular culture. Since the Jewish population has essentially been dis-persed throughout the world, Jewish food, and by extension the food of Israel, while centered in the Jewish dietary laws which were expounded in the Book of Leviticus, subsumes the cuisines of countries throughout most of the world. Unlike

The people went about, and gathered it, and ground it in mills, or beat it in mortars, and seethed it in pots, and made cakes of it; and the taste of it was as the taste of a cake baked with oil. And when the dew fell upon the camp in the night, the manna fell upon it. —Numbers 11:8–9

About four years ago, on an early-evening camel ride into the desert near Eilat, we passed a berry bush. I noticed that it was covered with a white gummy residue, which I later learned came from the tamarisk or "manna" tree. According to our guide, this sweet white resin is produced by aphids feeding on the shrubs. At night the resin hardens and can be shaken off in the early morning.

This is one theory about the origin of manna, the food which God supposedly sent down from heaven and settled on the earth like dew during the Children of Israel's forty-year trek through the desert. On the sixth day a double portion was sent down so that they would not have to gather it on the Sabbath. Another theory posits that manna is the biblical "coriander," the seeds of the cilantro plant that have been used as a seasoning throughout modern history—"And the house of Israel called the name thereof Manna: and it was like a coriander seed, white; and the taste of it was like wafers made with honey" (Exodus 16:31).

in France and Italy, for example, where cooking has been grounded in the same soil for thousands of years, in Israel the "new food" is a hybrid, inspired by every corner of the world, but with an increasing emphasis on native ingredients.

The original ingredients used by cooks in the land of Israel included the seven biblical foods mentioned in Deuteronomy—barley, wheat, figs, dates, pomegranates, olives, and grapes. *Mizrachi* or "Oriental" Jews—those who left Palestine for Babylonia at the time of the destruction of the First Temple, or those who stayed in the Middle East—have always maintained a cuisine more rooted in the original biblical ingredients. After the destruction of the Second Temple in 70 C.E., the Jews who migrated to Spain and Portugal adapted the new local foods to their dietary laws. Following the Inquisition, these people became known as Sephardic Jews, and their cuisine took on the tone of their new homelands of Greece, Morocco, and Turkey. So, too, Ashkenazic cooking developed, as other Jews made their journeys to central and eastern Europe. Today, all these foods are being embraced by many of the Jews returning from afar to the "land of milk and honey." Christian and Moslem cultures of the region have also contributed their own customs to Israeli cooking, so today Israel's emerging cuisine is truly global in scope.

Whenever I go to Israel, I am transporting myself, like a child playing make-believe, back to my ancestry. The first time this happened was thirty years ago, during a wonderful week spent in the sand dunes of the Sinai, where some Bedouins continue to live much as the nomadic Israelites did when they were wandering the desert. I couldn't help imagining myself as part of that ancient culture, sharing the stew that Sarah prepared for Abraham or the pottage of lentils that Jacob sold to his brother Esau. As I returned to Jerusalem after that

Introduction

Although many Israelis do not follow the Jewish dietary laws in their homes, the awareness of *kashrut* is second nature to them and is a defining element in Israeli cooking. Because the dietary laws prohibit the use of milk and meat together in one meal, breakfast and dinner have traditionally been dairy meals, and lunch, the main meal of the day, a meat meal.

Kashrut, the dietary laws given by God to Moses on Mount Sinai, many of which are explained in the Book of Leviticus, have been codified and elaborated upon by rabbis and scholars throughout the centuries. According to the rabbis' interpretations of the laws, observant Jews are permitted to eat meat only from an animal which has cloven hooves and chews its cud—"Whatsoever parteth the hoof and is wholly cloven-footed and cheweth the cud, that may you eat" (Leviticus 11:3). The biblical injunction includes cows, sheep, and goats and excludes rabbits, horses, dogs, cats, and—of course—pigs.

Edible fowl include turkeys, chickens, and doves, but not birds of prey. In addition, *kashrut*-observing Jews may eat only fish having both fins and scales, thus excluding all shellfish and monk- or catfish.

These dietary laws, which date back three thousand years, were a reaction against the sacrificial practices of paganism in the ancient world. They dictate that the flesh may not be torn from a living animal and that the killing of all animals and birds requires a *shochet,* a sage especially instructed in the ritual of slaughter so that the animal is killed instantly, with no suffering. After slaughter, the animal's lungs are checked for abnormalities. The *shochet* rejects cattle with certain types of adhesions, cuts, and bruises. The term "glatt kosher" refers to the smoothness of the lungs. Today, the very Orthodox use the term to define extremely kosher foods. The visitor to Israel on El Al, the Israeli airline, for example, can order a kosher or glatt kosher meal.

The Bible declares an absolute prohibition against the consumption of blood. "I said unto the children of Israel: No soul of you shall eat blood.... Ye shall eat the blood of no manner of flesh ... whosoever eateth it shall be cut off" (Leviticus 17:12, 14). To the Jew, blood is sacred, a gift of God as well as a means of atonement. "I have given it [the blood] to you upon the altar to make an atonement for your souls" (Leviticus 17:11).

After the animal is killed, the meat goes through a process called *melihah,* which consists of first soaking it in cold water, then covering it with coarse salt (fine-grained salt would dissolve instead of drawing out the blood). The salt is then shaken off, and the meat washed three times so that no blood remains.

Milchig (dairy) dishes must be cooked and eaten separately from *fleishig* (meat) dishes, because three times in Exodus and Deuteronomy the Bible states that a kid cannot be cooked in its mother's milk. However, neutral or pareve food such as fish and eggs may be eaten with either milk or meat. In the ancient land of Israel, all Jews used olive oil as the main cooking oil, causing no problems at dairy or meat meals. As Jews moved to countries in northern and eastern Europe, they had little access to olive oil. There they depended on butter or beef and poultry fats for cooking

week, at each fork in the road layers of civilization and thousands of years unwound before me like a newsreel.

I love discovering the connections between people and food, and nowhere more so than in Israel. Through culinary haunts one can uncover the enormously exciting story of how these pioneers transformed a harsh land to one bursting with new produce and culture. Some of their recipes are as old as the land; others are quite modern. Every recipe has a story, which is why I have written this book: to tell these stories, and through them the story of Israel and its peoples.

since lard, a pork fat, is forbidden to Jews. So they developed a system whereby they could assure that no milk and meat products would be mixed: one set of dishes is used, cleaned, and stored separately for milk meals, and another for meat meals. Observant Jews wait one, three, or six hours between eating meat and milk, depending on how strictly they observe *kashrut.*

In observant homes, no cooking is permitted on the Sabbath, the day of rest following the commandment: "Ye shall kindle no fire throughout your habitations upon the Sabbath day" (Exodus 35:3). Food prepared in advance can simmer for a long time under a low flame, like the traditional *cholent,* a robust stew, which cooks slowly in a low oven throughout the night.

Moslem dietary laws, as laid out in the Koran, have many similarities to those of the Jews. Moslems are also prohibited from eating pork products. Their form of ritual butchering is similar to that of the Jews, and they salt their *halal* meat in the same manner; in fact, in the city of Jerusalem, Jews and Moslems share the same municipal slaughtering house. Moslems do mix meat and milk, however, often serving *leben,* a form of yogurt, to wash down a heavy meal of meat and rice. Every day during the month of Ramadan, religiously strict Moslems fast throughout the day from sunrise to sunset, then eat a rather sumptuous meal in the evening. This Ramadan fast is central to their religious beliefs. They are also forbidden to drink alcohol.

Perhaps reacting against the strict Jewish dietary laws, the Christian communities in Israel have no daily dietary restrictions. In the New Testament, Jesus declares that all of God's foods may be eaten, that none are unclean or defiled until they enter the body. "'Nothing that goes into a person from outside can defile him; no, it is the things that come out of a person that defile him.... From inside, from the human heart, come evil thoughts...all these evil things come from within, and they are what defile a person'" (Mark 7:15–23). On another occasion, Peter tells an audience of a divine vision: "'...I saw four-footed beasts, wild animals, reptiles, and birds. Then I heard a voice saying to me, "Get up, Peter, kill and eat." But I said, "No, Lord! Nothing profane or unclean has ever entered my mouth." A voice from heaven came a second time: "It is not for you to call profane what God counts clean"'" (Acts 11:6–9).

However, during Lent, the forty-day period prior to Easter, as a penance some Christians abstain from certain foods. Members of the Greek Orthodox Church, for example, do not eat meat, fish, eggs, butter, milk, and cheese throughout the Lenten period. Some sects, like the Ethiopians, have as many as 270 fasts throughout the year.

Despite the prohibitions of their traditions, many Jews, Moslems, and Christians in Israel today do not adhere strictly to religious dietary laws, whereas some observe them to the letter. In fact, because of Israel's dynamism and inventiveness, there are probably more interpretations of every dietary law here than anywhere else in the world.

I have taken all practical measures to ensure that the recipes contained herein fulfill the requirements of *kashrut,* but within the many observant communities there are different views on the dietary laws. Accordingly, although rabbinic authorities have been consulted in the preparation of this text, the ultimate responsibility for ascertaining the conformity with *kashrut* of any particular recipe rests with the reader.

. . .

The hundreds of recipes and stories in this book reflect not only the varied influences of a Jewish population coming from ninety different countries, but also the Christian and Moslem traditions from throughout the Middle East. Israel is a land that transcends ethnic identity, where an immigrant's native tongue might be Russian or Farsi, Polish or Ladino, where some Jews came knowing how to bless bread in classical Hebrew but could not use modern Hebrew to buy bread and cheese.

Introduction

During a visit to Massada, one of Herod's hilltop fortresses, an archaeologist might pull out of his pocket a two-thousand-year-old olive or date pit which he found in an ancient garbage pile. On that same day, a new Israeli chef at Jerusalem's King David Hotel might prepare a modern *amuse gueule* of sushi made from seaweed filled with pine nuts and cured olives with a quail cooked in a date syrup. At the Levinsky Market in Tel Aviv, a Greek deli run by Holocaust survivors from Salonika stands across the street from a Turkish *burek* baker and a Persian market where the prices are written in Farsi, Hebrew, and Arabic. Meanwhile, every Friday grandmothers all over the country prepare traditional Libyan, Persian, Italian, and German Jewish meals for their families. The Sabbath, even in secular Israel, is the centerpiece of the week, with all meals leading up to it.

As I walk down Jerusalem's Jaffa Road to Mahane Yehuda, the Jewish marketplace, I see hundreds of tiny stalls filled with fresh spices and vegetables, some dating back to the biblical period and others as modern and sophisticated as anything in New York's gourmet markets. In some shops, expert hands mold and bake ornate artisan pita bread, called *aish tanoor*. In others, women sift couscous through their fingers, as they did in their native villages in Morocco or Tunisia. As I observe each ingredient, I play that same game I played in the Sinai, imagining the layers of history behind the foods. Which plants are native to the land and which came with conquerors or new immigrants? Did the sugar beet come with English Crusaders? Did the Turks bring green peppers?

This book is the story of the gathering in of foods and people which today form the basis for the new State of Israel. A typical Israeli main meal, as codified in the *Israel Defense Force Cookbook,* includes a Middle Eastern hummus or tahina, a central European turkey schnitzel with a Turkish eggplant salad, or a Hungarian goulash-type stew, with fresh native fruit for dessert. Over the years I have noticed that most tourists in Israel, when asked to name a local dish, usually mention only street food—hummus, *schwarma* (spicy rotisserie-grilled meat in a pita), and falafel, or the addictive sunflower and pumpkin seeds whose shells carpet some city sidewalks. In fact, few of these dishes can be identified solely as "Israeli"; hummus and falafel, for example, are certainly not Israeli, but are adapted from local Arab foods. While these street foods are indeed popular, it is important to consider also the multinational dishes that are so common in Israeli homes.

While Sabbath and holiday recipes increasingly reflect the diverse heritage of Jews from many parts of the world, there is a noticeable gap between generations: a Czech survivor of the Holocaust, for example, may make for her children a stuffed chicken from Prague as a tribute to a community that exists now only in her memory. But her children, who have grown up in Israel, have less of an emotional connection to their Czech heritage and more of a willingness to cook and eat foods native to Israel. Thus, traditional food is yielding both to the more modern everyday convenience food—frozen schnitzel, packaged hummus, and prepared soup—and to today's sophisticated restaurant cuisine, which increasingly plays with the bounty of the global market, resulting in a distinctly cross-cultural eating experience.

When I lived in Jerusalem in the early 1970s, only tourists, diplomats, or foreign journalists ate in restaurants. Grabbing hummus and falafel at a fast-food stand or dropping into a café for coffee and cake was the Israeli idea of "dining out." Food was scarce, and wasting time on such a bourgeois matter seemed contrary to the pioneering spirit of the country. In fact, the restaurants were so bad in those days that Henry Kissinger, engaging in his Middle East "shuttle diplomacy," once moaned, "Why can't a country with two and a half million Jewish mothers have better food?" Today, even Henry Kissinger might agree that that lament is a thing of the past.

The founding fathers and mothers of modern Israel had an idea of a melting-pot culinary style. David Ben-Gurion, Israel's first prime minister, envisioned that the country would have a distinct "Israeli food," like an "Israeli dance." But twenty years ago, in the country's adolescence, they realized that the melting-pot idea wasn't going to work. According to Dov Noy, professor of folklore at the Hebrew University of Jerusalem, "As the Oriental and Sephardic intelligentsia emerged in Israel, the idea of a kind of multiculturalism developed, and Israelis became aware that the Jewish people and other peoples in Israel have many languages and cultural ways. Then the melting-pot idea was given up. Now we think of Israeli food as a mosaic within the frame of the nation, where each dish is a different color and stands by itself."

For the past thirty or so years, an excitement inspired by this multiculturalism has been building in Israel's culinary community. The country has become an increasing presence in the international food world, contributing new and unusual products made from native ingredients. When I lived in Israel we ate kohlrabi and cauliflower but certainly not the blueberries and broccoli people eat today. The only lettuce we couldn't get was *hasa amerikait*, plain old American iceberg. Israel—known globally in the past almost solely for its Carmel tomatoes and Jaffa oranges—is now second to France for excellent foie gras. Ten years ago, there was little good local olive oil. Today, Jewish and Arab farmers in small, rural villages are pressing extra-virgin olive oil. With boutique cheeses being made throughout the country, kosher wines from the Golan Heights winning first-class competitions worldwide, and more cookbooks being written per capita than in almost any other country, Israel is bursting with culinary creativity. The interplay of cultures and cuisines has made eating an art such as it has never been in Israel before.

For a country the size of New Jersey, Israel offers not only an astonishing variety of food customs, but also an unusual abundance of historic and holy places. I often worry that visitors, so intent on a historic tour, do not have the time to linger in the local markets, in tiny out-of-the-way restaurants, in peaceful olive orchards and orange groves. To help travelers balance their itineraries, I have included an index of places mentioned in this book, as well as a glossary of terms in both Hebrew and Arabic. And, out of respect for those observing the dietary laws, both Jew and Arab, I have not included any recipes for pork and shellfish, nor any that mix meat and milk.

Readers should also note that the recipes here reflect my personal journeys to and from Israel over the years, and therefore sometimes include cities and territories—Nablus and Bethlehem, for example—which no longer lie within the country's borders. Like its cuisine, Israel's borders are constantly changing, and food is sometimes the sole recourse for remembering the connections that once existed within these lands.

Palestine in the Nineteenth Century

Spurred on by a religious fervor that was sweeping the "new" promised land and Europe in 1849, Clorinda Minor, a Seventh-Day Adventist from Philadelphia, moved to Artas, a farm in a fertile valley on the outskirts of Bethlehem. As the American writer Herman Melville wrote in his diary during his visit there in 1856 and 1857, Artas was to be "a kind of Agricultural Academy for Jews to prepare the Holy Land for assuming its position as the center of the earth in the End of Days." Armed with the seeds of various Western fruits and vegetables, including potatoes, mulberries, and even Jerusalem artichokes, Mrs. Minor and her companions worked the fields in an effort to restore Palestine to the agricultural promised land of the Scriptures, making way for the prophetic return of the Jews.

Later, Melville added that "the idea of making farmers of the Jews is in vain. In the first place, Judea is a desert with few exceptions. In the second place, the Jews hate farming. All who cultivate the soil in Palestine are Arabs. The Jews dare not live outside walled towns or villages for fear of the malicious persecution of the Arabs & Turks. Besides, the number of Jews in Palestine is comparatively small. And how are the hosts of them scattered in other lands to be brought here? Only by a miracle."

The miracle was to come, but the time was not yet ripe. The Jews who lived in Palestine then were for the most part poor, and they were often discriminated against by the Turks, who had been ruling Palestine for four hundred years.

Accounts abound of the lack of bread available to the Jewish people under the Turkish Empire. "The Effendis had bought up all the corn brought to market and stored it, to compel a rise in prices," wrote Elizabeth Ann Finn, wife of James Finn, the British consul from 1845 to 1862, in her memoirs. "Corn was not to be had. We showed to our visitors a specimen of the only bread which the poor could get; it was dry and of a dirty blue-grey color. Famine followed, and the people were found dead in the morning in the Jewish quarter from want. . . . The convents all had big stores and gave help to their people, and the rich Moslems gave help to theirs, but the Jews had no help at all."

Indigent, religious Jews from all over the world had come to pray and to die in the Holy Land. Rabbi Yosef Amdursky Mohliver, for example, journeyed from the Ukraine to Jerusalem in the 1840s. Seeing how needy the Jews of Palestine were, he started a kosher soup kitchen in the Old City. His son Yerachmiel later took over the kitchen and established the Amdursky Hotel Central near David's Tower (today the site of the Petra Hotel on David Street).

Although visitors to Palestine at the time spoke widely of its poverty and barrenness, there were in fact many fruits and vegetables available. Arab farmers employed techniques they had used for centuries to grow all kinds of crops, including radishes, sugarcane, American corn, and artichokes. Rabbi David Beth-Hillel noted that "cauliflowers now in their highest state of perfection were equal to the best English or American [ones]" but that "the uncultivated and unimproved Arab potato is now seen in great abundance." He also remarked that apples were inferior and that "several species of tobacco cultivated in Palestine were milder than that raised in the United States." The rabbi marveled that "every article mentioned in the calendar can be had from irrigated gardens for six, eight, or ten months of the year, and many, indeed, the entire year round."

American settlers wrestled with the problem of milling flour to bake the kind of loaf bread with which they were familiar. Scarcity of fuel was a larger problem; part of the reason that locals ate the flatbread *khubz* (eventually to be popularized throughout the world as "pita") was that it baked quickly and required little timber. "This is midwinter . . . though the natives build no fires (for merely warming themselves, except, perhaps, a few exposed out-door shopkeepers) contenting themselves throughout the winter with additional clothing," wrote Rabbi Beth-Hillel. "Charcoal is the principal fuel made use of for domestic culinary purposes. . . . In the large baking establishments, the only fuel used is green thorns, brushwood, and thistles in bunches the size of sage, brought from a considerable distance on donkeys, and great is the crackling of thorns under the pots. . . . All the village bakeries are heated by the excrement of cows and camels."

One of the groups most instrumental in improving milling and other agricultural techniques in the nineteenth century was a contingent of German Templars from farming communities in Württemberg, Baden, and Bavaria, who migrated to Palestine in 1869. Awaiting the Second Coming, they sought to live a more Christian and pacifist life than they had felt to be possible under Germany's increasing militarism. The Templars built solid stone houses, most of which still stand today in the "German" colonies of Jerusalem, Jaffa, and Haifa. Skilled in many trades, the first generation of Templars grew wheat and ground their own flour. They brought with them an agricultural tradition built around varied year-round farming.

The Templars' arrival corresponded with the establishment, in 1870, of the first *yishuv,* a Jewish agricultural settlement, in Mikveh Israel. Since the Jews coming from Russia and Poland had no agricultural experience and spoke Yiddish, it was natural for them to go to the German-speaking Templars for advice rather than to the local Arabs, with whom they had no common language. "The Jewish settlers learned from the Templars what it meant to lead the life of a farmer, and from German women occupations such as raising fowl and vegetables in home gardens," wrote Naftali Thalmann in *Introducing Modern Agricultures* (1988). "The Templar colonies were exemplary models for modern agricultural settlements in Palestine."

The grapevines they transplanted from Germany prospered so in the new land that the French wine-loving philanthropist Baron Edmond de Rothschild, touched by the plight of the Jews on his first trip there in 1887, consulted with the Templars. Although the Rothschild family had long been donating money to poor religious Jews living in Palestine, Edmond's financial commitment was focused on agriculture. Word of his generosity spread quickly, and soon almost all the new settlements were applying to him for help.

The baron devoted the next fifty years of his life to helping the Jews of Palestine, planting European-variety grapes there and strongly urging the settlers to use a great part of their land for the grape harvest. "Most of the farmers contented themselves with the safe income of the vineyards and developed no other crops," wrote Dan Giladi in his *Agronomic Development of the Colonies* (1975). "Nor did the very low price of fresh produce from the neighbouring Arab villages encourage them to grow their own food." By the end of the century, Rothschild vineyards covered more than half the land under cultivation in Palestine.

In 1891, the vineyards in Samaria and Galilee were attacked by phylloxera and had to be uprooted and replaced by pest-resistant plants from India. Like many of the other dreamers who came to Palestine, the baron had miscalculated. Not only did he overplant his grapes—people wondered who actually bought the vast quantities of his wine—but he established bottling plants at a time when wine was always shipped in wooden barrels.

Still, other agricultural experiments the baron initiated were successful, such as the planting of olives, figs, almonds, and citrus fruits—most notably, grapefruits. Thanks to Rothschild, many of these crops still thrive under the hands of Jewish farmers in Israel today.

The Rise of Zionism

While upper-class Jews like Rothschild were finding ways to help their kin in Palestine, the national and cultural self-determination movement known as Zionism was gaining force in Europe, in keeping with the romantic notions of nationalism sweeping the Western world. This movement to encourage the return of the Jews to the land of Israel sprang from a long tradition of messianic hope in an ultimate restoration of Zion, expressed by the prophets and in liturgy throughout Jewish history. Modern Zionism was conceived in the wake of the Russian pogroms in the early 1880s. First manifested in "Lovers of Zion" organizations in Russia and England, these groups sought to buy land in Palestine and to assist, from abroad, the pioneers' tilling of the soil.

A number of writers had helped set the stage for the new movement. Romantic literature, like Benjamin Disraeli's *Tancred* and George Eliot's *Daniel Deronda,* spoke to the plight of the increasing numbers of poor Eastern European Jews flooding London's East End and New York City's Lower East Side. In 1891 the Reverend S. Singer wrote of "the outcast Jews' desire to return to the Holy Land. . . . They love the very stones and favour the dust thereof; and they would deem themselves blessed indeed if they were permitted to till the sacred soil." Zionism became a matter of faith. "If England is for the English, Germany for the Germans, then the logical sequence is Palestine for the Jews," Singer continued.

In 1882 sixteen high school and university students from Odessa settled in Palestine. Members of the Lovers of Zion, they called themselves BILU, the acronym for the first Hebrew words of Isaiah 2:5 ("O house of Jacob, let us go in the light of God"). This migration was called the first *aliyah*, literally meaning "going up," a term used to describe the waves of Jewish immigration to the Holy Land. It lasted until 1903 and marked a turning point in Jewish immigration. These young, political Zionists, who came to the Holy Land for idealistic rather than religious reasons, had been politically active in Russia. They established moshavim (agricultural villages) made up of privately owned farms, most of which were eventually financed by Rothschild.

But despite the baron's help, life was tough. The settlers were lonely for their homelands and afraid of contracting malaria. They had no money and couldn't invest in improving their farms, so they were reliant on local Arab produce.

"The Arabs bring all sorts of things to sell: milk, eggs, chickens, wood, grapes and different kinds of fruit," wrote the wife of Kalman Kantor in a letter from Zichron Yaakov in 1889. "And everything is sold cheaply. . . . After all this, I still yearn for Russia. The heat and the *khamsin* (the desert wind) are very difficult for people from Russia; in the winter it is raining and this is the best time of the entire year, when we are able to live well. The winter season here is full of different types of vegetables and fruit which grow on trees. For food, we serve compote and eat bread. It's possible to live well here if God grants health and strength."

A year later, Mrs. Kantor was growing her own foods. "Every day I bring home a basket of eggs laid by my own hens; in the morning we drink good, fat milk from my cows; we have chicken every day for our noon meal, while over there we would only have such luxuries on holidays. . . . Our garden has every sort of fruit tree, even apples and cherries, but most of the vineyard is planted with grape vines."

The first *aliyah,* though mainly composed of Eastern European Jews, also included five thousand Jews from Yemen, who made up 6 percent of the new Jewish population. Unlike the Eastern European immigrants of this period, the Yemenites were motivated by the biblical commandment to return to Jerusalem. The men often found work in kitchens and as waiters, and they were most likely the first Jews to make falafel in the country. The women, mostly illiterate, worked as domestics, which provided a meager subsistence. Although they were not educated or sophisticated by European standards, they set an example of meticulousness in all aspects of housework, including the religious obligations taught by word of mouth: dietary laws, separation of challah, salting and koshering meat, the ritual immersion of utensils, blessings for meals, and candle lighting. They would rise before dawn to fetch water and to prepare the *gisher* (Yemenite coffee), grind flour, bake, and have breakfast ready when the men returned at sunrise from the prayer service in the synagogue.

Little by little, Yemenites and other Middle Eastern Jews started affecting the eating habits of the immigrants from eastern Europe, and different tastes and traditions began to coexist. For some, like those from eastern Europe, the idea of raw vegetables fresh from the soil seemed unhealthy. But their sense of curiosity prevailed: Yemenite soup with spicy sauces and the buttery layered bread called *malouach* very well may have been one of the exotic meals eaten by a group of well-heeled British Jews, organized by the Jewish industrialist Herbert Bentwich, who came to visit Palestine in 1897.

Four years before, in 1893, a French Jewish army captain had been arrested and degraded by an anti-Semitic mob in what came to be known as the Dreyfus Affair. The Viennese writer Dr. Theodor Herzl, so moved by this event, published his *Der Judenstaat* (The Jewish State), in which he foresaw the establishment of a homeland for the Jews. Shortly afterward, the first Zionist Congress took place in Basel, Switzerland.

A wagon laden with kegs of wine from Baron de Rothschild's cellars of Rishon le-Zion, 1911

In 1903, what was known as the second *aliyah* brought a new kind of immigrant, the Labor Zionist. This wave of thirty to forty thousand Russians was made up of young, single, mostly socialist *halutzim* (pioneers), often from middle-class families, fleeing a new round of pogroms in Russia in 1903 and the failed October Revolution, in 1905.

Overcoming extreme hardships as fledgling farmers, these predominantly male idealists, with no funds of their own, became the dominant force in the country for future generations. They insisted on speaking Hebrew as a revived tongue, making it the language of the new land. Straight-backed and self-reliant, they were the opposite of the downtrodden image of their religious brethren from the ghettos of Russia, who were not even permitted to own land. They believed in productive labor, and especially in agriculture. Their trademark was economic self-sufficiency and a rejection of the pattern set by the farmers of the first *aliyah,* with their dependence on Arab labor and foreign markets. Their children, the new native-born Israeli Jews, would be called *sabras* after the local prickly pear, which is sweet on the inside and tough on the outside.

The *halutzim* were a new breed of Palestinian Jew. Even in the kitchen, they shied away from the elaborate, table-centered habits of their predecessors from Russia, eating in a much more casual way, often with elbows on the table.

"Food was deliberately plain, consisting mainly of bread, olives, vegetables and soup, prepared in communal workers' kitchens," wrote Amos Elon in *The Israelis: Fathers and Sons* (1971). "Like American pioneers," he added in an interview, "ours had an attitude about obvious pleasures. They forsook pleasures for the hard pioneering life, thus tea and biscuits and a big bowl of vegetables on the table were more common than were overcooked, long meals with guests seated around a table for hours. Why would any of them take pleasure in food? Or in eating?"

In 1909—the year that Tel Aviv, "the all-Jewish city," was founded—Kibbutz Degania, located near the Sea of Galilee, was formed. Some of the original mem-

All the men in the *kvutza* [*sic*] worked happily from the beginning but at first the women were not happy.... [W]e still thought women could only cook and wash.... The women listened and were jealous, their work was quite different and the conditions for it were very hard. There were neither stoves nor kerosene—not to speak of electricity as there is now. They cooked in the open over a wood fire on two stones placed upright, the bitter smoke blowing in their eyes, and in the end the food tasted of smoke and was only half-cooked. They scrubbed and they sewed, they even saw to it that we washed and put on clean shirts for the Sabbath, but they had no part in our working lives.

One day they came to us. "Listen to us," they said. "We came to this country with the one idea in our heads—to work and to live with nature. But what now? You men are happy, you like your work, but we are worse off than our mothers were in their small town. What do you yourselves think of it? Should we continue in this way, with this difference between your lot and ours?"

We couldn't understand them. Our fathers had been breadwinners and our mothers had cooked. "How else can it be?" we asked. "Should a woman plough? Or should the men cook? What would other people think of us? We would be ashamed before everybody."

But our women gave us no rest. They insisted that things must change, that we should buy cows and chickens and grow vegetables so that there would be work for the women, and that more women should be sent for. It was a difficult problem, we couldn't understand it and it made us suffer. And how were we to have vegetable plots when we had no irrigation and every pail of water had to be brought up by mule or hand?

But in the end the women won. Gradually we understood and we changed. Now we know that women can do farm work, that they can even plough, and they can even fight. Not their words but their actions have proved it to us.

—Joseph Baratz, one of the founding members of Kibbutz Degania, in *A Village by the Jordan, The Story of Degania* (1954)

bers were women who had worked at Sejera, the first collective settlement founded by Manya Schochet. Here Jewish workers would be trained to work and live on land purchased in cooperation with the Jewish National Fund. As more and more pioneers settled on kibbutzim, culinary customs changed. In Europe the woman's realm had been only the kitchen, making heavy meals and long-cooking dishes that used potatoes, beets, and other root vegetables. In Palestine, Jewish women started growing and preparing vegetables such as tomatoes, eggplants, and green peppers brought by the Turks, a task which, for the most part, previously had been in Arab hands.

World War I meant the decline of the four-hundred-year-old Ottoman Empire and the beginning of the British Mandate. During the spring of 1917, there was a plague that destroyed the vegetable crop and damaged the orange groves. "The locusts swooped down on whatever vegetation was in sight, wheat and barley, wines, eggplants, cucumbers and watermelons," wrote Ruth Jordan in her memoir *Daughter of the Waves* (1983). "The earth, like the sun a few minutes earlier, went dark. The air trembled and reverberated with the beating of empty tins and the sound of munching and crunching, screeching and crackling. The locusts clung fiercely to the greenery and did not let go even when beaten with sticks and spades."

That same year, Zionism reached a critical turning point: Lord Arthur James Balfour, Britain's foreign secretary, wrote his famous declaration, favoring establishment of a national home for the Jewish people. Two months later, on the first day of Hanukkah, the Turks, who had sided with the Germans in World War I, handed over Palestine to the British. The British Mandate would last until 1948. (According to Teddy Kollek, had the French occupied Palestine instead of the British, Israeli cuisine would have had a better start.)

Zionism was growing much stronger, organizing itself both within and outside of Palestine. By the end of World War I, Tnuva, the agricultural arm of the increasingly powerful labor movement, began marketing the produce of all collective and cooperative settlements (kibbutzim and moshavim). It was Tnuva, for example, that started selling carp from the fish ponds in the Galilee and exporting bananas after World War II. Eventually, kibbutzim were producing so many chickens, ducks, and turkeys that Tnuva had them preserved in cans, and Israelis learned to prepare schnitzel with turkey instead of veal.

"We ate lots of turkey," recalled Dalia Carmel, who grew up in Palestine in the 1940s, "and we often cooked it in a pressure cooker. My mother used to make a rich soup out of turkey legs and necks, but then you had to eat the turkey legs, which had no taste. We called it laundered turkey."

During this time of heightened nationalism, consumers were encouraged to use "Jewish hands" and to buy Jewish products, including food cultivated by Jews in the kibbutzim, even though Arab farms contributed a heavy majority of fresh produce staples. It became unpatriotic throughout Palestine, for example, to stock Arab or foreign produce in one's grocery. "To encourage housewives to buy Israeli products was to let them know the other ones were inferior," wrote Mrs. Jordan in her memoir. "Buying from Jews was the lifeline of the new state."

In the 1920s and 1930s, Jewish Palestinians tried to re-create the pageantry of the biblical festivals, in which the first fruits of the harvest were brought to Jerusalem. One of the goals of these modern-day pageants, still celebrated at many kibbutzim today, was to show the superiority of Jewish products. Despite Herman Melville's prediction to the contrary, the Jews were slowly becoming farmers.

The enthusiasm for creating "Jewish" products from the land helped to strengthen the resolve of the Jewish population between the world wars. The Arab leadership, under Haj Amin el Hussaini, the mufti of Jerusalem, became concerned about the increasing Zionist presence. "There were complaints that the Zionists displaced Arab workers at the ports of Jaffa and Haifa, and from the orange groves," wrote Walter Laqueur in his *History of Zionism*. "That the Jewish trade unions consistently followed a policy of Jewish labour only." It was a complex issue. "If Jewish orange grove owners refused to employ Arabs they were bound to be charged with chauvinism," Laqueur continued, "but if they employed Arabs they were accused of exploiting cheap labour. When the Histadrut (labor federation) . . . attempted to organise Arab labour it was attacked for interfering in Arab politics. When it refrained from doing so it was charged with willfully neglecting the interests of the Arab worker."

Not only did the change from Ottoman to British rule require shifts in the emphasis on food production, it also altered eating habits. Jewish bakeries, for example, started making white loaf bread for breakfast and plum puddings at Christmas time. From leftover white bread, Moslem bakers created a kind of caramelized pudding with cream, to this day served as a treat during Ramadan. They call it *hisharaya,* which means "(British) policemen's bread."

The fourth *aliya,* which lasted from 1924 to 1932 (the third was from 1919 to 1923), while the British were still in control, was made up of petit bourgeois families from Poland, who moved into urban centers and increased the total Jewish population to 108,000. Because Egypt and Palestine were both occupied by the British, people traveled freely from one country to another, often going into business partnerships.

"On the train there were a number of Palestinian Jews, returning home after a visit to Cairo," wrote Antonia Fraser Futterer in *Palestine Speaks* (1931). "They carried with them small supplies of food, some sugar, hard-boiled eggs and chocolate. They explained that they were taking these things home for their families, and complained bitterly about the hunger and death in Palestine by comparison with Egypt."

Hunger and rough living conditions were a way of life in those days. "We workers were lonely men, and idealistic," recalled Samy Cohn, who came to Palestine from Romania and unloaded cargo in the port of Haifa in 1934. "It was a time of malaria. . . . We ate in this big kitchen that we used like a club, with long, long tables with benches. The man on duty brought us a pot of watered-down soup or lentils or barley. It was sometimes very, very salty. People ate it anyway, because they were hungry."

The fifth and last *aliya,* which spanned the years between 1932 and 1945, included more Labor Zionists like Samy Cohn, as well as middle-class refugees who fled the perils of Nazi Europe. Many of these middle-class immigrants, who came from Europe before the outbreak of war, used private capital to set up the country's large food establishments.

Typical of them was a German named Erna Myer, who wrote *How to Cook in Palestine* (1936), the first Palestinian Jewish cookbook. Written under the auspices of the Palestine Federation of WIZO, the Women's International Zionist Organization, it was published in a trilingual edition—German, Hebrew, and English. Two years later a *Dictionary of Kitchen Terms* was published, also in English, Hebrew, and German. Both books show the variety of ingredients used in the kitchen at that time. For example, various preparations were found for thirty-one kinds of fish. Curiously, there is no uniformity of measurements in these books, as if it was taken for granted that cooks would adapt the recipes to their native systems.

In 1931, Reuben Hecht, the pampered son of a Swiss-German Jewish shipping magnate, visited Palestine for the first time. A follower of Theodor Herzl, Hecht immediately saw that the burgeoning state would need more modern systems for storing and handling grain to feed the constantly growing population. Since his family owned flour mills with silos and food warehouses throughout the Rhineland, he had the expertise to help. His dream was to build a silo that could load and store both imported and domestic grain in bulk, and to improve the quality of grains used. The silo was finally constructed near the Haifa port in 1955.

Until then the developing state had been growing some grain and importing bagged flour from abroad. Moisture, heat, and insects had caused spoilage, ruining 10 percent of the import over time. With Hecht's silo—called *Dagon* after the ancient Canaanite god of earth, plant life, grain, and fertility—Israel was able to import huge quantities of barley, corn, soy, and rice, as well as darker grains like buckwheat and rye, to which Jewish immigrants from Central and Eastern Europe were accustomed.

· · ·

Then came World War II, and with it a blow to the agricultural export industry. Not only did commercial shipping stop, but the European market disappeared, virtually cutting off Palestine from Europe and eliminating the demand for citrus. To utilize the citrus crop, scientists converted oranges into chemicals, fertilizer, vitamin tablets, marmalade, oils, pectin, and alcohol. They developed condensed orange juice, and kibbutzim built up processing industries from the surplus of their fresh crop to produce it.

To help the local population adapt to food shortages and rationing, Lillian Cornfeld, a nutritionist and cookbook author from Montreal who settled in Palestine, created recipes for canned sardines and locally grown products like bulgur, lentils, barley, and eggplant, and she used her imagination to create eggless desserts to help satisfy the craving for sweets. She also cautioned her readers to taste their oil before using it and suggested that they buy it from Shemen, a Jewish company.

In 1936 the Palestine Broadcasting Service, patterned after the British Broadcasting Corporation, was founded. In the early 1940s Mrs. Cornfeld wrote and narrated a series of Zionist programs on ethnic foods in which she contrasted the heavy, meat-based cuisine from the "dark" Diaspora era (the thousands of years since the destruction of the Second Temple) with the more wholesome foods of contemporary Palestine under the Zionists.

"Common to them all is the consumption of large quantities of meat, and fat foods," she narrated. "And hence very little fruit and vegetables are eaten, particularly in a fresh and uncooked state. The cooking methods are very crude and are inclined to rob the fruit or vegetable of all its freshness through long and continuous cooking, exaggerated frying, use of much fat. Carrots, for instance, the one vegetable that most people from Poland eat willingly, is eaten only after it has entirely lost its original shape and form. The housewife is particularly proud that it is now prepared so that it is impossible to recognize it as carrots. Cooked in such a way, the carrots naturally lose any nutritive value they have had."

Through radio programs like Lillian Cornfeld's, as well as through posters and advertisements in movie theaters, the Zionists were trying to promote a new Jewish cuisine based in the Holy Land. World War II helped their cause. Import stoppages spurred the increased home cultivation of vegetables and the production of local dairy and poultry products.

By 1945, with the influx of survivors of World War II, the Jewish population had swelled to over 450,000. Despite the growing British opposition to new immigration, the country was flooded with the bedraggled victims of the Holocaust, who often arrived illegally. Between 1946 and 1953 the Jewish population doubled again with more survivors as well as immigrants from Romania and North Africa. No one thought about a "cuisine" in those days, nor were they concerned with table niceties. They just thought about having enough to feed the poverty-stricken from the concentration camps.

"Most of the survivors had rickets and were totally undernourished," recalled Dalia Carmel. "A few kids from Poland joined us in school in 1948–49. They were so skinny, their forearms and their thighs were the same width. Lacking totally any self-assurance, they never looked you in the face, they looked literally like frightened pigeons. I remember they would stand huddled in the corner, and they were brilliant. They learned Hebrew, I think, in half an hour. They used to steal our sandwiches which we brought in lunchboxes. Our teachers pleaded with us to have patience and not pick on them."

Reenacting the grape crushing of ancient Israel

The New State Reaches Out to Feed a New Nation

After the war, the British government, worn down by daily tensions and increasing pressure from abroad, decided to abandon its Palestine mandate, leaving the task of deciding its fate to the newly emerged United Nations. In the United States, wide sympathy was generated for the idea of a Jewish homeland as an answer to the plight of displaced Jewish persons, victims of the Holocaust who were stranded throughout Europe. When in May 1948 David Ben-Gurion, head of the Jewish Agency, declared Israel's independence, American president Harry S Truman, and shortly thereafter the Soviet Union, enthusiastically recognized the new state.

The face of the new nation changed, and gradually a new culinary picture emerged. But first the infant state found itself surrounded by enemies, and absorbing one hundred thousand immigrants a year. This time the wave was comprised not only of displaced survivors of the Holocaust, but of Jews from all over the Middle East. With each ethnic group came different styles of eating and cooking.

The massive immigration was a strain on the economy, so the period from 1948 to 1958 was a time of government-regulated *zena* (food rationing) and *mabarot* (makeshift dwellings). Women cooked with *khubeiza* (wild greens) from the fields; new foods, like Ben-Gurion's "Israeli couscous," were introduced to satisfy the needs of the multicultural population; and surplus vegetables, like eggplant, were ingeniously used to simulate meat. Israel's canning industry increased production, supplying canned tomato paste and puree, hummus, tahina, and mayonnaise in tubes.

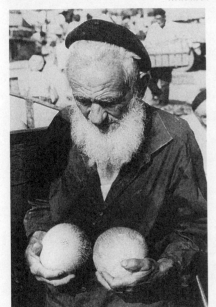

A newcomer from North Africa selects a perfect melon

One of the many issues to be resolved in this new Jewish country was the official position on the dietary laws. Ben-Gurion decided to remain with the "status quo" agreement, maintaining rabbinical supervision of *kashrut* in all government organizations, military service, schools, and hospitals.

Even the rabbis, however, had to compromise. The U.S. government, through the Agency for International Development, sent millions of pounds of preserved foods, such as dried eggs, dried skim milk, butter, dried codfish, and cheddar cheese. Maury Atkin, who worked at the newly created Israeli embassy in Washington at the time, recalled how the rabbis in Israel asked if the cheese was kosher. "We told them that cheddar cheese was the most wholesome cheese sold in America, even if it includes a small amount of nonkosher animal rennet. Because there were so many starving children, the Chief Rabbi of Israel issued an edict that the cheddar cheese sent over would be kosher for children up to the age of fourteen."

Kosher meat was scarce as well. Before the war it was often imported to Palestine from Romania. After the war, it was eventually supplied from Uganda, Argentina, and Brazil. The only kosher beef in the early years of the state came from male calves produced from the rapidly growing herds of dairy cows. Under a Jewish Agency program, thousands of heifers were being sent to Israel from the United States by plane and ship. It was not until the late fifties, however, when water sources had improved, that large herds of beef cattle were introduced into the Israeli agricultural economy.

After the Huleh Valley was drained, creating twenty thousand acres of highly fertile land, the menace of malaria was finally eliminated and internal agriculture developed. In addition, the nearby Jordan River was deepened and straightened, and the Jordanian and Negev water pipelines were built, providing the Negev Desert with the water to produce the crops that the country needed and to create more grass on which beef could graze.

Eliahu Navoth, the "father of the Israeli soybean," was sure that peace would come to Israel and its neighbors through the cultivation of soy, which would feed the increasing number of hungry mouths.

Arriving in Palestine from the Ukraine at the age of eighteen, in 1912, Navoth became one of the first farmers in Herzliyya, now a suburb of Tel Aviv. Because of the scarcity of water and food in Palestine, he was fascinated by the benefits of soy, a fodder crop of high nutritive value, which he was growing on his farm with seeds given to him by the British Mandatory Administration and later the United States Soy Bean Council. One scientist, Chaim Weizmann, who would become the first president of Israel, encouraged Navoth in his pursuit of peace by telling him that "soybean cultivation would be a great achievement, outstripping in importance the production of cannons or other weapons."

Through the years Navoth traveled the world, observing cooks and searching for the best strains of soy to grow in Israel. He learned to cook more than fourteen different soybean delicacies—salads, soups, cutlets, gravy, breads, cakes, falafel, and fish balls. His home became an experimental station for public nutrition and a test kitchen for new recipes. He was constantly preparing soybean meals for the public—once frying soy falafel for more than eight hundred children—never telling the unsuspecting guests that they were eating soy until they had tasted all the dishes.

Israel still leads the world in the use of soybean products, perhaps due in part to soy's potential as a dairy substitute. A full 85 percent of the country's cooking oil is made from soy, rather than from the more native olive. Soy also can be found in more than three thousand other products, from soap, celluloid, and lacquer paints to cattle feed, coffee, chocolate, and "cheese" puddings.

As the fertility of the land increased, so did the excitement of creating food to meet the needs of the growing population. "Israel is unique," said Shaul Homsky, author of *Fruits Grown in Israel*. "Within a small area, for example, a subtropical climate exists—near the Sea of Galilee, where mangoes, kiwis and bananas can grow—alongside a temperate climate in the mountains of Galilee and the Golan, where cherries and apples grow." Diversity of Israeli agriculture also has been affected by the constantly changing population; the European population that developed in the 1920s, '30s, and '40s was accustomed to eating apples, plums, and cherries, while later immigrants from Middle Eastern countries liked to eat and grow grapes, olives, and dates. "Because of the lack of a deep agricultural tradition," Mr. Homsky wrote, "farmers on the kibbutzim were ready to accept new techniques and experiment with new fruits and vegetables, unlike in a country like Greece, where for generations farmers have been tilling the soil in the same way and people have had the same diet."

Sometimes the experiments did not work. In 1961, Moshe Dayan, minister of agriculture, decided to replace Israel's favorite Marymont—a large, oval, and juicy tomato—with a thicker-skinned, cylindrical, and almost juiceless tomato, slightly larger than a cherry tomato. Dayan thought this "Moneymaker" would be heartier and cheaper to produce, and would appeal to the export market. In the transition from one strain of tomato to the other, five thousand tons of Moneymaker tomatoes were to be grown in the first season, half for local consumption and half for export. Farmers were encouraged to grow only Moneymakers. But the experiment was a failure both inside and outside the country, and the local press dubbed it Dayan's "assault" on agriculture.

Still, new fruits and vegetables had an increasing presence in the local market, and ambitious young chefs began to take advantage of their novelty. Chef Uri Guttman, who from the late sixties on was considered the ambassador of the Israeli kitchen, came up with innovative concoctions like a hot avocado soup; "St. Peter's fish" with mango and pomegranate; and crepes stuffed with pears, nuts, dates, and figs. Schooled in the French culinary tradition, Guttman traveled around the world representing Israel in cooking competitions and adapted unusual recipes to what was available in the country. He also developed menus for army bases and restaurants, using local products. "One of my dreams was to establish an Israeli cuisine," he said. "It is hard, though, with Jews coming from so many countries."

When the Golan Heights were annexed in 1967, apples, one of the few fruits that the Israelis were not adept at growing, were planted there and thrived in the cold nights and the high, dry altitude. Israelis also had the same success with grapes at the Golan Heights Winery, close to the Syrian border. These new varietals were of a much higher quality than Baron de Rothschild's plantings had been at his low-lying coastal wineries a hundred years earlier. The Golan Heights Winery, jointly owned by the nearby kibbutzim that supplied the grapes, introduced its first vintage in 1983, from grapes planted ten years earlier. These kosher wines have been winning silver and gold medals in international competitions ever since.

In 1973, Dr. Itzhak Adate, a scientist with the Vulcani Institute, in Rehovot, went on a professional tour to New Zealand where he tasted the kiwi, which had been introduced from China. Bringing a few cuttings and seeds back, he asked the kibbutzniks at Kibbutz Ammiad, located down the road from his home, to plant them. By 1980 the first kiwis had come to the market. With the abundant crop, Scottish-born Jeff Marks, a wine hobbyist and a member of the kibbutz, suggested that kiwi wine might taste as good as cordials made from pears, berries, and plums. Today, the kibbutz exports kiwi wine to countries throughout the world. Ironically, although Israel's agricultural industry is at the forefront of the global marketplace, kibbutz involvement has become proportionally less, with less than 2 percent of Israel's population now living on the kibbutzim.

Throughout the Middle East, where emotions run high, politics also plays a major role in the complicated global market. Since the 1980s, for example, when all trade with Iran was blocked, Israel has become the main exporter of Iranian variants of mint, parsley, and other herb seeds for Iranian-American growers.

In the past two decades, with a general rise in disposable income and the elim-

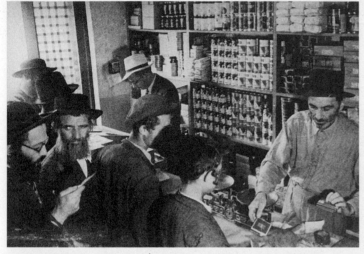

Carefully choosing provisions from abroad during the years of scarcity

Israel today has a total population of 6.3 million people, with close to 4.9 million Jews and 1.1 million Arabs. Of the Arab population, 842,000 people are Moslem, 183,000 Christian, and 95,000 Druse. Divided and subdivided into more than a hundred Jewish and Moslem groupings, and some thirty-two Christian denominations, the country is home to Jews from Chechnya, Ethiopia, and Yemen; Copts from Egypt; Greek Orthodox from Greece; Armenians from Turkey; and Moslems from the entire eastern Mediterranean world.

The first Moslems came to Israel in the seventh century. Today, representing one-fifth of the total population, Moslem communities are divided not so much by religion as by place of birth. The majority of Moslems in Israel are Sunni, one of the four sects of Islam. The Druse, a splinter group which left the Moslem religion after five hundred years, live in the north of Israel, traditionally in mountain villages.

The Christian communities fall into four main groups: Eastern Orthodox, Roman Catholic, Monophysite, and Protestant. Along with the local Arab Christian members of almost all the thirty Christian denominations, church dignitaries and heads of Christian communities reside in all parts of the Holy Land. The most important are the three patriarchs: the Greek Orthodox, the Armenian Orthodox, and the Latin (Roman Catholic). Christian representatives include thousands of monks, priests, and nuns; custodians of the holy sites in Galilee; the Baha'i Shrine in Haifa; teachers in the church-affiliated schools; nurses and doctors. In addition to the Moslems, Christians, and Druse are the ancient Jewish sects of Karaites and Samaritans.

There has been a continual stream of Jews into Israel since the time of David, a thousand years before Christ. Despite centuries of diffusion in the Diaspora, Jews have always yearned for Jerusalem, turning toward it in prayer throughout the world.

ination of travel taxes imposed on the struggling economy, Israelis have become open to new experiences in travel and food. After their two-year mandatory service, many young Israeli soldiers go abroad, most frequently to travel in East Asia or Latin America and to spend some time working in the United States. Many of these young people return home with new culinary tastes, as did American Peace Corps volunteers in the 1960s. A number of them have become chefs, schooled in international cuisine and influential in the development of modern Israeli cooking.

Despite their global lifestyles, the new Israeli chefs still cultivate a link to the foods of the Old Testament. Grapes, dates, lentils, and chickpeas are but a few of the ancient ingredients that have captured their imaginations in producing signature dishes. With constant waves of immigration, Israel is rapidly incorporating the native cuisines of its new populations. The story of Israeli food is not just a Jewish story—its recipes cross borders more easily than people do. It is also the story of a land that has overcome harsh natural deprivation to bring forth new agricultural produce. Because it constantly incorporates so much from the rest of the world, Israel may never boast of one "cuisine," but it will always retain a rich mixture of fine tastes. It reflects the modern mosaic of the country, embracing the culinary influences of its Arab neighbors and accommodating the varied tastes of the world's Jews.

Introduction

Breakfasts and Brunch Fare

I remember so clearly my first breakfast when I was volunteering on a kibbutz in the 1970s. Before the sun was up we started working, and at 7:30—breakfast time—all of us volunteers ran to a pump, splashed water on our faces and hands, and sat down in a huge shed in the middle of a field, hungry for breakfast. There was something so satisfying about a bowl of figs or pears picked that morning, with the dew still on them, and a basket of kibbutz cucum-

Above: "Tipat Chalav"—the "drop of milk" campaign to encourage Jews and Arabs to drink milk, circa 1920

bers, tomatoes, and green peppers. We could choose our own white cheese, or cottage cheese, yogurt, sour cream called *shemenet,* and kibbutz-baked rye bread or rolls, to craft our own meal. "I'll trade my tomato for your egg" was a typical barter between us hungry volunteers and kibbutzniks. We learned how to chop tomatoes and eggs in various ways to make the food seem different. The kibbutz breakfast was, and still is, a testament to what Israelis have done with the land.

According to Schmuel Federmann, one of the co-founders with his brother Yekutiel of Dan Hotels Corporation, the hotel dairy breakfast sprang from competition with small hotels in Safed and Tiberias, where three meals were included in a full pension. "Putting out a spread in the morning called the 'Israeli buffet breakfast,' which was included in the room price, made us able to compete with the small hotels," he said. "We started out with oranges, then apples, then pears, then prunes. We added more and more when we had more and more. Israel was, after all, the land of milk and honey."

The vast buffets were an instant hit. Even Eleanor Roosevelt, one of the early guests at the Dan Hotel in Tel Aviv, kept remarking about the breakfasts in Israel. "Although food didn't seem important when you were with Mrs. Roosevelt, she was amazed and pleased by the breakfasts we were served, the hard-boiled eggs, the herring, all kinds of breads, sliced and pickled cucumbers, since it was so unlike any breakfast we had ever seen," recalled her traveling companion, Trude Lash.

In the average Israeli home during the week, however, breakfast runs the gamut from a simple pita bread sprinkled with olive oil and *za'atar,* the ubiquitous Middle Eastern spice combination, to elaborate vegetable dips, milk and cheese products, and preserves spread over many kinds of bakery bread.

Although every kind of prepared cereal is available in supermarkets, Israel is not a major cereal-eating country. Some ethnic varieties like *jerisheh,* a cracked wheat turned into porridge, are often eaten in Arab villages. But Russian immigrants did not easily adapt to oatmeal and other hot cereals.

Sabbath breakfasts, however, are different. Iraqi Jews eat *sabikh,* a pita with fried eggplant, a hard-boiled egg, parsley, tahina, and mango pickle. Turkish Jews enjoy *burekas* (see page 28), those flaky finger pastries traditionally eaten on Shabbat after returning from the synagogue, or Yemenite *mahlouach* (see page 100). Central Europeans often make coffee cakes, or puffy pancakes like the Austrian *kaiserschmarrn* (see page 40) while Arabs, both Christian and Moslem, eat *kataif* (see page 38), pancakes filled with nuts or cream and bathed in a sugar syrup.

Today, Israelis buy most salads, milk products, and even ethnic breads ready-made in the supermarkets. Meals reflect the bounty of the land, with an amazing variety of yogurts, sour cream, cream cheese, cottage cheese, and goat cheeses, as well as spreads with chunks of olives and more than a dozen versions of the fruit preserves which are the pride of Israel.

Although this chapter features breakfast or brunch items, they can be prepared, as in Israel, for dinner as well. I have included some of my favorites, such as the North African *shakshuka,* a marvelous egg dish with tomatoes; figs stuffed with cheese; and a panoply of preserves. Israel has great jams, pulpier and less sweet than they are in the United States: date, pumpkin, star fruit, eggplant, sweet potato, orange, apricot, onion, beet—you name it, and all are legacies of the many immigrations to this new country.

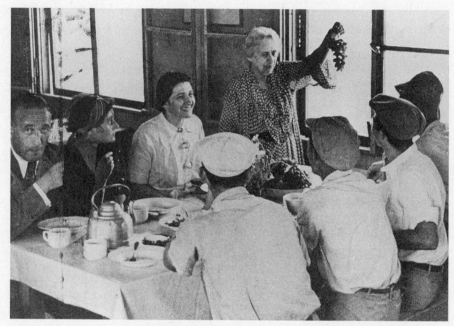

Henrietta Szold, founder of Hadassah, admiring grapes at breakfast on a kibbutz

In 1930, Simon Agranat, the chief justice of the Israeli Supreme Court, wrote to his aunt and uncle in Chicago: "I had my eighth successive egg meal during my three-day journey through the Emek (the valley)." Eggs have always been a main protein for people in Israel. When I lived in Jerusalem, I would make for my breakfast—or even for dinner—scrambled eggs with sauteed spring onions, fresh herbs, and dollops of cream cheese melted into the eggs as they were cooking. Probably the most popular egg dish in Israel is *shakshuka,* one of those onomatopoeic Hebrew and North African words, meaning "all mixed up." The most famous rendition of this tomato dish, which is sometimes mixed with meat but more often made in Israel with scrambled or poached eggs, is served at the Tripolitana Doktor Shakshuka Restaurant in old Jaffa.

Doktor Shakshuka, owned by a large Libyan family, is located near the antique market in an old stone-arched building with colorful Arab-tiled floors. "When I was a young girl at the age of ten I liked to cook," said Sarah Gambsor, the main cook of the restaurant and wife of one of the owners. "My mother told me that I should marry someone who has a restaurant." And she did just that.

Mrs. Gambsor, a large woman who clearly enjoys eating what she cooks, demonstrated that the dish starts with a heavy frying pan and tomato sauce. Then eggs are carefully broken in and left to set or, if the diner prefers, scrambled in as they cook. The *shakshuka* is then served in the frying pan at the table.

Shakshuka a la Doktor Shakshuka

YIELD: 6 SERVINGS

2 pounds fresh tomatoes, unpeeled and cut in quarters, or one 28-ounce can tomatoes

6 cloves garlic, roughly diced

2 teaspoons salt, or to taste

1 teaspoon sweet paprika

2 teaspoons tomato paste

1/4 cup vegetable oil

6 large eggs

1. Place the tomatoes, garlic, salt, paprika, tomato paste, and vegetable oil in a small saucepan. Bring to a simmer and cook, uncovered, over low heat until thick, for about 30 minutes, stirring occasionally.

2. Ladle the tomato sauce into a greased 12-inch frying pan. Bring to a simmer and break the eggs over the tomatoes. Gently break the yolks with a fork. Cover and continue to cook for about 3 to 4 minutes, until the eggs are set. Bring the frying pan directly to the table. Set it on a trivet and spoon out the *shakshuka.*

NOTE Alternatively, you can make individual portions, as they do at Doktor Shakshuka, by ladling some of the sauce into a very small pan and poaching one egg in it.

Burekas— My Favorite Breakfast Pastries

I remember with pleasure the Turkish spinach *burekas* we ate every Friday morning when I worked in the Jerusalem municipality. The ritual was as follows: Simontov, the guard at the front door downstairs, would appear carrying a bronze tray with Turkish coffee and the heavenly, flaky pastries filled with spinach or cheese, called *filikas* in Ladino. It is rare today to have such delicious *burekas* in Jerusalem or anywhere else in Israel. Most of the dough is commercially produced puff pastry, much thicker and less flaky than the home-made phyllo used to be. A few places, like Burekas Penzo in Tel Aviv (near Levinsky Street), which has been making the pastries by hand in the Turkish style for more than thirty years, produce a close second to those I remember from my days in Jerusalem. Various Ladino names like *bulemas* and *boyos* differentiate fillings and distinguish a Jewish *bureka* from a Turkish one. If you can find the thick phyllo dough, that works well. Otherwise, try this. My fifteen-year-old makes and sells them for fifty cents apiece. They are great!

YIELD: ABOUT 60 *BUREKA* TRIANGLES

1 cup (2 sticks) unsalted butter, melted

16-ounce package phyllo dough, thawed

Filling of your choice (see recipes below)

1 large egg

Black or regular sesame seeds for sprinkling

1. Preheat the oven to 350 degrees.
2. Using a pastry brush, coat the bottom of a cookie sheet with some of the melted butter.
3. Take a sheet of phyllo and cut lengthwise in strips, 4½ inches wide. Butter the strips, fold over lengthwise, butter again, and place a tablespoon of filling on the end. Then fold up right to left as you would a flag, so that the end result is a plump triangle, buttering the outside at the end. Repeat with the remaining filling and dough. Beat the egg, brush the *burekas* with it, and sprinkle sesame seeds over the tops.
4. Place on the cookie sheet and bake for 20 minutes or until golden in color.

NOTE You can also mold and freeze the *burekas* after forming. Defrost for 2 hours and then bake. You can fill any leftover phyllo with chocolate chips or Nutella and make triangular treats.

Three Ways to Fill a *Bureka*

Spinach Filling

YIELD: ABOUT 2 CUPS, ENOUGH FILLING FOR ABOUT 20 *BUREKAS*

2 pounds fresh spinach or Swiss chard leaves, washed well, or two 10-ounce packages chopped frozen spinach

2 large eggs, beaten lightly

1/2 cup crumbled feta cheese

1/2 cup grated cheddar cheese

1/4 cup chopped fresh parsley

2 tablespoons chopped fresh dill

8 scallions, diced

Salt and freshly ground pepper to taste

1. Place the fresh spinach or Swiss chard leaves in a frying pan with only the water that clings to the leaves, and cook briefly until they wilt. (If using frozen spinach, simply defrost.) Drain very well, squeezing out as much of the water as possible. Cool and chop.

2. Mix together the eggs, feta and cheddar cheeses, parsley, dill, and scallions. Add the spinach and salt and pepper to taste; mix well.

3. Use about 1 tablespoon of filling for each *bureka*.

Eggplant Filling

YIELD: ABOUT 2 CUPS, ENOUGH FILLING FOR ABOUT 20 *BUREKAS*

2 medium eggplants (about 2 pounds)

1/3 cup *kasseri* or feta cheese, crumbled

1/3 cup grated sheep or mozzarella cheese

1/4 cup chopped fresh cilantro or parsley

Salt to taste

1. Preheat the oven to 450 degrees. Prick the skin of the eggplants all over and roast on an oiled cookie sheet for 25 minutes, turning occasionally.

2. Remove the pulp from the skin, discarding the seeds and draining off any extra liquid. Cool slightly, then pat dry and coarsely chop. Combine the eggplant pulp, cheeses, and cilantro or parsley and mash well with a fork; add salt if needed.

3. Use about 1 tablespoon of filling for each *bureka*.

Cheese Filling

YIELD: ABOUT 2 CUPS, ENOUGH FILLING FOR ABOUT 20 *BUREKAS*

2 large eggs

1 cup grated cheddar cheese

1 cup crumbled feta cheese

Freshly ground pepper to taste

1. Beat the eggs in a small bowl. Add the cheddar and feta cheeses and pepper to taste. Mix well.

2. Use about 1 tablespoon of filling for each *bureka*.

Paula Ben-Gurion's
Kutch Mutch

Beneath the olive, sabra, and pomegranate trees near Kibbutz Sde Boker is David and Paula Ben-Gurion's "hut," the home to which Israel's first prime minister moved when he retired briefly in 1953. On December 30th of that year, Ben-Gurion wrote his daughter Geula a letter about the kibbutz. "Mother, of course, bought canned goods and bottles of wine. For the time being the wine just sits and only an occasional can is opened. There is a communal kitchen, of course, but mother is not keen on it. She neither likes the cleanliness of the tables nor the

· · · A LAND OF "YOGURT" AND HONEY · · ·

"*Tochdoo laba*," I echoed in a low voice. I knew it meant something like "Who will buy my yogurt?" but I did not rush out as quickly as I might have, for I wanted to hear the cry repeated. It was high-pitched, rhythmical, and clear, easily audible above the dull thud of the waves. The woman was tall and slim in her long black robe and smelled of sour milk and oven smoke. When she reached our veranda she put down her pot, uncovered a metal ladle from under her wide belt, and measured out the required quantity into a bowl my mother had provided. The village-made yogurt was sour and unsmooth, and I adored it.

—Ruth Jordan, *Daughter of the Waves* (1985)

And he said unto her: "Give me, I pray thee, a little water to drink; for I am thirsty." And she opened a bottle of milk, and gave him drink, and covered him.

—Judges 4:19

The "milk" referred to in this biblical passage was not the homogenized cow's milk available in stores today. More likely, it was *leben,* a refreshing, slightly acidic yogurt drink, thinned with water and made by shaking fresh goat's milk and salt in a goatskin or lambskin container and letting it ferment naturally, with the stale milk from previous use adhering to the skin. Claude Reignier Conder, in his *Tent Work in Palestine* (1878), wrote that *leben* was "generally considered a delicacy...refreshing to travelers, but has also a strange soporific effect, which was so sudden in its action on one English clergyman after a long ride that he thought he had been poisoned."

Yogurt evolved some six thousand years ago in the Middle East. A camel merchant or other nomad probably poured milk into a leather bag. By the end of a day of travel, the milk had turned into a custard-like, slightly acidic milk product. Thinned with water, it became a thirst-quenching drink. In later years people learned that yogurt could be made by inoculating one cup of warm fresh milk with a teaspoon or two of already prepared yogurt and leaving it out, covered, in a warm place overnight. *Labneh,* a drained yogurt product, sometimes made with cream or half-and-half and with salt added to taste, is delicious in dips or just sprinkled with *za'atar* (see page 62). At least three or four versions of yogurt or *labneh* mixed with vegetables are served with fruit at the Israeli breakfast table, or as one of the many appetizers at the beginning of lunch or dinner.

quality of the food nor the cooking. She hardly eats either in the kitchen or at home. How she manages, I don't know. I get used to nearly all the dishes and eat far more than I used to in Jerusalem or Tel Aviv."

Everyone has a story about Ben-Gurion's American-born wife, Paula. "The most important thing for Paula was David Ben-Gurion," said their grandson Elon Ben-Gurion. "She protected him like a child. I remember one day in Sde Boker. I walked in the house and he was sitting inside talking with Zalman Shazar, then the president of Israel. Paula walked in and told Shazar to sit outside so that Ben-Gurion could eat. He waited like a little kid until David Ben-Gurion had finished eating."

Paula's quirkiness is apparent today in the sparsely equipped kitchen of the Ben-Gurion home on the kibbutz, now a museum. There stands a table with an Osterizer, a bottle of fruit squash, which was diluted with water to make juice, and a few pots on the tiny stove. On the wall is a listing of the pills Ben-Gurion was to take, and a recipe for Paula's healthy and hated invention of *kutch mutch,* which she made him promise to eat every day for breakfast. This much-joked-about concoction included yogurt, white cheese, semolina, strawberry syrup, milk, and raw eggs. "When Paula passed away, Ben-Gurion, for whom food was a means to live, not an experience, made a commitment that he would eat it every day in her memory," said their grandson. "In my grandmother's mind it was a very healthy dish. I think his commitment to her was fabulous."

I have eaten versions of this much more palatable and equally healthy *kutch mutch* throughout Israel. Here is my adaptation with pecans, which I was surprised to taste in this dish in Israel since the nuts seemed so American to me.

YIELD: 4 SERVINGS

4 cups plain yogurt

6 tablespoons bran flakes

2 large apples, peeled, cored, and grated

1 tablespoon light-brown sugar, or to taste

2 tablespoons honey

3/4 cup chopped walnuts or pecans

1. Put the yogurt in a mixing bowl. Sprinkle the bran, grated apples, brown sugar, honey, and nuts over and mix well.
2. Serve as a breakfast dish, snack, or dessert.

NOTE   You can replace the apples with 2 cups of sliced fresh strawberries or other fruit of your choice.

I will never forget the breakfast I had at Meir and Nili Friedman's farm. For five generations, since 1881, Friedman family farmers have been living in the stone house built by Meir's great-grandfather in the picturesque village of Rosh Pina, one of the oldest settlements in the Galilee.

In 1882, the year after the first Friedman came from Romania and five years after the first settlers arrived from nearby Safed, Baron Edmond de Rothschild started a winery, a silk mill, and a tobacco plant in Rosh Pina, none of which succeeded. All that remains are the mulberry trees in the park across the cobblestone street from the Friedmans' home and some of the stone houses.

In the last ten years, this small mountain village of three thousand has had a renaissance. Many artists have come to live here, so Nili, a ceramist and artist, decided to turn some of the rooms in their house into a bed-and-breakfast. Their daughter Shiri, now in her twenties, does the cooking. She first learned to cook *ochel baladiya* (country food) from Wadia, the family's Arab Christian housekeeper, and then apprenticed with several chefs in France. Shiri has transformed the menu from simple farm fare into sophisticated food that is recognized throughout Israel for its freshness and its imaginative French approach.

Sitting at a farm table under a fig tree, with the Huleh Valley in the distance, we watched the cattle peacefully munch their hay. We drank our coffee and nibbled some of the Friedmans' home-cured olives, picked from their four-and-a-half-acre orchard and pressed in a village on the Golan Heights. The homemade breads, baked by Nili and Shiri, were presented on locally made ceramic platters with fresh goat cheese made by Nili's sister Amira, and a mushroom and mint omelet from the farm's fresh eggs.

To prepare the meals, the family worked together as a team. Shiri took turns with her brother Amit pitting olives to be baked in that evening's rolls. Amit, who studies industrial design in Tel Aviv, works weekends as his sister's sous chef. While Nili waited on the guests and answered the constantly ringing telephone, her husband, Meir, and the youngest son, Emanuel, were feeding the 150 head of cattle which they raise for breeding. Meir only stopped to chat when friends of their son Omer, who was still in the army, dropped by for coffee.

Of all Shiri's dishes, I especially liked her sweet and savory fresh figs stuffed with cheese and served with an apricot-mint sauce, a showstopper at any brunch.

Figs Stuffed with Cheese and Served on an Apricot-Mint Coulis with a Confit of Onions

With such a short season for fresh figs, Shiri sometimes substitutes poached dried figs or, in midsummer, fresh apricots. Shiri uses four kinds of cheese for this dish, including the famous variety from Safed (see page 242), and serves it over a confit of onions with fresh mint and her mom's apricot jam. This is a perfect brunch dish.

If you cannot find Safed cheese, use a Bulgarian feta. You can, of course, substitute store-bought apricot jam for the homemade variety, but chances are it will not have the same chunkiness or rich flavor.

YIELD: 6 SERVINGS

1 tablespoon Safed or Bulgarian feta cheese	3 tablespoons extra virgin olive oil
1 tablespoon goat cheese	2 large onions, sliced in thin rings
1 tablespoon Roquefort cheese	6 fresh figs
4 tablespoons cream cheese	¼ cup apricot jam (see page 35)
2 cloves garlic	1 tablespoon chopped fresh mint, plus whole mint leaves for garnish
1 teaspoon fresh thyme, chopped	

1. Put the cheeses, garlic, thyme, and 1 tablespoon of the olive oil in a food processor equipped with a steel blade. Puree and then refrigerate for a few hours.

2. Heat a frying pan and add the remaining oil with the onions; reduce the heat to low. Cook, uncovered, very, very slowly, stirring occasionally, until the onions become a rich golden brown, adding a little water if necessary. This may take up to 30 minutes. The longer you cook them, the more flavor your onions will have. This is called a "confit."

3. Trim the stems from the figs and cut crosses in the tops of the fruit, slicing almost to the bottom so that the fig will open like a flower.

4. Take a heaping tablespoon of the cheese mixture and place it inside one of the figs. Repeat with the remaining cheese and figs. This can be done several hours before serving and refrigerated.

5. To serve, mix the onion confit with the apricot jam and a tablespoon of fresh mint. Spoon a dollop of this confit on a small plate. Top with the cheese-stuffed fig.

NOTE You can substitute dried figs for fresh, or even, if you prefer, dried pears. Merely remove the stems, place fruit in enough water to cover, and simmer, uncovered, for about 20 minutes or until soft. Drain, wipe dry, and use as above.

In 1938, at the age of thirteen and a half, Ari Rath, former editor of the Jerusalem *Post*, came to Palestine. He was one of the lucky fifty to leave his native Vienna with Youth Aliyah, an organized immigration of German and Austrian Jewish children spearheaded by Henrietta Szold, the founder of Hadassah, the Women's Zionist Organization. Almost all of the remaining 175 applicants perished in concentration camps.

"I was a spoiled upper-middle-class boy," he said. "I was selected after writing an essay on 'why I want to go to Palestine.' At that age, I only knew that I wanted to go to a place where they wouldn't push me around anymore, so I went.

"The first shock for me came on the boat from Trieste to Haifa. My grandmother had presented me with a going-away gift of her honey cake and a jar of her marvelous homemade apricot jam. The first thing our leader told us was that we were going to a Socialist country and that we would pool all the gifts except for two or three good pieces, which we could keep for ourselves. I cut up four little pieces of the cake and put the jam on it. How I savored that jam.

"All of us acquired foster families in Israel to look after us. Again, we spoiled Viennese children wanted our *Jause*, the four o'clock coffee hour. So the leaders instituted it, with cocoa, tea, and bread with watered-down jam. Four o'clock coffee and cake is still a tradition in Israel.

"For five years we lived in tents and milked cows. The tent often fell down with the wind, and it was freezing. Our diet consisted mostly of bread and margarine and vegetables and pickled smoked herring. Once a week, for Shabbat morning breakfast, we had challah and one hundred grams of butter. Already they did a lot with eggplant, frying it like chopped liver. We had meat twice a week.

"I looked forward to having soup with potatoes or noodles, but the biggest delight was when we would get a slice of halvah—it was like a child having a piece of Godiva chocolate today. It was all in the mind, you could train yourself. It is not easy for a teenager to start life from scratch. It hardens you."

The Foods of
Israel Today

Nili Friedman's *Mishmish* Apricot Jam

*T*oocli *mishmish* is an Arabic phrase meaning that you must hurry to do something, otherwise you will lose the opportunity. In both Hebrew and Arabic, *mishmish* is the word for "apricot," which has one of the shortest ripe seasons of all fruits and therefore must be eaten and preserved very quickly. Besides eating them fresh from the tree during this time, Nili, like most Israelis, makes a chunky, compote-like apricot jam, traditionally eaten as a sweet with tea. Nili lets the cut fruit sit overnight before it is cooked down, bringing out a particularly full fruity flavor. When I make jam, I select firm apricots and let them sit a day until they start to soften. Beware of mushy, tasteless apricots!

YIELD: 4 CUPS

2 pounds fresh apricots (about 14)	1/4 cup water
1 cinnamon stick	2 cups light-brown sugar

1. Cut the apricots in half, removing the pits. Puncture a plastic bag with about five 1/2-inch slits. Put the apricots and the cinnamon stick in the bag and set in a bowl. Let sit out overnight.

2. The next day, transfer the apricots, their juice, and the cinnamon stick to a heavy casserole. Add the water. Simmer, covered, stirring occasionally, for about 1 hour. Stir in the brown sugar and immediately turn off the heat. The jam will caramelize naturally. Remove the cinnamon stick and cool. Put into jars and store, covered, in the refrigerator. It will last for several weeks.

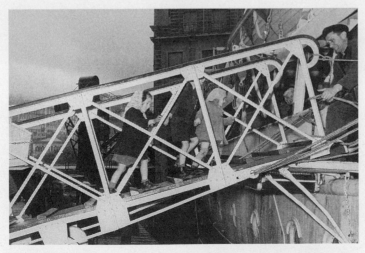

Youth Aliyah children arriving in Palestine in the late 1930s

Breakfasts and Brunch Fare

Coconut Jam

I first tasted this Egyptian Jewish coconut jam during Passover when I lived in Jerusalem. This is eaten like a jam with tea and is also tasty spread on a matzoh.

8 ounces unsweetened coconut flakes

1 tablespoon orange-blossom water

10 tablespoons cold water

1 cup sugar

1 1/2 teaspoons lemon juice

1/4 cup blanched almonds, chopped roughly

1. Place the coconut in a bowl and sprinkle with the orange-blossom water and 4 tablespoons of the cold water.

2. Fluff the coconut with your fingers and leave overnight to absorb the moisture. It will swell and become soft.

3. Put the sugar, lemon juice, and the remaining water in a small saucepan. Bring to a boil, reduce the heat, and let simmer for a few minutes until a thick syrup forms. (It should coat the back of a spoon.)

4. Add the softened coconut to the heated syrup, stirring constantly with a wooden spoon.

5. Remove the pan from the heat as soon as the coconut heats and becomes translucent. Allow the jam to cool, and stir in the almonds. Transfer to jars and refrigerate. It will last several weeks in the fridge.

Cheese *Levivot*— Pancakes

These cheese pancakes are typically served in Israel at Shavuot, the late-springtime festival which celebrates the time when Moses received the Ten Commandments on Mount Sinai. It is traditional to eat dairy at Shavuot because historically it was the only time when grass was growing in the parched land, thus producing more eggs and milk from the cows, goats, and chickens. Of the many other explanations for serving dairy at Shavuot, I particularly like this one: according to the mystics in Safed, eating pure dairy products is a reminder that those whose faith in the Torah is pure will attain paradise. You can also eat these cheese pancakes at Hanukkah—when, according to Jewish tradition, Judith ate them before decapitating General Holofernes to save the Jewish people.

YIELD: ABOUT 20 PANCAKES

2 large eggs	1 teaspoon plus 2 tablespoons sugar
2 cups cottage cheese	2 tablespoons unsalted butter
1/2 cup all-purpose flour	2 tablespoons vegetable oil
1/2 teaspoon baking powder	1/2 teaspoon cinnamon
1 teaspoon salt	

1. Beat the eggs with a whisk until fluffy. Add the cheese, flour, baking powder, salt, and 1 teaspoon of the sugar, and mix well.

2. Heat a griddle or a nonstick skillet; add 1 tablespoon of the butter and 1 tablespoon of the vegetable oil and heat until the butter is melted. Pour a heaping tablespoon of batter onto the skillet, flattening slightly with the back of the spoon. Cook in batches until golden brown, turn, and brown on other side. Repeat with the remaining batter, using the rest of the butter and oil when needed. Drain the pancakes on paper towels.

3. Mix the remaining sugar and the cinnamon in a small bowl. Serve the pancakes sprinkled with the cinnamon sugar.

Kataif—
Celebratory Pancakes

Whenever *kataif* are served, it signals a holiday in the Arab communities of Israel. I have tasted these light pancakes everywhere: at a break-the-fast meal after Ramadan in the Old City of Jerusalem, at street stands, and a particularly delicious version on a trip to the Moslem village of Arraba in Lower Galilee, where the pancakes were first fried on a Primus stove, then filled with caramelized sesame seeds and heated up in a taboon oven, which is fueled by dried goat manure and leftover debris from making olive oil, then covered with sand and set right into the ground. They are even sold ready-made.

Typically, these spongy pancakes are first fried on one side, then stuffed and folded into a crescent with all sorts of seasonal and symbolic fillings, then bathed in a mild sugar sauce. To break the daily fast of Ramadan, for example, *kataif* often contain fresh apricot jam; for the anniversary of the death of a family member the pancakes can be filled with caramelized sesame seeds, almonds, or walnuts; in the spring they are often filled with white curd cheese or *ushta,* a thick clotted cream made from the top of boiled goat's milk, or even ricotta.

Kataif is a great make-ahead dessert or a brunch dish. Fry the pancakes, fill them, and cover with plastic. The morning of the brunch, they can be heated in a pan in the oven and, just before serving, covered with the sugar syrup. The trick to making the perfect *kataif* pancake is to mix the batter very well—in some villages the batter is actually hand-mixed in a wooden churn. *Kataif* also must be fried on a very hot griddle and removed before they dry out.

YIELD: ABOUT 16 *KATAIF*

1 package dry yeast (1 scant tablespoon)

1 1/2 cups warm water

4 tablespoons sugar

1/2 teaspoon salt

1 1/2 cups all-purpose flour

1 cup sesame seeds or finely chopped walnuts

1 teaspoon ground cinnamon

2 tablespoons unsalted butter

1. Dissolve the yeast in the warm water in the bowl of an electric mixer. Using the mixer paddle, stir in 1 tablespoon of the sugar, the salt, and the flour, and mix very well, for at least 5 minutes. Cover with plastic wrap and let rise for an hour or two, until the batter starts to bubble.

2. Ladle about 1/4 cup of batter onto a very hot, greased frying pan, turning the pan to make the pancake an even circle, about 4 inches in diameter. When the pancake begins to bubble, remove it from the pan before the bubbles dry out, leaving one side uncooked. Repeat with the remaining batter, stacking the pancakes as you go and covering them with a damp cloth.

3. In a small bowl, mix the sesame seeds or chopped walnuts with the remaining 3 tablespoons sugar and the cinnamon. Melt the butter in a frying pan and add the sesame seeds or nuts, stirring for just a minute or two.

4. Spoon 1 tablespoon of filling onto the center of the raw side of each pancake, fold pancake over into a crescent shape, then pinch closed. Layer the *kataif* on a baking pan and cover with plastic wrap. Before serving, remove plastic wrap and bake in a preheated 350-degree oven for about 15 minutes, then spoon the cold sugar syrup (see below) over the pancakes.

Sugar Syrup

YIELD: ABOUT 3 CUPS

2 cups sugar

2 cups water

Juice of 1/2 lemon

1 teaspoon orange-blossom water (optional)

In a saucepan, dissolve the sugar in the water and bring to a boil. Skim off any foam that forms and boil for about 10 minutes, stirring occasionally, until liquid thickens ever so slightly. Squeeze the lemon juice and the orange-blossom water into the syrup and cool before drizzling over the *kataif.*

Vacationing at one of Israel's water parks

Kaiserschmarrn— Puff Pancake

When Seth Lipsky, then editor of the *Forward* newspaper, told me of his infatuation with *kaiserschmarrn,* I was embarrassed by my ignorance. I grew up eating *apfelschmarrn,* a puffy apple pancake. But *kaiserschmarrn?* I didn't have a clue.

So, I e-mailed my former boss Teddy Kollek, Jerusalem's ex-mayor and a self-proclaimed gourmand. "It is rather difficult to translate a taste into words," he wrote back. "Although this memory goes back to my childhood and youth, I still can feel on the tip of my tongue the taste of this delightful dessert, which often used to be part of our meals in Vienna."

Anxious to learn more, I called Teddy's good friend Erica Jesselson, who also grew up in Vienna, and who has two of the great kosher kitchens of the world, in her homes in Jerusalem and New York. Not only did she know *kaiserschmarrn,* cook it, and love it, she happened to have a picture and a recipe for it posted on her kitchen walls in both cities. A *kaiserschmarrn,* often called the "Emperor's nonsense" or the "Emperor's nothing," is a large puffy pancake that one tears apart with silver forks to serve.

Mrs. Jesselson, who visited Palestine for the first time in 1946 with her late husband, Ludwig, returned again and again, eventually taking up residence in Jerusalem. "When we first came if you could have an apple in Israel it was little and not much. Today we have too much. I used to make *kaiserschmarrn* for unannounced luncheon guests," she said, in her British-German accent. "You would serve it like an omelet with a *zwetschgen* (Italian plum) compote. I once had an Austrian guest for tea in Jerusalem, to whom I served pastries and then *kaiserschmarrn*. When the *kaiserschmarrn* came out, my guest was furious with me. Had she known, she would not have eaten all the other pastries!"

Kaiserschmarrn was named for the beloved Franz Josef I. This emperor of Austria and the king (*kaiser*) of Hungary granted the Jews civil rights and equality before the law. *Kaiserschmarrn—schmarrn* means "puff"—jibed with the abstemious lifestyle of this monarch, who ruled from 1848 until his death, in 1916, at the age of 86. He was known to rise early, go to bed early, and eat like the poorest of his peasants. "Everyone has eggs and flour in the house, so it is an easy dish to make for guests," said Mrs. Jesselson. Any tart fruit compote, or—perish the thought—prepared applesauce is a good accompaniment for this perfect brunch dish.

2 tablespoons raisins

3 tablespoons orange liqueur

4 large eggs, separated

4 tablespoons sugar

1/8 teaspoon salt

2 cups milk

1/2 teaspoon vanilla

1 cup cake flour

6 tablespoons unsalted butter

4 tablespoons confectioners' sugar

Fruit compote or plum jam

1. Soak the raisins in the orange liqueur for 30 minutes. Drain, discarding the liquid.

2. Beat the egg yolks, sugar, and salt together with a whisk until pale yellow and thick. Stir in the milk and vanilla extract, then gradually beat in the flour 1/2 cup at a time. Continue to beat until the batter is smooth. Stir in the raisins.

3. In another bowl or a mixer equipped with a whisk, beat the egg whites until they are stiff. Using a rubber spatula, carefully fold the whites into the batter.

4. Heat 1 tablespoon of the butter over low heat in a heavy 8-inch skillet. Pour in about one-third of the batter, enough to cover the bottom of the skillet to a 1/4-inch depth. Cook over low heat for about 4 minutes, or until the pancake has puffed up and browned slightly. (Test by lifting an edge with a spatula.) Using 2 spatulas, carefully turn the pancake out onto a plate. Add another tablespoon of butter to the pan, reheat, then slide the pancake back into the skillet, the uncooked side down. Cook for 4 more minutes. With 2 forks, pull the pancake into 6 to 8 pieces. Remove to a warm plate. Repeat twice more with the remaining batter.

5. Remove the *kaiserschmarrn* to a plate, sprinkle with the confectioners' sugar, and serve with a fruit compote or jam.

The first gas station–restaurant in Israel

Breakfasts and Brunch Fare

Pongyolas Alma— Apple in Pajamas

When Zehev Tadmor, a professor of chemical engineering and former president of the Technion (the Israel Institute of Technology) in Haifa, invited us for dinner, I never expected that he would actually cook the meal himself. Together with his wife, Tzippora, and two of their three children, he produced a first-class French meal. But when Zehev started to talk about the food he truly loves to cook, the subject was the Transylvanian fare of his childhood. One of his favorite recipes is for *pongyolas alma,* which can be translated as "apple in pajamas" or "dressed-up apples," a dish he makes on weekend mornings in his house high up on Mount Carmel. "I use two pans to speed up the process and make it more exciting," he told me over dinner. "The whole preparation is quick and simple and can be done in half an hour." Zehev dilutes any leftover batter with milk to make crepes. I use the batter with bananas as well as with apples.

YIELD: 24 SLICES, OR 6 SERVINGS

4 large full-flavored apples (like Granny Smith)

2/3 cup all-purpose flour

Pinch of salt

2 large eggs

1 tablespoon vegetable oil, plus oil for frying

1/3 cup milk

1/4 cup water

1/2 teaspoon cinnamon

2 tablespoons sugar

1. Peel, core, and slice each apple crosswise into 6 1/2-inch-thick rounds with holes in the center.

2. Put the flour and salt in a mixing bowl. Gradually whisk in the eggs, the tablespoon of vegetable oil, the milk, and water. Dip several apple slices in the batter. The batter should be just thick enough to adhere to the apple slices. If too thin, add more flour. If too thick, add more water.

3. Pour about an inch of vegetable oil into a large, heavy frying pan and heat to about 375 degrees.

4. Place the apple slices in the pan, 4 or 5 at a time, taking care not to crowd them. Fry for a few minutes until the coating is crisp on one side. Using tongs, turn the apples over, continuing to fry until the second side is crisp. Drain on paper towels.

5. Mix the cinnamon and sugar in a small bowl and sprinkle on top of the cooked apples before serving.

Lithuanian Cottage Cheese Coffee Cake

Hasia Noddle Vardi brought the recipe for this sweet cottage cheese coffee cake to Palestine from Lithuania in 1937. A Zionist youth, she followed her boyfriend, who had come earlier to help drain the swamps in the Huleh Valley.

YIELD: 1 LARGE COFFEE CAKE

1 package dry yeast	3 large eggs
1/2 cup warm water	2 cups cottage cheese, drained
2/3 cup sugar	2 teaspoons cinnamon
3 cups all-purpose flour (about)	1/4 cup (1/2 stick) unsalted butter
Dash of salt	

1. Dissolve the yeast in the water with 2 tablespoons of the sugar.

2. Place 2 1/2 cups of the flour in the food processor, add the salt, 2 of the eggs, and the yeast mixture, and process. Add flour as needed, continuing to process until you have a smooth and shiny dough. Remove to a greased bowl, cover, and let rise in a warm place for about 1 hour, until the dough has doubled in volume.

3. Turn the dough out onto a well-floured counter, punch down, and roll out into a large thin rectangle, about 12 by 16 inches. You may have to stretch the dough with your hands once you have rolled it out as thin as possible.

4. To make the filling, place the remaining egg in a bowl with 1/3 cup of the sugar, the cottage cheese, and the cinnamon. Mix well and then spread the filling over the dough, leaving an inch around the perimeter. Roll up the dough jelly-roll style, starting with 1 long side, and carefully place the roll in a greased and floured tube pan, seam side up.

5. To make a streusel topping, put the remaining 1/4 cup flour, the remaining sugar, and the butter in a bowl and crumble with your fingers. Brush water lightly over the top of the dough to moisten, and then spread the topping over the coffee cake.

6. Let rise, covered, for an additional hour. You can also place this in the refrigerator for several hours or overnight.

7. Preheat the oven to 350 degrees. Bake for about 45 minutes or until brown on top and hollow-sounding when tapped. Serve immediately.

Zvi and Hasia Vardi with their daughter Dalia in Jerusalem, 1942

Breakfasts and Brunch Fare

Halek—
Biblical Honey

During lunch at Jerusalem's Eucalyptus Restaurant, Chef Moshe Basson put a bowl of tahina (sesame-seed paste) on the table and swirled in a date syrup called *silan* or *halek,* which he explained was a biblical "honey," one of the seven foods in the land of Canaan cited in the book of Deuteronomy. Today, visitors can see a two-thousand-year-old date-honey press, similar to an ancient wine press but smaller, near the Dead Sea at Qumran, the site where in 1947 a Bedouin youth found the Dead Sea Scrolls hidden in earthen jars.

In ancient times, wild bees extracted honey from the flowers of prickly pears and the wild acacia tree, one of the few trees to live in the Arava Desert. In the springtime the acacia tree was like an umbrella, with its leaves shading the nomads from the hot sun, the long roots searching for water deep beneath the ground, and the green leaves providing plenty of protein to the wandering Bedouins and other desert peoples.

Called *dibs* in Arabic and *dvash* in Hebrew, honey is the term also used for a kind of molasses made from slowly cooked and sieved dates, pomegranates, tamarinds, figs, and carob. It is so common that Bertha Spafford Vester, in her memoir *Our Jerusalem,* recalled using grape honey as Americans would use maple syrup. "Sundays we frequently had pancakes with *dibs,* a molasses made of boiled-down grape juice," she wrote.

The date palm, whose height was a biblical metaphor for excellence and beauty, grew in the ancient land of Israel. The palm is so holy and fragile to the Moslems that one cannot uproot it; for Christians, the date palm is blessed and brought in procession the Sunday before Easter, representing Jesus' triumphal entry into Jerusalem. Not only is the palm said to ward off evil, but it symbolizes righteousness, love, and fertility. During the Jewish holiday of Sukkot, palm fronds are used for the roofs of the symbolic outdoor huts or *sukkot,* and a blessing is made over them, as they are one of the four species brought to the Temple during this pilgrim holiday. In the ancient world, they were used to make ceilings, as fans, and for cording and basket making. The hearts of the palm are a delicacy, as are the dates themselves.

The enthusiasm for replanting the land with the foods mentioned in the Bible inspired Benzion Israeli, one of the founders of Kibbutz Kinneret. Under the Mamelukes the date palms had declined terribly in Palestine through drought and neglect, and they needed to be replenished. Because dates cannot be promulgated from seeds, new seedlings, both male and female, had to be brought to the country. In 1933, dressed as an Arab, Israeli went to Iraq and smuggled nine hundred saplings back to Palestine. Making many more trips, he brought back more than seven thousand saplings from Iraq as well as from Iran and Kurdistan, of which only half took root. Later, another man, Shmuel Stoller, brought saplings from Egypt and Saudi Arabia. Because of the daring of these two men, date palms dot the landscape of Israel, especially in the Jordan Valley and Bet She'an. In the 1970s *mejdoul,* which means "unknown" in Arabic, and *deglet noor* varieties were also introduced from Coachella Valley in California. Date production is a sophisticated technology involving artificial pollination and a lengthy gestation period of five years before a tree bears its fruits. Today, scientists at the Vulcani Institute in Rehovot are trying to propagate dates from embryonic flowers taken from mature trees.

At Passover, Iraqi Jews serve date jam sprinkled with walnuts and almonds as their *haroset,* representing the mortar used by slaves in Egypt. Although many people make the following *halek* at home, Kibbutz Kinneret produces a commercial version which is exported abroad. *Halek* is especially tasty spooned onto vanilla yogurt or ice cream, sprinkled with halvah, a local tahina candy, or spread on a thick slice of bread with tahina or as a topping for pancakes.

When I was a child most of our dates came from Jericho.

—*Dalia Carmel*

YIELD: 4 CUPS *HALEK*

10 cups pitted dates, preferably *mejdoul*   2 teaspoons ground anise

4 quarts water

1. Put the dates, water, and anise in a large saucepan. Bring to a boil and simmer for about 1 hour, uncovered, stirring occasionally. The dates will soften, open up, and reach the consistency of chunky applesauce.

2. Press the date mixture through a food mill. Return the date syrup to a small saucepan and simmer slowly, uncovered, over a very low heat for about 3 hours, stirring frequently, until the syrup thickens enough to coat a spoon. Cool. Store in a jar in the refrigerator. The "honey" will keep for several months.

Breakfasts and
Brunch Fare

Finding a perfect *etrog* is no easy task.

Nahum Lurie and three of his eight children were packing *etrogim* to send to the United States when I dropped in on them at Kfar Habad, a Lubavitcher moshav just off the Jerusalem–Tel Aviv road. The *etrog,* thought by many to have been the true forbidden fruit in the Garden of Eden and mentioned as "the fruit of a goodly tree" in Leviticus 23:40, has always been admired for its beautiful color, perfect oval shape, and fragrant aroma rather than for its taste, which is extremely bitter. Carried with the *lulav,* the palm branch entwined with myrtle and willow, this bitter citron, a member of the lemon and orange family, is one of the four species waved and prayed over at Sukkot, the fall harvest festival.

"There are as many ways of looking at the four species as there are rabbis," said Levi Weiman-Kelman, rabbi of Congregation Kol Haneshma in Jerusalem. "For me they symbolize the Exodus and the entry into the land of Israel: the palm trees that grow in the desert, symbolizing the beginning of the wandering; the willows that need a lot of water, growing along the shores of the Jordan River; the myrtle, which grows in the hill region; and the *etrog,* the fruit of the tree grown by settled people that takes a commitment of years."

The *etrog,* prized in ancient times for its medicinal value, was supposed to enhance potency in men. According to one folk belief, a woman who bites into an *etrog* will become pregnant within a year. Botanically called *citrus medica* (Mediterranean), the *etrog* may have been brought by the Jews on their return from the Babylonian captivity.

By the time of the Second Temple, rabbis had ruled that the *etrog* had to be in as perfect condition as possible to be used with the *lulav* at Sukkot. Mr. Lurie explained that every *mitzvah* (religious duty or good deed) should be done in the best way possible, including picking the best *etrog* at Sukkot.

Although *etrogim* have always been cultivated in Palestine, another center for *etrog* cultivation was the island of Corfu, whose Jewish population under Venetian and later French rule acted as the broker of goods between Venice and the Levant. With anti-Jewish demonstrations in 1891 at Corfu, the *etrog* market switched to the agricultural settlements of Palestine, including Kfar Habad.

According to one Lubavitcher story, when God told Moses to make a *mitzvah* on the *etrog,* He sent him on clouds to Italy to get an *etrog.* To grow "pure" *etrogim* at Kfar Habad, the Lubavitcher rebbe brought seeds from a Calabrian *etrog.*

The Lurie family, in the *etrog* business for the past fifty years, picks about thirty thousand green *etrogim* and ships them to the United States, Canada, and Europe one month before Sukkot. In each shipment, the Luries include one apple which releases a chemical that turns the *etrogim* yellow.

Nahum Lurie packing his etrogim *at Kfar Habad*

After the holiday of Sukkot is over, the *etrog*'s thick skin is embalmed with cloves for fragrance at *havdallah,* the ceremony separating the Sabbath from the week. It can also be candied, pickled in vinegar, or added to grapefruit and orange peel to make citrus preserves.

Amira Ruben, a cheese maker and bread baker in Rosh Pina, makes this bright-colored chunky winter jam from *etrogim,* oranges, grapefruits, pomelos, the oblong grapefruit-like fruit with a thick skin popular in Israel, as well as its offspring, pomelite, a mixture of grapefruit and a pomelo, smaller with a thinner skin. Amira serves her jam slathered on her homemade bread with butter.

Amira's Triple-Citrus Marmalade

YIELD: ABOUT 6 CUPS

6 cups unpeeled, thinly sliced mixed citrus fruit like *etrog,* lemon, orange, pomelo, and grapefruit, seeds removed

3 cups sugar (about)

1. Put the fruit in a saucepan and add the sugar. Bring to a boil, then simmer slowly, uncovered, for about 45 minutes until the marmalade thickens, stirring constantly so that you do not caramelize the sugar.
2. Pour into jars, cover, and refrigerate.

Etrogim *for Sukkot at Mahane Yehudah*

Breakfasts and Brunch Fare

Israeli Onion Jam

Right from their early-morning arrival at Ben-Gurion Airport, some tour groups to Israel are taken directly to Neot Kedumim for a "Good Morning, Israel" program. This reconstructed biblical park in the Judean Hills is dedicated to reproducing the flora and fauna of the Bible. "Our forefathers were initially shepherds," said Helen Frenkley, the director of the park. "We study the period of their transition to farming. We are trying to research and illustrate the unbreakable bond between the ecology of Israel and the Bible, a real book about real people. By giving it the real natural setting, we can study the everyday life of our forefathers in their land."

After a self-guided tour through the park, establishing a sense of place for ourselves, we sat down to a biblical breakfast of goat cheese, yogurt, hyssop, walnuts, raisins, olives, yeastless pita, jams, cabbage salad, and celery. Nadav Granott, the cook at the park, also made an onion jam for us, unusual in that it included sugar, a more modern sweetener than honey.

YIELD: 4 CUPS

2 pounds sweet onions (Vidalia or Spanish), peeled and sliced in rounds

½ cup dry red wine

½ cup cider vinegar

4 cups sugar

Juice of 2 lemons

1. Place the onions with the red wine, vinegar, sugar, and lemon juice in a nonreactive bowl. Cover and let sit overnight.

2. The next day, transfer the onion mixture to a saucepan and bring to a boil. Simmer slowly, uncovered, for about 20 minutes. Do not overcook or the jam will harden. Store in a covered jar in the refrigerator. The jam will keep for several weeks.

Appetizers
In the Beginning

M y favorite part of a meal in the Middle East is the *mezze,*
the dozen or so appetizers laid out on the table before you sit down, a
legacy of the four-hundred-year Ottoman rule. Sipping *arrack,* the region's anise-
flavored liqueur, or the ubiquitous Coca-Cola, I love to slowly nibble each morsel
of the endless array of flavors set before me. Waiters tantalize my appetite with
glorious dips like hummus, the garlicky chickpea spread, or others made from
roasted eggplant flavored with tahina, garlic, and lemon; all are accompanied by

Above: Druse women serving mezze *at a wedding feast*

olives, pickles, or tiny stuffed vegetables. The menus read like a gastronomic "What's What in the Middle East": crisp Egyptian falafel; Iraqi *kubbeh,* torpedo-shaped meat-filled fritters; Armenian or Greek or Lebanese grape leaves stuffed with rice and pine nuts; a half dozen eggplant salads; and taboulleh, a light bulgur salad sumptuously seasoned with loads of fresh mint.

Mezzes are a way of life in Israel, from the vast breakfast spread offered at every hotel throughout the country to the first course served at restaurants to the hummus served at home as a snack or starter. Russian immigrants have brought their own version of *mezze,* called *zakuski.* So have Iraqis, Moroccans, and Turks. Many of these appetizers are as old as the lands from which they come. Take away the occasional modern addition of tomato, green pepper, or mayonnaise, and the ingredients are biblical basics. Originally pounded to a paste with a mortar and pestle, the dips, usually conveniently scooped up with a torn piece of pita bread, predate the fourteenth-century advent of the fork.

Because there is a spillover in the Middle East between salads and appetizers, I have included dips and finger food under Appetizers and fork food under Salads, so look there for additional ideas on how to create a modern *mezze* table.

Salat Hatzilim— Classic Israeli Eggplant Dip

One of my great pleasures when visiting Jerusalem is to spend Shabbat dinner with my good friends David and Dorothy Harman and their family. Once, during Hanukkah, some twenty people gathered at the Harmans' house to light the Sabbath and menorah candles, recite the blessings over the challah, and play dreidel. As an American mother, I was most impressed by the absence of Hanukkah presents and the fact that the children did not seem to expect any. Watching the flickering candles and celebrating the ancient Miracle of Lights together were the attractions for young and old alike.

Dorothy and I have a tradition, when I am in Jerusalem before the Sabbath, of visiting Brizel's Bakery in Mea Shearim to buy a crusty Chasidic challah that tastes divine dipped in David's signature dish, this distinctly Israeli eggplant salad. He grills his eggplants over a gas or charcoal grill.

YIELD: ABOUT 2 CUPS, OR 6 SERVINGS

2 large eggplants (about 2 pounds total)	1 tablespoon safflower or vegetable oil
3 cloves garlic, mashed	Juice of 1/2 lemon
3–4 tablespoons mayonnaise	Salt and freshly ground pepper to taste

1. Grill the eggplants over a gas or charcoal grill, turning them frequently, until charred all over. Put them in a wooden or ceramic bowl to cool. Remove the skins and drain off the liquid. The pulp should be soft to the touch.

2. Add the garlic, mayonnaise, oil, lemon juice, and salt and pepper to taste. Mix with a fork, mashing the pulp until it is the creamy consistency you want. Taste and adjust the seasonings; you may have to add more mayonnaise. The eggplant pulp can also be pureed in a food processor. Serve with challah or pita bread.

David Harman and Golda Meir

Appetizers

My mother was a wizard with eggplants, having learned the art of cooking them from the Arab peasant women who came to help with the weekly wash and the housework. She peeled them, cut them into flat round slices, and put them out in the sun to bake away their initial bitterness. Then she fried them and served them on slices of bread. Sometimes she grilled a large eggplant whole until it was slightly charred, spooned out the inside without the bitter seeds, mashed it with a hard-boiled egg, dressed it with lemon juice, olive oil, salt and garlic, garnished it with sliced tomatoes, and served it as a cold dish. At the beginning of summer, when eggplants were small and hard, she pickled them in large glass jars, having first sent us children scurrying in the field to pick up some dill. A washerwoman had told us that no Arab maid was worth her bride price until she was able to cook eggplants in seven different ways. Mother learned all seven, and I intended to do the same when I grew up.

—Ruth Jordan, *Daughter of the Waves* (1983)

I have heard many variations of the washerwoman's saying, one even asserting that a woman should know more than 101 ways to cook eggplant. Whatever the number of possible dishes, no *mezze*, and practically no meal in Israel today, is complete without at least one eggplant salad.

Having tasted so many variations in Israel throughout the years, I consider Israel to be the eggplant capital of the world. Eggplant was probably brought to the Middle East during the Middle Ages by Arab and Jewish traders. Easily grown in the region's hot climate, it has since become the most versatile vegetable in the eastern Mediterranean. Because of its firm texture, during difficult times eggplant could easily approximate some of the more expensive meat dishes with which Jews were familiar. Vegetarian chopped liver, for example, made with sautéed onions, fried eggplant, and hard-boiled eggs, reminded Jews of the flavor of traditional chopped liver. Fried eggplant can replace veal schnitzel, and, when smoked, can be eaten as "caviar."

Many soups and even cakes are made from eggplant. When I lived in Israel, a restaurant in Ramat Aviv boasted an entire menu of eggplant dishes. I have seen eggplant dips that include pickles, soy sauce, black olives, roasted peppers, mayonnaise—you name it.

Eggplants take on a lovely smoky taste when cooked in this fashion: First, grill the whole eggplant over charcoal or a gas burner, turning carefully with tongs, for several minutes. Continue grilling until soft or bake it on a cookie sheet (you can opt to cover with foil for easier cleanup) in a 450-degree oven until the pulp is soft, about twenty more minutes. If you want to skip the grilling, you can also merely prick the skin with a fork and bake the eggplant in a 450-degree oven for about thirty minutes or until it is soft, but the cooked eggplant will not have the same smoky flavor.

D alia's version of eggplant chopped liver is prepared as follows.

Eggplant Chopped Liver

YIELD: ABOUT 4 CUPS

2 large eggplants (about 2 pounds total)	1 large onion, chopped coarse
Kosher salt to taste	3 hard-boiled eggs
Flour for dredging	Salt and freshly ground pepper to taste
Vegetable oil for frying	

1. Peel the eggplants and slice in ⅓-inch-thick rounds. Sprinkle with kosher salt and set in a sieve over a bowl for about a half hour. Wipe the slices well with a paper towel, then dip in flour, shaking off any excess flour.

2. Fry the eggplant slices in a little oil, a few minutes on each side, until golden. Remove when done and drain well on paper towels.

3. In the same frying pan, fry the onions until golden and drain off any excess oil.

4. With a fork, coarsely mash the eggplant, onions, and eggs on a wooden board. You may use a food processor for this, but the texture should remain coarse, not mushy. Add salt and pepper to taste.

In the 1950s, during austerity in Israel, there was no meat and no money to buy meat. We didn't even have apples. It was a time of substitutions. We would make apple jam or compote from zucchini. My mother made meat patties from chopped fresh peanuts because we were growing them. Eggplant was cheap and we had a lot of it. One thing that became very popular was chopped liver made of eggplant. Later, people wanted to forget the food of the bad times and it more or less disappeared. About five or six years ago, eggplant chopped liver started to pop up again in unexpected places.

—Dalia Lamdani,
  retired food editor,
  La'isha magazine

Appetizers

Eggplant Caviar

Dr. Telhami, who now holds the Anwar Sadat Chair for Peace and Development at the University of Maryland, grew up in a small community of Arab Greek Catholics in a mostly Druse village near Haifa. Throughout the summer, Dr. Telhami's mother uses the family's olive oil in the following eggplant caviar recipe, as a refreshing salad and an accompaniment to meat dishes.

YIELD: ABOUT 2 CUPS

1 large eggplant (about 1 pound)	2 tablespoons lemon juice
1 clove garlic, mashed	2 tablespoons chopped fresh or
3 scallions, diced	$1/2$ teaspoon dried mint
$1/2$ green bell pepper, diced	Salt to taste
3 tablespoons extra virgin olive oil	Dash of cayenne pepper

1. Grill the eggplant over the gas grill or prick and roast in a hot oven until it is extremely soft inside (see page 52).

2. Mix the garlic, scallions, green pepper, olive oil, lemon juice, and mint with a little salt and cayenne pepper in a ceramic or other nonreactive bowl.

3. Peel the eggplant and place in a strainer to press out the juice. Chop the pulp into chunks and mix it with the other ingredients. Taste and adjust seasonings.

Baba Ghanouj—
Eggplant with Tahina

Baba ghanouj is one of the most sublime eggplant salads of the Middle East. Its name is curious: in Arabic, *baba* means "father" and *ghanouj* means "spoiled." Thus, the dish literally means "spoiled father," probably because it tastes so good that the father (or anyone) to whom it is served is spoiled with the flavors. The first time I tasted this flavorful eggplant salad was at a long-gone restaurant in East Jerusalem called Musswadeh. In those days, the sesame seeds were hand crushed in a factory nearby, and the eggplant roasted on an outdoor grill. Today, *baba ghanouj,* once thought to be of Lebanese origin, has become international and can be found everywhere.

At an upscale Lebanese restaurant in Washington, D.C., I recently tasted a stunning variation of this same recipe, made with two pounds of peeled and boiled beets instead of the eggplant.

YIELD: ABOUT 2 1/2 CUPS, OR 8 SERVINGS

2 large eggplants (about 2 pounds)

1/2 bunch flat-leaf parsley (about 1/2 cup), plus additional for garnish, finely chopped

1/2 cup tahina

4 tablespoons lemon juice, or to taste

2 cloves garlic, crushed

1 teaspoon salt, or to taste

Dash of cayenne pepper

2 tablespoons water (optional)

1. Grill the eggplant over a gas grill until the skin is completely charred or prick and place on a cookie sheet and bake in a preheated 450° oven for 20 minutes or until soft inside. Cool.

2. Cut the eggplant in half lengthwise, drain off the liquid, and scoop out the pulp. Press the pulp through a food mill or pulse in a food processor equipped with a steel blade.

3. Stir in the parsley, tahina, lemon juice, and garlic. For a thinner *baba ghanouj* that is whiter in color, add a little water.

4. Season with salt and cayenne pepper to taste and garnish with additional chopped parsley.

Eggplant Dip with Pomegranate and Tahina

Everyone in the Middle East loves pomegranates, one of the seven biblical species mentioned in the Old Testament. The prophet Mohammed said, "Eat of the pomegranate, for it purges the system of envy and hatred." Once thought to be the "apple" in the Garden of Eden, the pomegranate is considered by Jews to be a sign of fruitfulness. It is also said to have 613 seeds, equal to the number of commandments in the Bible. As an American Jew, I was surprised to see bowls of pomegranates on the Israeli Rosh Hashanah table, where we Americans use an apple dipped in honey to symbolize the first fruit of the new year.

The following delicious recipe comes from Adnan Abou Odeh, a Jordanian friend originally from Nablus. You can buy pomegranates when they are in season and store them whole in the refrigerator for up to a year. If you cannot find fresh pomegranates, use bottled pomegranate juice or syrup, diluting one tablespoon of pomegranate syrup in three tablespoons of water, and substitute dried cranberries or cherries for the fresh pomegranate seeds.

· · · TAHINA · · ·
THE PEANUT BUTTER OF ISRAEL

"In the Old City inside Damascus Gate there used to be a place where people stomped on the sesame seeds to extract the oil," recalled Aziz Shihab, author of *A Taste of Palestine* (1993). "Once the oil comes out, the residue forms balls. We used to buy the balls and eat them with *dibs*, the date syrup from Nablus."

To this day the hilltop city of Nablus is known for its good tahina, fruits, meat, milk, butter, and cheese. The secret to Nablus's culinary crown are the streams that rush down the hilltop and pass through the town. They help fertilize the area, provide water for the animals, and give water power to grind grain and sesame seeds. In many villages throughout Israel there was often, and occasionally still is, one villager who grinds the sesame seeds into a paste used in cooking.

Today, however, machines, similar to those used to produce peanut butter, usually grind the seeds. Sometimes when you buy tahina in stores, the sediment settles to the bottom with a film of oil on top, and it needs to be mixed well before using. I often blend the contents of a new jar in my food processor. But today, because most companies are putting an emulsifier in their tahina, this step is becoming unnecessary. The word *tahina*, meaning "ground sesame seeds," comes from the Arabic *thana* and Hebrew *tahina*, meaning "to grind." Known as a good digestive, some people eat it as we would Tums. A fresh tahina should have the smell of sesame seeds.

In the United States, it is familiar as an ingredient in hummus. But in Israel it is eaten as a dip by itself, mixed with parsley, garlic, and lemon juice, or it is used as we eat peanut butter, slathered on bread with a syrup made from pomegranates, carob, or dates (see pages 44–5).

2 large eggplants (about 2 pounds)

1 pomegranate

3 tablespoons tahina

1 tablespoon lemon juice, or to taste

½ teaspoon salt, or to taste

1 teaspoon crushed garlic

¼ cup chopped fresh parsley for garnish

1. Preheat the oven to 450 degrees.

2. Grill the eggplant over the gas grill or prick and roast in a hot oven until it is extremely soft inside (see page 52).

3. When cool, split the eggplant open and gently scrape the seeds out, using a melon-baller or large spoon. Pull away the skin, drain the liquid, and chop the pulp into ½-inch cubes.

4. This is my favorite way to peel a pomegranate without staining myself with juice: Gently score the outer skin into quarters. Then place the entire pomegranate in a large bowl filled with water. With your hands under the water, gently pull the skin off and remove the seeds, which will fall to the bottom. Drain off the water, discard the outer skin and fiber, dab the seeds dry, and proceed. Reserve ¼ cup of the seeds for garnish.

5. Place the remaining seeds over a sieve and press out the juice with your hands. You should have approximately ¼ cup of juice. Discard the pulp and seeds.

6. In a nonmetallic bowl, mix the eggplant with the pomegranate juice, tahina, lemon juice, salt, and garlic. Adjust the amount of pomegranate juice and lemon to your taste. In a food processor fitted with a steel blade, pulse the mixture until smooth but not mushy.

7. Spread mixture on a flat plate and sprinkle with chopped parsley and the reserved pomegranate seeds, dried cherries, or dried cranberries. Serve with pieces of warm pita for dipping.

Old City Tahina with Flat Italian Parsley and Lemon

One day I visited the onion-domed Greek Orthodox Church of the Seven Apostles at Capernaum on the Sea of Galilee. The priest had just baptized two children who were visiting from Jerusalem with their families and their local priest. They asked me to join them at their celebratory picnic, arranged on a table near the water. One dish that I particularly enjoyed was their tahina salad with fresh parsley and lemon. I had tasted something similar perhaps a hundred times, but that salad—perhaps because of the freshness of the ingredients, or the setting next to the biblical Lake Tiberias—was especially memorable. I have tried to reconstruct the perfect balance of tahina, parsley, and lemon that I tasted that day. Serve this with other salads, baked fish, or falafel.

YIELD: ABOUT 1½ CUPS, OR 4 SERVINGS

¾ cup tahina

½ cup lemon juice

1 clove garlic

2 tablespoons water, or as needed

1 cup roughly chopped Italian parsley

Salt and freshly ground pepper to taste

1. In a food processor fitted with a steel blade, puree the tahina, lemon juice, and garlic until smooth. If the tahina is still too thick, add a few tablespoons of water and it will thin down and become a pleasing white color.

2. Add the parsley and salt and pepper and pulse until blended. Adjust the seasonings and serve.

· · · ABU SHUKREI'S · · ·
A JERUSALEM HUMMUS HAUNT

Every Israeli has strong opinions, especially about hummus. And everyone likes to find a tiny hole-in-the-wall to call their own. My favorite place for the ubiquitous chickpea paste used to be Abu Shukrei's, located near the Fifth Station of the Cross at the bottom of the Via Dolorosa in Jerusalem's Old City. Opened in 1948 by the late Abu Shukrei it was a tiny restaurant with Formica tables, scraps of paper for napkins, and white vaulted ceilings. In the seventies, Abu Shukrei stood at the back of his shop, his fez perched on his head, stirring a deep cauldron full of bubbling chickpeas which had simmered slowly all night long. Today, I only go very early in the morning; otherwise it is overrun by tour buses!

Almost every time I have visited the restaurant since 1970, Abu Shukrei, and more recently his son Fathi Taha, has told me a little bit more about hummus. The word *hummus* means "chickpea" in both Arabic and Hebrew. Fathi Taha, who has been working at the restaurant since he was fifteen, uses a large wooden mortar and pestle to grind the warm chickpeas and blend them with garlic, parsley, lemon juice, salt, water, and tahina. According to him, the chickpeas must be ground while still warm, and any good tahina, well stirred, will do. When I asked for an exact recipe, he answered, "Use your eye, and use your heart."

Fathi Taha mixing his hummus

· · · OTHER HUMMUS HAUNTS IN JERUSALEM · · ·

Recently, more and more places seem to have good hummus. Here are some of my favorites in Jerusalem:

Abu-Taher Restaurant, an Old City favorite established before 1948, is located on Jaffa Road at Al-Lahamin Market 16. Their fresh hummus is very lemony.

Lina's, a hole-in-the-wall on the Via Dolorosa in the Old City of Jerusalem, was started by a former chef at Abu Shukrei's.

Nazmi is another tiny place in the Old City. It is located on Jeweler's Street (Rehov Hazorfim), one block down from Butcher's Street.

Pinati, at 13 King George Street at the corner of Ben Hillel, was founded almost thirty years ago.

Rachmo's, a storefront with Formica tables, has been in the same spot in Mahane Yehuda (2 HaEshkol), Jerusalem's open-air market, for almost forty years. Rachmo's Syrian hummus is especially garlicky.

Ta'ami, at 3 Shammai Street in Jerusalem, near Ben Yehuda Street, has also been around for a while—almost fifty years—and is very popular

For hummus haunts outside Jerusalem, see page 61.

A popular Jerusalem hummus haunt

Hummus

I have been making hummus for years and have concluded that despite the temptation to use canned chickpeas, the flavor is much better when it is made with dried chickpeas found at Middle Eastern or Indian food stores. First I soak a large quantity overnight, cook some, and then drain and freeze the rest in two-cup batches in plastic bags. Whenever I need them for hummus, falafel, or for the many chickpea soups and stews in this book, I just take them out of the freezer. When substituting canned beans, figure that one cup of raw chickpeas equals two cups of cooked or canned. Some old-time cooks in the Middle East either peel cooked chickpeas or pass them through a food mill before using them. I find there is no need for this laborious extra step. I add to my hummus a little bit of cumin, which blends beautifully with the garlic and lemony flavor.

YIELD: ABOUT 4 CUPS, OR 6 TO 8 SERVINGS

1 cup dried chickpeas	1/2 teaspoon ground cumin, or to taste
1 cup tahina	3 tablespoons extra virgin olive oil
1/2 cup lemon juice, or to taste	2 tablespoons pine nuts
2 cloves garlic, or to taste	Dash of paprika or sumac
1 teaspoon salt	2 tablespoons chopped fresh parsley or cilantro
Freshly ground pepper to taste	

1. Put the raw chickpeas in a bowl with cold water to cover and soak overnight.

2. Drain and rinse the chickpeas, then place them in a heavy pot with enough cold water to cover. Bring to a boil, then simmer, partially covered, for about an hour or until the chickpeas are soft and the skin begins to separate. Add more water as needed.

3. Drain the chickpeas, reserving about 1½ cups of the cooking liquid. Set aside ¼ cup of the cooked chickpeas for garnish. In a food processor fitted with a steel blade, process the remaining chickpeas with the tahina, lemon juice, garlic, salt, pepper, cumin, and at least ½ cup of the reserved cooking liquid. If the hummus is too thick, add more reserved cooking liquid or water until you have a paste-like consistency.

4. Heat a frying pan and add 1 tablespoon of the olive oil. Spread the pine nuts in the pan and stir-fry, browning on all sides.

5. To serve, transfer the hummus to a large, flat plate, and with the back of a spoon make a slight depression in the center. Drizzle the remaining olive oil on top and sprinkle the reserved chickpeas, pine nuts, paprika or sumac, and parsley or cilantro over the surface.

6. Serve with cut-up raw vegetables and warm pita cut into wedges.

NOTE   You can also add cayenne pepper to the hummus. Sometimes leftover hummus tends to thicken—just add some water to make it the right consistency.

Coussa B'Leben— Zucchini with Yogurt

Anyone who gardens is bound to have bumper crops of zucchini and will welcome this zucchini, tahina, and yogurt dip. I first tasted it at the Abu Ahmad Restaurant in Amman, which serves traditional Palestinian food. You can also substitute eggplant for the zucchini.

YIELD: ABOUT 3 CUPS, OR 6 TO 8 SERVINGS

4 medium zucchini (about 3 pounds total)

Olive oil for brushing

5 cloves garlic, mashed

1 cup plain yogurt

6–8 tablespoons tahina

Juice of 2 lemons

Salt to taste

1/2 medium tomato, peeled and diced

2 tablespoons fresh parsley, chopped

1 tablespoon crushed dried hot pepper for garnish

1. Brush the zucchini with olive oil and grill over an open flame, or bake in a 500-degree oven about 15 minutes or until tender. Cool slightly, and squeeze gently to remove excess liquid. Remove any charred skin, then mash the pulp.

2. Mix together the zucchini pulp, garlic, yogurt, 6 tablespoons tahina, the lemon juice, and salt to taste, stirring well. Add more tahina depending on taste, and garnish with the tomato, parsley, and hot pepper.

· · · OTHER HUMMUS HAUNTS OUTSIDE JERUSALEM · · ·

By definition a good hummus joint is usually a hole-in-the-wall establishment that serves absolutely fresh hummus and usually has only a very few tables.

Akko
 Hummus Foul Said, inside the market in the Old City

Galilee
 Abu Salakh, near Ammiad Junction
 El–Leali, in a small village called Gush Halav

Haifa
 Abu Yousef II, 1 Hamaginim Boulevard
 Faraj, 29 Hamaginim Boulevard
 Um Amir, 37 St. John Street, located in Wadi Nisnas

Jaffa
 Ali Carayan, (also called **Abou Hassan**), 1 Dolphin Street
 Kalabuni, Rehov Yefet

Nazareth
 Naz Hummus A Sheik, Afifi Building, Iksal Street

Tel Aviv
 El–Gal, 5 Mikveh Israel Street
 Hummus Akram, Yermiahu Street
 Tsnobar, Ben Yehudah Street

61

· · · ZA'ATAR · · ·
THE SPICE COMBINATION THAT OPENS UP THE MIND

In search of an authentic *za'atar*, the popular Middle Eastern spice combination, I visited Rabai Ariedi in the Druse village of Ma'ghar in the Galilee. "We eat *za'atar* for breakfast, sprinkled on pita with olive oil from our village," said Mrs. Ariedi, the mother of five children, as she opened a jar of her homemade *za'atar* for me to taste. "My parents told us that *za'atar* opens up our minds and makes us more alert as students."

Za'atar, named for both the herb and the mix, is made from *origanum syriacum*, a wild oregano called hyssop in the Bible and whose flavor is a cross between Greek oregano and thyme. Symbolic of humility and modesty, it is possible that *za'atar* was the last food that Jesus ate. "After this, Jesus, aware that all had now come to its appointed end, said in fulfillment of scripture, 'I am thirsty.' A jar stood there full of sour wine; so they soaked a sponge with the wine, fixed it on hyssop, and held it up to his lips. Having received the wine, he said, 'It is accomplished!' Then he bowed his head and gave up his spirit" (John 19:28–30).

Commercial *za'atar* mixes abound throughout Israel and can be purchased in Middle Eastern markets in the United States. Nevertheless, in April and May Mrs. Ariedi and the other women in her village drive to the hills behind her home to pick large quantities of the wild herb. (Wild *za'atar*, considered an endangered species by the Hagenat Hatevah, the Society for the Protection of Nature in Israel, may only be picked at specified times during the year.)

After the women have gathered the *za'atar*, they wrap the branches in bundles and dry them on the flat roofs of their houses. With the twigs removed, they sift the leaves and run them through their fingers, crumbling them into little pieces. Sometimes sesame seeds, salt, and sumac (a sour-tasting desert herb not related to the American poisonous variety) are added to the herb. Today, commercial *za'atar* is ground to a powder and often mixed with lemon salt or citric acid rather than the more costly sumac. The redder the *za'atar*, the more sumac has been included.

After one trip to Israel, I decided to make my own *za'atar* using the Greek oregano and thyme growing in my herb garden in Washington, D.C. It tasted so good that I continue to make it; stored in a cool, dark place, the blend will keep for several months. I pick the oregano just before it blooms and dry it with the thyme either on a flat basket or on a table in my kitchen. I buy the sumac from a local Middle Eastern market and preroasted sesame seeds from a Chinese market—you can also toast your own sesame seeds in your oven. My version is not the purist's *za'atar*, perhaps, but it is a flavorful first cousin. I sprinkle the blend on pita bread with a little olive oil to make a Middle Eastern breakfast *bruschetta*. It can also be used as a topping for pizza and pasta, or as a dry marinade for chicken or fish, and is a tasty addition to salads and vegetables. Today, you can buy a *za'atar* mix commercially in most Middle Eastern and other supermarkets.

YIELD: ³/4 CUP

¼ cup dried oregano and thyme	¼ cup roasted sesame seeds
2 tablespoons dried sumac	Salt to taste

1. Removing any twigs, crumble the oregano and thyme between your fingers into a bowl.
2. Add the sumac, sesame seeds, and salt to taste. Stir well.

This typical Israeli dip from my friend Liz Magnes is always a hit.

Labneh with Za'atar and Sun-dried Tomatoes

YIELD: ABOUT 10 SERVINGS

2 cups sun-dried tomatoes

2 cups plain *labneh* (see page 30)

1 teaspoon *za'atar,* or to taste (see page 62)

2 cloves garlic, mashed

Juice of 1 lemon

Salt and freshly ground pepper to taste

1 tablespoon extra virgin olive oil

1. Put the sun-dried tomatoes in a bowl and cover with hot water. Let sit for 5 minutes, then drain and chop roughly.

2. Place the *labneh,* ½ teaspoon of the *za'atar,* the mashed garlic, lemon juice, and salt and pepper to taste in a small mixing bowl. Mix well. Just before serving, fold in the sun-dried tomatoes, reserving a few for garnish. Drizzle with the olive oil and sprinkle with the remaining *za'atar.* Serve with crudités or wedges of toasted pita.

Herbs for za'atar in the Old City

Appetizers

Avocado Spread with *Labneh* and Pine Nuts from Israel's "Mahler in the Kitchen"

Avocado, a ubiquitous fruit on the Israeli dinner table, came to Palestine in the 1920s from South America, when farmers planted trees at the agricultural school of Mikveh Israel. In the 1950s, a few experimental avocado trees were grown as a commercial food crop for export. By the 1970s, those trial trees filled thirty thousand acres, with much of the crop being exported to the European market as fruit and as paste and oil used for skin medications. Today, Israel is second only to Mexico in per capita consumption of avocados.

In Israel, avocado is served in salads, as a soup, as an ice cream, or in a spread. Somehow, the concept of guacamole and chips has not caught on. A typical Israeli avocado spread comes from octogenarian food hobbyist Jacob Lishansky, the first male honored as Israel's "Queen of the Kitchen." After tasting his first avocado on a trip to London in 1956, he created fifty recipes for a pamphlet for the Israel Department of Agriculture, with such exotic combinations as avocado halvah with tahina and honey.

While serving as the military governor of the Galilee in the 1950s, Mr. Lishansky met and became lifelong friends with the late Leonard Bernstein who, after a dinner at his home, dubbed Lishansky "Israel's Mahler in the Kitchen."

YIELD: ABOUT 3 CUPS

3 avocados (about 3 cups mashed)

Juice of 1/2 lemon, or to taste

4 cloves garlic, mashed, or to taste

3 tablespoons olive oil

1/4 cup *labneh* (see page 30) or plain yogurt, strained well

Salt and freshly ground pepper to taste

1/2 teaspoon hot or sweet paprika

1 tablespoon pine nuts

1. Peel and puree the avocado in a food processor equipped with a steel blade with the lemon juice, garlic, and 2 tablespoons of the olive oil. Add the *labneh* or yogurt and continue mixing until the ingredients are fully incorporated. Add salt and pepper to taste and adjust seasonings, adding more lemon juice if needed. Sprinkle with the paprika.

2. Fry the pine nuts for a minute or 2 in the remaining tablespoon of olive oil and sprinkle on top of the avocado. Serve as a dip with bread or raw chopped vegetables.

Moroccan Cigars Stuffed with Jerusalem Artichokes

In Israel, Moroccan *cigares,* rolled-up pieces of phyllo dough shaped more like cigarettes than cigars, are usually filled with meat, but many people prefer a vegetarian version. Rutabaga, turnips, or celeriac, alone or blended with mashed potatoes, may be substituted for the Jerusalem artichokes in Israel Aharoni's recipe.

YIELD: ABOUT 36 CIGARS

2 pounds Jerusalem artichokes, peeled

8 whole shallots, peeled

10 whole garlic cloves, peeled

20 sprigs fresh or 1 teaspoon dried thyme

2 large eggs

Salt and freshly ground pepper to taste

18 sheets phyllo dough, at room temperature

$\frac{1}{2}$ cup olive oil

1. Preheat the oven to 350 degrees.

2. Spread the Jerusalem artichokes, shallots, and garlic cloves on a greased pan. Strew the thyme sprigs or sprinkle the dried thyme on top, and cover with aluminum foil. Make 3 or 4 holes in the foil and bake for an hour. Remove the sprigs of thyme.

3. Put all the vegetables in the bowl of a food processor fitted with a steel blade. Pulse until blended but not pureed. Add the eggs and salt and pepper to taste, and mix well.

4. Lay 1 phyllo sheet out on a work surface and brush it with oil. Cover with 2 more phyllo sheets, brushing each with oil.

5. With scissors, cut the phyllo rectangle in half to form two $8\frac{1}{2}$-by-13-inch rectangles. Then cut each rectangle in thirds to make 3 long strips, about 8 inches long and $4\frac{1}{3}$ inches wide. Place 1 tablespoon of filling in a line along 1 long edge. Fold each long edge in about half an inch, then roll up like a cigar, encasing the filling. Brush again with oil and place on a baking pan. Repeat with the remaining phyllo and filling.

6. Increase the oven temperature to 400 degrees and bake the cigars for about 15 minutes or until golden brown.

Balkan *Burikitas* with Eggplant

Chinese cooking was just a hobby for Israel Aharoni until he went to Taiwan. There he got hooked. After an eighteen-month stay, he returned to Tel Aviv to open three Chinese restaurants, employing Vietnamese and Thai immigrants as his helpers. Now he is the chef-owner of four restaurants, a weekly columnist for the afternoon newspaper *Yediot Aharonot,* and a major cookbook author. When Aharoni, whose parents emigrated from Bukhara, came to Washington to prepare the hors d'oeuvres for a fund-raiser for the fiftieth anniversary of Israel, old fans from Israel and new ones from the United States could not miss this bearded gentleman, dressed in a Mandarin-style jacket, with one long black braid trailing down his back. One remarked, "Aharoni, he is Israel's number one!"

These *burekas* filled with eggplant are a specialty of the Ottoman Empire, and this version is a distinctly Sephardic delicacy. I have tasted them in Istanbul, Izmir, Washington, and Tel Aviv. What makes these tiny *burekas* or *burikitas* Balkan is the crust made with yogurt. Any leftover filling makes a great dip.

YIELD: 25 *BURIKITAS*

FILLING

- 2 large eggplants (about 2 pounds)
- 1 whole head garlic (about 15–20 individual cloves)
- 1/3 cup extra virgin olive oil
- Salt and freshly ground pepper to taste
- 2 tablespoons feta cheese
- 2 tablespoons cream cheese

DOUGH

- 4 cups all-purpose flour
- 1 teaspoon baking powder
- 1 tablespoon salt
- 2 large eggs
- 1/2 cup olive oil
- 1 1/2 cups plain yogurt

GLAZE

- 1 large egg yolk
- 1 tablespoon water
- 2 tablespoons black caraway seeds

1. Preheat the oven to 350 degrees and grease a cookie sheet.

2. Cut the eggplants in half lengthwise and brush them with olive oil. Place on the cookie sheet and bake about 10 minutes.

3. Meanwhile, smash the garlic cloves with the side of a heavy kitchen knife to make it easier to remove the skins. Peel, and enclose the cloves in aluminum foil. Bake along with the eggplants, another 30 minutes, or until the eggplants are soft.

4. Remove both from the oven. Cool the eggplants slightly and scoop the pulp from the skin. Shake the pulp gently in a colander to drain. Transfer the pulp to the bowl of a food processor fitted with a steel blade, add the roasted garlic cloves, olive oil, salt, pepper, feta, and cream cheeses, and pulse to mix. Set aside to cool.

5. Meanwhile, prepare the dough. Put the flour, baking powder, and salt in a mixing bowl. Add the eggs, olive oil, and yogurt and blend to form a soft dough. Let it rest for about 15 minutes.

6. Divide the dough into 4 pieces and roll each out to a thickness of $\frac{1}{8}$ inch. Using a cookie cutter, cut circles 2 inches in diameter. Place about 1 tablespoon of the filling on each circle.

7. To make the glaze, blend the egg yolk with the water. Using your index finger, put some of the glaze around the perimeter of each circle. Fold into a semicircle and crimp the edges. Brush the *burikita* tops with more of the glaze. Sprinkle the black caraway seeds on top and bake on the middle rack of the oven for 25 minutes or until golden.

The mighty olive, one of the seven species of Canaan mentioned in the Book of Deuteronomy, served as food, fuel, and anointing agent for the people of the Fertile Crescent throughout history.

During an early November visit I made to the western Galilee, Arabs, Druse, Bedouins, and Jews were shaking trees with sticks, as described by Isaiah in the Old Testament. The olives fell to the ground onto colorful woven tarpaulins. At the end of the day the harvesters tied the corners of the canvas and brought the best of the olives home to be cracked and cured in brine with garlic, lemon, and herbs. The others were to be brought "from the tree to the stone"—an Arab adage urging a quick pressing for good oil.

In the village of Tamra in the Lower Galilee, Waffik Abu Roomi operates a two-year-old Italian Pieralisi steel olive press. Olive pressing here, as throughout the Galilee, takes on a festive market-like air. Outside Mr. Abu Roomi's press, lines of people wait with their empty plastic tins and jerry cans to collect the oil from their olives. Payment is in biblical tithes, a tenth of the produced oil to the owner. Inside, the press's fan blows out the leaves and the dirt; then the machine crushes and kneads the olives before separating the water from the oil.

Arabs working during the olive harvest

"I wanted to go into the pickle business," said Mr. Abu Roomi. "But my father urged me to do this instead. A family that presses olives is blessed." As overseer of this annual production, he offers his customers pita to be dipped in the newly pressed oil; Turkish coffee; and the white cheese for which his family's dairy-processing plant is famous throughout Israel. "Olive pressing is a thirty- to forty-day sideline for me," said Mr. Abu Roomi. Above the levers to the press hangs a good luck message from the Koran and a strand of garlic, another ancient symbol of good fortune.

Recently Jewish Israelis, too, have begun pressing their own oil. One of the earliest was Oded Yanai, who in 1970 bought a ranch in Upper Galilee and planted olive trees. "One day, we'll have our own olive oil," he told his grandson Ayal at the time. The Yanais have been producing an organic oil for the past six years using a cold steel press imported from Italy. "I make my oil according to the Bible, by letting the oil drip from the press," said Ayal. The difference is that five thousand years ago, the stone lever and weight press were hand-operated.

"Olive oil was much more important in the seventh century B.C.E. than petroleum is today," said Seymour Gitin, director and Dorot Professor of Archaeology at the Albright Institute in Jerusalem. Dr. Gitin and Trude Dotan, a professor at Hebrew University, led a team of researchers who unearthed in Ekron, near Ashkelon, the largest olive oil production center prior to the Roman period, dating back more than twenty-seven hundred years. "Oil was used as protection from the sun, for coal, for medicine, for anointing kings, for ablutions on the priests before entering the Tabernacle in Jerusalem, and of course, as today, for cooking and lighting," said Dr. Gitin. Olive oil was so important in the biblical period that priests brought the first crush of the "purest and finest" oil in sealed cruses as an offering to the Temple in Jerusalem.

"Can you imagine how many olives were crushed to make the oil for the Temple?" wondered David Eitan, founder of the Israel Oil Industry Museum in Haifa. "And how hard it was to crush them into basins by hand?" In modern times olives are crushed and then pressed, producing a greater yield of oil.

Caramelized Green Olives

In her 1882 memoir *A Home in the Holy Land,* Elizabeth Anne Finn had this to say about the olive: "We have a saying that, to a stranger, the taste of the first olive is detestable, the second he can endure, and the third he likes so much that ever after he is an olive-eater. Once, during a siege of Jerusalem, our whole diet consisted of rice and olives. We could get nothing else, and were truly thankful to have them in store in our house, otherwise we should have been badly off."

It doesn't take hard times to appreciate cured olives. If you have ever sampled a raw olive, you know how distasteful it is; olives must be cured. First they are crushed with a hammer. Then they are covered with water and salt, which is changed every day for five to six days. Then the juice and peel of whole lemons can be added, along with diced garlic, sometimes hot pepper, and enough salt that the water tastes like the sea. The olives are then covered with olive oil and left to cure for a few weeks to six months.

Although I am usually a purist when it comes to the flavor of cured olives, I love these caramelized olives baked in brown sugar, which Israeli cookbook writer Nira Rousso introduced to me. Don't use canned olives for this recipe.

YIELD: 2 CUPS

²/₃ cup light-brown sugar

3 tablespoons water

1 tablespoon butter or pareve margarine

Dash of powdered ginger

2 cups pitted, good-quality cured green olives (about 1 pound)

1. Preheat the oven to 350 degrees. Put the brown sugar, water, and butter or margarine in a small saucepan. Simmer just long enough to dissolve the sugar. Add the ginger.

2. Spread the olives in a cake pan large enough to fit them in 1 layer. Sprinkle the olives with a few tablespoons of their own juice. Cover with the brown sugar mixture.

3. Bake for about 40 minutes, stirring occasionally, until the sugar is caramelized. Serve warm or at room temperature as an accompaniment to a meat meal.

My Favorite Falafel

Every Israeli has an opinion about falafel, the ultimate Israeli street food, which is most often served stuffed into pita bread. One of my favorite spots is a simple stand in the Bukharan Quarter of Jerusalem, adjacent to Mea Shearim. The neighborhood was established in 1891, when wealthy Jews from Bukhara engaged engineers and city planners to plan a quarter with straight, wide streets and lavish stone houses. After the Russian Revolution, with the passing of time and fortunes, the Bukharan Quarter lost much of its wealth, but even so the area retains a certain elegance. There, the falafel is freshly fried before your eyes and the balls are very large and light. Shlomo Zadok, the elderly falafel maker and falafel stand owner, brought the recipe with him from his native Yemen.

Zadok explained that at the time of the establishment of the state, falafel—the name of which probably comes from the word *pilpel* (pepper)—was made in two ways: either as it is in Egypt today, from crushed, soaked fava beans or fava beans combined with chickpeas, spices, and bulgur; or, as Yemenite Jews and the Arabs of Jerusalem did, from chickpeas alone. But favism, an inherited enzymatic deficiency occurring among some Jews—mainly those of Kurdish and Iraqi ancestry, many of whom came to Israel during the mid 1900s—proved potentially lethal, so all falafel makers in Israel ultimately stopped using fava beans, and chickpea falafel became an Israeli dish.

The timing was right for falafel in those early years, with immigrants pouring in. Since there was a shortage of meat, falafel made a cheap, protein-rich meal—and people liked it.

Jerusalem's Shlomo Zadok, a veteran falafel maker

Rachama Ihshady, daughter of the founder of another favorite Jerusalem falafel joint, Shalom's Falafel on Bezalel Street, told me that her family recipe, also of Yemenite origin, has not changed since British times. Using the basics taught to me by these falafel mavens, I have created my own version, adding fresh parsley and cilantro, two ingredients I like and which originally characterized Arab falafel in Israel. Give me mine wrapped in a nice warm pita bread, swathed in tahina sauce and overflowing with pickled turnip and eggplant, chopped peppers, tomatoes, cucumbers, *amba* (pickled mango sauce)—and make it *harif*, Hebrew for "hot." The type of hot sauce used, of course, depends on the origin of the falafel maker.

YIELD: ABOUT 20 BALLS

1 cup dried chickpeas	1 teaspoon cumin
1/2 large onion, roughly chopped (about 1 cup)	1 teaspoon baking powder
	4–6 tablespoons flour
2 tablespoons finely chopped fresh parsley	Soybean or vegetable oil for frying
	Chopped tomato for garnish
2 tablespoons finely chopped fresh cilantro	Diced onion for garnish
	Diced green bell pepper for garnish
1 teaspoon salt	Tahina sauce
1/2–1 teaspoon dried hot red pepper	Pita bread
4 cloves garlic	

1. Put the chickpeas in a large bowl and add enough cold water to cover them by at least 2 inches. Let soak overnight, then drain. Or use canned chickpeas, drained.

2. Place the drained, uncooked chickpeas and the onions in the bowl of a food processor fitted with a steel blade. Add the parsley, cilantro, salt, hot pepper, garlic, and cumin. Process until blended but not pureed.

3. Sprinkle in the baking powder and 4 tablespoons of the flour, and pulse. You want to add enough bulgur or flour so that the dough forms a small ball and no longer sticks to your hands. Turn into a bowl and refrigerate, covered, for several hours.

4. Form the chickpea mixture into balls about the size of walnuts, or use a falafel scoop, available in Middle Eastern markets.

5. Heat 3 inches of oil to 375 degrees in a deep pot or wok and fry 1 ball to test. If it falls apart, add a little flour. Then fry about 6 balls at once for a few minutes on each side, or until golden brown. Drain on paper towels. Stuff half a pita with falafel balls, chopped tomatoes, onion, green pepper, and pickled turnips. Drizzle with tahina thinned with water.

NOTE Egyptians omit the cilantro and substitute fava beans for the chickpeas.

Harissa—
Tunisian Hot Chili Sauce

This hot sauce, which varies from village to village in Tunisia, Morocco, and even Algeria, is delicious on falafel and grilled meat—and a teaspoon of it will cure the worst cold!

YIELD: ABOUT 1 CUP

4 ounces dried hot red New Mexican chili peppers (about 18), stems removed

1/2 cup extra virgin olive oil (about)

7–8 cloves garlic

1/2 teaspoon cumin

1/2 teaspoon ground coriander

1 teaspoon coarse salt, or to taste

1. Soak the peppers in warm water until soft; drain and squeeze out any excess water. Then grind them, as North African Jews do, in a meat grinder, or process in a food processor with a steel blade with 1/4 cup of the olive oil, garlic, cumin, coriander, and salt. The consistency should be a thick puree, the color of deep red salmon. Place in a jar, pour on the remaining olive oil, cover, and refrigerate.

2. Let sit for a few days before using, until the *harissa* becomes less opaque. Use sparingly, as it is very hot.

The following excerpts are from an interview with Natan Sharansky, former Soviet refusenik who lived for eight years in solitary confinement. The most famous of the "prisoners of conscience," he now lives in Israel with his wife and his two daughters, where he serves as the minister of the interior of Israel and the head of the Israel B'Aliya Party.

"When I was in prison those eight years, I learned that the less you are thinking about food, the better. You ate when you got food because you might never have it again. There were eighteen levels of diets, with less and less calories. 9B3 was three cups of water and three pieces of bread a day. When they really wanted to punish me they gave me only three cups of water a day. Twenty years have passed. The KGB has gone. I still have the taste of those years. Thinking about food was torture, so I tried not to think about it. . . .

"After I was released, I went to Germany before I came to Israel. They took me to a *dascha,* a German country house. All the time I thought I was in a dream. So many times in my sleep I had dreamt of leaving. Then I entered the house and smelled the coffee. I knew it was not a dream. Coffee was the first smell of freedom for me. . . .

"When I came to Israel there was a press conference, and they gave me salads and tastes of all kinds of fruits. I remember the first time I saw artichoke, kiwi, avocado, they were especially exotic. One of the journalists asked, 'Do you like falafel?' I asked, 'What is falafel?' The next day a big sack of falafel appeared at my door from a neighbor who was a falafel man. In those days our two-room apartment was the headquarters of my wife's struggle to set me free. The first days in paradise."

The author with photographer Nelli Sheffer,
editor Judith Jones, and friends sampling falafel

Afula

On the main street in Afula there are several places that sell great falafel, considered by many to be the best in the country. While there look for Garinei Afula, which literally means "seeds (*garinim*) from Afula," sunflower and other seeds for snacking.

Haifa

Michel Falafel has won prizes for the best falafel and *schwarma* (see pages 307–8) in Israel.

Jerusalem

Shalom Falafel, at 36 Bezalel Street, is a Jerusalem landmark, founded more than fifty years ago. Watch closely or you'll walk right by it. Eat the falafel in the *aish tanur,* the large pocketless pita. Shalom Falafel has two more branches, one in Emek Rafaiim, and another in Talpiot.

Yosef Falafel, at 7 Shlomo Moussaieff Street, is a tiny stall located in the Bukharan Quarter. It's my favorite in Jerusalem.

Melech Ha Falafel, at 10 King George Street, has been around for forty years and is owned by a Kurdistani family.

Falafel Ma'oz, on King Street (across from the Mashbir Department Store).

Ha Gingi, in Mahane Yehuda.

Pardess Hanna serves the original Dvorah falafel. Although other people call their falafel Dvorah, this place is the one and only real thing. It is known for its Yemenite falafel, which is delicious stuffed into the famous soft pita.

Rosh Pina

Assoul Falafel, at the entrance to the town, has one of the most flavorful falafels I have tasted in Israel. It's made with cilantro and stuffed into pita with great pickled vegetables.

Tel Aviv

Dr. Sa'adyah, at 45 King George Street.

Malkot Ha-Felafel, at 85 Yehuda Halevi Street, is supposed to be a very "in" place. They serve several different flavors of falafel, including the standard "green" (made with cilantro and other herbs) variety and a falafel made with sweet potatoes.

Felafel Yosef, at 3 Beit Lechem, Shuk Bezalel, off King George Street behind Allenby Street.

Mango *Amba*— Mango Pickle Sauce

Almost as important as the falafel are the condiments which accompany the crisp balls: sauerkraut, eggplant salads, diced cucumbers, pickled vegetables (see page 176), tahina sauce, hot sauces like *z'hug* and *harissa* (see pages 139 and 72), and my favorite, mango *amba*.

The mango, a tropical tree born in India, was brought from Egypt to Palestine at the turn of the century. The cultivation of mango started in Israel after a long period of research to find appropriate places with semitropical conditions, since the mango is sensitive to frost. Although most mangoes are sold fresh—processing is expensive—this mango sauce has become a favorite Israeli accompaniment to falafel. I like to have it in my refrigerator for falafel, and to serve with grilled chicken or fish.

YIELD: ABOUT 4 CUPS

6 firm mangoes, peeled and cut into ¼-inch chunks

2 lemons, unpeeled and cut into ¼-inch chunks

2 tablespoons salt

1 tablespoon ground curry powder

1 teaspoon turmeric

1 teaspoon ground fenugreek

1 teaspoon sweet paprika

4 cups white vinegar

1. Place the mango and the lemon in the bowl of a food processor equipped with a steel blade. Sprinkle with the salt, curry, turmeric, fenugreek, and sweet paprika, and pour the vinegar over all. Process to the consistency you like—either pulse on and off for a chunky sauce, or puree.

2. Pour or pack the fruit mixture into a jar and store in refrigerator. It will last several weeks.

Varda's Kurdish *Kubbeh*

Varda makes about twelve varieties of *kubbeh*. This mixture of meat and bulgur, traditionally ground together with a mortar and pestle, can be served large or small, stuffed with meat and rice or vegetables, or used in soups (see pages 142–5). A flat, layered version called *kibbi* (see pages 320–1), served as a main course, is prevalent in Lebanon and northern Israel; the following version, stuffed with rice and pine nuts, is served deep-fried as a finger food for special occasions.

Varda first soaks the bulgur in salted water for half an hour. According to her, the dough separates if no salt is used. Onions and meat are sautéed, and the soaked bulgur is kneaded for half an hour. Varda makes vast quantities of these torpedo-shaped fritters and serves them on the Sabbath and for special occasions. Arabs call this version *kibbi nabulsia*—*kubbeh* from Nablus. During the British Mandate, the British called them "Arab torpedoes."

· · · CRAFTING KURDISH *KUBBEH* · · ·

Until recently, the art of crafting *kubbeh*, which can be served as either a dumpling or a torpedo-shaped fritter, was considered to be one of the prerequisites of a young Kurdish woman's education. Varda Shilo would agree. Born in Zacho, Kurdistan, which is now part of Iraq, she has lived in Jerusalem most of her life. But her great passion is still the history, culture, and cuisine of the Kurdish Jews. Mrs. Shilo, who never finished high school, has written an Aramaic Syrian dictionary, a collection of stories about the Jews of Zacho, and a Kurdistani cookbook (1986).

When we visited her apartment, the table was set with her best china and covered with a silk scarf that Varda's mother had hand carried from Kurdistan. Nearby hung her parents' *ketubah* (wedding certificate), another treasured possession from the old country. In her kitchen she had fashioned a cardboard Kurdish village, with each house centered around a communal courtyard where the cooking was done. On Varda's windowsill sat a clay pitcher, like the ones often used in Kurdistan.

Varda recalls, "We brought Zacho with us. It was the Jerusalem of Kurdistan. We lived in clay *pise* huts with straw roofs. Twice a day we made bread over a coal stove. All our pots were made from clay, and we sat on the floor. Everybody spoke Aramaic, like they did Yiddish in eastern Europe.

We were big Zionists. For twenty-five hundred years we sat on our suitcases because we wanted to go to Jerusalem. We didn't know the name Israel—only Jerusalem. When the state was created, we left everything and came, first by bus to Baghdad, then a train, and then a plane to Lod. When we arrived in 1951, we were herded into buses like sheep into the mountains of Castel, close to Jerusalem. They gave us iron beds with straw mattresses and a gray army blanket. I keep the blanket as a memory of those difficult times. It was very cold, the beginning of April. We danced all night to get warm. We had no food but we were happy because Kurds know how to survive. We ate herbs from around Jerusalem. We pickled and dried them and survived on vegetables. After we arrived we ate only tea, vegetables, and bread. Until 1960 we were hungry. We had about one-quarter kilo of meat per month. Ben-Gurion said, 'The Kurdish Jews know how to work, they survive, they don't demand much, they work hard. They built the land of Israel in quiet.'

"I married at the age of sixteen. My mother married at twelve. My mother cried because the moon came with us, and left her parents behind. I love Israel but I want to remember the past, so I make Kurdish food. When I grew up we didn't eat a lot but we ate well. We covered our table with a tablecloth of love and holiness."

SHELL

2 cups medium bulgur

2 teaspoons salt

$1/4$ cup semolina flour

$3/4$ cup water

FILLING

2 tablespoons vegetable oil, plus oil for frying

1 onion, finely diced

$1/2$ pound ground beef or lamb

4 tablespoons chopped fresh parsley

2 tablespoons currants

2 tablespoons pine nuts

$1/2$ teaspoon cardamom

$1/4$ teaspoon turmeric

$1/2$ teaspoon cumin

$1/2$ teaspoon ground ginger

$1/2$ teaspoon ground cinnamon

2 teaspoons salt

Freshly ground pepper to taste

1. Put the bulgur in a bowl and cover with hot water and 1 teaspoon salt; let sit for a half hour, stirring occasionally. Then squeeze the water out.

2. Heat the 2 tablespoons of oil in a frying pan. Sauté the onions until transparent, then add the meat along with the parsley, currants, pine nuts, cardamom, turmeric, cumin, ginger, cinnamon, 1 teaspoon of salt, and pepper to taste. Sauté about 5 to 8 minutes more or until meat is cooked, breaking up the meat as it is cooking. Remove from the heat and cool slightly.

3. For a traditional preparation, knead the bulgur for about 10 minutes and add the flour and the water, continuing to knead until you have made a soft, pliable dough. You can also put the bulgur, flour, and water in a food processor fitted with a steel blade and pulse until a tacky dough is formed.

4. Wet your hands with cold water. Take a piece of dough about the size of an egg in 1 hand, smooth it into a ball, then make an indentation with your thumb, hollowing out the center to a thickness of about $1/8$ inch. Put a tablespoon of the meat filling into the opening and close the hole, using your first and second finger dipped in cold water to seal any cracks. Using your palms, form the *kubbeh* into a torpedo shape. The outer shell should be smooth so that no filling escapes during frying. Repeat with the remaining dough and filling.

5. Heat about 3 inches of vegetable oil in a heavy pot or wok to 375 degrees. Deep-fry about 5 *kubbeh* at a time, about 5 or 6 minutes on each side, turning once with a slotted spoon. Drain on paper towels. Serve hot.

NOTE   I like to fry the *kubbeh,* drain, cool, and freeze them. To reheat, defrost slightly, place on a cookie sheet, and bake in a preheated 350-degree oven for about 15 minutes. Serve them as an hors d'oeuvre, as is or with 1 or 2 sauces like *z'hug* (see page 139) or mango *amba* (see page 75).

Vegetarian *Kubbeh* with Mint and Potatoes

Rajar's vegetarian version of *kubbeh,* except for the modern addition of potatoes, is as old as the region from which it comes. The women stoop down to knead the softened bulgur into the potatoes, then deftly mold the mixture into thin sausage-like shapes, which they deep-fry.

YIELD: ABOUT 30 *KUBBEH*

1 cup medium (#2) bulgur (2 1/2 cups after soaking)

1 pound potatoes

Salt and freshly ground pepper to taste

3 tablespoons dried mint

1/2 teaspoon paprika

1/2 teaspoon cumin

1/2 teaspoon dried marjoram

Vegetable oil for deep-frying

· · · A DAY IN RAJAR · · ·
A SYRIAN ALAWITE VILLAGE ON THE NORTHERN BORDER

It is 11 a.m., and the Kahmuz family is sitting on their front porch drinking cold water, taking a break from the summer tasks of drying and preserving food for the winter. Instead of fighting the heat as Americans do in their air-conditioned homes and offices, this family has to move with and even enjoys the slow summer rhythm. Every few minutes a loud bomb startles only us, the American visitors. "The bombs are like music here, like Michael Jackson," said Samira, 21. "We would be uncomfortable without them."

Bombs and barbed wire are a way of life in Rajar (pronounced "gha-jar"). Originally a gypsy village (*rajar* means "gypsy" in Arabic), the majority of the inhabitants of Rajar are now Syrian Alawite. The village is located in the northeast finger of Israel, bordering Lebanon only eight feet away on two sides. Nearby guns are aimed at the Hezbollah guerrillas in southern Lebanon. Yet except for these military "intrusions," life takes on an almost biblical beat among the seventeen hundred residents of the town.

It is unusual for Syrian Alawites to be living in Israel. Most of the million or so members of this Moslem sect, an offshoot of the Shiite sect, live in southern Turkey, northern Syria, parts of Lebanon, Iraq, and Iran. The Kahmuz family

originally came from Iskenderun on the Turkish-Syrian border during World War I. After the 1967 war, they were given the option to stay in Israel or cross over into Syria or Lebanon. "For three months we were like the Vatican after the war," said Mahmud, 28, the eldest son of the twelve children, who spoke to me in Hebrew. "We waved a white flag above the village and told the Israelis that we were Syrian." Half of the villagers decided to stay in Israel. "I hope there will be peace. It will come."

Before 1967, the village, a finger of Syria that entered Lebanon, had no electricity or running water. According to Mahmud, the women used to walk down to the Wazzani Spring, one of the three tributaries feeding into the Jordan, to haul up water, which they then carried home on their heads. Today a pump from the spring brings water to the homes.

For the most part, the villagers cook vegetarian fare. During the fall, when the river is not as dry as it was on the day of my visit, they add fresh fish to their diet. On special occasions, chickens, ducks, quail, and other fowl, which used to be raised in cages right next to the barbed wire border, are served as well. Lamb and beef, from the sheep and

1. Cover the bulgur with about 1¼ cups of cold water, and let sit for half an hour, until the water is absorbed, draining off any excess.

2. Meanwhile, peel the potatoes, cut each in half, and cover with cold water in a saucepan. Bring to a boil and simmer until cooked through, about 15 minutes. Drain, cool, dice, and season very well with salt and pepper.

3. Add the potatoes, mint, paprika, cumin, and marjoram to the bulgur and season liberally with more salt and pepper to taste. Knead the mixture for a few minutes, or until the dough has a tacky consistency. Refrigerate for 1 hour.

4. Using about 1 tablespoon of dough, form a sausage-like shape about 2 inches long. Repeat with the remaining dough.

5. Heat a couple of inches of oil in a deep frying pan or wok to 375 degrees. Gently insert the *kubbeh* and fry 1 or 2 minutes on each side, turning with a slotted spoon or tongs. Drain on paper towels.

---

cattle grazing nearby, are reserved for particularly special meals.

Earlier in the week of my visit, the women had made *shanklish,* a yogurt cheese which, before it is dried and rolled in *za'atar,* resembles a saltier mozzarella. There was also homemade *labneh,* covered in olive oil.

The day I was in Rajar, I saw bulgur being prepared as a winter food, drying on large sheets on the flat rooftops of stone houses. During the weeklong drying period, the women occasionally ascend to the rooftops to separate the grains with their fingers. Once dried, the grains are taken down to the village and shelled in a special machine, then crushed to the required fineness at the mill. The larger grains, the size of broken rice, are used for *mujeddra,* a lentil and bulgur stew with sautéed onions. Smaller kernels are used for taboulleh (see page 164) and *kubbeh* (see page 76). The finest crushed wheat, called *jerisheh,* is used for a hot breakfast cereal. Large sacks of the different grades of bulgur, along with tomatoes, garlic, avocado, and zucchini, are kept in the storeroom next to the kitchen.

Adiba Kahmuz, Mahmud's mother, often sits under a fig tree in the backyard, kneading a kind of gruel called *kishk,* made from fine bulgur mixed with *labneh,* salt, and aniseed. The mixture is left to ferment for several days, then kneaded and formed into small balls of *kishk* which are brought to the rooftop to dry in the sun for seven days. This convenience food will be stored throughout the winter to be eaten as a snack, mixed with garlic, *za'atar,* and onion, and soaked with water to make a gruel, a soup, or a sauce for meat dishes. Today you can buy the *kishk* as a powdered, yogurt-based mix in Middle Eastern import stores.

Most of the men in the village of Rajar work in factories and construction, in kibbutzim or at nearby Kiryat Shmoneh. But seven years ago, Mahmud decided to stay home and start a family business of feeding tour groups. At 1 p.m. the day I was visiting, the five sisters and sisters-in-law geared up for the rush: kneading the dough for the *kubbeh,* the fritters filled with diced potatoes and spices; and pounding the hummus, which they sprinkle with sweet red pepper. Crouched down, they worked on the stone floor, mixing the ingredients and dishing them out on flat plates to serve to their guests.

The members of the tour group were seated in a shady garden, surrounded by lemon, pomegranate, plum, olive, and fig trees, grapevines, mulberries (called white berries or tree berries in Israel), zinnias, marigolds, and geraniums. Plates of *kubbeh,* taboulleh, hummus, *labneh,* and olives appeared without end. For dessert, anise-flavored cookies fried in olive oil were served with fresh fruit and tea made from dried ginger, anise, cinnamon, and cumin. In this northernmost corner of modern-day Israel, I felt somehow transported to biblical times.

Fongelom—
Cochin Vegetable
Fritters

It seems that throughout Israel, each ethnic community has one or two designated cooks. They are called upon to prepare the food for weddings, bar mitzvahs, even funerals. One such woman is Rachel Ephraim, a native of Cochin, India, a city which at one time had a large Jewish population. Most of them, except perhaps a handful, now live in Israel. Rachel, who lives in Rechasim, a moshav (collective village) in the western Galilee, makes the traditional food of her native land, like these festive fritters she prepared when I was visiting her relatives in nearby Kfar Hassidim.

YIELD: ABOUT 35 *FONGELOM*

1 small butternut squash (about 1½ pounds)

1 medium potato (about ½ pound)

1 medium onion, finely chopped

½ cup grated coconut

1 fresh serrano pepper, finely chopped

3 stems fresh curry leaves,* finely chopped (or 2 teaspoons curry powder)

2 teaspoons salt, or to taste

1 large egg

2 cups cake flour

1 teaspoon baking powder

Vegetable oil for frying

1. Peel the squash and remove the seeds. Grate it and the potato into a large bowl.

2. Add the onions, coconut, serrano pepper, curry leaves or powder, salt, and the egg; mix well. Gradually fold in the flour and baking powder and continue mixing until fully incorporated. The batter will be slightly sticky.

3. Shape the mixture into balls about 1½ inches in diameter, and flatten each slightly to make a patty.

4. Heat 2 inches of oil in a deep frying pan to 375 degrees. Using a slotted spoon, carefully slip some of the patties into the hot oil and fry until golden, turning once. Do not overcrowd the pan.

5. Drain on paper towels, and serve immediately.

*Available at Indian markets

T hese chicken- and potato-filled turnovers, which Rachel Ephraim also prepared for me, are another Cochin specialty.

Kartala Pastels—
Chicken and Potato
Turnovers

YIELD: ABOUT 32 *KARTALA PASTELS*

FILLING

¼ cup vegetable oil

2 medium onions, finely chopped (about 2½ cups)

1 small potato, cut into ½-inch cubes

1 hard-boiled egg, crumbled

2 tablespoons chopped fresh parsley

1 chicken breast, cut into ½-inch cubes

½ teaspoon turmeric

1 teaspoon freshly ground pepper

1 tablespoon balsamic vinegar

PASTEL DOUGH

2¼ cups unbleached all-purpose flour

3 cups water

3 large eggs

1 tablespoon vegetable oil or pareve margarine

1 teaspoon salt

Vegetable oil for frying

1. To make the filling, heat the oil in a large sauté pan. Add the onions and cook over low heat until translucent. Add the potato, increase the heat to high, and cook until golden brown. Put the onion and potato in a bowl and mix with the hard-boiled egg and parsley.

2. Put the chicken, turmeric, pepper, and vinegar in the same sauté pan over medium heat, stirring occasionally until the chicken is fully cooked, about 5 minutes. Add the onion and potato. Remove from the heat, cover, and set aside.

3. To make the dough, whisk together the flour, water, and 2 eggs in a large bowl, to the consistency of a thin cake batter. There should be no lumps.

4. Heat 1 teaspoon of oil or margarine in a medium nonstick frying pan over a low flame; swirl to coat the entire pan. Ladle in 2 tablespoons of the batter, then quickly tilt the pan to form a thin 4–5 inch circle of batter.

5. When the sides of the *pastel* begin to pull away from the bottom of the pan, flip it over with a spatula, cook for a few more seconds, then remove to a paper towel to drain. The *pastel* will be pale in color; if the dough gets too brown, the pan is too hot. It may take a few attempts before you master the art of *pastel*-making. Repeat the process until all the batter is used up, adding a small amount of oil or margarine after every 3 or 4 *pastels*.

6. Beat the remaining egg with the salt.

7. Place 1 heaping tablespoon of the filling near the edge of a *pastel*. Fold the bottom edge over the filling, fold in the sides, then roll into a rectangle. Repeat with the remaining *pastels*. Brush the outside of each with the beaten egg.

8. In a deep frying pan, heat 1 inch of vegetable oil. Gently slip a few of the filled *pastels* into the frying pan and cook until golden brown, turning. Do not overcrowd the pan. Drain on paper towels and serve immediately.

Appetizers

Fennel Finger *Burekas*

I was thrilled when Tel Aviv–born caterer Hava Volman invited me to her Brooklyn, New York, home to taste her cooking. A student of fine arts, she changed careers several years ago and began catering for the Israeli consul general and the ambassador to the United Nations. Married to Greek Israeli artist Artemis Schwebel, Hava lives in a Brooklyn row house, where she has a white Spartan stucco kitchen with blue tiles and high-tech stainless-steel equipment. Out back, near their one mulberry tree, Artemis crafted an Argentinian grill where the couple often barbecues, serving the food on pottery plates that Hava made when she worked as a ceramist. Even though Hava has the ethnic world of Brooklyn as her vegetable basket, *za'atar* is still her "holy spice combination." These fennel *burekas* are her Israeli variation of the traditional Greek spanakopita.

YIELD: 12 SERVINGS

3 fennel bulbs (about 2 pounds total)

4 tablespoons olive oil

2 bunches scallions, chopped (about 2 cups)

1 tablespoon fennel seeds

2 tablespoons *za'atar* (see page 62)

1 teaspoon dried sumac

1/2 pound feta cheese, crumbled

1/4 pound fresh spinach, chopped (about 2 cups)

1/2 cup raisins

1/2 teaspoon cinnamon

Salt and freshly ground pepper to taste

6 sheets of phyllo dough (or 12 sheets if making individual triangle-shaped *burekas*)

1/2 cup (1 stick) unsalted butter, melted

1. Preheat the oven to 450 degrees. Cut the fennel bulbs into quarters, removing the tough core and stems. Place the fennel on a greased cookie sheet and drizzle 2 tablespoons of the olive oil over the pieces. Roast on the middle rack of the oven for 35–40 minutes or until tender. When cool, chop the fennel into bite-size pieces.

2. Heat the remaining olive oil in a large sauté pan. Add the scallions and cook over medium heat until soft, about 2 minutes.

3. Lower the oven temperature to 400 degrees and grease another cookie sheet.

4. In a large bowl, fold together with a rubber spatula the fennel, cooked scallions, fennel seeds, 1 tablespoon of the *za'atar,* the sumac, feta, spinach, raisins, cinnamon, and salt and pepper.

5. Spread out 1 sheet of the phyllo with the long side parallel to the edge of your work surface. Put a damp towel over the remaining phyllo to keep it from drying out.

6. Brush the phyllo with melted butter, cover with a second sheet, and brush that with butter. Spoon ⅓ of the fennel filling in a pile along 1 long edge of the dough, leaving a 1-inch border around the outside. Fold the short sides in and roll up jelly-roll style. Place on the greased cookie sheet seam side down, and brush the top with butter. Repeat with the remaining sheets of phyllo and filling.

7. Brush once more with butter, then sprinkle the remaining tablespoon of za'atar over the logs. Bake on the middle rack for 25 minutes or until golden brown. Divide each log into 2-inch slices. Serve immediately.

NOTE To make individual triangle-shaped burekas, brush a sheet of phyllo with butter and cover it with a second sheet; brush again with butter. Cut the dough lengthwise into 6 equal strips. Place a teaspoon of filling at the bottom of each strip, then fold each strip as you would a flag, forming triangles. Repeat with the remaining phyllo and filling. Yield: 36 triangles.

Fennel at Mahane Yehudah

Shortcut Potato
Burekas

This cross between a *bureka* and a knish is very popular throughout Israel. I learned how to make a faster version, using storebought dough, in the border city of Bet She'an, at the home of American-born Ziona Levy, the daughter-in-law of former foreign minister David Levy, who is of Moroccan origin. "When I married Jacky, it was a culture shock," said Ziona. "I had to learn to cook. I had married into a family of twelve children and I was the only non-Moroccan. And he was the first son. So I hung around in the kitchen to watch the women. I was expected to make his mother's food. At our home we had traditional Ashkenazic Jewish chicken soup, roast, and one salad for Shabbat, but here they had ten different kinds of salads, fish, *pastels,* and *burekas.* I take all kinds of shortcuts, like using frozen pastry for potato *burekas.*" These are tasty with a mushroom and tomato sauce, the recipe for which follows.

YIELD: 12 *BUREKAS*

3 large onions, diced

4 tablespoons butter

2 pounds baking potatoes (about 4 medium)

Salt and freshly ground pepper to taste

1/2 teaspoon turmeric (optional)

1/2 cup chopped fresh parsley

3 large eggs

1 sheet commercial puff pastry

1 tablespoon water

1 tablespoon sesame seeds

1. Sauté the onions in 2 tablespoons of the butter until golden.

2. Meanwhile, peel the potatoes, cut them into quarters, and cover with cold water in a large pot. Bring to a boil, then simmer about 15 minutes or until the potatoes are cooked through. Drain and mash them with a fork. Add salt, pepper, turmeric, parsley, the remaining butter, and 2 of the eggs. Mix thoroughly.

3. Preheat the oven to 400 degrees and grease a cookie sheet.

4. Place the sheet of commercial puff pastry on a floured board and roll out as thin as possible, until it is about 8 inches by 12 inches. Spoon the potato filling along one long side, leaving a 1-inch border all around. Roll into a tight jelly roll. Using the side of your hand near your pinky, press down on the dough to cut it. Do this at 2-inch intervals. The dough should naturally enclose the filling. (Press the sides to make sure the filling is thoroughly enclosed.) Place the *burekas* on a cookie sheet.

5. Mix the remaining egg with the water in a small bowl. Brush the *burekas* with this egg wash.

6. Sprinkle sesame seeds on top and bake on the middle rack of the oven for 10 minutes. Reduce the heat to 350 degrees and continue baking 15 to 20 minutes or until golden brown. Serve with the tomato-mushroom sauce.

NOTE You can also add 1 cup of cottage cheese, ¼ cup Parmesan cheese, or ½ cup feta cheese to the potatoes.

Tomato-Mushroom Sauce

YIELD: ABOUT 2 CUPS

1 large onion, chopped

2 tablespoons vegetable oil or unsalted butter

1 pound mushrooms, chopped

3 tablespoons tomato sauce

Salt and freshly ground pepper to taste

Red pepper flakes to taste

Sauté the onions in the vegetable oil or butter until soft. Add the mushrooms and continue sautéing until the onions are golden. Stir in the tomato sauce and add salt, pepper, and pepper flakes to taste.

Piles of hot pepper at a market on Levinsky Street

Yalanchi Sarna— Armenian Stuffed Grape Leaves

I would venture to guess that there are more ways to stuff a grape leaf in Israel than in any other country in the entire world. Every Middle Eastern immigrant has his or her own recipe. Some, like chef Moshe Basson of the Eucalyptus Restaurant in Jerusalem, use cabbage and the large Jerusalem sage leaves instead. If I had to choose one preparation, it would be the following *yalanchi sarna,* brought to Jerusalem by Armenian immigrants from Turkey. *Yalanchi sarna* means "fake grape leaves," thus no meat is used in this dish. I first tasted these tart grape leaves filled with gently sautéed onions, crunchy pine nuts, dill, and tomato many years ago when visiting dignitaries in the Armenian Quarter of Jerusalem. The leaves, picked young in the summer, are best for stuffing when fresh. Some are, of course, traditionally cured in a brine for the winter, but many cooks I interviewed throughout Israel have switched to freezing the fresh, tender leaves for use throughout the year. This allows the leaves to retain their bright green color.

Another variation of grape leaves I especially like comes from Margaret Thayer, a Tunisian Jew who owns a restaurant in Jaffa. Margaret serves hers, similar in flavor to the Armenian version, on a bed of one cup of warm, rich yogurt or sour cream mixed with one-quarter cup buttermilk, with olive oil drizzled on top and a sprinkling of fresh mint and lemon juice.

YIELD: ABOUT 60 STUFFED GRAPE LEAVES

1/4 cup plus 2 tablespoons olive oil

6 cups diced onions (about 3 medium)

1/3 cup pine nuts

1/3 cup currants

3/4 cup chopped parsley

1/4 cup snipped fresh dill

1 tablespoon dried or 2 tablespoons diced fresh mint

1/2 teaspoon cinnamon

1/2 teaspoon allspice

1 teaspoon ground cardamom

1 tablespoon salt, or to taste

1/2 teaspoon freshly ground pepper

1 cup short-grain Egyptian or other white rice, uncooked

2 cups water

1 tablespoon sugar

1 1/2 cups diced fresh tomatoes, juices reserved

Juice of 2 lemons

70 grape leaves, fresh or jarred, stems removed

1. Heat 1/4 cup of the olive oil in a large covered skillet, and add the onions. Cover and steam (this is called "sweating" the onions) for 20 minutes.

2. Uncover the skillet, add the pine nuts and currants, and sauté until the onions are golden and the pine nuts slightly browned. Stir in the parsley, dill, mint,

cinnamon, allspice, cardamom, salt, pepper, rice, 1 cup of the water, sugar, and tomatoes. Cover and simmer for 15 minutes, until the rice is almost cooked. Uncover, squeeze 1 of the lemons over the mixture, replace the cover, and continue cooking for 5 more minutes. Remove from the heat, let cool, then chill while you are preparing the grape leaves.

3. If using grape leaves bottled in brine, soak them in cold water, changing the water several times, to remove some of the salty taste. Pat the grape leaves dry with paper towels.

4. Line the bottom of a heavy 6-quart pot with 10 leaves, dull side up.

5. Place 1 leaf on a flat surface, dull side up, with the stem end toward you. Spoon on 1 tablespoon of filling near the stem end of the leaf and flatten the filling to the width of the leaf. Fold the stem end over the filling, then fold the sides into the center and roll away from you. Repeat with the remaining leaves and filling.

6. Arrange the stuffed grape leaves, seam sides down, in rows along the bottom of the lined pot, then stack them on top of each other. Pour the remaining cup of water over the leaves and place a small plate on top to keep the leaves weighted down. Cover the pot and bring to a boil; reduce the heat and simmer for 20 minutes. Uncover and simmer 10 minutes more. Allow to cool in the pot, then drain.

7. Serve warm or at room temperature as an appetizer, sprinkled with the juice of the remaining lemon and the remaining 2 tablespoons of olive oil. If you like, you can also top them with yogurt.

Israeli Revisionist
Haroset

This *haroset* recipe, which comes from eighth-generation Jerusalemite Hemda Friedman, includes apples, an influence of the Eastern European Jews, alongside the dates and raisins of the Middle Eastern Jews.

YIELD: ABOUT 4 CUPS

2 cups raisins

1 cup pecans, toasted

1 cup blanched almonds, toasted

1 cup date paste (or 1 cup dried dates, chopped)

3 Granny Smith apples, cored and cut into chunks

2 teaspoons cinnamon

$1/4$ cup sweet red wine, or to taste

1–2 tablespoons lemon juice

Using a food processor fitted with a steel blade, coarsely grind together the raisins and nuts, pulsing so as not to overprocess. Add the date paste or chopped dates, the apples, and the cinnamon and mix well. Add wine and lemon juice to taste.

· · · PASSOVER *HAROSET* · · ·

To me, *haroset,* the fruit and nut paste symbolic of the mortar used when the Jews were slaves in Egypt, is the ultimate appetizer. The first food eaten at the Passover seder, it, more than gefilte fish or hard-boiled eggs, whets the appetite for the rest of the meal.

Since biblical times, throughout the Mediterranean, a portion of summer fruit like figs, grapes, and dates has always been set aside at harvest and dried on strings to be prepared for *haroset* at Passover. Because foods were difficult to come by in Israel's early days, immigrants made do using peanuts, bananas, or whatever fruits and nuts they could find. An Israeli recipe that includes bananas and peanuts appears in Molly Lyons Bar-David's seminal *Israeli Cook Book* (1964).

Even today, many people save a pomegranate or other fall fruit in the hope that it will not dry out before it can be stirred into the Passover *haroset*. Before the advent of the food processor, these fruits were pounded with a mortar and pestle or ground with a manual chopper, often combined with spices like cinnamon, cardamom, or ginger, and some sweet wine or even Passover vinegar, which cleanses the fruit. Spices vary according to the country of origin. Yemenites, for example, might include cloves and pepper, while Israelis of eastern European origin often add cinnamon.

Soofer Family Iranian-Israeli *Haroset*

This flavorful version, with so many nuts, reminds me of the Talmudic suggestion as to the symbolism of *haroset:* that it represents the fruit trees under which Jewish women slaves enticed their husbands to make love, and thus propagated the Jewish people.

YIELD: ABOUT 10 CUPS

1/3 cup shelled pistachio nuts	1 1/4 cups pomegranate juice
1/3 cup unblanched almonds	3 cups sweet red wine (about)
3/4 cup cashews	1 teaspoon cinnamon
1/3 cup hazelnuts	1/2 teaspoon cayenne pepper, or to taste
3/4 cup walnuts	1 teaspoon ground cardamom
2 pears, peeled and quartered	1/2 teaspoon ground cloves
2 red apples, peeled and quartered	1 teaspoon ground coriander
3 cups seedless black raisins	1 teaspoon cumin
1 cup seedless golden raisins	1 teaspoon ground nutmeg
2 3/4 cups dates, pits removed	1 teaspoon ground ginger

1. Roast the pistachio nuts, almonds, cashews, hazelnuts, and walnuts by placing them in the microwave on medium power for about 5 minutes, stirring frequently.

2. Place the roasted nuts in a food processor fitted with a steel blade and process until coarsely ground. Add the pears, apples, raisins, and dates and pulse until the nuts are finely ground and the fruits coarsely chopped. Gradually add the pomegranate juice, continuing to process until thick. Add the wine and the spices and process once more to incorporate, adjusting to taste.

Breads

When I cried as a child,
my grandmother put
me on a table while she
was making bread.
I remember how she
moved her hands; it is
so deep in me that
I move my hands the
same way.

—Amira Rubin, bread
baker in Rosh Pina

In the Negev, south of Be'er Sheva', at one of the last Bedouin
villages in Israel, veiled women of the Azzazma tribe kneel by their goatskin
tents to grind wheat between two stones. They mix the resulting flour with salt
and water and roll out the dough with practiced hands. Dressed in flowing black
gowns with beautiful embroidery at the yoke, they slap the rolled dough onto a
concave metal disk similar to an inverted wok and quickly bake it over coals of
camel dung and olive pits, on the ground. Watching them is like going back thousands of years to Sarah and Abraham's tent near Hebron. Sarah, as a gesture of
hospitality to three visiting men, measured three portions of choice flour and
made thin, flat, chewy unleavened cakes (Genesis 18:5).

"The unleavened desert bread, which is essentially matzoh, is the staple of the

---

Above: Matti Lendner, a Jerusalem challah maven

Bedouin diet, which they bake three times a day," said Clinton Bailey, author of *Bedouin Poetry from Sinai and the Negev* (1991) and Israel's foremost authority on Bedouin culture. "It was not until the Israelites were enslaved in Egypt that they ate leavened bread. Still today, to the Bedouin, yeast is the sign of a settled people, of contamination in the city," said Bailey. "Pure bread for them includes no yeast because there is no leaven in the desert."

Throughout history, bread, both leavened and unleavened, has been the central food in Israel, the home of the mother of wheat, the genetic strain of emmer from which all contemporary wheats derive. Before each meal, observant Jews bless *lehem,* the "bread from the earth," as symbolic of all food that grows from the earth. Jesus frequently referred to himself as the "bread of life," and in Arabic the word for bread is *khubz,* which also means life. "Bread is sacred in Palestine, as the main article of food," wrote Estelle Blyth in 1927, in her memoir *When We Lived in Jerusalem.* "I have often seen an Arab stop in the road to pick up a piece of bread that had fallen there, touch his forehead with it as a token of respect, and carefully place it in a cleft of the wall so that it may be safe from passing feet."

Pilgrim, visitor, and immigrant alike have brought to Israel their personal concept of bread. Some, like the German Templars, came in the late nineteenth century with their own millers and planted the kinds of grains with which they were familiar in the Rhineland. Others, like Kreshe Berman, who came with her husband and children in 1875 from Lithuania, started baking black bread, darkening it with molasses made from the local carob tree, and selling it to the Russian Orthodox pilgrims on their way to the Church of the Holy Sepulchre. Today, pushcarts still sell Berman bread in the Old City, the company being the second largest commercial bakery in Israel.

Breads in Israel go back almost to the dawn of civilization. The earliest matzoh or flatbread derives from the Babylonian *ma-as-sa-ar-tum,* meaning "barley," the first grain harvested in the Middle East. It was in use many centuries before wheat, which was first grown around 4000 B.C.E. The barley was ground with a flat stone; the stone was then heated with a flint stone until it was hot enough to cook the bread. The barley was also dried, as mentioned by the threshers during the barley harvest in the Book of Ruth. If the household had a hearth, the dough was roasted in the ashes. "Yea, also I have baked bread upon the coals thereof" (Isaiah 44:19).

When the Jews settled in Canaan after the return from Egypt, they preferred hard wheat bread to barley bread. These flatbreads, similar to pita, were easier to make because they cooked quickly, requiring less wood than thicker breads. For centuries the best bread was made from the purest flour and brought as an offering, with the purest olive oil, to the Temple in Jerusalem.

I am told that most of the grain of the Holy City and Palestine is turned into flour by hand-mills at home. Some flour is imported and some is ground in mills run by camels or donkeys. The Jew of Jerusalem seldom buys grain. He uses imported flour. In baking bread the dough is kneaded at home and brought in great lumps to the public ovens. These are to be found in almost any street. They are cave-like vaults running down below the street level. Olive wood is used as fuel, and the oven floor is marked out in blocks, so that the baking of each family is put on a separate block. The loaves are about an inch thick and of the size of a tea plate. They have a hole in the centre. The baker makes them from the dough, bakes them, and returns them hot from the oven to the customers.

—Benjamin L. Gordon, *New Judea* (1919)

Three thousand years ago, in the City of David, the first breads were small and round, slightly raised in the center and about as thick as a finger. Three breads per person were eaten at each meal. Thus, at the meal Abigail prepared for David and his men, she served two huge jugs of wine and two hundred loaves of bread. "Then Abigail made haste, and took two hundred loaves, and two bottles of wine, and five sheep ready dressed, and five measures of parched corn, and a hundred clusters of raisins, and two hundred cakes of figs, and laid them on the asses" (I Samuel 25:18).

These flatbreads were the kinds of bread that were eaten in Jesus' time. It was probably the same bread that he multiplied so that five loaves fed five thousand people, with bread left over (Matthew 14:17–21). On the night he was betrayed, Jesus ate unleavened bread—matzoh (I Corinthians 11:23).

A version of this flatbread is the kind still baked in a clay *tabunah* oven. Jerusalem's Eliyahu Cohen makes Iraqi pita in one of these wood-fired clay ovens. His bakery, just big enough to hold the oven and one or two customers, is located in the Bukharan Quarter. The dough, stretched by hand, is placed on a gigantic pot holder that looks like a pillow and is pressed onto the clay oven wall; a few minutes later it is peeled off. This crisp flat loaf, popular throughout Israel as *aish tanur,* is eaten by Iraqis for all meals, even on the Sabbath, when they eat it for breakfast as *sabikh,* stuffed with roasted eggplant, a hard-boiled egg, parsley, and tahina.

A few blocks away from Cohen's is Nahama, a Persian bakery on the outskirts of Mea Shearim. Fourth-generation baker David Nahama uses the same dough as the Iraqis, but he presses it into more bulbous, oval shapes, the surface indented with fingerprints. Black and white sesame seeds are sprinkled on top before the loaves are transferred to long wooden paddles and shoved into the wood-fired oven. The Sabbath challah for Persians, like that of the Iraqis, is just a different form of their everyday bread. Today, these Oriental flatbreads sit side by side on the Sabbath table with the Ashkenazic twisted sweet challah in many multicultural homes in Israel.

Modern Israel has an amazing array of breads, representing the polyglot culture of the country: flatbreads, twisted breads, croissants, scores of variations on challah, and—in the last few years—even bagels.

Pita Bread

In Hebrew the generic term for bread is *lehem.* A piece of dough broken off to make a small bread is *pat,* which comes from the Aramaic. Some think that the Greek and modern Hebrew word *pita* is also Aramaic. Others, like food historian Charles Perry of the Los Angeles *Times,* say that *pita* comes from *pkakous,* the Greek flatbread from about 300 C.E. Whatever the origin, pita, or as the Turks call it, *pide,* was born. According to Perry, the word *pita* was borrowed from Judeo-Spanish, the language of the Sephardic Jews, who picked it up in a Balkan country—he thinks Romania, where four-fifths of the Balkan Jewish population lived at the beginning of this century. Today, throughout the world the word *pita* has come to describe a particular type of pocket bread.

Replicating authentic pita bread is difficult with our conventional ovens. I have tried different versions with varying degrees of success. My editor, Judith Jones, shared her method with me, and the breads were surprisingly like the bread I ate in the villages of Galilee. If the bread becomes stale, pop it in the microwave or a medium oven, slice, and stuff. It is a great pocket bread for sandwiches.

YIELD: 12 PITAS

1 package dry yeast (1 scant tablespoon)	1 teaspoon salt
1 1/2 cups warm water	3 1/2 cups all-purpose flour (about)
1 tablespoon olive oil	

1. Sprinkle the yeast into a large bowl and pour the warm water on top. Stir until the yeast is dissolved; add the olive oil and salt and mix well. Add enough flour until the dough is difficult to stir.

2. Turn the dough onto a floured surface and knead for about 10 minutes, adding more flour as necessary to make a firm, elastic dough. You can also use a food processor, or an electric mixer with a dough hook. Place the dough in a greased bowl and let rise, covered, for about 1 1/2 hours or until doubled in bulk.

3. Turn the dough out onto a large floured surface and cut into 12 equal sections. Using your hands, form each section into a ball about the size of a ping-pong ball. Cover with a towel and set aside for 5 minutes.

4. Flour the work surface lightly. Using a rolling pin, roll out each ball to a disk 6 inches in diameter. The dough will be very elastic, so roll firmly, adding a little more flour as necessary to keep the dough from sticking. Repeat with the remaining balls of dough. Cover the circles and let rest for 15 minutes.

5. Meanwhile, preheat the oven to 500 degrees, lining one rack with baking tiles or a baking stone. (If you do not have either, heat a baking sheet.) If you have a bread paddle, dust it with flour and transfer 2 of the rounds to it, then slide them onto the hot tiles or stone, keeping the remaining balls covered. Otherwise, gently pick up the disks with your fingers and toss them onto the tiles. Bake for 3 minutes. Remove the pitas with tongs or a spatula. Repeat with the remaining rounds.

Fa'toy'yeh B'sbaanegh—
Pita Spinach Turnovers

When I dropped in on Fathima Zeidan Salah in the village of Salim, she was picking wild greens by the wayside to insert in the pita dough she bakes daily for her six children. Like all the Bedouins in the Lower Galilee, the family no longer lives in tents, but in houses with plumbing. "Life is better for us than it was before," said her husband. "We were the last holdouts in tents."

They also may be the last holdouts to resist prepackaged food. "I can't tell what is in sacks or packages," said the four-foot-five-inch Fathima, flashing her engaging smile and shaking her curly brown hair. Fathima picks her own wheat, brings it to a mill for grinding, and watches the miller put the flour in sacks. Throughout the winter the sacks are kept in a storeroom in her home with other staples such as lentils, chickpeas, and tiny pickled eggplants with pimientos. In her kitchen, outfitted with a cooktop but no conventional oven, she stores other staples like onions, carrots, tomatoes, *za'atar,* and, of course, oil from olives that she has picked and her husband has crushed and pressed.

But bread is the centerpiece of each meal, as it was for the lunch that she prepared for us. Combining flour, water, salt, and a little bit of leavening, she works the dough, lets it rise, and molds it into balls. Then she places a rolled-out piece of dough on a lazy Susan–type disk set over a fire in her wood-burning stove. She pats the dough down and, after it has puffed up and browned, flips it over and bakes it a few more minutes. The bread is served hot from the oven, often sprinkled with olive oil and *za'atar.* Some dough is shaped in triangles, filled with wild greens like arugula, dandelion greens, scallions, and the stems and leaves of wild herbs, all gathered in the nearby fields. One she uses in the springtime is *murrar,* a bitter herb which was probably the bitter green called *maror* eaten by the Israelites in the desert at Passover. The fragrant greens, embedded in the dough over the fire, are steamed so slightly that they retain their very fresh flavor. Served with some of the flatbread, *labneh,* fresh fava beans sautéed in olive oil and garlic, and other greens like sautéed *hashook* (wild celery), *akouba* (wild artichokes), and *khubeiza* (wild mallow), the meal was so basic, yet as modern in its simple flavors as any I have tasted throughout the world.

Each time I taste more sophisticated Lebanese versions of this spinach turnover in Washington, D.C., Rio de Janeiro, or even Buffalo, New York, I think of its origins, with people like Fathima picking their own fresh greens for steaming inside the dough. These turnovers make a great finger food at lunch or an afternoon snack. Eat some and freeze the rest.

3 tablespoons extra virgin olive oil

1 bunch scallions, diced (green and white parts)

6 pita dough balls, uncooked (see recipe, page 93)

¼ teaspoon allspice

½ teaspoon dried sumac

½ teaspoon salt

3 cups chopped fresh spinach, chicory, arugula, dandelion greens, or a combination

Juice of 1 lemon

¼ teaspoon *za'atar* (see page 62) (optional)

Cornmeal for dusting

1. Preheat the oven to 350 degrees.

2. Sauté the scallions briefly in 2 tablespoons of the olive oil, until soft.

3. Roll out the pita dough to 6-inch rounds and brush with olive oil.

4. Sprinkle the allspice, sumac, and salt over each pita and divide the scallions among them.

5. Place about ½ cup of the greens in the center of each pita and squeeze the lemon juice over all.

6. Brush the perimeters of the pita circles with water. Pull the edges of the dough up to form a triangle around the filling and pinch the 3 corners together, overlapping the dough so that the filling is completely enclosed.

7. On a baking sheet sprinkled with cornmeal, bake the pita triangles for 15 minutes. Eat immediately as is, or brushed with more olive oil and sprinkled with *za'atar.*

Rayah from Pekiin making pita

Breads

Abouelafia's Sunny-Side-Up *Za'atar* Pita Pizza

When I visited the Abouelafia bakery in Jaffa, Khamis showed me how to make their most popular flatbread—pita drizzled with olive oil, *za'atar*, and feta cheese, sometimes with olives or tahina, and with an egg baked sunny-side-up in the dough. After learning of a similar concoction served at a pizza joint in Safed, I changed the dough slightly, adding semolina and whole-wheat flour.

YIELD: 4 PITA PIZZAS, SERVING 4 TO 8 PEOPLE

1 package fresh or dry yeast (1 scant tablespoon)

1/4 cup warm water

1 tablespoon honey

1 teaspoon salt

5 tablespoons olive oil

3/4 cup water (cold in summer, warm in winter)

2 cups all-purpose flour (about)

3/4 cup whole-wheat flour

1/4 cup semolina

4 teaspoons *za'atar* (see page 62)

2 tablespoons Safed or feta cheese

8 large eggs

· · · JAFFA'S ABOUELAFIA · · ·
THE FLATBREAD FANTASY WORLD

In 1880, Said Abouelafia started making pita right behind the clock tower in Jaffa. In those days Jaffa was the main seaport of the region, and the Arab-owned Abouelafia bakery was one of the first places where visitors and Jewish immigrants went to buy their bread.

Today, open twenty-four hours a day, the bakery, with a steady stream of visitors lined up outside, sells at least eighty different kinds of stuffed breads. One of the most famous bakeries in Israel, Abouelafia produces breads that reflect historical immigrant trends. "Every two or three years we try to add a new kind of bread. Behind each bread is a story," said Khamis Abouelafia, son of the bakery's founder and a seventh-generation baker. "After the

Khomeini revolution in the 1970s, thousands of Iranian Jews came here. They lived near the old central bus station in Tel Aviv. One day a few newcomers came searching for their *naan*. I asked them what they wanted. They told me they were trying to find a bread similar to their bread and couldn't find any. They agreed to come and show my employees how to make the bread. Now we sell it."

By 1948, the majority of Abouelafia's neighbors were Jewish. "When my father realized the switch in population," said Khamis, "he decided to close the bakery at Passover, trying to show that the basis of a relationship is respect." Today, sixty-five employees—Christian, Jewish, and Moslem—pride themselves on this bakery and its roots.

1. Dissolve the yeast in the warm water; stir in ½ teaspoon of the honey and set aside for 10 minutes.

2. Mix the remaining 2½ teaspoons of honey with the salt, olive oil, and water and set aside.

3. Put the flours and semolina in the bowl of a food processor fitted with a steel blade. With the motor running, slowly pour in the honey-oil mixture through the feed tube. Then pour in the dissolved yeast. Process until the dough forms a ball on the blade. If it is too sticky, sprinkle on a little more all-purpose flour.

4. Scrape out the dough onto a lightly floured surface and knead a few times, until smooth. Transfer to an oiled bowl, cover, and let rise for 1 hour, until doubled in bulk.

5. Divide the dough into 4 walnut-sized pieces. Roll each piece into a smooth, tight ball. Put on a flat sheet or dish, cover with a damp towel, and let rise for another hour.

6. Preheat the oven, preferably with a pizza stone inside, to 500 degrees, or oil and flour a baking sheet.

Finishing off a bread sandwich at Abouelafia's

7. Roll or stretch each ball of dough into a 6-inch circle. Put the circles on the baking sheet, or slide them onto your pizza stone, and bake about 3 minutes, until the dough starts to dry slightly.

8. Remove the partially baked disks from the oven and brush with olive oil to within 1 inch of the edge. Sprinkle on the *za'atar* and the feta. Break 2 eggs in the center of each bread and bake in the oven for 5 minutes, or until the crusts are golden brown and the eggs are baked. Do not overcook. The pizzas should be slightly soft.

Breads

"The Yemenite people were very poor, so they invented ten kinds of bread, which they ate with radishes and onion or dipped into their soupy stews, the way we would use a spoon," Hadassah Gariwaany Hamdy told me when I visited her at home in the Kiryat HaYovel section of Jerusalem. "We grew up without spoons and forks."

Mrs. Hamdy, now in her late eighties, is known for her *ka'ak* (pretzel-like rings) and *kubannah* (a Yemenite overnight bread, made especially for the Sabbath), which she prepared every Friday morning in her tiny apartment. Her parents, like so many Yemenites, followed their dream to live in the biblical Promised Land. When they finally arrived safely in Jaffa, after a journey by water from Beirut and by land from Yemen, they just sat in the road all day; no one came to meet them. Eventually a Yemenite passerby heard them talking and took them to the Yemenite Quarter in Jaffa, and then to Rehovot, where Mrs. Hamdy grew up.

"We were very poor and didn't have much to eat," she said. "My father used to harvest the wheat in the south for farmers, who gave him some wheat that we ground to make bread. The cycle of the week revolved around this bread. On Monday or Tuesday we soaked the durum wheat in water for three days. Then we drained and ground the wheat again like for a porridge. On Thursday night we prepared the yeast. Friday morning we baked for the Sabbath in an outdoor clay oven.

"I knew a Yemenite woman in Jerusalem who sang songs when she ground her wheat into flour," she recalled. "Her son-in-law thought he could help her. He was ashamed by her primitive work so he motorized the mill. She was happy for a week or two but then she went back to the old ways. 'Yes,' she told me, 'maybe it's easy, but I can't sing when I prepare bread that way.'"

Mrs. Hamdy's parents arriving from Yemen in the 1880s

Old Jerusalem *Ka'ak*— Mizrachi Bagels

Round rolls with a hole have been in existence since yeast was first discovered in ancient Egypt. They are usually either soft like the sesame-studded *bagala* or hard like the following *mizrachi* or Middle Eastern pretzel-like *ka'ak,* a perfect snack-food. Bagels have only recently become a popular item in Israel, brought there by American immigrants and perhaps regarded as a rare luxury, considering the amount of water needed for boiling.

YIELD: 50 TO 55 *KA'AK*

1 package dry yeast (1 scant tablespoon)

1 cup lukewarm water

1/2 teaspoon sugar

1 teaspoon salt

3 1/2 cups unbleached all-purpose flour

1/2 cup (1 stick) unsalted butter or pareve margarine at room temperature, plus 2 tablespoons butter or margarine, melted, for brushing

3/4 cup sesame seeds, lightly toasted

1. Put the yeast, water, and sugar in a small bowl. Let stand for 5 minutes, until the yeast has dissolved.

2. Pour the dissolved yeast into another bowl and add the salt, flour, and 1/2 cup of butter or margarine. You can also use a food processor fitted with a steel blade, although Mrs. Hamdy does not use one. Mix or process until a soft dough is formed, adding more flour as needed.

3. Remove dough from the bowl or the food processor and knead in the toasted sesame seeds until thoroughly incorporated.

4. Put the dough in a bowl, cover, and let rise in a warm place for about an hour, until doubled in bulk.

5. Preheat the oven to 375 degrees and grease 2 baking sheets. Divide the dough into balls a little smaller than walnuts. Roll into pencil-thin, snake-like pieces about 10 inches in length and 1/2 inch in diameter. Twist into rings, pinching the ends together, and place on the baking sheet.

6. Lightly brush the rings with the melted butter or margarine.

7. Bake on the middle rack of the oven for 20 minutes or until golden brown. I store them in airtight containers for hungry teenagers.

VARIATION An Egyptian version includes ground anise, cumin, black caraway seeds, and *mahlep* (ground cherry-pit centers) instead of the sesame seeds. Egyptians also make a sweet *ka'ak,* flavored with vanilla or anise and sugar.

We were fed dough rings and raisins, and given hard-boiled eggs that are round and have no beginning or end, and gently taught the laws of mourning word by word.

—A. B. Yehoshua,
   Mr. Mani (1992)

We drove up the *sabra*-lined road to Nelli'im, an Arab village on the way to Jerusalem, right near Modi'in, the second century B.C.E. home of the Maccabean brothers. The aroma of the figs and the *sabras* (known in the United States as prickly pears), both kissed by the steaming sun of late July, filled the air. It was close to noon, and we heard the village *muezzin* call the people to prayer. As we drove on, we noticed an arch with three symbols embedded in the stone—a six-pointed Star of David, a flower, and a serpent. As the story goes, the Khawaijas—a name that means "foreigner" or "gentleman" in Arabic—were one of the five main families of the village. The first Khawaija, a Jew who came to the village some four hundred years ago, although married to a Moslem, put the Star of David on the house. (Of course, the hexagonal star may have been merely decorative, as the six-pointed star has been a widespread sign of the Jewish people for only the last two hundred years.)

Ghada Khawaija, the mother of three young children, had just finished setting tiny okra to dry on a straw mat in the hot sun on her terrace overlooking the Judean Hills. In the winter, Mrs. Khawaija reconstitutes the okra in hot water, then bathes it in olive oil. As we spoke, she offered us a cold drink, a slice of whole-grain flatbread, a plate of *sabras,* and the most flavorful figs I have ever eaten. "You can taste the sun in the fruit," she said. Her village, she told us proudly, is famous for its figs, olive oil, and *sabras*. Mrs. Khawaija sometimes serves the figs sprinkled with pine nuts or walnuts and honey. We liked them just the way they were.

When we asked to see the oven in which she baked the bread, she led us to a vaulted stone room with a hole in the ceiling; on the floor beneath the flue, a fire had been built using charcoal, avocado wood, olive pits, and animal dung for kindling. The dough is baked on stones, which rest on the heated coals. The women make the bread each morning and eat it throughout the day, as we did, sprinkled with their own olive oil and *za'atar* or *labneh* and *sabra* honey. Twice a day, or as needed, the women grind the whole-wheat flour between stones, but the white flour they buy by the sack in the market.

Next we visited Abou Esar, an elderly beekeeper who brought us to his hives. He showed us how the bees build their own honeycombs, taking the nectar from the *sabra* flowers. Honey from natural honeycombs, he explained, will strengthen the gums when rubbed into them, and, if applied to a burn, will aid healing and scarring. As we watched Mr. Esar bringing out the bees and caring for the honey, cattle and chickens roamed the field. Before we left, Mr. Esar offered us some tamarind juice spiked with rose water, one of the oldest drinks known to mankind.

Whole-Wheat *Khubz*

Although the Arabic word for bread is usually *khubz*, in Egypt it is called *aish*, which comes from *aisha*, meaning "life." This particular bread is much thicker than the typical pita. Stone-ground whole-wheat flour works best in this recipe and I have added honey to my version.

YIELD: 2 LOAVES

1 package dry yeast (1 scant tablespoon)

3 cups warm water

¼ cup honey

3 cups unbleached all-purpose flour

4 cups whole-wheat flour (about)

1 tablespoon salt

Semolina

1. Mix together the yeast, water, and 1 teaspoon of the honey in a large bowl. Gradually stir in the all-purpose flour, 3 cups of the whole-wheat flour, the remaining honey, and the salt. Turn the dough out onto a floured surface and begin kneading, adding more whole-wheat flour as needed. When the dough is smooth, place it in a greased bowl, cover it, and let it rise, for about 2 hours or until doubled in bulk.

2. Divide the dough into 2 pieces and form into rounds. Cover and let rise again for another hour.

3. Preheat the oven to 400 degrees and sprinkle semolina on a baking sheet. The dough may be baked on the baking sheet or, if you want to replicate the Nelli'im method, gather some small stones, heat them on a cookie sheet in the oven, brush with olive oil, then place the dough on top of them and bake for about 30 minutes or until the bread sounds hollow when tapped.

4. Remove the bread from the oven, cool, and serve as a centerpiece with dips (see Appetizers). I like it slathered with butter.

Mahlouach—
Yemenite Pancakes

"*Baruch Hashem, yesh li lehem* (Praise be to God, I have bread)," said Mazal Cohen-Nehemia, whose parents came to Palestine from Yemen, when I visited her home. To this day Mrs. Cohen-Nehemia lives in a world of good luck omens: garlic strands, blue stone amulets to ward off the evil eyes, and photos of rabbis adorn the walls of her tiny Jerusalem apartment. Nahlaot, where Mrs. Cohen-Nehemia raised her family, was a poor Sephardic and Oriental neighborhood near Mahane Yehudah, the Jewish marketplace. Although gentrified today, it was once an area teeming with large families and donkeys. Yet wonderful smells wafted throughout its courtyards from the kitchens and communal ovens. Recipes were exchanged in Ladino, the common Spanish Hebraic language of the neighborhood.

Mahlouach (pronounced "mah-lou-wach") sounds suspiciously like *mallah*, an Arabic precursor to phyllo dough. This puff pastry–like pancake bread is served fried, both in Yemenite restaurants and in homes. Like the Yemenite Sabbath breads *kubbanah* (see page 117) and *jahnoun*, *mahlouach* is so popular with Israelis that it is made commercially and sold frozen in supermarkets around the country. Eat as is, dipped in hot sauce or soup, or filled like a crepe with spinach or meat.

YIELD: 6 *MAHLOUACH*

3³⁄4 cups unbleached all-purpose flour

1 cup water

1 tablespoon vegetable oil

1 teaspoon white-wine vinegar

1 teaspoon salt

1 teaspoon sugar

1–2 sticks unsalted butter or pareve margarine, at room temperature

1. Mix together the flour, water, oil, vinegar, salt, and sugar. Knead lightly for about 10 minutes. Cover with a towel and let rest for 30 minutes.

2. Divide the dough into 6 pieces and roll out 1 piece to a 9-by-9-inch square. Spread 1–2 tablespoons of butter over the surface (more butter will make the finished bread richer and more flaky). Fold the dough in half to form a rectangle. Repeat with the remaining 5 pieces of dough. Pile the rectangles on top of each other, cover, and refrigerate for 30 minutes.

3. Roll each piece again to a 9-by-9-inch square and fold in half. Stack, cover, and place in the refrigerator for 30 minutes. Repeat this procedure 3 more times. After the final fold, wrap the pieces in plastic wrap and refrigerate overnight.

4. Roll out each piece of dough to a 9-inch circle. In a 9-inch frying pan with a lid, heat the remaining tablespoon of butter over a medium-low flame.

5. Place 1 dough circle in the pan, cover, and cook for 3 minutes. Turn the dough over, cover, and cook another 3 minutes, or until golden brown. Remove and drain on paper towels. Repeat with the remaining dough. (You will not have to add more butter for frying, as the raw *mahlouach* are already quite buttery.)

Hanoch's Olive Bread

I met Hanoch Bar Shalom in Israel several years ago at a photo shoot for a story I was writing for *Food and Wine* magazine. A self-taught chef and food stylist, Hanoch has that natural gift of making food look and taste good. In his home, he whipped up an absolutely beautiful and delicious meal, which he served with his favorite olive bread. "This bread is ugly to look at, a wet dough, which makes the good flavor," he told us. "It is a very rich bread. The higher the quality of olives used, the better the flavor. I like to soak bread in beautiful olive oil and then have people eat it. Israel is like a big village, you can get everything anywhere all the time."

Although this hearty bread will not win any beauty contests, I prefer it to all the artisan olive breads made today. Serve it with a salad and you'll have a meal.

YIELD: 5 SMALL LOAVES, SERVING 2 TO 3 EACH

5 cups unbleached all-purpose flour, plus 2 teaspoons for sprinkling

1 package dry yeast (1 scant tablespoon)

1¼ cups water

1 to 1½ cups Mediterranean black olives, pitted and chopped

1 to 1½ cups Mediterranean green olives, pitted and chopped

½ teaspoon salt

1 tablespoon dried oregano

2 tablespoons melted butter or pareve margarine

1. Put 4 cups of the flour into a mixing bowl and make a well in the center.

2. Dissolve the yeast in 1 cup of the water and pour into the well. Incorporate the flour into the liquid, then turn dough out onto a board and knead until smooth. Return the dough to the bowl, cover, and let rise for 1 hour.

3. Punch down the dough, then work in the olives, salt, oregano, ¼ cup of water, and remaining cup flour. Knead again for a few minutes and let rise, covered, in the same bowl for another hour.

4. Divide the dough into 5 portions and form into ovals about 6 inches long and 2½ inches wide. Using a sharp knife or razor, cut 3 slits horizontally across the tops and allow to rest, covered, for 20 minutes.

5. Preheat the oven to 375 degrees and grease 2 cookie sheets. Brush the tops with the melted butter or margarine and sprinkle with the remaining 2 teaspoons of flour. Place the loaves on the cookie sheets.

6. Bake for about 45 minutes or until the breads sound hollow when tapped. Serve warm.

NOTE   This bread freezes well. Remove from freezer an hour before serving and heat in a 350-degree oven for about 20 minutes.

Tahinli—
Armenian
Sesame Bread

On every trip I make to Jerusalem, I visit the Armenian Quarter of the Old City. This quiet neighborhood, with its colorful ceramic artwork, beautiful churches, and stunning stone library, has been a presence in the Old City of Jerusalem since 62 C.E., when Saint James the Less, a disciple of Jesus, built the Armenian monastery. The Armenians are the guardians of the Church of the Holy Sepulchre, said to be the center of the Christian world.

With the Turkish massacres of 1914, the Armenian monastery offered sanctuary to refugees in its compound. Now, with the independence of Armenia from the former Soviet Union, new immigration and an increase in Armenian tourists have rejuvenated this community.

I first tasted *tahinli,* one of the world's great breads, many years ago, when I accompanied Mayor Teddy Kollek on a visit to the Armenian archbishop. A few years later, the late Rose Sanasarian and her friends at the St. James Armenian Apostolic Church of Watertown, Massachusetts, showed me how to make it. Laced with sesame-seed paste and sugar, it is a delicious breakfast bread with coffee.

YIELD: 8 LOAVES

2 teaspoons dry yeast	1 cup sugar
2/3 cup warm water	4 cups unbleached all-purpose flour (about)
2 large eggs	
1/2 cup lukewarm milk	1/2 teaspoon salt
4 tablespoons butter, melted	1 cup tahina
2 1/2 tablespoons melted vegetable shortening	1/4 cup vegetable oil
	1/4 cup sesame seeds

1. Mix together the yeast and the water in a small bowl. In the bowl of an electric mixer fitted with a paddle, beat 1 of the eggs; add the dissolved yeast, milk, butter, shortening, and 2 tablespoons of the sugar. Mix well.

2. Slowly add 3 cups of the flour and the salt to the wet ingredients. Switch to the mixer's dough hook and knead for about 6 minutes, adding more flour if necessary, until smooth.

3. Turn the dough out onto a board and shape into a ball. Place in a greased bowl. Cover with plastic wrap and leave in a warm place to rise for about 2 hours or until doubled in bulk.

4. Punch the dough down and divide into 4 pieces, each about the size of your hand. Cover and let rise about 30 minutes, until doubled.

5. Mix together the tahina, vegetable oil, and remaining sugar until smooth. If the tahina mixture is lumpy, puree it in a food processor fitted with a steel blade until it is the consistency of thick cream.

6. On a floured board, roll out each ball of dough to a 10- to 12-inch circle.

7. Drizzle ¼ cup of the tahina mixture over each round of dough and smear evenly with the back of a spoon.

8. Starting at 1 end of the circle, roll up like a jelly roll. Pinch the ends closed. Gently roll the dough back and forth with the palms of your hands, stretching the roll as thin as possible, to about 18 inches in length. Twist the dough lengthwise, then roll up like a snail. Place flat on a parchment-lined cookie sheet. Repeat this process with the remaining dough, placing 4 doughs on each cookie sheet. Let the bread rise, uncovered, 1 hour more.

9. Preheat the oven to 350 degrees.

10. Slightly flatten each bread with a rolling pin and prick with a fork. Beat the remaining egg and brush each bread with the egg wash. Sprinkle with sesame seeds. Bake 30 minutes or until golden. *Tahinli* freezes well.

Ye shall dwell in booths seven days; all that are home-born in Israel shall dwell in booths; that your generations may know that I made the children of Israel to dwell in booths, when I brought them out of the land of Egypt.

—Leviticus 23:42–43

One Sukkot, the fall harvest festival when the Jewish people are supposed to reside in booths, Benjamin Tsedaka, a leader in the Samaritan communities of Holon and Mount Gerizim near Nablus, invited me to his family home on the outskirts of Holon, south of Tel Aviv. The biblical Samaritan sect—which adheres literally only to the Torah (the Five Books of Moses), treating Moses as the only prophet—has about 630 followers today. When I visited the Tsedaka home, I was surprised to see decorations of fresh fruit hanging from the ceiling of their living room rather than in an outdoor *sukkah* like those traditionally built by most Jews during the fall Feast of Tabernacles. A typical *sukkah* is built outside and covered loosely with branches so that the sky is visible from inside; most are decorated with cornstalks and strings of fruit and nuts, all reminders of the harvest period in ancient Israel.

Mr. Tsedaka explained that the Samaritan custom of decorating the inside ceiling of one's house began during the Byzantine rule. Afraid that their Sukkot decorations would be too visible in the primarily Christian religion, between the fourth and sixth centuries C.E., the Samaritans made their *sukkah* inside.

As we went from home to home, we were given tea with crackers and cookies, including the following crispy sesame thins, which are mentioned in the Old Testament.

The Foods of
Israel Today

Samaritan sukkah *with peppers, papaya, pomegranates, and other fruits hanging beneath the ceiling*

This quote, as well as the Book of Leviticus's description of the meal-offering baked in the oven for the tabernacle or Temple, refers to *rekikey,* unleavened wafers spread with olive oil. Batya Tsedaka's recipe for these sesame thins comes from the *Cookbook of the Samaritans,* which she wrote in Hebrew with her sister Tzipora Sassoni. These sesame thins can be bought commercially today as lavash crackers.

Rekikey Sumsum—
Samaritan Sesame Thins

YIELD: ABOUT 36 SESAME THINS

1 1/2 cups unbleached all-purpose flour

3 cups whole-wheat flour

2 teaspoons salt

1/2 cup plus 1 tablespoon sesame seeds, lightly toasted

1 1/2 cups water

1 tablespoon olive oil

1. In a food processor fitted with a steel blade, mix together the flours, the salt, 1/2 cup of the sesame seeds, and water. Pulse for 15 seconds to form a pliable dough, somewhat smooth but not too soft or sticky. Turn the dough out onto a floured board, divide into 3 pieces, cover with plastic wrap, and let rest for 30 minutes.

2. Preheat the oven to 400 degrees.

3. Roll 1 piece of the dough on the floured board into a rectangle about 8 inches by 6 inches, or as thin as possible. Using a knife or cookie cutter, cut the dough into 12 circles, triangles, or squares, about 2 inches wide, turning often so the dough does not stick to the surface. Repeat with the remaining dough.

4. Brush the pieces with olive oil and sprinkle on the additional sesame seeds. You may also sprinkle with coarse salt, Parmesan cheese, or *za'atar.*

5. Bake 8 to 10 minutes on a nonstick cookie sheet; turn wafers over and continue baking 2 to 3 minutes more, until edges begin to curl. Stack the wafers as they come out of the oven.

NOTE   For smaller, cracker-size thins, cut each third of the rolled dough into approximately 30 squares or circles and follow steps 4 to 6 above. Yield: 90 small sesame thins.

After the Patt brothers came to Palestine from Poland at the turn of the century, the Turks sent them, like many other Jewish men, to Cairo. There they worked in a bakery. Returning to Palestine after the British Mandate in 1920, the brothers opened Cafe Patt Conditorei in Ramat Gan, Haifa, and on the Street of the Prophets in Jerusalem, right near the original Hadassah Hospital.

During the period just before independence, the Patts not only offered the doctors and nurses at Hadassah cake and coffee, often on credit, but the bakery was also the center of a major arms cache hidden under the flour sacks. "When I was about eight years old," recalled Gideon Patt, former member of Knesset and cabinet minister, "I went on the roof to chase pigeons in the big water tanks. When I looked into one tank, I saw huge packages wrapped in rubber. I was so excited that I ran downstairs and said to my mother that the water wasn't clean. She slapped me to keep me quiet. A British officer had just come in. She knew that ammunition was hidden in those rubber packages."

In those days white loaf bread was a rarity. "The British officers, who trusted my mother, asked her to bake white bread for the British and the sick," recalled Mr. Patt. Every morning there were lines of people holding small cards saying that they were entitled to several breads each day. The Patt family would punch a hole in the ticket and give them a white bread, challah, and cakes.

"Once a British policeman named Frank Edy was playing cricket and got a ball into his mouth and lost all his teeth," said Mr. Patt. "Because he couldn't eat solid food, my mother made sure they would make porridge for him. He was a very nice man who was lonely. When my mother died, we called the policeman and he came from England for the funeral."

Petites Galettes Salées from Sefrou

Several years ago I went to Morocco on an Oldways Historic Trust Preservation trip. One evening, driving from Fez to a Moslem home in Sefrou for dinner, we passed a sign for a Jewish cemetery. When I asked my host if there were any Jews living in Sefrou, he said that there were none now, but that before 1948 half the population was Jewish. I later discovered that writers also described Sefrou as a half-Jewish city. "Sefrou is a pool of fertility, lush, shimmering with laughter and water," wrote Colette in *Places* (1970). "Pomegranate trees are ablaze with color, cherries swell, fig trees smell of milk, the grass oozes sap at the slightest bruising. . . . It is a place of handsome young men and young, smooth-skinned Jewesses with shining hair and eyes."

One of them was Rosette Toledano, whose family lived in Sefrou for generations until she emigrated to Netanya in 1971. Although Mrs. Toledano's everyday life is Israeli, her kitchen is not. Her freezer is loaded with Moroccan baked goods, like these buttery, salted crackers awaiting unexpected visitors. She cuts them in rectangles; you can also use cookie cutters to make inventive shapes. No matter how you cut them, these *galettes* will melt in your mouth.

YIELD: ABOUT 60 *GALETTES*

8 tablespoons (1 stick) unsalted butter	4 teaspoons baking powder
4 tablespoons vegetable shortening	1 1/2 teaspoons salt
1 tablespoon sugar	1 tablespoon anise seeds
2 large egg yolks	1 tablespoon sesame seeds
2 cups unbleached all-purpose flour	1/4 cup iced water

1. Using a food processor equipped with a steel blade, place the butter, vegetable shortening, and sugar in the bowl and process. Gradually add the egg yolks, 2 cups of the flour, the baking powder, salt, anise seeds, and sesame seeds, and process with the iced water until a ball is formed, adding more flour if needed.

2. Let the dough rest, covered, in the refrigerator for about 15 minutes. Preheat the oven to 375 degrees and grease 2 cookie sheets.

3. On a floured surface roll the dough out to a rectangle about 1/8 inch thick. Using a dull knife cut the dough into 1- by 2-inch rectangles or use a cookie cutter to cut into tiny shapes. Place on cookie sheets. Prick the crackers all over with a fork.

4. Bake in the oven for about 20 minutes or until golden.

Cheese *Beiguele*

The slightly sweet, slightly salty Shavuot *beiguele* is an example of serendipity. *Beiguele,* which means "small bread" in Yiddish, was probably first made as a cheese knish in Bessarabia or Lithuania, undergoing a local transformation when the recipe traveled with Jewish refugees to Argentina in the late 1800s. There, at the Clara Agricultural Colony, founded by the philanthropist Baron Maurice de Hirsch, the Jews made the farmer cheese used for this dish, which was not previously known in Argentina. Daniel Furman, a descendant of the first settlers in the Jewish colony, brought the recipe with him when he came to Israel in the 1970s.

"Other than people from that part of Argentina, no one eats it," said Daniel when we spoke about the flaky cheese-filled pastry. "All my extended family made it. These people used to have cows and at first made their own milk products. Eventually they were made at a cooperative called El Fondo Communal."

Although most filled finger food in Argentina is shaped like the half-moon *empanada,* this roll is formed like the eastern European strudel dough. It is made in Israel with the farmer cheese available there. Serve the cheese *beiguele* fresh from the oven or at room temperature, topped with sour cream if you like. You can also substitute Bulgarian feta or ricotta cheese for the farmer cheese.

YIELD: 3 CHEESE *BEIGUELE*, 12 SLICES

DOUGH

1½ cups plus 1 teaspoon unbleached all-purpose flour

7 tablespoons butter or pareve margarine, at room temperature

½ teaspoon salt

½ cup boiling water

½ teaspoon white vinegar

FILLING

1 large egg

1½ pounds farmer cheese

1½ teaspoons salt

1 teaspoon unbleached all-purpose flour

1 tablespoon sugar

5 leaves (green part only) of scallions, chopped (about ¼ cup total)

1. In a food processor fitted with a steel blade, process the flour and the butter or margarine until smooth. Add salt, boiling water, and vinegar and process until a dough is formed.

2. Divide the dough into 3 balls, cover with plastic wrap, and refrigerate for 2 hours.

3. Preheat the oven to 325 degrees and grease a baking sheet.

4. Beat the egg well in a mixing bowl and add the farmer cheese, salt, flour, sugar, and scallions. Mix well.

5. On a lightly floured surface, roll out each ball of dough to a rectangle about 10 by 12 inches. On each rectangle, spread ⅓ of the filling in a 3-inch strip lengthwise down the center of the dough. Fold each rectangle lengthwise over the filling, then roll up jelly-roll style; pinch the edges together firmly, using water if necessary to seal the ends completely.

6. Place the rolled doughs seam side down on the prepared baking sheet and bake for 1¼ hours or until golden in color. Cool slightly, then cut with a serrated knife into 2-inch slices.

NOTE   If you like a creamier consistency for the filling, you can substitute 1 cup cream cheese for 1 cup of the farmer cheese.

Oceanus's Oversized Pita with Oregano and Rosemary

We have the best ingredients in the world," said Eyal Shani, chef-owner of the highly praised Oceanus Restaurant in Jerusalem and Herzliyya. "The soil is not easy, but the warmth of the sun gives our food strong feeling." Chef Shani, a former filmmaker in his early forties, looks at food the way others look at fine paintings.

When I prepare this bread, a great showstopper at his restaurants, I often serve one loaf with a variety of cooked salads and dips as an hors d'oeuvre, and the second I use as a base for the Palestinian *mousakhan* (page 302), creating a stunning main course. Start the dough about three hours before you plan to serve it.

YIELD: 2 LOAVES, EACH SERVING AT LEAST 6 HUNGRY PEOPLE

2 packages dry yeast (2 scant tablespoons)

1 teaspoon sugar

2–2½ cups lukewarm water

8 cups all-purpose flour

1 tablespoon sea salt, plus extra for sprinkling

3 tablespoons finely minced fresh rosemary

3 tablespoons finely minced fresh oregano

Olive oil

1. Dissolve the yeast and sugar in 2 cups of the water and let sit about 10 minutes, or until the yeast begins to bubble.

2. If you are working the dough by hand, put the flour, salt, and 2 tablespoons each of the rosemary and oregano in a large bowl. Add the yeast mixture and enough additional water to make a sticky dough. Turn out onto a floured work surface and knead for about 10 minutes by hand. Let rise in a greased bowl, covered with plastic wrap, for 1 hour. If you are using an electric mixer, put the yeast mixture in the mixing bowl. Add the flour, salt, and 2 tablespoons of the rosemary and oregano and, using the mixer's dough hook, work the dough for 15 minutes. Turn into a greased bowl and let rise, covered with plastic wrap, for 1 hour.

3. Punch the dough down and knead 10 minutes by hand or 5 minutes in the machine. Turn the dough into the greased bowl and let it rest again, covered, for another hour. It should be very elastic.

4. Preheat the oven to 450 degrees and grease 2 cookie sheets.

5. Divide the dough in half and form 2 balls; let rest, covered, 15 minutes. Roll out each ball of dough, then stretch it as thin as possible, to a rough circle about 18 inches in diameter. Place on the cookie sheets and bake for a total of 8 minutes, turning once after 4 minutes and again after 3 minutes, switching racks if using one oven.

6. Flip once more, then brush the top with olive oil and sprinkle with remaining rosemary, oregano, and sea salt. Return to the oven for another 30 seconds or until slightly golden.

7. Place the bread on the table and let your guests use their hands to tear it apart. Serve immediately.

Oceanus's oversized pita straight from the oven

Erez's Double Chocolate Braided Bread

Lehem Erez, run by Erez Komarovsky, is one of the best of the upscale bakery/restaurants that have recently sprung up in Israel. Like many young Israelis, Erez learned about cooking in the army. After his military service, he traveled abroad. In California he became a food stylist; in Japan he studied Asian cooking; in Paris he learned how to make croissants. With an artistic bent and a love of his native land, he decided to return to Israel, and he opened Lehem Erez in an industrial park in Herzliyya. Bouquets of bare light bulbs hanging from wires light the restaurant. The silverware is set on beige paper napkins like the first step in a three-strand braid. The sandbox outside, within sight of parents inside, is reserved for toddlers; they also can play with a lump of dough, which the friendly waiters will pop into the oven. The artisan breads, croissants, and bistro-like foods have that earthy feel so often found in Israel.

This double chocolate braided bread is a knockout. Instead of using regular chocolate chips, something available only recently in Israel, Erez uses chopped-up bittersweet chocolate. You can use either. Hot from the oven, the chocolate melts in your mouth. I find it somewhat reminiscent of the *pain au chocolat* I ate as a student in France.

YIELD: 2 LOAVES

2 packages dry yeast (2 scant tablespoons)

½ cup sugar

2 cups lukewarm water

3 tablespoons unsalted butter, softened

1 large egg yolk

7 cups all-purpose flour (about)

1 tablespoon salt

2 tablespoons unsweetened cocoa powder

1 cup ½-inch chunks of bittersweet chocolate, or large chocolate chips (8 ounces)

Semolina for dusting

1. Dissolve the yeast and 1 tablespoon of the sugar in the water in the bowl of an electric mixer. Let sit a few minutes, then add the butter and egg yolk and stir with the paddle. Slowly add 6 cups of the flour, salt, remaining sugar, and cocoa. Change to the mixer's dough hook and knead until the dough becomes smooth.

2. Turn the dough onto a floured board, knead the chocolate chunks or chips into the dough, and form into a smooth round. Put in a greased bowl, cover, and let rise for 2–2½ hours, until the dough doubles in bulk.

3. Punch the dough down and divide into 6 equal parts on a floured board. Let rest for 20 minutes.

4. Roll 3 pieces of dough into sausages about 12 inches long and 2 inches wide. Line up the 3 pieces side by side and braid, then pinch the ends together. Repeat with the other 3 pieces. Place the 2 loaves on a cookie sheet sprinkled with semolina. Cover with a moist towel and let rise for an hour, until the dough doubles again.

5. Preheat the oven to 375 degrees. Fill a pan with hot water and place on the lower shelf of the oven. Bake the breads on the upper shelf for 20 minutes. Then lower the oven to 350 degrees and bake another 20 minutes or until the bread sounds hollow when tapped. Serve warm.

· · · CHALLAH IN THE HOLY LAND · · ·

"The Ashkenazic challah is the best. When I was in the army, I could smell newly baked challah two miles away. It was pouring rain, we walked to the bakery in town and knocked on the door. We were dripping wet, but the baker gave each of us a fresh challah and we walked back to the Wadi. What else on earth tempts you like that? The smell of bread gave us power and comfort."

—Meir Shalev in an interview

According to Leviticus, God instructed Moses to place twelve round loaves, probably made of flour with a texture similar to present-day semolina, on a table before the Lord, in two rows of six flat round loaves each, in the Tent of Meeting on Mount Sinai. So it was done "regularly every Sabbath day—it is a commitment for all time on the part of the Israelites."

After the Romans destroyed the Temple in Jerusalem in 70 C.E., the home table became a metaphor for God's table, still a tradition today. Gradually the Sabbath bread in the home assumed a number of symbolic meanings, and eventually it became the Ashkenazi's sweet egg bread.

The concept of a sweetened bread probably began in the Mediterranean, but it was not just a Jewish phenomenon. The Greeks serve a rich, braided egg bread at Easter; so do the Portuguese. In Eastern Europe, the Russian nobility ate a rich egg bread for special occasions. The Ashkenazic Jews probably adopted this tradition, using a similar bread to usher in the Sabbath.

Thus, by the late Middle Ages, when twisted breads came into vogue in central and eastern Europe, the twelve round loaves described in Leviticus became two loaves with at least six braided strands in each, representing the two rows of six loaves described as offerings in the Temple. These breads came to be known as challah, a reminder of the biblical injunction to throw a piece of the Sabbath bread, challah, into the oven to burn as a symbol of the portion given to the *kohanim* (priests). Later the practice came to be symbolic of the destruction of the Temple.

As Jews from all over the world came to Palestine in the nineteenth and twentieth centuries, they brought with them their many versions of Sabbath bread. In Israel today all the prayers and customs accompanying the mitzvah of making a special bread for the Sabbath provide the four-thousand-year link from contemporary times back to the Book of Leviticus.

Dabo—
Ethiopian Shabbat Bread

For Ethiopian Jews, coming to Israel has entailed many transitions. In their native land, these *falasha* (exiled people), also called *Betai Israel* (House of Israel), used clay cooking pots over an open fire throughout the year. Just before Passover, they broke the pots, then made new ones to use for the next year, starting at Passover. *Injerra* is the daily bread prepared from *teff,* a grain fermented in water for several days. The dough is ladled onto a flat griddle.

For the Sabbath, Ethiopians often prepare *dabo,* a loaf bread made from flour, water, yeast, turmeric, black caraway seeds, and a little oil. In Ethiopia the bread was baked over a fire on a flat disk or in a frying pan. In Israel, even though today most people do have ovens in the home, *dabo* still is usually made in a frying pan.

I first tasted this bread at the home of an Ethiopian family in Beit Shemesh. The mother had awakened at 6 a.m. to start the dough for me, because it traditionally rises for 6 hours. *Dabo* is often served Friday night with *doro wat,* a spicy chicken dish (see pages 292–3), and on Shabbat morning with cottage cheese.

YIELD: 3 SMALL OR 1 LARGE *DABO*

1 package dry yeast (1 scant tablespoon)	5–6 cups unbleached all-purpose flour
2 cups warm water	1 tablespoon salt
2 tablespoons sugar	1 teaspoon black caraway seeds (*nigella*)*
2 tablespoons vegetable oil	½ teaspoon turmeric

1. Put the yeast in a large bowl or in the bowl of a mixer equipped with a dough hook. Add the water, sugar, and vegetable oil and mix well.

2. Gradually add 4 cups of flour, the salt, caraway seeds, and turmeric; using your hands or a dough hook, knead until the dough is smooth, adding more flour if needed.

3. Place in a greased bowl and cover. Let rise for about 2 hours. (Ethiopian cooks let the dough rise for about 6 hours at this point, but I've found that 2 hours is plenty.)

4. Punch down the dough, divide it into 3 pieces, and flatten each piece into a round. Heat an ungreased 12-inch frying pan and place 1 round in the pan. Cook over a low flame for about 10 minutes on 1 side, flip, and continue cooking for several minutes. Repeat with the other 2 portions of dough. A more modern, less labor-intensive method is to place the whole dough in a greased, 10- to 12-inch round baking pan and bake for 30 minutes in a preheated 375-degree oven, or until the bread sounds hollow.

*Black caraway seeds, also called *chernuska,* are members of the pepper family. You can buy them at health food stores or Middle Eastern markets.

Yemenite *Kubbanah*— Sabbath Overnight Bread

This Yemenite Sabbath morning bread, traditionally made with flour soured in water, was originally cooked overnight in the embers of a fire. Although aluminum *kubbanah* pots, specially designed for this bread, are sold in Israel, any six-cup or larger ovenproof casserole with a cover will do. The Sephardic *huevos haminadav,* the Sabbath breakfast hard-cooked eggs, are baked atop the bread in the *kubbanah* pot. Serve the *kubbanah* with tomatoes, *z'hug,* a Yemenite hot sauce, or the fenugreek *hilbe* (see page 140).

YIELD: 1 *KUBBANAH*

1 package dry yeast (1 scant tablespoon)	1 tablespoon salt
1½ cups plus 2 tablespoons lukewarm water	1 tablespoon black caraway seeds (*nigella*)
1 tablespoon sugar	½ cup (1 stick) unsalted butter or pareve margarine
4–5 cups all-purpose flour	5 eggs

1. Dissolve the yeast in 1½ cups of water mixed with the sugar. Place 4 cups of the flour, salt, and caraway seeds in the bowl of a standing mixer and form a well in the middle. Pour the yeast mixture into the well and, using the dough hook of the mixer, incorporate into the flour.

2. Pour the additional 2 tablespoons of water into another bowl. Remove the dough to this second bowl and let sit in the water, covered with a damp towel, in a warm place for an hour.

3. Turn the dough out, punch it down, and knead again, gradually adding the remaining cup of flour as necessary to make a slightly tacky yet smooth dough. Return the dough to the bowl, cover, and let rise for 1 more hour.

4. Melt the butter or margarine in a casserole fitted with a lid, or in a metal *kubbanah* pan.

5. Punch down the dough and divide into 4 balls. Place the balls in the casserole side by side on top of the butter, rolling them in the butter to coat them. Cover with the lid and let rise another 30 minutes.

6. Preheat the oven to 375 degrees.

7. Wrap the eggs in a piece of aluminum foil and place on the lid of the covered *kubbanah* pan or casserole. (If it does not have a flat lid, as the traditional *kubbanah* pan does, place the wrapped eggs on a baking sheet next to the bread.)

8. Bake, covered, for 30 minutes in the lowest part of the oven. Lower the oven temperature to 150 degrees and continue baking overnight or for at least 8 hours. Serve hot in the morning, pulling off hunks of bread with your hands. Peel the eggs and eat them with diced tomatoes and the bread.

NOTE If you prefer to make 2 *kubbanahs,* use smaller casseroles and divide the dough into 8 pieces.

Moroccan
Pan de Casa

It is 6 on a Friday morning in the northern Israeli town of Bet She'an. Kneeling next to her bathtub, Hannah Zritoun, an elderly woman from Morocco's Atlas Mountains, is already kneading a huge amount of dough. Each Friday she wakes up at 4, checks her flour carefully, and mixes it with water, yeast, salt, and a few handfuls of anise and sesame seeds before molding the dough with her weathered hands. I watch her as she fires up her taboon, an outdoor clay and straw oven, with olive wood. By the time the dough has risen, the fire is ready for baking, and she places flat stones in the oven. First, following biblical tradition, she pulls off a wad of dough, "the *challah,*" symbolic of the offering to the high priests, and tosses it into the fire. Then she shapes round loaves and bakes them on the hot stones, sometimes glazing the loaves with egg.

Mrs. Zritoun, who can neither read nor write, bakes at least twenty loaves every Friday for her children and grandchildren. Her robust, crusty loaf is very different from the Moroccan Jewish bread I tasted at a Shabbat dinner in Marrakesh. Although also flavored with anise and sesame seeds, the bread in Marrakesh, called *pain petri* ("bread kneaded at home"), is sweeter, more sophisticated, enriched with eggs, and oval in shape.

Hannah Zritoun shoveling a loaf into the oven for Sabbath bread

"When we arrived in 1950, we bought bread but found it wasn't clean; we wouldn't eat it because there were bugs and worms in it. No one was cleaning the flour," explained Mrs. Zritoun. "A woman in Bet She'an who came from the Atlas Mountains taught us how to build the oven. We built it with big stones, mud, and straw, made a floor from tiles, and covered the door with a brick. We used mud so the heat wouldn't escape from the oven, and used round stones from the sea for baking." Today the oven still sits under the lemon and mango trees in her backyard.

In the Atlas Mountains, baking was different. There, Mrs. Zritoun had a fifty-pound sack of flour in her home and would make bread several times a week, kneading it, marking it, and putting it in a straw basket that she would send to a communal oven shared by about twenty families. Called *pan de casa* in Hakita (a combination of Spanish, Arabic, and Hebrew), this robust version is spiked with anise and sesame seeds, which hark back to its roots in the small mountain villages. For a more citified version of this bread, see page 120.

1 package dry yeast (1 scant tablespoon)   1 tablespoon salt

2 tablespoons sugar   1 tablespoon anise seeds

1³/₄ cups warm water   1 tablespoon sesame seeds

5 cups all-purpose flour

1. Dissolve the yeast and sugar in the water in the large bowl of a standing mixer.

2. Using a dough hook, stir the flour, salt, anise seeds, and sesame seeds into the yeast mixture and knead until smooth.

3. Place dough in a greased bowl and let rise, covered, for an hour and a half.

4. Turn the dough out and knead again. Grease 2 cookie sheets. Divide the dough into 3 rounds and let rise, covered, for another half hour on cookie sheets.

5. Preheat the oven to 375 degrees. If you want to make this the old-fashioned way, take uneven stones and heat them in the oven on cookie sheets.

6. Bake the rounds in the oven for 30 minutes or until the rounds sound hollow when tapped. If using stones, brush them with oil first, then place the rounds on top.

Displaying the finished loaves

Breads

Sefrou Sabbath Bread

This recipe, from Rosette Toledano (see page 109), is a more sophisticated, "citified" version of the Moroccan Jewish Friday-night bread (see pages 118–19).

YIELD: 2 LOAVES

1 package dry yeast (1 scant tablespoon)	3 large eggs
½ cup sugar	½ cup vegetable oil
1 cup warm water	1 tablespoon anise seeds
1 tablespoon salt	4–5 cups all-purpose flour

1. In a large bowl or the bowl of an electric mixer fitted with a dough hook, dissolve the yeast and 1 tablespoon of the sugar in the water.

2. Add the remaining sugar, salt, 2 of the eggs, oil, and anise seeds and mix. Gradually add 4 cups of the flour. Knead with the dough hook or turn the dough out onto a floured board and knead by hand until you have a soft, smooth dough. Transfer to a greased bowl and let rise, covered, for an hour and a half.

3. Punch down the dough, divide in half, and shape into 2 rounds. Place the rounds on a greased cookie sheet and brush with the remaining egg beaten with a little water. Preheat the oven to 375 degrees.

4. Let rise for another half hour and brush again with the egg wash.

5. Bake the breads 30–35 minutes or until golden.

· · · SHABBAT WITHOUT A LENDNER'S CHALLAH IS NO SHABBAT · · ·

One Friday at dawn, when I was challah-hopping in Mea Shearim, the ultra-Orthodox neighborhood in Jerusalem, a Chasid told me that in his family, Shabbat without a Lendner's challah is no Shabbat. He then directed me to a narrow alley just below Mea Shearim Street, where the aroma of freshly baked bread filled the air.

There I met Matti Lendner, a tall, white-haired man wearing a white baker's hat and apron, who ushered me into his office. On the wall was a portrait of his grandfather, Moshe Dov Lendner, who came from Romania in 1894 and shortly thereafter founded the bakery.

In the nineteenth and early twentieth centuries, Moshe Dov Lendner became famous both for his bread and for his generosity to the poor people of Jerusalem. The story goes that Mr. Lendner met a rabbi who wore no shoes, so he took off his own and gave them to him.

Across from the bakery was Mr. Lendner's synagogue.

Until his death at the age of eighty-three, he would stoke the woodstove in his synagogue each morning at 3 for the early prayer service. Then he mixed his ingredients and returned to the synagogue to pray while the dough rose.

After showing me the photos and reminiscing about his past, Matti Lendner ushered me down to the white brick oven with the baker's pit below, the last of its kind in Jerusalem. He pulled out two huge, brown, braided challahs, which had been prepared for a wedding later that day.

Unlike most American challahs, Lendner's, and the majority of Jerusalem challahs, have no egg in the dough. "In old Jerusalem people were poor and mostly dependent on outside contributions," said Mr. Lendner, as he shellacked his loaves with a mixture of cornstarch and water. "Eggs and sugar were out of the question. Even in my family's part of Romania, challah rarely included eggs. It was already a luxury to have a bread with white flour for the Sabbath."

Lendner's Romanian Challah

Although I show how to braid this challah with four braids, you can make it with three, six, or even twelve braids!

YIELD: 2 CHALLAHS

1 package dry yeast (1 scant tablespoon)	7 1/2 cups all-purpose flour (about)
2 1/4 cups warm water	Semolina for dusting
1/2 cup sugar	1 teaspoon cornstarch
4 tablespoons vegetable shortening	Poppy or sesame seeds for sprinkling
1 tablespoon salt	

1. Dissolve the yeast in 2 cups of the water in a large bowl of a mixer with a dough hook. Add the sugar, vegetable shortening, salt, and 7 cups of the flour and knead well, with your hands or the dough hook, until smooth and soft. (If kneading by hand, mix the ingredients in a large bowl and turn out onto a floured surface to knead.)

2. Turn the dough out onto a floured board and continue to knead until smooth, adding additional flour if needed. Then place dough in a greased bowl. Cover and let rise for 1 hour. Punch down, cover, and let rise for another 45 minutes.

3. On a floured board, cut the dough into 2 equal parts. Cover 1 and set aside. Divide the other dough into 4 pieces. Roll out these pieces into snakes about 17 inches long and 1 inch in diameter. Cut each snake into 2 pieces, 1 about 12 inches and the other 5 inches long.

4. Place the 4 longer strands next to each other and pinch together at 1 end. Pick up the far left strand and weave it over the next strand, under the third, and over the fourth. Pick up what is now the furthest left strand and weave it over, under, and over. Continue weaving this way, keeping the braids taut, until you have braided the entire challah. Pinch the ends together and tuck under.

5. Repeat this process with the 4 smaller pieces. Place the smaller braid on top of the larger, gently pinching down throughout to attach. Repeat the whole procedure with the second ball of dough, forming a second loaf.

6. Preheat the oven to 375 degrees and sprinkle a baking sheet with semolina.

7. In a small bowl mix the cornstarch and the remaining 1/4 cup water; brush the loaves with the mixture, transfer them to the baking sheet, and let them rise another half hour. Immediately before baking, brush again with cornstarch mixture and sprinkle poppy or sesame seeds over the top.

8. Bake for 45 minutes or until the loaves are golden brown and sound hollow when tapped. Remove the loaves from the oven and immediately brush again with cornstarch and water.

Jacob Itzhak Beigel left Poland in 1937 for Israel, where he became a baker. His sons founded Beigel & Beigel, which manufactures strictly kosher crackers and cookies, now served on El Al flights in and out of Israel. In Crakow where the rest of his Bobover Chasidic family remained, the Beigels owned five bakeries at the beginning of the Nazi occupation in 1939. Like many others in the flour or baking business, they were able to help their fellow Jews. In the beginning, the Germans let Jacob's father, Rabbi Fishel Beigel, buy flour, salt, and yeast, ordering the family to make bread for the German soldiers as well as for the Jews in the ghetto. With potatoes and some root vegetables bought on the black market, the Beigel women cooked and cooked. Having special permission to go out from the ghetto, the family would carry soup and bread to the camps and factories where Jews worked. Later, when the Germans sealed the ghetto, Jews sometimes sneaked into the Beigels' apartment, where tables and benches were set up with steaming soup and bread.

"Everybody knew us from the ghetto," said Nehama Wis- licki, Jacob's sister, who now lives in Borough Park, Brooklyn. "We were risking our lives to cook, but we had to do it. Once a German policeman found all our stored goods and took away the flour. We didn't give up and started again. My mother gave her last piece of bread to someone who was starving. It was unbelievable." Aware of the tragic irony, she continued, "There is no such law in the Torah that if we are hungry we have to give our last piece of food, but we did."

On the memorable eve of Yom Kippur in 1942, some fifty people hidden in the Beigel home were preparing for the fast. "Our rebbe, Schlomo Halberstam, came to us with his mother, his mother-in-law, and his sister, because they didn't have anywhere to go," said Mrs. Wislicki. "My mother didn't have anything to cook. She served the noodles with water so they wouldn't be so dry, and maybe a piece of bread. There was nothing else." Several months later, the Germans liquidated the ghetto and sent the Jewish population, including the Beigel family, to the Plashow concentration camp and then to Auschwitz, where Mrs. Wislicki's parents and sister died in the gas chambers.

Beigel Family Challah

This challah recipe, given to me by members of the Beigel family, is one of the best I have ever tasted. I have included instructions on how to make a six-braided challah, one that my family prepares each week for the Sabbath.

YIELD: 2 CHALLAHS

1½ packages dry yeast (1½ scant tablespoons)

1 tablespoon plus ½ cup sugar

1¾ cups lukewarm water

½ cup vegetable oil

5 large eggs

1 tablespoon salt

8–8½ cups all-purpose flour

Poppy or sesame seeds for sprinkling

1. In a large bowl, dissolve the yeast and 1 tablespoon of the sugar in the water.

2. Whisk the oil into the yeast, then beat in 4 of the eggs, 1 at a time, with the remaining sugar and salt. Gradually add 8 cups of the flour. When the dough holds together, it is ready for kneading. (You can also use a mixer with a dough hook both for the mixing and the kneading.)

3. Turn the dough onto a floured surface and knead until smooth. Clean out the bowl and grease it, then return the dough to the bowl. Cover with plastic wrap and let the dough rise in a warm place for 1 hour, until almost doubled in bulk. The dough may also rise in an oven that has been warmed to 150 degrees and then turned off. Punch down the dough, cover, and let rise again in a warm place for another half hour.

4. To make a 6-braided challah, take half the dough and divide into 6 balls. Roll each ball with your hands into a strand about 12 inches long and 1½ inches wide. Pinch the strands together at 1 end, then gently spread them apart. Move the outside right strand over 2 strands. Then take the second strand from the left and move it to the far right. Regroup to 3 on each side. Take the outside left strand and move it over 2 to the middle, then move the second strand from the right over to the far left. Regroup and start over with the outside right strand. Continue this method until all the strands are braided, tucking the ends underneath the loaf. The key is to always have 3 strands on each side so you can keep your braid balanced. Make a second loaf the same way. Place the braided loaves in greased 10-by-4-inch loaf pans or on a greased cookie sheet with at least 2 inches in between.

5. Beat the remaining egg and brush it on the loaves. Let loaves rise another hour.

6. Preheat the oven to 375 degrees and brush the loaves with egg again. Sprinkle on poppy or sesame seeds.

7. Bake for 35 to 40 minutes or until golden and loaves sound hollow. Cool the loaves on a rack.

From Baguettes to *Bejma*—The Tunisian Friday-Night Bread

About ten years ago, an Israeli from Tunisia invented a baguette-making machine. Today baguette bars dot Israel, competing with falafel stands. Sandwich slabs of deli meats with sauces are compacted into slices of fresh-from-the-oven French loaves, with customers discussing the variety of hot and mild sandwich spreads the way Americans do ice cream flavors. Although these Tunisian Jews have created a cross-culturalism with their French baguette sandwiches, I hope that they also will start exposing Israelis to the traditional Tunisian *bejma,* these delicious triangular breads made from three bulbous balls, which they serve in their own homes on Friday night.

YIELD: 3 LOAVES, ABOUT 8 SERVINGS PER LOAF

2 packages dry yeast (2 scant tablespoons)

¼ cup sugar

1½ cups lukewarm water

4 large eggs

¼ cup vegetable oil

2 teaspoons salt

7 cups unbleached all-purpose flour

1. Dissolve the yeast and 1 teaspoon of the sugar in 1 cup of the water in a large bowl or the bowl of an electric mixer. Stir, and let sit for 10 minutes.

2. Stir into the yeast mixture 3 of the eggs, oil, salt, and the remaining water and sugar. Slowly knead in enough flour to make a soft, tacky dough. Using your hands or the dough hook on the mixer, knead for 10 minutes or until smooth. Turn the dough out onto a floured board, place in a greased bowl, and let rise, covered, for 1 hour.

3. Punch down the dough and divide into 9 rounds about the size of tennis balls. Place 3 rounds together on a greased cookie sheet, touching, to form a triangle. Repeat with remaining dough. Let rise, uncovered, for about 30 minutes.

4. Preheat the oven to 375 degrees.

5. Beat the remaining egg with a little water and brush the dough. Bake for about 20 minutes or until golden and loaves sound hollow.

Levi Kelman, rabbi of Congregation Kol Haneshama in the Baka section of Jerusalem, used to make this challah while living in a Jewish communal house at the University of Wisconsin. "The recipe has gone all over the world," he said. "I use the yeast as a metaphor for education—it needs not too much and not too little nurturing. I make this every week with my kids. It is distinctly Jewish, but has an American sixties flavor to it."

A Rabbi's Whole-Wheat Challah

YIELD: 2 CHALLAHS

3 cups whole-wheat flour

4$\frac{1}{4}$ cups unbleached all-purpose flour (about)

1 tablespoon salt

2 packages dry yeast (2 scant tablespoons)

1 teaspoon sugar

1$\frac{3}{4}$ cups warm water

4 large eggs

$\frac{1}{3}$ cup vegetable oil

$\frac{1}{2}$ cup plus 1 teaspoon honey

1. Place the whole-wheat flour and 4 cups of the all-purpose flour with the salt in a large bowl or the bowl of an electric mixer, and make a well in the middle.

2. Dissolve the yeast and the sugar in $\frac{3}{4}$ cup of the water and pour into the well. Gradually, using a spoon or the dough hook of the mixer, work in 3 of the eggs, the oil, $\frac{1}{2}$ cup of the honey, and the remaining cup of water. Either knead in the mixer or turn out onto a floured board and knead, adding all-purpose flour as needed until a soft, elastic dough is formed.

3. Cover the dough with a towel and let rise for 2 hours. Punch down, divide into 6 pieces, and roll them out to 2-by-18-inch ropes. Place 3 pieces together, pinch ends, and braid. Repeat to make a second loaf. Beat the remaining egg with the remaining teaspoon of honey and brush on the challah. Place on a greased cookie sheet.

4. Preheat the oven to 375 degrees and bake challahs for about 45 minutes or until the loaves are golden and sound hollow when tapped.

Breads

Soups

There are probably more kinds of soup in Israel than anywhere else in the world—and they are almost always mopped up with bread. In the hot climate, rich vegetable and meat broths replenish the body's moisture and minerals. Since the biblical period, Jewish immigrants have brought and cooked their favorites from Transylvania, Tashkent, and Tennessee. I will never forget one evening before the fast of Yom Kippur, in the mid-1970s. I was a guest at the home of a Yemenite family in Jerusalem, and as the main course of the dinner, we were offered a soupy stew flavored with spices quite unlike anything I'd tasted in my mother's chicken soup at home. It was served with an unusual Yemenite bread, which we dipped into a variety of spicy sauces, then into the soup.

Jerusalem may also be the soup-kitchen center of the world. During the Turk-

Above: A communal kitchen in Jerusalem during the Ottoman Empire

ish Empire, the effendi distributed a kind of soupy gruel made of flour, water, and salt to the servants, the Moslem pilgrims, and the poor living in the city at the time. The tradition continues today. Every Wednesday, Tova Cohen, a tiny woman with a scarf wrapped around her head, makes her flavorful native Yemenite chicken soup. Seasoning it with cumin and turmeric, with the spice combinations of *z'hug* and *hilbe* as condiments, she gives it to the needy who come to the synagogue across the street from her home in Jerusalem.

Today, with modern technology, Israel has perfected the art of packaged soup mixes, which are so good that many chefs use them as the bases for their restaurant soups: mushroom barley, green pea, borscht, potato, vegetable, onion, celery, asparagus, tomato—even a Hebrew Alef-Bet soup, in which the letters float from right to left. Throughout this chapter, I often call for vegetable or chicken broth, which most Israelis would buy prepared.

Another Israeli custom is to float crispy croutons, called mini and maxi *mandelen,* meaning "nuts" or "soup cheeks," in the soups. Originally homemade, these

Chef of the late King Abdullah, one of the many soup masters of Jerusalem

were developed commercially by the Osem noodle factory in the 1950s (see page 246). "My father thought of using his noodle machine to make something that would float on top of soup," said Gad Propper, son of the founder. "So he cut the noodles into smaller cubes and fried them."

As has been a tradition in the land of Israel since that first soupy stew that Sarah served Abraham, many of these soups can serve as the center of a meal. On a cold winter night, try the Yemenite Chicken and Beef Soupy Stew or the Afghan Friday-Night Chicken and Chickpea Soupy Stew with Meatballs. For warm weather, a lighter meal might include Bukharan Tomato Gazpacho with Garlic and Cilantro, Judith Tihany's Transylvanian Green Bean Soup, or a more traditional Ashkenazic cold borscht. And soups offer the perfect opportunity to meld unusual combinations of foods, as in the Iranian Beet, Plum, and Celery Soup or the more modern Hummus Soup, with fresh herbs from Kerem Restaurant in Tel Aviv or the Pan-roasted Cherry Tomato Soup from Michael Andrew Restaurant in Jerusalem.

Soups

Palestinian Fruit Soup

When Samy Cohn, born in Romania and now a Brazilian businessman, arrived in Haifa in 1934, eighteen years old and penniless, he found an inexpensive boardinghouse. For meals he ate at a nearby workers' kitchen where, as he wrote in his autobiography, the food was "healthy and cheap. The specialty was a fruit soup, and the meal was invariably spiced with heated discussions of world matters, especially on how to bring our Zionist dream to fruition. The debates often lasted till the early hours."

I first saw a recipe for this Palestinian fruit soup in the *Fairmount Temple Cookbook* from Cleveland, Ohio. It came from Rebecca Aaronson Brickner, who had traveled to Palestine in the 1930s, where she found it the dish most often offered to visitors. The soup started as a fruit compote, but the addition of water and sometimes wine transformed the condensed dessert into a main-course soup in Palestine, where fruit and vegetables were often in surplus when other food was scarce.

YIELD: 6 SERVINGS

1 cup pitted prunes

2 oranges, peeled and diced (about 2 cups)

2 stalks rhubarb, cut in ¹/₂-inch pieces (about 2 cups)

2 cups diced fresh pineapple or peeled, diced peaches

1 cup diced strawberries

1 cup pitted cherries

5 cups water

1 cup light-brown sugar

¹/₂ teaspoon salt

1 cinnamon stick or ¹/₂ teaspoon ground cinnamon

Juice of ¹/₂ lemon

1 cup sour cream

1. Mix together the fruit and the water in a large soup pot and bring to a boil. Add the sugar, salt, cinnamon, and lemon juice. Reduce the heat and simmer, covered, for 20 minutes, or until the fruit is tender.

2. Pulse in a food processor fitted with a metal blade, or in a blender, until the fruit is broken up but not pureed.

3. Chill and mix in the sour cream before serving.

NOTE Other fruits may be substituted, but use a combination of tart and sweet. You should have a total of 9 cups of mixed fruit.

Like George Konrad, many others returned to their homes in Europe after the war only to find that the communists had taken over. There was no longer a place for them in their own countries, so they came to Israel.

This splendid and unusual soup came to me from one such Holocaust survivor, Judith Tihany, the mother of restaurant designer Adam Tihany. Although Mrs. Tihany ate this soup as a child, she learned to cook it from other survivors in Jerusalem after the war.

At a recent dinner at the Israeli ambassador's home in Washington, I asked Congressman Tom Lantos of California if he remembered this green bean soup from his childhood in Hungary. Did he ever! It was his favorite childhood summer dish—and for good reason, as it is beautifully colored and flavored with red peppers and fresh-picked green beans. Mrs. Tihany thickens hers with flour, as is customary in the Romanian Hungarian kitchen. "In Israel everyone wants things so light," said Mrs. Tihany, "but I like it this way."

Untergeschlugenah— Judith Tihany's Transylvanian Green Bean Soup

One early summer day in 1949 the Jews all closed their stores and workshops and hung out their BACK SOON signs. At the edge of town they boarded a truck. By way of the Czechoslovak border it was still possible to reach the U.S. occupation zone in Austria, and from there the State of Israel. Most of them settled in the same town in Israel. For the rest of his life, Janko Kertesz, the cobbler, continued to gossip in Hungarian, sitting on his three-legged stool in that new little town on the coast of the Mediterranean, just as he used to do back in Ujfalu. His customers were almost the same, and so were his friends: the people with whom he had gone to school and synagogue, served in the army, suffered through the labor camps, mourned wives and children. Today there is only one Jew left in town, a baker. It was not altogether unintentional, this consigning of the memory of the Jews of Ujfalu to oblivion.

—George Konrad,
  A Feast in the Garden (1989)

YIELD: 6 TO 8 SERVINGS

5 cups vegetable broth or water	Lemon juice to taste
2 pounds fresh green beans, cut into 1-inch pieces	Dash of sugar
1 red bell pepper	Salt and freshly ground pepper to taste
2 tablespoons butter	Paprika to taste
2 medium onions, diced (about 2 cups)	1/2 cup chopped fresh parsley
2 tablespoons unbleached all-purpose flour	1/2 cup snipped fresh dill
	Sour cream for garnish (optional)

1. Bring the broth or water to a boil and add the beans. Simmer for about 5 minutes.

2. Using a vegetable peeler, remove the outer skin of the pepper; scrape out the pith and seeds. Grate by hand or use the grating blade of a food processor. Add to the soup and simmer for an additional 5 minutes or until the beans are tender. You can also use roasted and peeled peppers instead.

3. Heat the butter in a small frying pan and sauté the onions until translucent. Stir in the flour and cook for several minutes, stirring occasionally. Add the flour-thickened onions to the broth and bring to a boil. Adjust the seasonings with lemon juice, sugar, salt, pepper, and paprika to taste. The final soup should be a little sweet and sour.

4. Just before serving, add the fresh parsley and dill. Serve as is or with a dollop of sour cream.

Soups

129

When I walked up the flight of stairs to Zahava and Shmuel Nissan's apartment in Holon, south of Tel Aviv, I did not know what to expect. As soon as I entered, three women wearing long, flowing Bukharan robes and hats greeted me. The table was set for Shabbat. The women had lit two candles each, leaving two for me, and the house was quiet. Thankfully, Israel slows down for that one day of the week—cell phones off, cars parked, quiet everywhere.

The women, who had been cooking all day, were putting the last touches on the salads for dinner. The food for the Sabbath was on top of a warming plate and covered with a huge flat pillow. A large samovar was heated for tea, and on top the eggs were cooking slowly for the next day's Sabbath breakfast after synagogue.

In a few minutes Mrs. Nissan's brother and her husband, partners in an electric component store, arrived, and we sat down at the table together, where the men said the blessings over the wine. For this one night of the week, their simple table was transformed into a throne. First, the men placed both sweet and varietal wine in a cup, adding a little water and letting it pour over into the saucer. Then, saying a blessing, they sipped the wine. They explained to me that they use both water and wine to show the overabundance of their good fortune at having the Sabbath, and the hope that this luck will spill over into the new week.

Then they placed two oblong, flat loaves of Bukharan bread bottom to bottom and turned them over and over.

After reciting the traditional blessings over the bread, they tore away morsels, dipped them in salt, and gave them to each person at the table. They explained that *lehem* (bread) has many meanings, and that the root for the word *lehem* is in the word for war, *milhama*—bread is so important that wars are fought over it. Before the men said the blessings, they put their hands palms upward in front of them to thank God for the bread, while chanting "*poteach et yadekha umasbia lekhol chai ratzon*" (God opens his hands and sustains all who desire). They also explained that all ten fingers are involved in making bread, and that there are ten transformations from the planting of the wheat to the final baking of the bread.

The meal started with fresh tomato soup with cilantro (the recipe for which follows), a variety of eggplant salads, and *taboulleh*, with *z'hug* on the table. The next course included Bukharan carp steaks with garlic and lemon juice; a carp filled with vegetables; a Bukharan form of *petscha*, calf's foot cooked for four hours until it gels and served with crunchy chickpeas; lemony stuffed grape leaves; smoked meat; and *barsch*, the traditional Bukharan rice dish for Friday nights and holidays (see page 230). Dessert included watermelon, a big bowl of fruit, and raisins and nuts, as well as a Bukharan half-moon *samosa* pastry, filled with nuts, and Chinese tea. In between courses they sang the enchanting Sabbath music for which Bukharan Jews are famous.

The Foods of
Israel Today

This refreshing cold tomato soup is a lovely way to start a midsummer meal. I recommend making it with very fresh tomatoes.

Bukharan Tomato Gazpacho with Garlic and Cilantro

YIELD: 6 SERVINGS

3 pounds fresh tomatoes

3 cloves garlic

½ teaspoon salt, or to taste

2 tablespoons extra virgin olive oil

¼ cup diced onion (optional)

½ cup chopped fresh cilantro

1. Drop tomatoes into a large pot of boiling water. After approximately 30 seconds, remove and peel.

2. Put the peeled tomatoes and garlic in a food processor bowl and blend until smooth. Strain to eliminate seeds. Add salt and olive oil, blend again until frothy, and refrigerate.

3. Before serving, blend once more, adjust the seasonings, and sprinkle onion and cilantro on top.

Ottoman legacy of tomatoes, peppers, and eggplants

Soups

Bulgarian Eggplant Soup with Yogurt

In the 1970s, Melech Hahatsilim, a Bulgarian restaurant in Ramat Aviv, just north of Tel Aviv, prided itself on being the "king of eggplants." Although the restaurant has been closed for years, I tracked down Arnold Beinisch, the owner, now in his seventies. In addition to making divine dishes with the purple-skinned vegetable, he used to give gifts of eggplant charms to his restaurant guests. My most vivid memory is of this soup in which, Bulgarian-style, he swirled cold yogurt into the hot eggplant.

YIELD: 6 SERVINGS

3 large eggplants (about 3 pounds total)

3 garlic cloves

3–3½ cups vegetable broth

1 teaspoon white vinegar

1 tablespoon sugar

Salt and freshly ground pepper to taste

1 cup plain yogurt

1. Grill the eggplants over a flame or under the broiler, turning them with tongs until charred on all sides (see page 52). While they're still hot, plunge them into a plastic bag, close tightly, and let them steam for about 15 minutes to loosen the skin.

2. Scrape the flesh from the skin and shake the pulp in a colander to remove excess liquid.

3. Puree the garlic with the eggplant pulp in a food processor. Add 2 cups of the vegetable broth, process, and then strain the contents into a bowl.

4. Adjust to the consistency of a creamy soup by adding more vegetable broth if necessary, and season with vinegar, sugar, and salt and pepper to taste.

5. Spoon a ladleful of hot soup into the bottom of serving bowls, cover with dollops of yogurt, and continue to layer in this manner.

ichael Katz, typical of the new breed of Israeli chefs, apprenticed abroad before opening his restaurant, Michael Andrew, in an idyllic setting overlooking the Western Wall in Jerusalem. In the fashion of others I have interviewed, he treats cooking kosher as a cultural and creative challenge, serving dishes like sea bream with phyllo and saffron risotto, and this extraordinary cherry tomato soup.

Michael Katz's Pan-roasted Cherry Tomato Soup

YIELD: ABOUT 10 SERVINGS

6 tablespoons olive oil

4 large onions, sliced into rounds

4 pints cherry tomatoes

1 tablespoon salt

Freshly ground pepper to taste

2 stalks celery, chopped

1 tablespoon coriander seeds

12-oz can peeled plum tomatoes, with juice

6 cloves garlic, chopped

1/2 cup balsamic vinegar

1 bay leaf

1 handful of fresh parsley, chopped

2 sprigs thyme

4 cups water (about)

2 tablespoons sugar, or to taste

1 cup heavy cream (optional)

4 tablespoons chopped fresh basil

1. Heat 3 tablespoons of the oil in a 6-quart soup pot and sauté the onions until golden, about 20 minutes.

2. Meanwhile, in a large frying pan, fry the cherry tomatoes, in 2 batches, in the remaining olive oil. Cook until the skin starts to split, about 8 minutes, seasoning with salt and pepper.

3. Add the celery, coriander seeds, and a few grinds of pepper to the onions. Cook for a few minutes, then add the canned tomatoes, half the garlic, and the fried cherry tomatoes. Cook for another few minutes, stirring occasionally, then add the vinegar, bay leaf, parsley and thyme, and 4 cups of water. Bring to a boil and simmer over low heat, uncovered, for about 40 minutes, tasting once or twice to adjust the seasonings. Add sugar to taste to offset the acidity.

4. Cool slightly, fish out the bay leaf and the thyme sprig, and add the remaining garlic.

5. To make the soup frothier, transfer it to a blender and puree in 2 batches. Put the soup through a food mill, return it to the pot, and bring to a boil. Adjust the seasonings, swirl in the cream (if you like), garnish with fresh basil, and serve hot.

Cold Beet Borscht with Dill and Chives

I was sitting in a garden lush with bananas, green papaya, guava, *etrog,* pomelo (a local species of grapefruit), and lemon at a home in Caesarea, one of Herod's cities on the Mediterranean. The table was set with napkin holders made out of ceramic handles from two-thousand-year-old Byzantine pots collected during walks on the nearby beach. The food was an array of Scandinavian salmon and flatbreads, Israeli olives, white cheese with *za'atar* and olive oil, black sesame-seed bread, egg rolls made by the Filipino housekeeper, and this cold summer borscht.

YIELD: 6 TO 8 SERVINGS

4 large beets (3 pounds with greens)

1 medium onion, chopped

1 teaspoon salt

1½ tablespoons sugar

2 cups cold water

Juice of ½ lemon

1 cup sour cream or plain yogurt

1 tablespoon snipped fresh dill, plus additional for garnish

1 tablespoon chopped chives

1. Preheat the oven to 450 degrees and trim the leafy tops of the beets to ¼ inch. Wrap the beets individually in aluminum foil, place in a pan, and roast in the oven for 30 minutes or until tender. Cool, peel, and cut into large chunks.

2. Put the beets, onion, salt, sugar, 1 cup of the water, and the lemon juice in the bowl of a food processor equipped with a steel blade and process. Stir in ¾ cup of the sour cream or yogurt and 1 tablespoon of the dill. Thin as desired with the remaining cup of water. Chill for at least 2 hours before serving. This soup can be made 2 to 3 days in advance. Adjust seasonings and serve garnished with the remaining dill and the chives and, if you like, with an additional dollop of the sour cream or yogurt.

Maya's Melon Soup with *Arrack*

One of the meals I cherish in Jerusalem is the relaxed Saturday-afternoon lunch. Eating at the home of Bedouin specialist Clinton Bailey (see page 91) and his wife, Maya, the art director of the Jerusalem Theater, stands out in my memory. One Saturday we all sat around a table on their patio while Maya cooked up a storm for us and other guests, mostly expatriate Americans who live in Israel. A native of Buffalo, New York, Clinton came to Israel in 1958 as a young student and fell in love with Maya. Maya, who loves to cook, is influenced by the foods of her native Israel and of nearby Greece. (The two own a summer home on a Greek island.) This soup reflects her talent and her travels, as well as her principle of making each flavor count. In Greece she uses ouzo and in Israel *arrack;* both are grape-based liqueurs flavored with anise.

YIELD: 8 SERVINGS

2 ripe cantaloupe or honeydew melons (about 2 1/2 pounds each)

1 cup sour cream or plain yogurt

2–3 tablespoons sugar

1 cup milk

1/4 cup ouzo or *arrack,* or to taste

Several sprigs of fresh mint for garnish

1. Peel and cube the melon; puree in a food processor equipped with a steel blade.

2. Add the sour cream or yogurt, sugar, milk, and ouzo or *arrack.* Mix well and refrigerate a few hours or overnight.

3. Thin with additional milk if necessary. Garnish with a sprig of fresh mint.

Hummus Soup

In the nineteenth and early twentieth centuries both Jerusalem and Jaffa had active American colonies, inhabited by Christian immigrants from the United States. Keren, one of Tel Aviv's finest restaurants, is housed in a totally renovated New England–style timber house, built by Christian immigrants from Maine more than one hundred years ago in what was called the American Colony, on the Tel Aviv–Jaffa border. From here pilgrims would start their ascent to Jerusalem.

Haim Cohen, the restaurant's chef, gave me his recipe for hummus soup, which he serves at the restaurant. "I thought to myself, if everyone takes their inspiration from the food around, like in Provence, although we are much smaller than Provence, why not make a hummus soup?" he said. "My mother is from Turkey and my father from Israel, so I was familiar with chickpea soup, but not like this one." Nor was I. The earthy colors of the soup are welcoming, especially in winter. Instead of garnishing it with fried calamari and herbs, as Mr. Cohen does, I have used only fresh oregano or thyme.

YIELD: 8 SERVINGS

5 cups vegetable broth, or more if necessary

10 cups well-cooked chickpeas (see page 60)

3 tablespoons grated Parmesan cheese

Salt and freshly ground pepper to taste

3 tablespoons extra virgin olive oil

Juice of 1 lemon, or to taste

Small leaves of fresh oregano or thyme for garnish

1. Bring the vegetable broth to a boil in a soup pot and add 8 cups of the chickpeas. Return to a boil and simmer, uncovered, for 10 minutes.

2. Puree the chickpeas and the broth together in a food processor or blender until very smooth. Pass through a fine sieve (the finer the sieve, the smoother the finished soup will be), adding more broth as necessary to ease the chickpeas through, and return to pot.

3. Bring the puree back to a boil, adding more broth if the soup is too thick. Add the remaining chickpeas and the Parmesan cheese and cook for 10 minutes. If you want a thicker soup, lower the heat and simmer for a longer time. Season with salt and pepper to taste.

4. Drizzle a little olive oil and lemon juice over each serving and garnish with oregano or thyme leaves.

Then will come the supper, served to the men in one room and to the women in another. At supper [at a Yemenite wedding] there will be meat and thick soup. The meat together with the soup will be served in a single bowl, and they'll eat as the children of Israel ate the paschal lamb, not letting the food cool and devouring it in a hurry; nor will God's gift be defiled by a fork. The soup will be sopped up with soft 'pittes' and you may be sure that not a drop will go to waste.

—Yehoash, *The Feet of the Messenger* (1923)

The closest a modern Jew can come to genuine biblical eating is to attend a holiday meal at the Yemenite home of Rabbi Yosef Zadok, the 111-year-old head of Jerusalem's Yemenite community. A master silversmith whose grandfather made coins for the king of Yemen, Rabbi Zadok continued to practice the craft until about twenty years ago. A portrait of him draped in a flowing white robe, and with long, twisted white forelocks, hangs in his family shops around Jerusalem.

Several legends attempt to explain the Jews' two-thousand-year presence in the tip of Arabia. The Yemenites themselves maintain that their ancestors arrived during the first century of the common era, following the destruction of the Second Temple by the Romans and the dispersion of the Jews from Judea. For centuries, the Yemenites held firm to the belief that one day a great bird or a magic carpet would take them back to the Holy Land. In 1948, the great birds appeared in the shape of transport planes. The Zadok family, along with about thirty-four thousand other Yemenite Jews, fulfilled their dream when the silver birds came to pick them up and airlifted them to Israel, in what was known as Operation Magic Carpet.

On holidays, the Zadok family gathers in the living room of the rabbi's apartment, above his workshop near the Mea Shearim neighborhood. Rabbi Zadok presides, sitting barefoot and cross-legged on a pillow atop his usual corner bench at the dining table. Yemenites eat a diet of grains,

*Rabbi Zadok celebrates
his one hundredth Hanukkah*

nuts, and a small amount of meat, including the genitals, tails, legs, bellies, and udders of lambs and cows. In Yemen, roasted locusts are a special treat.

Occasionally, a festive meal will begin with fish served with a hot pepper sauce. The main course is almost always a stew consisting of chicken, beef, and vegetables. Years ago Rabbi Zadok pointed out to me that the only "new" ingredients in the stew are potatoes and tomatoes, brought to Yemen by the Turks in the seventeenth and eighteenth centuries. The stew is made with and accompanied by *hawayij*, *z'hug*, and *hilbe*, spice combinations that have become mainstream ingredients in Israeli cooking today. *Hawayij* is peppery and colorful, with black pepper, caraway seeds, cumin, coriander, cardamom, and turmeric. *Z'hug*, a spicy mixture of chiles, garlic, cilantro, cumin, and cardamom, is as Israeli as catsup is American. *Hilbe* (Arabic) or *urbiya* (Hebrew) means "to be fruitful and multiply." It is made from soaked fenugreek seeds—which symbolize fertility in Yemenite folklore and are mentioned in the Talmud—mixed with *z'hug* and other ingredients.

Before and after eating the stew, each person nibbles on *ga'le*, a combination of raisins, pomegranates, pecans, walnuts, roasted peanuts, and chickpeas.

When the meal is over the rabbi always sits back to rest a little and says, "Blessed be the Name. We have always eaten little but well of what God has given us."

Yemenite Chicken and Beef Soupy Stew

I have made my own additions to the soup the women of the Zadok family taught me more than twenty years ago. They serve meat with the bones, but I prefer to scrape off the meat. I usually start the soup one day and finish it off just before serving time.

YIELD: 8 TO 10 SERVINGS

8 cups water

1/2 pound beef shoulder or ribs, fat removed

2 pieces of marrow bone

8 garlic cloves, peeled

2 large onions, peeled and quartered

1 large tomato, almost quartered but not cut all the way through

1/4 cup chopped fresh parsley

1/4 cup snipped dill, plus dill for garnish

1 chicken, cut into 8 pieces

2 large carrots, peeled and left whole

4 celery stalks

1 teaspoon curry powder

1/2 teaspoon ground cumin

1 zucchini, diced in 1-inch pieces

3 potatoes, peeled and diced in 1-inch pieces

1 tablespoon *hawayij,* or to taste (see page 140)

Salt and freshly ground pepper to taste

Juice of 1 lemon

8 cups boiled rice

1 cup chopped fresh cilantro

2 tablespoons *z'hug,* or to taste (see facing page)

1/3 cup *hilbe,* or to taste (see page 140)

1. Pour the water into a soup kettle and add the beef and marrow bones. Bring to a boil, skimming the foam from the surface.

2. Lower the heat and add the garlic cloves, onion, tomato, parsley, and 1/4 cup dill. Cover and simmer 20 minutes.

3. Add the chicken pieces. Bring to a boil and skim the foam from the surface. Add the carrot, celery, curry powder, and cumin. Cover and simmer another 20 minutes or until the chicken pieces are cooked. You can do this a day ahead and refrigerate overnight.

4. Remove the marrow bones and the fat that has formed on the top of the pot and fish the chicken and beef out of the soup. Cut the meat into bite-size pieces and scrape the skin and bones from the chicken. Return the meat to the soup pot. Dice the cooked celery and carrots and return to the pot.

5. Add the zucchini, potatoes, *hawayij,* and salt and pepper to taste and simmer, covered, another 10 minutes or until the vegetables are cooked. Pour the lemon juice over the soup.

6. To serve, place a portion of rice in each soup bowl and top with the chicken, vegetables, and broth. Garnish with the fresh cilantro and the remaining dill. Serve the *z'hug* and *hilbe* in separate bowls. Add them according to your taste.

Z'hug—Yemenite Hot Sauce

Some like it hot! This Yemenite hot sauce is used like Tabasco, but more often—in soups, as a condiment with eggs, as a spice rub on fish or chicken, as a sauce for gefilte fish instead of horseradish, or even sprinkled on yogurt for a tasty dip. There are two kinds of *harif* (hot sauce in Israel): red and green. The red, also called *harissa* (see page 72), includes only red peppers, with no herbs. The typical fresh Yemenite green *harif, z'hug,* has lots of cilantro, garlic, hot serrano or jalapeño peppers, cumin, and cardamom. The key to this sauce is always to use extremely fresh ingredients.

YIELD: ABOUT 1/2 CUP

4 ounces fresh green serrano or jalapeño peppers, stems removed

1 whole head garlic

1/2 cup fresh cilantro, well rinsed and dried

1/2 cup fresh parsley, well rinsed and dried

1/4 teaspoon whole black peppercorns

1/2 teaspoon cumin

2 green cardamom pods, peeled

1 teaspoon salt, or to taste

1/4 cup olive oil, plus additional to cover

1. Place peppers with the garlic, cilantro, parsley, peppercorns, cumin, cardamom, and salt to taste in the bowl of a food processor. Chop until almost pureed, then add 1/4 cup olive oil and puree.

2. Remove the contents to a glass jar and cover with additional olive oil. The *z'hug* will keep for several months, covered in an airtight jar, in the refrigerator.

Peeling garlic to make z'hug at Tel Aviv's Carmel Market

Soups

Hawayij—Yemenite Spice Combination

This traditional Yemenite spice combination varies from family to family. One can find old-time spice merchants in Tel Aviv's Carmel or Hatikva markets and Jerusalem's Mahane Yehuda hawking their unique blends. I like this particular combination of peppercorns, caraway, cumin, cardamom, coriander, and turmeric. Although many recipes call for more saffron, it is so expensive that most people use turmeric instead or, as I have done, just a dash of saffron. Use this as a seasoning for soups, stews, vegetables, rice, fish, and meat.

YIELD: ABOUT 1/4 CUP

2 tablespoons whole black peppercorns

1 tablespoon black caraway seeds

1 teaspoon cumin seeds

1 teaspoon coriander seeds

1 teaspoon cardamom seeds

Pinch saffron (optional)

2 teaspoons turmeric

Pound all the ingredients together using a mortar and pestle, or use a coffee grinder reserved for grinding spices. Store in an airtight container.

Hilbe—A Yemenite Fenugreek Sauce

This is a peculiarly creamy Yemenite sauce which is often added to soup. Fenugreek, mentioned in the Bible, is a medicinal herb that the Yemenite Jews most likely learned to use from the Indians. Traditionally, one would use whole fenugreek seeds ground with water into a paste; I use fenugreek powder because it is so readily available. Many Yemenite Jews in Israel today add chopped tomato to their *hilbe,* clearly a modern addition to an ancient sauce.

YIELD: ABOUT 1/3 CUP

3 tablespoons fenugreek powder

1/2 cup water

1 generous teaspoon *z'hug*

Juice of 1/2 lemon

Salt to taste

1. Soak the fenugreek powder in the water for at least 3 hours.
2. Drain off some of the water, leaving a gelatinous paste. Using an electric hand mixer or a whisk, beat until smooth. Add *z'hug,* the lemon juice, and salt. Adjust seasonings to taste. The sauce should be very spicy.

Chickpeas were a protein staple for early Zionists like the late Golda Meir, who learned to use them in Israel. For others, like Margalit Shemesh of Bat Yam, a Bukharan Jew whose husband hails from Afghanistan, chickpeas have always been a basic staple in their cuisine. On Friday nights Mrs. Shemesh makes her husband's soup and her family's *barsch* (see page 230). From her I learned this tip for storing and peeling chickpeas: soak a large quantity of chickpeas in water overnight, drain, then freeze in two-cup quantities. Defrost as needed, then cover with water. If your recipe requires it, peel chickpeas by squeezing the outer coat off as you would do when peeling almonds. In Israel, Mrs. Shemesh uses turkey wings in this soup, though chicken wings are easier to find in the United States. If you can find them, throw in a few dried Iraqi limes from Basra for flavor.

Chelov— Afghan Friday-Night Chicken and Chickpea Soupy Stew with Meatballs

YIELD: 8 TO 10 SERVINGS

1 cup chickpeas	1 cup chopped celery leaves
3–4 beef soup bones	Salt and freshly ground pepper to taste
3 chicken thighs	1/2 teaspoon turmeric
2 turkey or 4 chicken wings	2 pounds ground turkey
10 cups water	1 large onion, grated
2–3 dried limes, pierced (optional)	1/2 teaspoon cinnamon
2 cups chopped fresh cilantro	2 tablespoons matzoh meal
1 cup chopped leeks (about 1 large leek)	Juice of 1 lemon, or to taste

1. Soak the chickpeas in water to cover for several hours or overnight. Drain.

2. Put the soup bones and the chicken pieces in a large soup pot and add the water. If you like, prick the dried limes and add them. Bring to a boil, skimming off the foam that rises to the top.

3. Add the chickpeas and simmer, covered, for about an hour. Add 1 cup of the cilantro, the leeks, celery leaves, salt, pepper, and turmeric and bring back to a simmer.

4. To make the meatballs, mix together the ground turkey, onion, cinnamon, salt and pepper to taste, and matzoh meal. With wet hands, form balls the size of walnuts. Drop them into the soup and let simmer for about 10 minutes.

5. Add the remaining cilantro and simmer 10 minutes more. Adjust the seasonings and serve in soup bowls with a squeeze of the lemon juice. This soup is traditionally served over rice.

One of the main meals was chick peas soaked in water for twenty-four hours, then cooked with onions for soup. "The same concoction served for cereal," said Golda, "and later still in the evening, we ground it with onions as salad." A greater favorite was fried onions with bits of hard-boiled eggs.

—Ralph G. Martin, *Golda* (1988)

Kurdish *Kubbeh*— Semolina and Bulgur Dumplings

To learn how to make *kubbeh,* the ubiquitous Kurdish and Iraqi soup dumplings, I visited Tzivia Gamlieli in Moshav Aminadav, just outside Jerusalem. Mrs. Gamlieli was married to her husband, Yosef, in Kurdistan, now part of Iraq, when she was fourteen. Now in her late seventies, Mrs. Gamlieli told me the story of how they rode on two separate horses to their wedding, with her future husband filling in details half in Aramaic and half in Hebrew. "My mother was his aunt," she casually explained while molding balls out of bulgur and semolina. With her finger, she tunneled out the center, which she filled with ground lamb, onion, spices, and nuts.

Each week she makes about sixty *kubbeh* for her children and grandchildren, who come to the Gamlieli home for the Sabbath. Wednesday she grinds the meat and makes the filling; Thursday she mixes the outer bulgur and semolina dough, molds the *kubbeh,* and stuffs them with meat; Friday she makes the soup and simmers the *kubbeh* for the Sabbath afternoon meal. Forming the *kubbeh* is always done sitting cross-legged on a blanket on the floor, the telephone within easy reach, her hair covered in a large net. It is a great time to talk about recipes, about the past, and about her eight children, twenty grandchildren, and six great-grandchildren.

Tzivia and Yosef Gamlieli on their wedding day in Kurdistan

YIELD: 12 DUMPLINGS

2 cups fine bulgur

2 cups semolina (smead or sulet)

1 teaspoon salt

1/2 medium onion, chopped fine

1 tablespoon olive oil

1/2 pound chopped beef or lamb

2 tablespoons pine nuts

1/4 teaspoon allspice

2 tablespoons chopped fresh parsley

1. Soak the bulgur in warm water to cover for about an hour.

2. Squeeze the bulgur dry and mix with the semolina and salt, kneading well with your hands, adding water as necessary to form a malleable dough. For a smoother dough, pulse in a food processor fitted with a steel blade.

Mrs. Gamlieli mixing the kubbeh *dough*

3. Sauté the onions in the oil until translucent, then add the beef or lamb. Sauté about 5 minutes, breaking up the meat until it is cooked through. Drain off any excess fat.

4. Add the pine nuts, allspice, and chopped parsley.

5. Divide the dough into 12 rounds about 2½ inches across. Dip your hands in cold water and tunnel out the center so that the walls are about ¼ inch thick.

6. Insert a heaping teaspoon of the meat mixture into the hole and enclose to form a round ball. Refrigerate for about an hour or until ready to cook.

Filling the kubbeh

"This soup soothes me," said a customer from Haifa who comes each week to the tiny Morduch Restaurant in Jerusalem's Mahane Yehuda marketplace, a simple restaurant with only eight Formica tables. "These ingredients are so primordial that they connect me to ancient times, and to what I am as a Jew. It is a real Aramaic dish, close to the Talmud. Who knows, it may have traveled from Jerusalem to Babylonia at the destruction of the First Temple, and now it's back again."

Morduch's *Hamusta*— Aramaic Chicken Soup with Squash and *Kubbeh*

YIELD: 10 TO 12 SERVINGS

12 cups chicken broth

2 celery stalks with leaves, cut into 2-inch chunks

5 small zucchini, cut into 2-inch chunks

4 dried limes (optional)

Salt and freshly ground pepper to taste

Juice of 2 lemons, or to taste

12 *kubbeh* (see following recipe)

2 tablespoons chopped fresh basil or dill

1. In a large pot, bring the chicken broth to a boil.

2. Add the celery, zucchini, dried limes, salt and pepper, lemon juice, and *kubbeh*. Cover and simmer about 25 minutes or until the *kubbeh* are soft.

3. Add the basil or dill and adjust the seasonings of the soup, adding more lemon juice as needed.

4. Simmer a few minutes more and serve immediately, giving each person 1 large dumpling and plenty of zucchini.

Soups

Iranian Beet, Plum, and Celery Soup with *Kubbeh*

I spent one day watching Ora Matalan in the kitchen of her charming white stucco house, a stone's throw from the Carmel market in Tel Aviv. As she cooked Iranian versions of soup floating with *kubbeh,* we listened to men praying in the tiny synagogue next door. Although she follows the recipes her mother taught her, she now uses a food processor for the meat filling instead of the meat grinder she used in her native Kirmanshah.

Mrs. Matalan's repertoire of *kubbeh* includes a semolina dumpling and for Passover a fried *kubbeh* made from pounded white-meat chicken and rice. While the dumplings are traditionally prepared with lamb, Mrs. Matalan often uses beef in Israel. With any leftover meat filling she makes large *ktzitzot* (meatballs), which she floats in this delicate broth of beets, plums, and celery. Sometimes she substitutes dried apricots for the plums.

YIELD: ABOUT 36 *KUBBEH*, OR 18 SERVINGS

3 cups fine semolina (smead)

$1\frac{1}{4}$ teaspoons salt

2 cups hot water (about)

6 small onions

5 garlic cloves, diced

2 tablespoons vegetable or olive oil

$\frac{1}{4}$ cup diced celery root

3 beets, peeled and diced

6 small red plums, pitted and diced

6 cups cold water

$\frac{1}{4}$ cup chopped celery leaves

2 cups chopped fresh Italian parsley or cilantro

$\frac{3}{4}$ pound ground beef

1 teaspoon freshly ground pepper

1 teaspoon dried or 1 tablespoon chopped fresh mint

1 tablespoon sugar (optional)

1. Put the semolina, $\frac{1}{4}$ teaspoon of the salt, and the hot water in a bowl and mix with a fork. Set aside.

2. For the soup, dice 1 of the onions and sauté with the garlic in the oil for a few minutes. Add the celery root, beets, and plums and sauté, covered, for about 15 minutes. Add the cold water and simmer slowly, covered. This can be done ahead of time.

3. To make the *kubbeh* filling, process the remaining 5 onions, celery leaves, and parsley or cilantro in a food processor fitted with a steel blade until finely chopped but not pureed.

4. Add the beef, pepper, and remaining teaspoon salt to the processed onions and mix well with your fingers.

5. Knead the semolina until very pliable. With wet hands, take a walnut-sized portion of the semolina dough and flatten it in your palm. Place 1 teaspoon of

the meat mixture in the center of the circle. Using your thumb and forefinger, completely enclose the meat with the dough and roll it into a ball between your hands. Repeat with the remaining dough and filling. Keep your hands wet throughout the entire process.

6. Place the dumplings in the soup and bring to a boil. They will sink to the bottom and thicken the soup. Cover and simmer slowly about 30 minutes or until cooked through. Add water if the soup becomes too thick. Adjust seasoning with additional salt, pepper, and the mint and the sugar.

NOTE   The *kubbeh* can be frozen on cookie sheets and stored in freezer bags. Do not thaw before placing in the simmering soup.

*Ora Matalan in her kitchen next to the
Caramel Market in Tel Aviv*

· · · FINK'S · · ·
THE HARRY'S BAR OF JERUSALEM

"At the Eichmann trial in 1966 the city was flooded with foreign journalists who all went to Fink's. Al and I always met there for dinner at 10 p.m. That was when everybody was finished filing their stories and we had goulash soup and good talk. The Brits were always broke. They were a very rackety bunch and I was once there when one of them tried to swap his watch for drinks and goulash soup. Dave [Rothschild] examined the watch and said, 'For you very good, for me, never mind.' He added the journalist's name to the tab, which is still in the back of the tiny bar to this day."

—Judith Rosenfeld, widow of NBC's Alvin Rosenfeld

Fink's is to Jerusalem what Harry's Bar is to Venice. Not only is it steeped in history, but its wraparound bar and half dozen tiny tables are always filled with the who's who of journalism and politics. Because it is so small, heads go up as soon as someone enters. Located at 13 Hamelech George, right off the Ben-Yehuda Pedestrian Mall in the heart of New Jerusalem, it has been in existence since 1932, when a Mr. Fink opened a small café. In the early 1940s Dave Rothschild, a native of a small town in southern Germany, started working there and bought the place. He operated it for fifty years, until his death in 1995. Today his daughter, Edna Azrielli, and her husband, Moulli, run Fink's with the same bar and tables. The signature dish is a rich goulash soup, which simmers constantly in a double boiler to enrich and thicken it. This fragrant soup evolved during the period of the British Mandate in Palestine, a time of austerity. The meat used then for goulash was British corned beef, and plenty of potatoes were added to make the dish both cheap and filling. According to Moulli, "people didn't have money, and the restaurant didn't have meat. Regulars would come to Mr. Rothschild and give him their meat-ration coupons. With the coupons he would purchase meat and make goulash soup. If you gave him a coupon, you'd get a serving." To attest to Fink's place in Jerusalem, Moulli recently received the honor of *Yakia Yerushalaim,* the worthy of Jerusalem.

Fink's Goulash Soup

Although I (and many others) have been trying to get Fink's recipe for goulash soup for years, the family is still guarding the secret. I have made some progress, however, since I first tasted it in 1970. Moulli was willing to tell me which ingredients they use. Here is my best guess as to how much and how to put them together.

YIELD: 6 TO 8 SERVINGS

3 medium onions, diced

2 tablespoons vegetable oil

2 pounds top round beef, cut into 1-inch cubes

1 tablespoon paprika

Salt and freshly ground pepper to taste

6 cups water

1 tablespoon tomato paste

2 medium potatoes, peeled and diced

2 medium carrots, peeled and diced

1 cup diced butternut squash, peeled

1 cup diced zucchini

1. Sauté the onions in the vegetable oil until golden but not crisp.

2. Add the beef and brown lightly. Sprinkle on paprika, salt, and pepper.

3. Pour the water over the beef and bring to a boil, skimming off the foam that forms on the top. Stir in the tomato paste and simmer slowly, covered, for about 2 hours.

4. Fold in the potatoes, carrots, and butternut squash, replace the cover, and simmer lightly another 10 minutes. Then add the zucchini and continue cooking, covered, until the potatoes are tender, about 5 more minutes. Adjust the seasonings and serve immediately or remove to the top of a double boiler and simmer, covered, very slowly for several more hours.

NOTE   If you like, you can thicken the soup with a little flour dissolved in water.

Eucalyptus's Jerusalem Artichoke Soup with Lemon and Saffron

In the Old City of Jerusalem, just inside the Damascus Gate and near what was once the American Colony, there is a huge patch of Jerusalem artichokes. Originally an American tuber, the Jerusalem artichoke may have been brought to Israel by American visitors in the nineteenth century. Not related to the more familiar globe artichoke, the Jerusalem artichoke is a member of the sunflower family. Curiously, the word "Jerusalem" in the vegetable's name does not come from the name of the city, but rather from the Italian *girosel,* meaning "sunflower." In the United States, Jerusalem artichokes are also known as California sunchokes. Although many people in Israel tunnel out the center and stuff the knobby vegetables with meat and rice, Chef Moshe Basson of Jerusalem's Eucalyptus Restaurant (see page 300) prefers to serve them in a lemony soup flavored with saffron. Eucalyptus is a kosher meat restaurant, so in order to finish off the soup with a creamy effect, Chef Basson grinds blanched almonds in a little water and folds the paste into the broth, following an age-old Sephardic tradition.

YIELD: 6 TO 8 SERVINGS

2 medium onions, diced in ½-inch pieces

2 tablespoons extra virgin olive oil

1 clove garlic, minced

1½ pounds Jerusalem artichokes, peeled and quartered

4 cups chicken broth

Salt and freshly ground pepper to taste

10–12 blanched almonds

2 tablespoons water

Pinch saffron

Juice of ½ lemon

2 tablespoons chopped fresh Italian parsley, with stems

1. Using a heavy casserole with a cover, sauté the onions in the olive oil over low heat, covered, about 20 minutes. (This is called "sweating" the onions.) Uncover, add the garlic and the artichokes, and increase heat. Continue to sauté for a few more minutes.

2. Add the chicken broth and salt and pepper to taste. Bring to a boil and simmer, covered, for 30 minutes.

3. Grind the almonds in a spice grinder and mix with the water. Whisk the mixture into the soup along with the saffron strands and the lemon juice. Reheat, sprinkle parsley on top, and serve.

NOTE   You can replace the Jerusalem artichokes with artichoke hearts; or make a dairy soup by replacing the chicken broth with vegetable broth and substituting ½ cup of heavy cream for the almonds and water. The vegetables may also be pureed before serving.

The jams of Rosh Pina

Above: A festive dinner at Zahava and
Shmuel Nissan's apartment in Holon

Opposite, top: Fathima Zeidan Salah
collects herbs in the hills outside Salim

Opposite, bottom: Her husband Zeidan serves
breakfast in their home in Salim in the Galilee

Above: Salads at Eucalyptus Restaurant

Opposite, top: Pita making at Damascus Gate

Opposite, bottom: Abu Thayer hummus place

Above: Breads of Amira in Rosh Pina

Opposite: Sandra Rosenfeld putting the finishing touch on her husband Michael Katz's Pan-roasted Cherry Tomato Soup, page 133

Bagele vendor in front of the Church of the Holy Sepulchre

Lentil Soup with Tomatoes

In the quotation at right, the word *edom* is a play both on the word *adom,* which in Hebrew means red, and *idam,* meaning brown in Arabic. Actually, the dish was probably a yellow-brown color. In Hebrew the word for lentil is *adash* (*adas* in Arabic), which means "to tend a flock." Lentils, it seems, were food for peasants and shepherds. The pottery remnants at Tel Anafa, in Israel's Huleh Valley, suggest that its third-century-B.C.E. inhabitants subsisted on lentil soup, porridge, and similar soupy dishes. Esau's pottage may have included most of the ingredients for the following lentil soup, except for the New World ingredient of tomatoes.

YIELD: 8 SERVINGS

4 tablespoons olive oil

2 medium onions, chopped (2 cups)

2 cloves garlic, crushed

1 stalk celery, chopped

1 large carrot, peeled and chopped

1 cup red or brown lentils

28-ounce can crushed plum tomatoes with juice

8 cups chicken broth, vegetable broth, or water

¼ cup plus 2 tablespoons chopped fresh parsley

¼ cup plus 2 tablespoons chopped fresh cilantro

1 teaspoon ground cumin

1 teaspoon turmeric

Salt and freshly ground pepper to taste

Juice of 1 lemon or 1 preserved lemon, diced (see pages 179 and 180)

1. Heat the oil in a large saucepan and sauté the onions and garlic gently until the onions are soft. Add the celery and carrots and continue to sauté a few more minutes.

2. Add the lentils, tomatoes, broth or water, ¼ cup each parsley and cilantro, cumin, turmeric, and salt and pepper to taste. Bring to a boil then lower heat, and simmer, covered, for 1 hour or until the lentils are tender. For a thicker soup, puree half the contents of the pot in a food processor equipped with a steel blade. Return the puree to the pot and stir well. Adjust the seasonings, add the lemon juice or diced preserved lemon, and serve with the remaining parsley and cilantro sprinkled on top.

When the boys grew up, Esau became a skillful hunter, a man of the outdoors; but Jacob was a mild man who stayed in camp. Isaac favored Esau because he had a taste for game; but Rebekah favored Jacob. Once when Jacob was cooking a stew, Esau came in from the open, famished. And Esau said to Jacob, "Give me some of that red stuff to gulp down, for I am famished"—which is why he was named Edom. Jacob said, "First sell me your birthright." And Esau said, "I am at the point of death, so of what use is my birthright to me?" But Jacob said, "Swear to me first." So he swore to him, and sold his birthright to Jacob. Jacob then gave Esau bread and lentil stew; he ate and drank, and he rose and went away. Thus did Esau spurn the birthright.

—Genesis 25:27–34

Israel Aharoni's Chicken Soup with Matzoh Balls Stuffed with Chicken Liver

Israel Aharoni, one of Israel's major cooking personalities (see pages 66–7), caused quite a stir in the newspaper *Yediot Aharonot* when he published a recipe for matzoh balls stuffed with chopped liver. "Usually matzoh balls are rather dull," he said. "You want to have something different? Why not still keep them traditional but stuff them with nice chopped chicken liver? It is wonderful with onions, chopped roughly, fried in *schmaltz,* and then stuffed inside a typical matzoh ball." He sometimes serves them as a side dish simply fried in *schmaltz,* which is rendered goose or chicken fat.

Although many Israelis welcomed this new way of preparing matzoh balls for Passover, others rebelled. "Don't tamper with my matzoh balls," complained the writer Meir Shalev when his wife prepared Aharoni's version for their Seder. He pleaded with her to return to his mother's recipe. "I like tradition," he said, "especially on holidays."

Aharoni defends his recipe. "There is a revolution of food in Israel," he said. "Until a few years ago it was kind of a shame to eat good food. It was too bourgeois. With Holocaust survivors and idealism, fine dining was not the right thing to do. Revolutions come from young people. In Israel we were born to foie gras and want to enjoy life like the rest of the young people in the world. Our young professional chefs came with cooking habits from all over the world. At first Israelis substituted canned tomatoes for fresh, beef for lamb, ethnic foods were devalued. Until ten years ago we all used vegetable oil; olive oil was an Arab thing. Then Italian food became special and now we are trying everything, even matzoh balls stuffed with chopped liver."

YIELD: 10 TO 15 MATZOH BALLS

1 1/3 cups matzoh meal	1 cup water
2 large eggs	1 medium onion, chopped
1/4 cup chopped fresh parsley	1/4 pound fresh chicken livers
3 tablespoons rendered chicken fat or vegetable oil	10 cups chicken broth
Salt and freshly ground pepper to taste	

1. Put the matzoh meal in a mixing bowl with the eggs, parsley, 1 tablespoon of the oil or chicken fat and salt and pepper to taste. Mix well with a fork. Add enough water to make a soft dough. Cover with plastic wrap and refrigerate for an hour.

2. Sauté the onions in a second tablespoon of the rendered fat or oil until soft; add the livers. Continue sautéing about 7 minutes or until the liver is cooked through. Cool slightly and remove the liver and onions to the bowl of a food processor. Pulse, using a metal blade, until coarsely chopped.

3. Roll about 2 tablespoons of the matzoh dough between your palms into a ball. Using your finger, make a hole in the center of the ball and stuff a heaping teaspoon of the liver filling into the hole. Then roll the dough back into a ball, closing the hole. Repeat with the remaining dough and filling.

4. Fry the matzoh balls in the remaining tablespoon of chicken fat or oil until lightly browned.

5. In a soup pot, bring chicken broth to a boil. Place the browned matzoh balls in the simmering liquid and cook for about 12 minutes.

Aharoni tampers with Israel's matzoh balls

Galilee Spinach Soup

I first tasted this simple soup at the home of Umm Joseph ("Mother of Joseph," in Arabic) in the Christian Arab village of Deir Hanna in the eastern part of the Sachnin Valley in the Galilee. The area is mentioned in the Mishnah, the rabbinic code of law dating from 200 C.E. When the valley became Christian during Byzantine times, so did the village. Then a Moslem population settled there some four hundred to five hundred years ago.

When I visited, Umm Joseph brought out an array of fall dishes for sampling. I especially liked this one, which her family had eaten on a recent visit to Egypt. *Meloohiya* is a Middle Eastern green similar to spinach. She picks it in the early spring and fall and uses it interchangeably with spinach. I have made the soup just with spinach in this country and it is delicious.

YIELD: 6 TO 8 SERVINGS

1 pound chicken breast, cut into 1-inch cubes

2 tablespoons vegetable oil

2 tablespoons olive oil

10 cloves garlic, crushed

3/4 pound *meloohiya* or spinach leaves, chopped

8 cups chicken broth

1 teaspoon salt, or to taste

1 teaspoon nutmeg

Juice of 2 lemons

Cooked rice

1. Sauté the chicken in the vegetable and olive oils until golden.

2. Add the garlic and the spinach and press down with a spatula, releasing the water from the spinach.

3. Add the broth, salt, and nutmeg and bring to a boil; cover and simmer 15 minutes. Squeeze the lemon juice onto the soup.

4. Serve in a bowl over rice.

Umm Joseph and her family after lunch in Deir Hanna in the Galilee

Harira— Moroccan Holiday Vegetable Soup

Harira, which means "mixed" in Arabic, is a lemony Moroccan vegetable soup with lentils and chickpeas, eaten with a plump date to break the daily fast during the month of Ramadan. The Jews in Morocco adapted the soup from their Moslem friends to break the fast of Yom Kippur. In Israel, cumin and vegetables like carrots, celery root, and sometimes squash and turnips have been added to the soup. This particular version is popular at Le Tsriff Restaurant in the YMCA in Jerusalem, a branch of Le Tsriff in the Russian Compound (see page 216). I have added a whole pickled lemon mashed to a pulp in the food processor to give the soup a Moroccan flavor. Although *harira* is sometimes served thickened slightly with flour, or with paper-thin vermicelli cooked in the soup just a few minutes before serving, I like it as it is, with a delicate broth.

YIELD: 10 TO 12 SERVINGS

1 cup dried chickpeas	10 cups water
2 tablespoons vegetable oil	1 cup lentils
1 large onion, diced (about 2 cups)	1/2 cup chopped fresh parsley
2 leeks, diced	1/2 cup chopped fresh cilantro
3 celery stalks, diced	1/2 teaspoon ground cumin
1/2 celery root (about 1/2 pound), peeled and diced	Salt and freshly ground pepper to taste
3 medium carrots, peeled and cut in rounds	1 whole fresh or preserved lemon (see pages 179 and 180)
1 pound beef soup bones (optional)	3 large tomatoes
	Juice of 1 lemon

1. Soak chickpeas overnight in water to cover. Drain.

2. Heat the oil in a heavy-bottomed soup pot and sauté the onions, leeks, celery stalks, celery root, and carrots. Add the soup bones if you like, stir well, and continue to sauté for a few minutes.

3. Add the water and drained chickpeas and bring to a boil. Skim off the froth and continue to simmer for another 30 minutes, removing the froth every few minutes.

4. Add the lentils, half the parsley, half the cilantro, the cumin, and salt and pepper to taste. Continue to simmer, uncovered, for a half hour.

5. Cut the fresh or preserved lemon in half, discard the seeds, and put the halves in the bowl of a food processor. Quarter the tomatoes, remove the seeds, and add to the food processor. Pulse until the lemon is chopped. Add the lemon-tomato mixture to the soup and continue to simmer for a few more minutes or until the lentils are tender.

6. Remove the soup bones (if using) and add the lemon juice and the remaining parsley and cilantro. Adjust the seasonings to taste.

When I visited ninety-seven-year-old Shoshana Kleiner at her apartment, she had just finished preparing gefilte fish for the Sabbath. One of the last living members of the fourth *aliyah*, Mrs. Kleiner, who came to Palestine in 1925, ran Neve Shoshana, a boardinghouse in the Jerusalem garden suburb of Beit Hakerem, from 1948 until the late 1980s. Here are some of her memories of the early years in Palestine:

"I was a pioneer, a *halutz*. Thirty of us came together by foot from Galicia through Czechoslovakia, where we snuck over the border and took a train to Vienna. We stayed in Austria for a long time working on a farm, until we received our *laisser passers* and took a cargo boat to Palestine.

"At Brindisi two of our group went to buy some bread and vegetables. No food was served on board. The boat left early and the two were left on the deck yelling, '*Cellio, Cellio!*' which was the name of the boat. Those of us on board had no food, so the captain gave us each a half loaf of bread until the next port. We met our friends again in Alexandria. At the port in Jaffa representatives from the Jewish Agency met us and gave each of us a half a herring, half a package of halvah, and some bread.

"They sent us to Binyamina, where we slept in tents near the railroad station. In the winter foxes came. Most of our things from Poland were lost on the way. We used our coats as blankets. The tent flaps flew in the wind. There was no water, so we stole water from the water tanks at the railway station. It seems as if we never ate. If there was bread, it was already good. We didn't have a job so we helped build the road from Binyamina to Zichron Yaacov with stones. It was a lot of work and they cheated us when they weighed the stones. With the money we were able to buy some black or white bread from a Jewish baker. Eventually, we moved to a wooden shack that was at least better than a tent. We still had no food. I started doing wash for a Jewish woman, working eight hours a day for twenty-five *grush*. For that we could buy twenty-five loaves of bread.

"Then we went to Herzliyya, which was an American settlement. After my husband, Abraham, and I married, we lived in a wooden house, converted from a chicken coop, and had a little farm with chickens, cows, and vegetables. . . . Because the Jewish laborers didn't work as well as the Arabs in the orchards, I worked as a maid and my husband a house painter. Our children had milk and I made bread and fed them a little. We had no furniture, so we took orange crates and built a bed and cooked on a Primus stove made from a cut-up tin container with a kerosene lamp inside. I cooked a soup on top from potatoes, meat, and any vegetables available from the garden. We felt rich in those days."

Girls unloading the potatoes they have dug from the field behind

Remembering more difficult times, Mrs. Kleiner still puts to use all the leftover ingredients from her vegetable soup. She recycles any leftover potatoes into potato-egg salad, and any celery and onions become the filling for stuffed cabbage. Her directions for cooking are: "Cook until cooked!" The celery root makes an interesting addition to this hearty soup.

Fourth *Aliyah* Vegetable Soup

YIELD: ABOUT 12 SERVINGS

12 cups water

1 celery root (about 1 1/4 pounds), diced

3 stalks of celery, halved

3 medium onions (1 pound), halved

5 medium carrots, peeled and left whole

4 sprigs fresh dill, plus snipped dill for garnish

4 sprigs fresh parsley, chopped, plus extra for garnish

4 sprigs fresh cilantro, chopped, plus extra for garnish

1 tablespoon salt, or to taste

1/2 teaspoon freshly ground pepper, or to taste

1/2 cup dry lima beans

1/4 cup barley

1/4 cup lentils

2 white potatoes (about 1 pound), diced

2–3 zucchinis (about 1 1/4 pounds), diced

1 sweet potato (about 1 pound), peeled and diced

1/2 pound fresh mushrooms, sliced

1. Put the water, celery root, celery, onions, 3 of the carrots, dill, parsley, cilantro, and salt and pepper in a 12-quart pot. Bring to a boil and simmer, uncovered, for half an hour. Skim off the froth that builds on the surface of the broth.

2. Add the lima beans, barley, and lentils and continue to simmer for another half hour.

3. Dice the remaining 2 carrots and add them with the potatoes, zucchini, sweet potato, and mushrooms; simmer, uncovered, for about 15 minutes or until the potatoes are tender. Skim off any foam that has developed. Fish out the whole celery, whole carrots, and pieces of onion and discard them (or recycle as Mrs. Kleiner does). Adjust the seasonings; serve garnished with the fresh dill, parsley, and cilantro.

Meir Shalev's Hot Meat Borscht with Cabbage and Beets

I am sentimental about Russian Jewish food, about borscht," reflected the Israeli writer Meir Shalev one evening at his apartment in the German Colony of Jerusalem. "We have it often on Friday evenings when I meet for dinner with my siblings. My grandfather used to say that the secret to a good borscht was the lemon juice. I also eat it with one clove of garlic wrapped in bread." Shalev, one of Israel's leading novelists, was an ambulance driver, and the host of a popular television talk show until age forty. As he reminisced about the foods of his childhood, we ate some leftover borscht from the refrigerator. "Soup is something like bread," he said. "It makes your body more relaxed. When I feel weak, I take a slice of bread with salt and soup. It gives me some kind of home feelings." Here is his basic recipe, very similar to my own.

YIELD: 10 TO 12 SERVINGS

6 cups water

2 pounds beef brisket

2 beef soup bones

2 pounds beets (about 6), peeled and quartered

2 medium carrots, peeled

1 large onion, quartered

3 stalks celery

1 green bell pepper, quartered, seeded, and pith removed

1 red bell pepper, quartered, seeded, and pith removed

1 potato, peeled and quartered

1 small green cabbage, shredded

3 garlic cloves, minced

14-ounce can tomatoes, with juice

Salt and freshly ground pepper to taste

2 tablespoons sugar

Juice of 1 lemon, or to taste

1 whole sprig oregano

Fresh dill for garnish

1. Bring the water to a boil in a large soup pot. Add the brisket and soup bones and cook gently over medium heat until a foam rises to the surface. Skim off the foam and continue cooking, uncovered, for 1 hour.

2. While the meat is cooking, grate the beets, carrots, onion, celery, peppers, and potatoes. You can use a food processor fitted with a grating blade or grate them by hand. Add the grated vegetables to the meat along with the cabbage, garlic, and the tomatoes with their juice. Season with the salt, pepper, sugar, lemon juice, and oregano. Cover and cook over low heat for another hour. Adjust the seasonings.

3. Remove from the heat. When the soup is cool, discard the soup bones and the oregano sprig. Remove the brisket to a wooden board and cut into bite-sized pieces. Return the meat to the pot, reheat, and serve garnished with the dill.

Salads

From Eden and Other Gardens

To the *halutzim,* the pioneers who came to Israel at the turn of the century, food was meant to satiate the body, not the soul. Restaurants were luxuries, and many newcomers lived on kibbutzim, partaking only of the foods they grew themselves. Today, although the traditional kibbutz is becoming an anachronism, with common dining rooms rarer and rarer, you can still find

Above: Early Nahalal women planting tomatoes

Making salad is a creation that gives you pleasure. Watch the kibbutznik with a big heap of fresh vegetables in front of him. Very slowly, with deep intention, he designs personally his own salad, a corner of individualism in the heart of a commune.

—Amos Keynan,
The Book of Pleasures (1997)

those marvelous tables with large bowls filled with the fruits of the seasonal harvest—whole cucumbers, tomatoes, green peppers, hard-boiled eggs, and olives with salads personally crafted.

But off the kibbutzim, Israelis have come to appreciate food as art and entertainment rather than simply as sustenance. Hanoch Bar Shalom, an innovative caterer, food stylist, and food writer, agrees that food has become one of life's pleasures in Israel. "For a long time Israelis ate for survival," he told me as we lunched in his Tel Aviv apartment. "Israel didn't have the culture of the pleasure of food. For the last ten years people have begun to think food is something beautiful in itself; it is joyful and should be fun." And did he prove his point! Lunch was an array of homemade salads: bright red tomatoes with goat cheese and basil

---

· · · LADY MONTEFIORE'S PALESTINE SALAD · · ·

I would reply, "Carry out simply what they themselves have suggested; but begin in the first instance with the building of houses in Jerusalem. Select land outside the city; raise, in the form of a large square or crescent, a number of suitable houses, with European improvements; have in the centre of the square or crescent a synagogue, a college, and a public bath. Let each house have in front a plot of ground large enough to cultivate olive trees, the vine, and necessary vegetables, so as to give the occupiers a taste for agriculture."

—*Diaries of Sir Moses and Lady Montefiore* (1890)

Sir Moses Montefiore, the English philanthropist whose wife, Judith, was a Rothschild, started the first housing settlement of Jews outside the Old City walls in 1858. Abandoned in 1948 because of its proximity to the Jordanian border, the neighborhood—called Yemin Moshe and Mishkenot Shaananim—was restored after the Six-Day War. It housed a windmill—whose construction Montefiore supervised—which the residents could use to grind their flour. Montefiore visited Palestine seven times during his lifetime. His last trip was in 1875, at the age of ninety-one, when the Jewish population had increased to twenty thousand. He was a great gourmet—he brought bottles of wine, loved eating out, and had his own *shochet* (a sage especially instructed in the ritual of slaughter) traveling with him.

Although Montefiore had hoped for the immigration of sturdy, energetic, self-sufficient people, the Jews in Jerusalem more often were elderly people who had come to die in the holy city, as well as religious students and poor Sephardic Jews who lived off charity collected at synagogues and institutions throughout the world.

Montefiore was frequently accompanied by his wife, whose 1846 *Jewish Manual* was the first kosher cookbook in the English language. The couple visited Palestine for the first time in 1827, bringing back many recipes which are in her cookbook. Jerusalem artichokes appear in a Palestine soup with sausage and veal, as well as in the refreshing Palestine Salad. "Take a dozen fine Jerusalem artichokes," wrote Lady Montefiore. "Boil til tender, let the water strain off, and when cold cut them in quarters, and pour over a fine salad mixture; the artichokes should lie in the sauce half an hour before serving. This salad is a very refreshing one, and has the advantage of being extremely wholesome." My guess is that the "fine salad mixture" most probably would have been a lemon vinaigrette.

over mint and red rose petals in a stone bowl; roasted garlic marinated in olive oil; and roasted peppers with cinnamon, oregano, balsamic vinegar, and olive oil, topped with good goat cheese. Each of these creations, served on a separate plate, was an elaboration on the kibbutznik's theme, one step above the simple kibbutz vegetable salad.

In nearly every part of Israel, from every culture represented there, I have tasted extraordinary salads, like Lebanese *fettush,* Druse taboulleh with mint, Bulgarian celery root and carrot salad, and myriad Moroccan pepper, carrot, and eggplant salads, many prepared ahead by women who, in honor of the Sabbath, God, and their families, begin elaborate preparations on the day after Shabbat, a week before the next day of rest. See my other cookbooks for additional Israeli salad ideas.

Kibbutz Vegetable Salad

Sometimes called Turkish Salad, this typical Israeli salad, served at almost every meal, has many variations. But one thing remains the same: the tomatoes, onions, peppers, and cucumbers must be cut into tiny pieces, a practice of the Ottoman Empire. Two types of cucumber are common in Israel: one, like the Kirby cucumber, goes by the name of *melafofon* in Hebrew and *khiyar* in Arabic; the other, called *fakus* in Arabic, is thinner, longer, and fuzzy, and is eaten without peeling.

YIELD: 4 TO 6 SERVINGS

1 green bell pepper	Salt and freshly ground pepper to taste
1 red bell pepper	Juice of 1 lemon
1 yellow bell pepper	2 cloves garlic, minced
2 tomatoes	3 tablespoons olive oil
1 onion	1/2 teaspoon ground sumac or *za'atar* (optional)
1 cucumber	

1. Remove the pith and seeds from the peppers and dice them along with the tomatoes, onion, and cucumber. Toss together in a wooden or ceramic bowl.

2. In a separate small bowl, stir together the salt, pepper, lemon juice, and garlic. Slowly whisk in the olive oil. Pour over the vegetables, mix, sprinkle with sumac or *za'atar,* and serve.

Salads

Tomato, tomato, only yesterday we arrived by ship, today it went into our salad and our meatballs.

—An old Israeli folksong

Whenever Eliezer Ben Yehuda, the father of modern Hebrew, created a new word, his next job was to introduce it to the public. After breakfast he would give his family the newest word of the morning and tell them to use it in conversation with other Jerusalemites, most of whom spoke Yiddish, Ladino, or Arabic.

"Our home was the laboratory for the Hebrew Language of Eliezer Ben Yehuda," said Dola Ben Yehuda Wittman, his last surviving child, during an interview in Jerusalem. "We were his guinea pigs and his soldiers, and couldn't speak anything but Hebrew at home and with our friends. Our family was the first since the time of the First Temple that spoke only Hebrew. My father wanted us even to eat like in the Bible. He looked all over the world for words, and if he didn't find them he made them up. Ben Yehuda made a sort of linguistic ghetto for us."

Her father's new words usually were accepted by the public, but some were completely rejected except by members of his family. One such word was the one he selected for the tomato, also known as the "love apple," a New World fruit introduced to Palestine in the eighteenth century by the Turks. The common word used was *aghvania*, from a Hebrew root that means "to love sensuously," mentioned in a poem by the Israeli poet Nahman Bialik. Because Ben Yehuda did not like the word *aghvanit* (the plural)—he felt it was too sexually suggestive—he turned to colloquial Arabic, as he often did, and coined the word *badura*.

After he announced the word in his newspaper column, his "soldiers" received their marching orders. From then on, whenever any member of the Ben Yehuda family went into a shop to purchase a tomato, he or she was to ask for a *badura*. If the shopkeeper didn't know what *badura* meant, the family member would point to the tomato. Although this way of introducing new words into modern Hebrew usually worked, the public did not take to the word *badura*, preferring the more sensual *aghvania*. After a few years the only people who used *badura* were members of Ben Yehuda's family, including Mrs. Wittman, now in her nineties, who shared this story with me.

Rachama's Eggplant Salad with Tomato

I tasted this typically Israeli salad during a recent speaking engagement at the Mandel Jewish Community Center in Cleveland, Ohio. To my surprise, Rachama Ihshady, cook at the JCC restaurant, comes from one of the leading falafel families of Jerusalem. She shared with me her family's secret recipe for falafel (see pages 70–1), as well as this eggplant salad.

"I look for lightweight, dark-purple, and smooth, almost black eggplants," she said. The intense tomato flavor in this dish comes from the generous use of tomato paste, which Americans usually add as a thickener to canned tomatoes. Israelis have used it as a sauce since the early 1920s, when tomato paste was one of the first canned products sent as aid from the United States to Israel, so I am always struck with how strongly this salad tastes of Israel. Moroccan women, who never used the canned paste in their native land, prepare at least two kinds of tomato-eggplant salad for the Sabbath, one baked and one fried, as done here. This salad lasts for at least one week in the refrigerator.

YIELD: 6 TO 8 SALAD SERVINGS

3 large eggplants (about 3 pounds), unpeeled

2 tablespoons coarse salt, or to taste

1/2–3/4 cup vegetable oil

2 6-ounce cans tomato paste

1 1/2 cups water

2 cloves garlic, minced

Freshly ground pepper to taste

1/4 cup fresh lemon juice

1 teaspoon sugar

2 tablespoons fresh parsley, chopped

1. Wash the eggplants and slice into 1/2-inch-thick rounds. Put in a strainer set over a bowl and sprinkle liberally with salt. Drain for half an hour. Rinse the eggplants in very cold water to remove excess salt and pat them dry with paper towels.

2. Heat 1/4 cup of the oil in a frying pan and sauté the eggplant rounds until golden, adding more oil as needed. Drain the rounds well and cut them into quarters, reserving any remaining oil in the pan.

3. Stir the tomato paste into a bowl with water and dissolve. Stir in the garlic, pepper, lemon juice, and additional salt to taste. Add to the frying pan, adding a tablespoon or so of oil. Add the eggplant and simmer slowly for 2 minutes or until heated through. Drain off any excess oil. Arrange on a platter and serve warm or cold. Before serving, sprinkle with the parsley.

Hannah Zrihen, a dedicated mother, cook, and breadwinner, is typical of many Jewish women I have met. The mother of ten, she came to Israel in 1956 from Marrakesh, where she worked as court seamstress, sewing robes for the king and buttons and caftans for his wife, the queen. "Everyone was coming to Israel then," she said during a Sabbath dinner at her home in Ma'alot, a development town in the north of Israel. When Hannah and her husband, Amram, came to Israel, they settled immediately in a *ma'abarah,* a tent city where new immigrants stayed before finding permanent housing.

"I had heard about Eretz Israel," said Amram. "I was like a king in Marrakesh, I had a store in the *mellah* (Jewish Quarter), and I had strength, I was young, *baruch haShem* (blessed be the Lord). There was nothing here when we came. We worked hard in the cotton fields, we were too busy to think how hard it was. We were together with mostly Moroccans from Marrakesh and the Atlas Mountains."

Even after thirty years, Mrs. Zrihen cannot forget Morocco. "In Marrakesh I had truffles, saffron, and organic vegetables," she said. "When I heard about immigration to Israel, we came, but we knew if we didn't like it we would go back." Like many women of her generation, Mrs. Zrihen cannot read, nor can she tell time, so she cooks by instinct. And does she cook!

As she told me her story, her children came in one by one, kissing her for the Sabbath. The Zrihens' simple stucco home, the original two-room house that they lived in after moving from the *ma'abarah,* has been expanded little by little, thanks to the men of the family. "We all helped build the house," said her thirty-nine-year-old son, Moshe, an

Hannah Zrihen and her family at their Shabbat-laden table in Ma'alot

electrician. "I remember the terrorist raid on our town, when a busload of children were killed. We were small kids. I was nine years old and we all hid in the army room. It was a room in the basement ready for this kind of thing. We didn't go to school. We heard about another family that got killed. Helicopters and the army came close to our house, readying us for evacuation."

Since that time Mrs. Zrihen has sent five sons to the army. "I send my soul to my children. I send them and their entire army unit little containers of food. While they were in the army, I was here. But in my heart I was with them wherever they were. Now, thanks to God, we live very well. The only thing that is missing is true peace."

The Sabbath food was already on the table or heating in the oven, portions set aside for her daughters-in-law, who do not cook the old-fashioned, start-from-scratch way, to take home. Like most women of Mrs. Zrihen's age, she starts preparing for Shabbat early in the week. This is her way of honoring the Sabbath. "God knows what will happen with my recipes," Mrs. Zrihen said. "As long as I stand on my feet I will do it." The *hamim,* or *skeena,* an overnight stew with chickpeas and beef or lamb, rested on the stove beneath two blankets to keep it warm throughout the Sabbath. Inside the oven warmed the Yemenite *kubbanah* (see page 117), a Sabbath morning bread which Mrs. Zrihen learned to make from a Yemenite friend at the community center. The table, covered with a red-checked cloth, was laden with an Ashkenazic challah; her Sabbath fish with red peppers and fava beans (see pages 268–9); and a variety of make-ahead salads, including the following *matbucha.*

Moroccan *Matbucha—Salat Mivushal,* Cooked Tomato and Pepper Salad

In Israel there is a saying for *matbucha,* "*Ata margish et ha esh*"—You feel the smoky fire when you eat it. I love this salad, made in the summer with ripe tomatoes or in the winter with canned ones. In Morocco, Mrs. Zrihen used oil from the argan tree; it is one of the best oils in the world for cooking, and can cost seven or eight times more than good extra virgin olive oil. In Morocco the oil traditionally is roasted and homogenized from the argan kernels collected from the feces of goats grazing near the trees. In Israel, the only country outside Morocco to cultivate the tree, an oil is being created that does not require the goat; instead, the kernels are roasted and compressed in a cold press. If you are lucky enough to find argan oil, drizzle it on the salad just before serving. Otherwise, dress the salad with a good olive oil. Whichever tomato or oil you use, make sure to cook the salad slowly, as Mrs. Zrihen says, "until the eye eats."

YIELD: 6 SERVINGS

- 4 green bell peppers
- 1/4 cup vegetable oil or extra virgin olive oil
- 3 pounds very ripe fresh tomatoes (about 8), peeled, seeded, and diced, or one 32-ounce can diced tomatoes, drained
- 6 cloves garlic, minced
- 1 teaspoon sugar
- 2 teaspoons sweet paprika
- 2 teaspoons salt, or to taste
- Freshly ground pepper to taste
- 1 tablespoon argan or extra virgin olive oil for drizzling

1. Put the whole peppers on a baking tray under the broiler, turning frequently with tongs, until they are charred on all sides, about 20 minutes. Place them in a tightly closed plastic bag for 10 minutes to allow the skins to loosen. Peel the charred skin from the peppers, discard the seeds, and cut into 1-inch squares.

2. Heat the oil in a heavy skillet, and add the peppers, tomatoes, garlic, sugar, paprika, salt, and pepper to taste. Simmer over a low flame, stirring occasionally and mashing the vegetables with a fork until the liquid begins to evaporate. Continue cooking until the salad has a thick, sauce-like consistency. Mrs. Zrihen mashes the vegetables with a potato masher before serving, but they can also be left as is.

3. Drizzle with the argan or olive oil and serve at room temperature.

Druse Taboulleh

The Book of Exodus recounts that one of the daily offerings on the altar in the Temple in the Wilderness was *solet chitim*, a kind of gruel made of three parts crushed wheat smeared with one part pure olive oil. The gruel is possibly the root of modern-day taboulleh, which is made from bulgur, olive oil, garlic, lemon juice, and chopped fresh herbs.

I stumbled on this recipe for taboulleh in a tiny restaurant in the village of Bukarta Ramat on the Golan Heights near the Lebanese border. It includes parsley, red bell pepper, and fresh and dried mint, but no garlic. "Garlic is forbidden in taboulleh," insisted B'sass Salwa, the cook, who lives in a nearby Druse village. She showed me how to scoop up the salad with pieces of cabbage, romaine lettuce, or fresh grape leaves. Not being a purist, I like the taboulleh with or without the garlic.

YIELD: 10 TO 12 SERVINGS

1 cup medium (#2) bulgur

1½ cups chopped scallions (green and white parts)

1 red bell pepper, diced

4 cucumbers or 2 European cucumbers, peeled (if waxed), seeded, and diced

4 ripe tomatoes, seeded and diced, or 1 pint cherry, grape, or pearl-drop tomatoes, halved

½ cup lemon juice, or to taste

2 cloves garlic, minced (optional)

Salt and freshly ground pepper to taste

¼ cup extra virgin olive oil

1 tablespoon dried mint

½ cup chopped fresh mint

1 cup chopped fresh parsley, with stems

1. Soak the bulgur in a bowl with water to cover for at least 1 hour. Drain and squeeze out the excess water.

2. Transfer the bulgur to a large salad bowl and add the scallions, pepper, cucumbers, and tomatoes.

3. Mix the lemon juice, garlic, and salt and pepper to taste in a small bowl. Whisk in the olive oil. Pour the dressing over the taboulleh, sprinkle with the mint and parsley, and toss gently with your hands. Adjust seasonings and serve. You can use a fork, or cabbage, romaine, or grape leaves as an edible scoop.

Pomegranate Taboulleh

This unusual taboulleh comes from Pini Levy, chef-owner of Pini Bahatzer (Pini's Courtyard), nestled in the Nahlat Shiva Quarter of Jerusalem near Jaffa Road. A born and bred Jerusalemite, Pini is praised by chefs throughout Israel for his expertise in making fresh salads. His potato salad, for example, is so simple, mixed with scallions and cilantro and dressed with olive oil and vinegar. I especially like his taboulleh because of the tasty and colorful addition of pomegranate seeds. You can substitute dried cherries or cranberries when pomegranates are not in season.

YIELD: 4 TO 6 SERVINGS

1 cup medium (#2) bulgur

2 cups chopped flat-leaf Italian parsley, including a few stems

Seeds of ½ pomegranate

1 clove garlic, crushed

Juice of 1 lemon, or to taste

Salt and freshly ground pepper to taste

3 tablespoons extra virgin olive oil

1. Soak the bulgur in water to cover for at least 1 hour. Drain and squeeze out the excess water. Put the bulgur in a serving bowl.

2. Add the parsley and pomegranate seeds.

3. Put the garlic, lemon juice, and salt and pepper in a separate small bowl. Whisk in the olive oil. Pour over the bulgur and toss gently with your hands. Allow to marinate, refrigerated, for several hours.

Eating the harvest at a kibbutz

Salads

165

Tzatziki—Armenian Cucumber Salad

This Armenian rendition of cucumber salad is a perfect cool dish for a hot day. Sometimes, in the winter, I add walnuts, raisins, and even apples; in the summer, I add fresh tomatoes, green bell pepper, and onions. Because I like the intensity of dried mint as well as the flavor of fresh, I use them both in the salad.

YIELD: 4 TO 6 SERVINGS

2 medium cucumbers (about 1¼ pounds)

1 teaspoon salt

1 cup plain yogurt

2 cloves garlic, crushed

1 teaspoon dried mint

2 tablespoons chopped fresh mint

1. Peel the cucumbers if their skin is waxed. If not, draw the tines of a fork lengthwise through the skin. Cut lengthwise, remove the seeds, and slice paper-thin. Place the cucumber slices in a colander over a bowl and sprinkle with the salt. Let sit for 30 minutes. Squeeze gently to remove the excess liquid.

2. Mix together the yogurt, garlic, and dried mint in a bowl. Add the cucumber and stir to coat. Chill well and garnish with the fresh mint.

Concia—Marinated Fried Zucchini with Basil

This Roman Sephardic specialty is served as an appetizer at Angelo's Restaurant in Jerusalem. When chef-owner Angelo Di Segno was a child in Rome, he always brought it with him as a filling for a sandwich at the beach. I have tasted it served as an appetizer in the Italian province of Puglia, where they substitute fresh mint for the basil. When I lived in Israel in the 1970s, I could rarely find zucchini; we used a lighter-colored, less dense green squash called *kishouim*. Today zucchini is grown all over the country.

YIELD: ABOUT 3 CUPS

2 pounds young zucchini

About 2½ cups vegetable oil, for deep-frying

2 tablespoons cider vinegar

6 cloves garlic, chopped

¼ cup chopped basil

¼ cup chopped flat-leaf Italian parsley

Salt and freshly ground pepper to taste

1. Slice the zucchini into thin rounds and deep-fry in the oil until golden brown. Drain on paper towels.

2. Put the fried zucchini in a salad bowl. Sprinkle vinegar, garlic, basil, and parsley over it and toss. Let marinate until ready to serve. The salad will keep, covered, in the refrigerator for a week.

Israeli Carrot Salad

I have been making variations of this quintessentially Israeli salad for almost thirty years. Not only does it taste and look good, but it is so easy to prepare that I make it for last-minute dinner guests when I have no lettuce in the house. (Somehow my fridge is always stocked with raw carrots.)

YIELD: 6 SERVINGS

2 cloves garlic

8 sprigs (1/2 bunch) fresh parsley, stems removed

1 pound carrots, peeled

2 tablespoons lemon juice

2 tablespoons orange juice

4 tablespoons extra virgin olive oil

1/2 teaspoon salt

Several grinds of pepper

Place the garlic and the parsley in the bowl of a food processor equipped with a steel blade and chop or julienne. Add the carrots, lemon juice, orange juice, oil, and salt and pepper. Pulse until the carrots are well chopped but not pureed. Adjust the seasonings and serve.

NOTE You can add orange slices and/or radish slices to garnish this salad. Add grated or julienned celery root with the carrots in winter.

· · · FROM COTTON TO CARROTS · · ·
SAM HAMBURG PLANTS THE DESERT

It was David Ben-Gurion's dream for the Jews of Israel to move south in the desert, the way Americans moved west, to develop their land. In the early 1950s, Sam Hamburg, a desert farmer from California, was seduced by Ben-Gurion's idea of making the desert bloom. Hamburg flew between Israel and California several times a year, often bringing home samples of cotton, hybrid corn, peanuts, sugar beets, winter tomatoes, and carrots in his luggage. He also improved methods of growing almonds and introduced new varieties of tomatoes for canning.

On a visit to Be'er Tuvya, a moshav in the Negev origi-nally founded by the Rothschilds, Hamburg noticed new immigrants from Yemen picking weeds along the road. According to Ruth Gruber, in a show she wrote about Hamburg for the Eternal Light radio program in 1958, he had with him seeds that he had brought from America—carrots, a vegetable that they may have known but had not culti-vated—and he taught the Yemenites how to plant and grow them. Soon they were packaging the carrots in cello-phane bags and selling them to the American troops in Germany. Suddenly there was employment, and the immi-grants were moving from tents into stucco houses.

"Papaya tastes best when eaten ripe and raw or in a fresh fruit salad," said Hungarian-born Rose Bilbool, who is eighty-seven years old. She should know. For fifty-five years, Dr. Papaya, as she is called, a licensed pharmacist with a doctorate in biochemistry, has been experimenting with the enzymes extracted from papaya in her laboratory in Jericho.

Born in Transylvania, Dr. Bilbool came to Palestine in 1938. Because of her photographic memory, she found work memorizing maps for the Hagana in 1939 and 1940. One day she was visiting Jericho when she saw an overturned jeep and decided to come to the victim's aid. The driver's flesh was cut up, and it occurred to her to use what was available. Earlier that day she had bought a papaya, a curiosity in those days. She cut it open and pressed it into the open cut. By the time the two arrived at a hospital, the bleeding had stopped.

The experience inspired Dr. Bilbool to explore the healing properties of papaya. She started with six papaya bushes in Jericho and propagated them into more than twenty-two hundred bushes. She makes cholesterol-reducing medicine, some cosmetics, and other items from the papayas she grows. Even during the height of the *intifada*, which lasted from December 1987 to the signing of the Oslo Accords, in 1993, when most Israelis did not feel welcome on the West Bank, Dr. Bilbool continued to drive alone to the laboratory six days a week. "The Arabs accept me, I love my work, and I am never afraid," she said. "If you breed goodness you will be part of the greatest kingdom—the human being's heart."

The Foods of
Israel Today

"Guacamole is the most un–Israeli recipe," said Gideon Meir, grandson of the late Golda Meir, prime minister of Israel from 1969 to 1974, when we spoke at a café in Tel Aviv. "Avocado is usually served in Israel simply chopped with lemon juice and sometimes garlic." Gideon, a harpsichordist, makes a wonderful salad with avocados, cucumbers, persimmons, and papaya. It is colorful, refreshing, and flavorful—a perfect salad for a party buffet. I serve it in a bowl lined with bright red radicchio leaves.

Avocado Salad with Cucumbers, Persimmons, Papaya, and Citrus

YIELD: 6 SERVINGS

1 persimmon, peeled and diced

1 papaya, peeled, seeds removed, and diced

1 long, crisp cucumber, sliced in rounds

1 grapefruit, peeled and diced

1 orange, peeled and diced

Juice of 2 lemons

1 clove garlic

1 tablespoon honey, or to taste

1/2 teaspoon salt, or to taste

Several grinds of pepper

4 tablespoons olive oil

1 avocado, peeled and diced just before serving

1/2 head radicchio

1. Put the persimmon, papaya, cucumber, grapefruit, and orange in a large nonreactive bowl.

2. Put the lemon juice, garlic, honey, salt, and pepper in a small bowl. Whisk in the olive oil, taste and adjust seasonings, then pour over the fruits. This can be done hours in advance. Add the avocado just before serving and blend well with your hands.

3. Serve in a salad bowl lined with the radicchio leaves.

Restaurant Diana's Fried Eggplant Salad

On a trip to Nazareth, where Jesus lived for thirty years, we visited the Church of the Annunciation. When the priest who was guiding us in the Grotto—Mary's home and the site of the Annunciation—learned that I was interested in food, he led us down to the crypt, where archaeologists had discovered the remnants of a stone fireplace that had been used as a kitchen in the time of Jesus. The priest showed us the charred area around the fireplace, indicating where vegetables and meat were roasted. He then directed us to Restaurant Diana, known in the city for great roast meats (see page 332) and for this eggplant salad.

YIELD: 4 TO 6 SERVINGS

2 large eggplants (about 2 pounds)

2 tablespoons kosher salt or other coarse salt

Olive oil for frying

1 medium onion, diced

1 hot green pepper, diced

4 cloves garlic, pressed

Salt and freshly ground pepper to taste

Juice of 1 lemon

12 ½-inch strips of roasted red bell pepper (see page 163)

2 tablespoons chopped fresh parsley or cilantro

1. Cut the eggplants into 2-inch cubes and put them in a colander. Sprinkle with the salt and let sit for about half an hour.

2. Rinse off the salt with cold water and pat the eggplant dry.

3. Heat about half an inch of olive oil in a heavy frying pan, then sauté half the onions and half the eggplant for about 7 minutes. Add half of the hot pepper and sauté for about 3 minutes more. Drain very well. Repeat with the second half of ingredients.

4. Put the eggplant in a ceramic or other nonreactive bowl with the garlic, salt and pepper to taste, and lemon juice. To serve, arrange the eggplant on a flat serving platter and decorate with the strips of roasted red pepper. Sprinkle with the fresh parsley or cilantro.

Jews from Romania and Transylvania are known for using garlic in mixed-meat grills and in salads, especially those with peppers and tomatoes, like this cook-ahead summer salad.

Transylvanian Pepper and Tomato Salad with Dill

YIELD: 4 TO 6 SERVINGS

2 tablespoons vegetable oil

2 large onions, diced (about 4 cups)

3 large green bell peppers, seeds removed, and cut in strips

3 large red bell peppers, seeds removed, and cut in squares

5 medium tomatoes, peeled and diced (3 cups)

1 tablespoon tomato paste

3 cloves garlic, finely chopped

Salt and freshly ground pepper to taste

2 tablespoons snipped fresh dill

1. Heat the oil in a frying pan and sauté the onions until translucent.

2. Add the green and red peppers and sauté until the liquid evaporates.

3. Add the tomatoes, tomato paste, and garlic and simmer for 15 minutes, stirring occasionally. Season with salt and pepper to taste. Let cool.

4. Arange the salad on plates or a platter and garnish with the dill before serving.

Tomatoes, peppers, and cucumbers—ingredients for an Israeli salad

It was a rule with my Romanian dressmaker that on Fridays she wouldn't work. One Friday I begged to come to try on clothes. The house smelled of garlic. She apologized that on Friday at noon she and her husband eat garlic with a lot of onions. She said, "We did this in Romania, and we do it in Israel. For years it has been found that garlic is very good for the stomach and cleaning the blood."

—Kena Shoval

Salads

171

Apio Ilado—
Bulgarian Celery Root and Carrot Salad with Dill and Pistachio Nuts

When Missada Bulgarit, the oldest grill restaurant in Be'er Sheva', opened in 1949, no one knew what a "grill restaurant" was in the then-desert army outpost. "The soldiers were afraid that our food was evil, that grilled meat might cast a spell on them," said Itzhik Halio, son of the founder and the present owner of the restaurant. "One brave soldier came alone and said, 'Either I'll die in the war or here,' so he ate in our restaurant." At the time Mr. Halio's partner decided the restaurant business was so risky that he got a job selling tickets at the only outdoor movie theater in town to supplement his meager income. Each evening when the movie was over, he stood outside telling the viewers they could eat delicious grilled food down the street; the hungry moviegoers headed to the restaurant for grilled meats, fresh vegetables, and pickles. Later, soups, fish, and salads were added to the menu.

One staple at the restaurant is the following Bulgarian salad, which appears in many versions throughout Israel. Sometimes the celery root and carrots are julienned, and sometimes they're cut in squares or in rounds, as they are in this recipe. Fresh dill and green pistachio nuts are sprinkled on top.

YIELD: ABOUT 6 SERVINGS

1 celery root (about 1 1/4 pounds), peeled

3 cups hot water

Juice of 2 lemons

1 tablespoon extra virgin olive oil

Salt and freshly ground pepper to taste

1 teaspoon sugar

6 coriander seeds

4 medium carrots, peeled and cut into 1/8-inch rounds

1/4 cup snipped dill

2 tablespoons whole green pistachio nuts, peeled

1. Peel the celery root and cut into 1/8-inch-thick slices, then, using a cookie cutter, into rounds 1 inch in diameter. Put in a bowl and cover with 2 cups of the hot water and the juice of 1 lemon.

2. Place the remaining cup water, the olive oil, remaining lemon juice, salt and pepper to taste, sugar, and coriander seeds in a medium saucepan and bring to a boil.

3. Drain the celery root and add, along with the carrots, to the boiling water. Simmer, covered, until al dente, about 10 minutes.

4. Strain the vegetables, reserving 1/2 cup of the cooking liquid. Discard the coriander seeds and place the vegetables in a small bowl with the reserved cooking liquid. Chill overnight to let the flavors blend. Sprinkle with dill and pistachio nuts before serving.

Fettush—Arabic Caesar Salad

*F*ettush is a Lebanese and northern Israeli salad made with roughly cut tomatoes, green bell peppers, onions, scallions, fresh mint, parsley, and watercress, or any wild green in bloom. The dressing is made with lemon juice, garlic, and olive oil. It sounds at first like any Israeli salad, but the addition of pita bread brushed with olive oil, sprinkled with *za'atar* (see page 62), and baked until crisp adds to the texture and flavor of this Arabic version of a Caesar salad. According to Adnan Abu Odeh, a Jordanian adviser to the king originally from Nablus, bread is not baked every day during Ramadan, so *fettush* was created as a way to use up day-old bread, soaking it in the dressing and serving it with the vegetables to break the daily fast. Today it is eaten during Ramadan and throughout the year. Many Jewish Israelis make a form of *fettush* with matzoh during Passover.

YIELD: 4 TO 6 SERVINGS

- 2 whole pita breads (or 2 matzohs)
- 3 tablespoons extra virgin olive oil
- 1 teaspoon *za'atar*, or to taste
- 2 tomatoes
- 1 green bell pepper
- 1 cucumber
- ½ medium onion
- 2 scallions, chopped (white and green parts)
- 1 cup watercress or any wild greens
- 1 handful (about ¼ cup) coarsely chopped fresh mint
- 1 handful (about ¼ cup) coarsely chopped fresh cilantro or parsley
- 1 clove garlic, minced
- 2 tablespoons lemon juice
- 1 teaspoon salt, or to taste
- ¼ teaspoon freshly ground pepper, or to taste

1. Preheat the oven to 350 degrees. Brush the pita breads with 1 tablespoon of the olive oil and sprinkle with ½ teaspoon of the *za'atar*. Bake on a cookie sheet for about 5 minutes or until crisp but not browned. (If you are using matzoh, follow these directions but toast in a 200-degree oven.)

2. Dice the tomatoes, pepper, cucumber, and onion into 1-inch chunks and put them into a salad bowl. Add the scallions, watercress, mint, and cilantro or parsley and toss together.

3. Put the garlic, lemon juice, salt, and pepper in a small bowl. Whisk in the remaining olive oil. Just before serving, pour the dressing over the vegetables and sprinkle with the remaining *za'atar*. Break up the pita and toss gently with the vegetables. Adjust seasonings and serve immediately.

Arcadia's Winter Endive and Walnut Salad with Goat Cheese

This salad comes from the Arcadia Restaurant in Jerusalem, located in a nineteenth-century stone house in a courtyard off a tiny winding street. The restaurant is run by two young Israeli chefs who, at astronomical prices, are turning out dishes like grilled foie gras with vanilla oil and quince and fish carpaccio with three kinds of oil. Born to an Iraqi family in Jerusalem, chef Ezra Kedem studied at the California Culinary Institute in San Francisco and at the French Culinary Institute in New York before returning to Israel. His partner, Tamar Blay, is a self-taught Israeli chef of Egyptian background. When they opened the restaurant together in 1995 it was an immediate success.

"I grew up with olives, sumac, the authentic foods of Jerusalem," said Ezra. "My neighbor was a Christian Arab. I smelled the flavors and spices of their home every day and was always fascinated by them. This led me to my interest in other kinds of food." What I like about this recipe is that Ezra pairs sophisticated, imported ingredients like Belgian endive and balsamic vinegar with local greens, local cheeses, and a pinch of local sumac, which adds color and flavor to the salad. He also uses *rashad,* wild greens from the mustard family.

· · · BIBLICAL GOATS AND THEIR CHEESE IN THE JUDEAN HILLS OF JERUSALEM · · ·

In most countries, food is separate from politics. But in Israel, *nothing* is separate from politics. Shai Seltzer became a cheese maker because of the 1973–1974 Yom Kippur War. Until then, this bearded man in his late fifties was a botanist at the Hebrew University. Today he raises about one hundred Nubian goats, the kind mentioned in the Bible, in a meadow in the Judean Hills, and he makes and sells his own goat-milk yogurt and cheeses. "I came here because I realized during the war that everything I did in my life was slipping through my fingers," he recalled while making yogurt, using a generator for electricity to heat the milk to the right lukewarm temperature. "Here I simply raise the goats, and with the milk I make the cheese."

On another visit, he waxed poetic as he showed me how to taste one of his aged goat cheeses wrapped in grape leaves. "Our mouth has a lot of senses," he said. "Put the cheese on the edge of your mouth. Feel how the tastes come along your mouth. Swallow and then feel the aftertaste, feel what the cheese contains."

His Tommes de Pyrenees, Gorgonzola, Camembert, and Limburger cheeses are so good they were served to a delegation of visiting American chefs. When asked why he is making kosher French cheese in Israel, he replied, "I can make anything here. There is not yet an Israeli cuisine. It is like somebody moving into a new house and moving his furniture all the time because he doesn't know how it fits. Is it a Moroccan dish or is it a Polish dish? Our cuisine is so mixed it will take another four generations to make a true Israeli food."

Meanwhile, Seltzer—and Israel—will keep experimenting, serving salads like the ones in these pages, accompanied by the delicious native cheese.

3 Belgian endives

1 bunch curly endive or chicory (about 2 cups)

1 bunch mustard greens, wild arugula, or watercress (about 2 cups)

¼ cup walnuts

6 ¼-inch slices goat cheese (about 4 ounces)

2 tablespoons balsamic vinegar

1 tablespoon fresh orange juice

1 tablespoon fresh lemon juice

6 tablespoons extra virgin olive oil

1 shallot, finely diced

Salt and freshly ground pepper to taste

Pinch of dried sumac

1. Rinse and dry the Belgian endives, curly endive or chicory, and greens, then cut them into bite-size pieces, leaving some of the chicory leaves whole for garnish. Place the greens in a salad bowl or on individual plates. Sprinkle with walnuts and top with the slices of goat cheese.

2. Put the vinegar, orange juice, and lemon juice in a separate bowl. Whisk in the olive oil and add the shallot, salt and pepper to taste, and sumac. Drizzle the dressing over the salad and serve.

Watercress and Herb Salad with Pine Nuts and Pomegranates

I first learned about this salad from chef Johanne Killeen of Al Forno Restaurant in Providence, Rhode Island, who tasted it on a trip to Jerusalem. Although Shai Seltzer uses wild greens, like *khubeiza,* I make it with watercress, arugula, purslane, and other leafy greens.

YIELD: 6 SERVINGS

8 cups of mixed greens—watercress, arugula, purslane, or other leafy greens, washed and dried well

4 tablespoons chopped fresh parsley

2 tablespoons chopped fresh dill

2 tablespoons chopped fresh basil

1 tablespoon chopped fresh mint

1 clove garlic, crushed

Juice of 1 lemon (about 2 tablespoons)

4 tablespoons olive oil

Salt and freshly ground pepper to taste

4 tablespoons pine nuts, toasted

4 tablespoons fresh pomegranate seeds

1. Cut the greens into 1-inch pieces. Add the parsley, dill, basil, and mint and toss well.

2. Mix the garlic, lemon juice, and 3 tablespoons of the olive oil together in a small bowl. Add salt and pepper to taste, and pour over the greens.

3. Heat a frying pan and pour in the last tablespoon of olive oil. Stir-fry the pine nuts in the pan until golden. Then sprinkle with the pomegranate seeds over the greens.

Salads

Hamutzim—
Pickled Vegetables

Pickling is very much part of life today in Israel. Cooks pickle everything from cucumbers to olives to baby eggplants to mango to carrots and cauliflower. But the Sephardic way of pickling vegetables in vinegar is rapidly replacing the more time-consuming classic method that people like Israeli author Meir Shalev's grandmother used to use.

This typical Kurdish recipe for *hamutzim* (pickled vegetables) comes from the late Naima Levy, known for her simple yet amazing vegetable alchemy.

YIELD: 2 QUARTS PICKLED VEGETABLES

About 5 pounds of vegetables, such as celery, carrots, cabbage, cauliflower, kohlrabi, zucchini, baby eggplant, winter squash, or bell peppers

6 quarts water

2 cups citrus vinegar

1 tablespoon turmeric

½ tablespoon hot paprika

2 tablespoons kosher salt

2 tablespoons dill, plus the dill head

1 head garlic (about 12–15 cloves), halved

1. Wash and prepare the vegetables. Cut the celery and zucchini into chunks or long, thin pieces. Peel and slice the carrots. Shred the cabbage into ½-inch slices. Separate the cauliflower into flowerets. Peel and slice the kohlrabi. Slice the squash or peppers into 2-inch slices. Cut off the stems of the eggplants, leaving them whole.

2. Heat the water in a large pot. Just before it comes to the boil add the celery, then the carrots. As soon as the water comes to a full boil add the vinegar, turmeric, hot paprika, salt, and the other vegetables. Return to boil, then turn the heat off.

3. Drain the vegetables, reserving the liquid, and place in two 2-quart jars. Tuck the dill, the dill head, and the garlic into the jars, then cover the vegetables with some of the vinegar-water solution. Close the jars tightly and refrigerate overnight before using.

NOTE   You can also add, as Syrian Jews do, a peeled and sliced beet to this solution, which will color the vegetables.

My grandmother made pickles in the Russian way, from cucumbers, salt, dill, and water. She never used vinegar. She placed the cucumbers in boiling water with 1 teaspoon salt so they would stay very crisp. Then she would take an egg from a henhouse. If the egg floated, there was too much salt. If it sank there was too little. She lined the pickles up on the window. My grandmother drank the cucumber water because she thought it was healthy.

—Meir Shalev

Moroccan Eggplant Salad with Pickled Lemon

I first tasted this elegant eggplant salad at a Sabbath dinner in Marrakesh, Morocco, at the home of Charles and Raymonde Elfassi, the last members of a famous rabbinic family still living in Morocco. The rest of the family, like the majority of Moroccan Jews, have emigrated to France or Israel, taking their family traditions and recipes with them. The Israeli branch of this family uses fresh lemon in the salad instead of the more common preserved lemon. Busy Israeli cooks have also begun to replace the carefully selected spices used in Morocco with the generic Yemenite spice combination of *z'hug*, the Moroccan *harissa*, or the Israeli *tavlanim*, which often includes cumin, coriander, and cinnamon.

YIELD: 6 SERVINGS

2 large eggplants, unpeeled (about 2 pounds)

2 tablespoons salt

Vegetable oil for frying

Juice of 1 lemon

4 cloves garlic, peeled and crushed

1 teaspoon ground cumin

1 teaspoon paprika

Dash of hot pepper flakes

2 tablespoons diced preserved lemon (see recipes below)

2 tablespoons chopped fresh parsley

1. Peel one of the eggplants and cut them both into ½-inch cubes. Toss them with the salt in a colander in the sink and allow to stand for 30 minutes. Rinse well with very cold water, squeeze the eggplant gently, and pat dry.

2. In a large frying pan, heat enough oil to coat the bottom of the pan. In 2 batches, stir-fry the eggplant until golden on all sides, about 7 minutes per batch, adding more oil as needed. Drain well on paper towels.

3. Toss the eggplant with the lemon juice, garlic, cumin, paprika, pepper flakes, and preserved lemon in a serving bowl. Let sit in the refrigerator for a day to absorb the flavors. Just before serving, sprinkle with the parsley.

And every meal-offering of thine shalt thou season with salt; neither shalt thou suffer the salt of the covenant of thy God to be lacking from thy meal-offering; with all thine offerings, thou shalt offer salt.

—Leviticus 2:13

All the heave-offerings of the holy things, which the children of Israel offer unto the Lord, have I given thee, and thy sons and thy daughters with thee, as a due for ever; it is an everlasting covenant of salt before the Lord unto thee and to thy seed with thee.

—Numbers 18:19

Salt is perhaps the most essential ingredient, its importance a constant throughout human history. Even the origin of its name attests to its significance; *milhama,* the word for "war" in Hebrew and Arabic, is rooted in the Hebrew word *melach* (salt). When the early Israelites were nomads, they used salt not only for seasoning and preserving foods but also as a sacred element in certain ritual practices. The Dead Sea Scrolls, documenting life in Qumran, once called the Salt City, illustrate the significance of salt. Today, the Bedouin tribes in the Negev Desert continue some of these ancient traditions, breaking bread and eating meat under a "salt covenant," which sanctifies an alliance among those present at the meal.

In a *midrash* that comments on the story of Lot and his wife in the Book of Genesis, Lot's wife goes to fetch salt for the angels who came to visit them in Sodom. Later, as she and her husband flee the burning city, she turns into a pillar of salt when, according to some interpretations, she cannot help looking back to gaze at the home she is leaving behind. A pillar of rock salt in the shape of a human figure still attracts visitors to the spot where Lot's unnamed wife is thought to have met her end.

Lot's city of Sodom was adjacent to the Yam Ha Melach (Sea of Salt), known as the Dead Sea, which contains eight times more salt than ocean water does. The Dead Sea is so dense with minerals, in fact, that it is impossible for a swimmer to sink. Today, the Dead Sea has become a spa center, as salt is also thought to cure many ailments.

The "salt covenant" between God and Israel, referred to a number of times in the Bible, recalls the salting of sacrifices in the Temple of Jerusalem. With the destruction of the Temple, the home table is as much God's table as the altar once was. Not only does salt recall the purity of God

and the Temple, it also can ward off evil spirits. In observance of the covenant, newborn infants were once rubbed with salt as a protection against demons, and many Jews sprinkle salt on bread when saying a prayer before each meal, and, on the Sabbath, dip challah in salt.

Alongside its religious significance, salt has been put to much practical use throughout the history of the land of Israel. In the hot climate of the region, the custom of salt-curing fish, vegetables, and meat was, before refrigeration, essential to the survival of the population.

Samaritans salting meat for sacrifice at Passover

Preserving lemons with salt is an ancient custom, one raised to a high art in Moroccan cooking. I love the flavor of the lemons, and I add them to many dishes. They are delicious in salads, in chicken with olives (see page 286), in a marvelous Moroccan brisket (see pages 310–11), and stuffed into the cavity of a simple roast chicken with garlic and fresh herbs. Long ago the lemons were weighted with stones to keep them submerged in the preserving liquid. In the following more contemporary method, the lemons sink with the weight of the salt. Because the lemon is preserved, you may eat the skin as well. I pickle a dozen at a time and keep them on my counter throughout the year, adding them to salads, fish, and meat recipes.

Classic Moroccan Method for Preserving Lemons in Salt

YIELD: 7–10 PRESERVED LEMONS

12–15 lemons

1/2 cup kosher salt (about)

1. Cut 7 of the lemons lengthwise, almost into quarters, leaving them intact at one end. You can also slice them thin.

2. Using your fingers, stuff as much salt as possible inside the lemons, close them, and place in a sterilized wide-mouthed 2-quart jar. Squeeze the juice of at least 4 lemons into the jar. Allow to stand, half covered, at least 1 week on the counter, shaking the bottle each day, or until the peels sink with the weight of the salt in the jar. Then add a few more salted lemons, lemon juice, and, if you like, olive oil to cover.

3. Close the jar and leave out on the counter for at least 3 weeks before using. When using the lemons, merely rinse with water, remove the seeds, and chop up for your recipes. Refrigerate after opening.

NOTE   For a flavorful variation, I sometimes add 4 crushed garlic cloves and 1 teaspoon of sweet paprika to the lemons.

Quick Method for Preserving Lemon

Once, in a panic, I called my friend Najmieh Batmanglij, the Persian cookbook writer—I needed preserved lemon for a recipe I was serving that night. She taught me this short-cut version of preserving the lemons, using salt and vinegar, which hastens the process. It worked just fine.

YIELD: 3 PICKLED LEMONS

3 lemons

3 tablespoons kosher salt

3 tablespoons white vinegar

3 cups spring water

1. Make a slit in each of the lemons halfway through the middle and stuff each with 1 tablespoon of the salt. Place the lemons in a sterilized wide-mouthed pint jar. Add the vinegar and water, leaving 1 inch at the top. Close.

2. Place the jar in a large pot filled with enough water to reach the neck of the jar. Bring the water in the pot and the water in the jar to a boil; reduce the heat and simmer for 30 minutes. Remove the bottle from the water, dry, cool, and use the lemons immediately.

Tunisian Squash Salad

Winter squash is a surprising ingredient in a salad, but this one is particularly delicious. This is one of those recipes where the intensity of the flavor of the squash or pumpkin makes or breaks the salad. I advise using a flavorful squash and adjusting the seasonings carefully before serving.

YIELD: 6 SERVINGS

1 pound butternut, calabash, kabocha, or buttercup squash

1/2 teaspoon sweet paprika

2 garlic cloves, pressed

1/2 teaspoon cinnamon

1 teaspoon sugar, or to taste

1 teaspoon salt

1 tablespoon olive oil

Juice of 1 lemon

1. Peel, seed, and dice the squash. Then cook in boiling water until tender, about 15 minutes. Drain, put in a mixing bowl, and mash coarsely with a fork.

2. Add the paprika, garlic, cinnamon, sugar, salt, olive oil, and lemon juice. Adjust the seasonings to taste. Serve chilled, on its own or with the couscous on page 237.

Jacqueline and Amran Dahan, owners of this popular Moroccan restaurant in Eilat, came to Israel from Casablanca in 1956, after the Sinai Campaign. Today their menu offers more than two dozen cooked salads. This is a versatile salad, in which you can substitute unpeeled eggplant for the zucchini, if you like.

Hallelujah Restaurant's *Marmouna*— Spicy Zucchini, Pepper, and Tomato Salad

YIELD: 6 TO 8 SERVINGS

2 tablespoons vegetable or olive oil

½ cup diced onion

2 large zucchini, cut in 2-inch strips

2 garlic cloves, halved

1 hot pepper, cut in strips

2 green bell peppers, sliced into thick rounds

4 large tomatoes, quartered, or one 28-ounce can of whole peeled tomatoes, with their juice

1 teaspoon sugar

1 teaspoon salt

¼ teaspoon saffron

¼ cup water

Fresh olives for garnish

1. Heat the oil in a large skillet and sauté the onion and zucchini until golden. Add the garlic, hot pepper, green peppers, tomatoes, sugar, salt, saffron, and water and bring to a boil. Reduce heat and simmer, very slowly, covered, for 1 hour. Uncover and cook slowly until the sauce thickens.

2. Serve at room temperature, garnished with olives.

Selecting squash in Mahane Yehudah

Salads

181

Israeli Lemony Cabbage Salad

I first tasted a version of this recipe at a now-closed Israeli restaurant in Philadelphia when I was leading a tour of the city's Jewish food sites for the International Association of Culinary Professionals. Our group, which included Julia Child, was served an Israeli breakfast with pita bread, *shakshuka* (see page 27), and this cabbage salad, which America's first lady of food kept praising. Since then I have tasted it many times in Israel, most recently at Zwilli's Fish Restaurant in Be'er Sheva'. A sweeter, American version of this salad, without oil or American mayonnaise, is called Health Salad. (See my *Jewish Cooking in America*.) It is made with lemon salt (ascorbic acid), often used to provide a lemony flavor, even when fresh lemons are available.

YIELD: 8 SERVINGS

1 whole cabbage (about 2 pounds), shredded

1 teaspoon lemon salt

Juice of 1 1/2 lemons

3 garlic cloves, crushed

1 tablespoon sugar

4 tablespoons vegetable oil

2 tablespoons chopped fresh parsley

1. Toss the cabbage with the lemon salt in a nonreactive bowl.

2. Mix the lemon juice, garlic cloves, and sugar in a small bowl and whisk in the oil. Pour the dressing over the cabbage and toss well. Cover and marinate in the refrigerator for several hours or overnight.

3. Just before serving adjust the seasonings and sprinkle the parsley on top.

J ust off the highway between Acre and the Amiad Junction, east of the turnoff to Safed in Upper Galilee, is Ein Camonim, one of the first cheese farms in Israel. Outside, near the barns and the cheese store, country-like tables are always laden with a welcoming basket of vegetables, an assortment of cheeses on a wooden platter, and homemade breads; classical music adds to the serene setting. Inside, a wood-burning stove warms winter guests, who nibble on the attractively prepared food that includes *labneh,* cheeses, and ice cream, all made on the premises. This is my version of the salad served to most visitors to Ein Camonim; it is delicious with a platter of cheeses.

Cabbage Salad with Capers at Ein Camonim, the Cheese Lover's Paradise in Upper Galilee

YIELD: 8 SERVINGS

- 1/2 head cabbage, shredded (about 1 pound)
- 2 carrots, peeled and grated (about 1 cup)
- 1 medium onion, grated (about 1 1/4 cups)
- 1 red bell pepper, grated
- 1 green bell pepper, grated
- 4 tablespoons balsamic vinegar
- 2 tablespoons sugar, or to taste
- 2 teaspoons Dijon mustard
- Salt and freshly ground pepper to taste
- 1/4 cup vegetable oil
- 1/4 cup extra virgin olive oil
- 2 tablespoons crushed olives
- 1 tablespoon capers

1. Put the vegetables in an attractive salad bowl.
2. Mix the vinegar, sugar, mustard, and salt and pepper to taste in a small bowl, then whisk in the oils. Spoon the dressing over the vegetables. Sprinkle the olives and the capers over the salad and toss well.

Salads

Asparagus with Jaffa Orange and Ginger Vinaigrette

This Israel-inspired recipe is good for a Passover seder, or for any springtime meal.

YIELD: 6 TO 8 SERVINGS

2 pounds fresh asparagus

4 tablespoons fresh orange juice

1 tablespoon fresh lemon juice

1 large clove garlic, crushed

1 teaspoon grated fresh ginger

Salt and freshly ground pepper to taste

4 tablespoons extra virgin olive oil

Black and white sesame seeds for garnish

1 orange, sliced, for garnish

1. Break off the bottom ends of the asparagus with your hands. Cook the spears in boiling salted water until tender, about 5 to 7 minutes. Remove with tongs and quickly transfer to a large bowl of ice water so the asparagus will retain its brilliant green color. Drain on paper towels and refrigerate, wrapped in a towel, up to 4 hours before serving.

2. Put the orange and lemon juices, the garlic, ginger, and salt and pepper in a small mixing bowl. Whisk in the oil.

3. Arrange the asparagus on a plate and drizzle with the vinaigrette. Garnish with the sesame seeds and orange slices.

Vegetables and Vegetarian Dishes

Not one vegetable is included in the seven crops mentioned in the Book of Deuteronomy. But through the ages, Crusaders, Ottoman conquerors, and pilgrims of all kinds coming to the Holy Land brought new vegetables, like onions, garlic, leeks, eggplant, tomatoes, and squash. In its more recent history, through immigration and irrigation, the land of Israel has come to yield almost every fruit and vegetable known to mankind.

Through trial and error, the early pioneers learned how to become effective, inventive farmers in the hot, dry climate. By the late nineteenth century, visitors who came to Palestine would remark on the number of different vegetables available, many of which were unknown in Europe at the time. These hot-weather vegetables included a light-green marrow squash often served stuffed, kohlrabi, and all kinds of wild greens including the most famous, a mallow called *khubeiza*.

And the parched land shall become a pool, and the thirsty land springs of water.

—Isaiah 35:7

Above: Preparing eggplants in so many different ways!

Bertha Spafford Vester, an American who grew up in Jerusalem at the beginning of the twentieth century, wrote in her wonderful memoir, *Our Jerusalem* (1950), "We had no potatoes, but rice and cracked wheat, cone sugar—solid and very pure—and plenty of vegetables. We never ate anything raw that was not peeled, or lettuce unless it was grown in our own garden. But we had radishes, and a squash called *coussa,* like vegetable marrow." Equally bountiful in modern Israel is the eggplant, served stuffed, baked, stewed, or roasted, in incarnations as varied as the Israeli cooks who prepare it.

In the early 1950s, with an influx of immigrants and the resulting demand for more advanced agricultural techniques, Israeli agronomists traveled abroad to learn more about farming. Upon their return, they introduced innovative techniques for cross-pollination and cross-breeding and began to expand the farmers' agricultural horizons. Now, decades later, endless varieties of ginger root, avocados, boutique tomatoes, and peppers are cultivated for use at home and abroad. Scientists at Ben-Gurion University in Be'er Sheva', for example, have begun to cultivate the Moroccan *terfeze,* a white truffle with a similar aroma to the European one but much milder, and intended to be eaten like a potato. Always pursuing new challenges, they are also starting to experiment with European black truffles.

Each vegetable's journey to Israel is a story in itself. Take the tomato exported under the Carmel brand name, one of Israel's signature crops. The boutique tomato was developed by Eddie Peretz, who was determined to make the Israeli tomato into a gastronomic star. Born in England, Mr. Peretz was raised on the Channel Islands of Guernsey and Jersey, which were famous for their greenhouse tomatoes. Although his Polish-born father believed that agriculture was an inappropriate occupation for a nice Jewish boy, Peretz persisted. He left the Channel Islands and spent the next twenty years building up the tomato industry in New Zealand before coming to Israel in 1968.

With the assistance of the Israeli government, Peretz traveled throughout Israel, searching for the right mixture of topography, soil, rainfall, and temperature until he found Yesha, a moshav established by Egyptian Jews near the Gaza Strip. He and his wife moved into a tiny house on the moshav, built a greenhouse, and planted their first crop. Eventually, their years of experience led them to a tomato that would stay red and flavorful for weeks. Even in the winter, when U.S. grocery stores are a tomato wasteland, Carmel tomatoes are ripe and available to those who will pay the price.

Today, because people are more health conscious and the climate in Israel is more conducive to a diet light on meat—which is expensive in this part of the world—many second- and third-generation Israelis of all backgrounds have gravitated to the lighter vegetarian cooking style of the Sephardic and Oriental Jews.

Rosh Pina Eggplant with Ginger and Soy Sauce

Since the eggplant was unfamiliar to many immigrants during the first half of the century, there was much ado as to how to prepare it appropriately. Dr. Erna Meyer, in her cookbook *How to Cook in Palestine,* wrote, "It is a prejudice that the bitterness of the egg plant can be removed by salting slices and drying in the sun. Egg plants which have been insufficiently watered while growing have a bitter taste and that is very difficult to remove. But such plants are not put on the market. If you understand by 'bitter' the characteristic taste of egg plant, that is, indeed, removed by salting. But with it are also removed valuable mineral substances and what is ultimately served is nothing but fried cellulose. Consequently: Deal with the egg plant as with every other vegetable according to the given recipes."

In Rosh Pina, I tasted this crisp eggplant dish as one of many antipasto salads at a tiny restaurant called Ja'uni, located in a nineteenth-century stone house built by Baron Edmond de Rothschild.

YIELD: ABOUT 6 SERVINGS

2 pounds baby eggplants (or 2 large eggplants), peeled

Olive oil for frying

1 inch ginger root, grated

2–3 tablespoons soy sauce

2 tablespoons honey

1. Cut the eggplant into julienne slices about 5 inches long.
2. Pour about 2 inches of olive oil into a frying pan or wok and heat to 375 degrees. Using about ½ cup of eggplant at a time, fry the strips until crispy, about 2 to 3 minutes per batch. Drain on paper towels, then place in a serving bowl.
3. Whisk together the grated ginger, soy sauce, and honey. Pour over the eggplant and mix well. Serve the dish immediately so that the eggplant stays crispy.

Until the twentieth century, many eastern European Jews were afraid to eat tomatoes. Some believed that because of its red color, the "love apple," as it was called, was filled with blood, and was therefore not kosher.

The Israeli author Shmuel Yosef Agnon came to Palestine from Galicia in 1908. In his slightly autobiographic novel *T'mol Shilshon* (Only Yesterday), set in Palestine, the main character, Itzhak, experiences a culinary culture shock. Part of his adjustment to the country is learning to eat its staples, such as olives and tomatoes:

"Itzhak did not know tomatoes are a food for humans, for in his town [in Galicia] people used to call tomatoes 'foolish apples' and clever people would avoid them. All of a sudden, Itzhak was hosted by others, and tomatoes were placed before him. All of a sudden, hunger came and told him—eat! He took a piece of bread and a few olives, one of the seven species with which the land of Israel is blessed, but could not touch a tomato. When he tasted the olives, he distorted his face in dislike. When his host saw him, he smiled and said, 'Just as you distorted your face from them today, so you will be happy for them tomorrow because you will be so hungry . . . there is nothing else to eat. Take a tomato and eat.' After Itzhak ate a slice of tomato, he could not continue. He thought, 'I will have none of your sweet and none of your sour acid.' His friend responded, 'If you want to be a son of the land of Israel, you must eat whatever you find.'" And so Itzhak, and immigrants like the author Agnon, became accustomed to the tomato, often cooked with fried eggplant . . . or with the biblical olive.

Maronite Bishop Paul Nabil Sayyah on his rooftop

The Foods of
Israel Today

Old City Eggplant with Tomato Sauce

Eggplant baked in tomato sauce may sound Italian, but it is also a universal everyday dish in Israel. Before tomatoes were cultivated in Israel in large quantities, people relied on canned tomatoes from the United States, either stewed or as paste. Today tomatoes are cooked fresh, or they are canned at home.

I spent one afternoon in the kitchen of the Maronite Church, just steps from the Jaffa Gate. This enchanting stone structure, tucked inside the Armenian Quarter, is also a hostel for visitors to Jerusalem. After I had tea with the bishop on a rooftop porch with a splendid view of the Old City, he led me into the kitchen, where his staff was making this typical Jerusalem eggplant casserole. The beauty of this version is that it doesn't involve deep-frying, as so many Middle Eastern eggplant recipes do.

YIELD: 6 TO 8 SERVINGS

2 large eggplant (about 2 pounds)

1 tablespoon salt, or to taste

2 tablespoons extra virgin olive oil

2 large vidalia or Spanish onions, sliced in rings

2 cloves garlic, minced

3 pounds fresh tomatoes (about 5 medium)

2 tablespoons tomato paste

1/2 teaspoon cinnamon

1/2 teaspoon freshly ground pepper

1/2 teaspoon sumac

1. Slice the eggplant lengthwise, then into 1/2-inch-wide strips. Put them in a colander over a mixing bowl, sprinkling salt over each layer. Let sit for a half hour.

2. Meanwhile, heat the olive oil in a frying pan. Sauté the onions until soft, about 5 to 7 minutes, stirring occasionally. Then add the garlic and sauté until the onions are golden and the garlic fragrant, about 5 more minutes. Place the onions and garlic in a 6-cup pot or flameproof casserole. Squeeze out the liquid from the eggplant and add it to the onions.

3. Remove the stems and quarter the tomatoes. Place the unskinned quarters in a food processor or blender and puree until smooth. Stir in the tomato paste, cinnamon, black pepper, and sumac. Pour over the eggplant and onion mixture. Bring to a boil, reduce the heat, and simmer slowly, uncovered, for 1 hour. Adjust seasonings to taste.

Bamiya (Okra) with Tomato

The first time I ever saw a garland of the seed pods of *bamiya,* or okra, drying on a string was in the market of the Jewish Quarter of Izmir, Turkey, many years ago. I brought some okra home, and they decorated my kitchen for almost a year. Since then, I have seen okra drying in homes in villages throughout Israel, hanging or spread out on flat baskets during the summer, the height of the okra season.

I tasted the following dish in Isfouiya, a Druse hilltop village near Haifa, where brothers Ruken and Yusef Mansur run a restaurant out of their home. Their mother, Haifa Mansur, is in her sixties and does the cooking in their family kitchen. Everything is home-cooked, including the bread, which is baked in an outdoor taboon oven. The Mansurs, whose family has lived in this village for five hundred years, still dress in traditional garb. On the day I visited, Mrs. Mansur was in a long blue dress and a white hat, sitting barefoot in their salon. Through an interpreter, she told me that she learned to cook from her mother. One of the important techniques to use when cooking okra, she said, is to dry them as she does and

Yusef and Ruken Mansur at their restaurant in Isfouiya

make sure the vegetable remains whole so that it does not become sticky or slimy. The tiniest are the tastiest. This recipe is equally delicious if you substitute eggplant or green beans for the okra, as the Mansurs sometimes do. It tastes great served with rice.

YIELD: 4 TO 6 SERVINGS

2 tablespoons extra virgin olive oil

1 large onion, diced

1 pound fresh okra

1 teaspoon dried oregano

1 teaspoon dried sage

2 tablespoons snipped fresh dill

2 tablespoons tomato paste

1 teaspoon sugar

1 teaspoon salt, or to taste

A few grinds of pepper

2 cups chopped, peeled tomatoes, fresh or canned

1. Heat the olive oil in a frying pan with a cover. Add onions and sauté until transparent. Add the okra, oregano, sage, dill, tomato paste, sugar, salt, and pepper, and cover with the tomatoes.

2. Simmer over low heat, covered, for 1 hour or until the liquid is almost evaporated.

Milhouliya or Swiss Chard with Fava Beans

When I visited Ghada Khawaija in her village of Nelli'im (see pages 100–1), she had just finished drying her okra and *milhouliya,* a green commonly used in Egyptian cuisine, which she often cooks with fava beans, garlic, olive oil, and lemon juice. Although many people in Israel today freeze vegetables, Ghada prefers to dry them. "It is healthier to follow what the old women do in this village," she said. Though *milhouliya* can be found in many Middle Eastern markets, I often substitute Swiss chard or fresh spinach.

YIELD: 6 SERVINGS

1 pound fresh or frozen *milhouliya* or fresh Swiss chard or spinach

1 pound fresh shelled, or frozen, fava beans

3 garlic cloves, crushed

2 tablespoons extra virgin olive oil

Juice of 1 lemon

1 teaspoon salt, or to taste

A few grinds of pepper

3/4 cup water

2 tablespoons chopped fresh cilantro

1. Clean the greens if fresh, pat dry, and chop. If frozen, defrost and squeeze out the liquid.

2. Place the fava beans, garlic, olive oil, lemon juice, salt, and pepper in a small saucepan with the water. Simmer, covered, for about 15 minutes or until the beans are tender.

3. Add the *milhouliya,* Swiss chard, or spinach with the cilantro and simmer gently another 5 minutes or until the greens are tender. Drain if necessary and serve hot or cold with rice.

Maachshi or Mimoulaim— Old Jerusalem Stuffed Vegetables

When I told Pini Levy, chef-owner of the restaurant Pini Bahatzer, that I was in search of the best stuffed vegetables in Israel, he said he didn't know about the whole country, but he promised me the best cook in Jerusalem. "The woman I know uses simple ingredients," he said. "But somehow her stuffed vegetables are the best of any I have ever tasted."

We set out to meet Esther Mizrachi at her daughter's apartment in French Hill, overlooking the Judean Hills. Mrs. Mizrachi, now in her late seventies, grew up in the Old City before the War of Independence. "Everything was hand prepared at home, including the macaroni and noodles," she recalled as she brought her stuffed vegetables out from the oven.

Esther Mizrachi with a clay cooking pot

"We didn't buy anything packaged and cooked on a Primus stove. There wasn't even a refrigerator. We made tomato sauce, wine from raisins and figs, and of course stuffed vegetables. My father had many Arab friends— they were neighbors, and worked together."

After the War of Independence in 1948, in which her father and her brother were both killed, Mrs. Mizrachi's family left the Old City and moved to Nahlaot, a stone courtyard community near the Jewish Mahane Yehuda market. She married and raised ten children, earning a living as a laundress. "I remember how things were so scarce that we stood on line for hours for water. If there was extra water, we used it for a shower. Then we washed the floor with it." All the time while she worked, she quietly found ways to stretch limited ingredients like bulgur, rice, and onions to feed her family. I asked if anyone knew about her cooking talent. "In those days, when you cleaned for other people, they were not interested in what you cooked for your own family," she said as she served us the following stuffed vegetables, which are simple yet sublime.

4 large onions	1/4 cup vegetable oil
5 baby eggplants	3 teaspoons salt, plus more for sprinkling
4 small zucchini	1/2 teaspoon freshly ground pepper
3 medium tomatoes	1 teaspoon powdered vegetable bouillon
2 cups short-grain rice	6 cups water, or to cover
1 stalk celery with the leaves, diced	1/2 teaspoon lemon salt (ascorbic acid)
2 heaping tablespoons tomato paste	

1. Bring 4 cups of water to a boil in a pot. Immerse onions in the boiling water for 5 minutes. Drain, cool slightly, and push out the inner rings, using a grapefruit knife if necessary, leaving 2 to 3 layers of rings on the outside. Sprinkle the inner layers with salt and set aside.

2. Prepare the other vegetables for stuffing. Cut off the stems of the eggplants and the zucchini and tunnel them out with an apple corer. Using a grapefruit knife or a spoon, remove and reserve the pulp, leaving a 1/2-inch wall.

3. Cut off the tops of the tomatoes and scoop out the insides, again reserving the pulp.

4. Dice the reserved onion pieces and place them in a mixing bowl with the rice. Add the celery, 1 tablespoon of the tomato paste, vegetable oil, salt, pepper, and bouillon and mix well. Dice the reserved pulp from the eggplant, zucchini, and tomato and add to the rice. Stuff the vegetable skins with the filling, using about 1/4 cup of filling per vegetable, depending on their size. Be sure to leave about an inch—or, as Mrs. Mizrachi says, "the space from the first joint on your thumb to the top of your nail"—to allow the rice to expand.

5. Layer the vegetables in a flameproof casserole. Stir the remaining tomato paste into 1 cup of the water and add the lemon salt. Pour over the vegetables, then add more water to cover. Set a heatproof plate on top to weight down the vegetables, then cover the casserole and bring to a boil on top of the stove. Lower the heat and simmer for a half hour.

6. Preheat the oven to 450 degrees. Move the pan of vegetables to the oven and bake, covered, for an additional half hour. Then reduce the temperature to 350 degrees. Uncover, remove the plate, and bake for about 1 hour more or until most of the water has evaporated.

Vegetables and
Vegetarian Dishes

Armenian Baby Eggplants Stuffed with Garlic and Cooked in Tomatoes

"My ancestors came here as a broken people from the Armenian massacre," said Haig Hagopian during a conversation I had with him in the Armenian Quarter of the Old City of Jerusalem. Today about fifteen hundred Armenians live in Jerusalem, with another two thousand scattered throughout the country. With the creation of the independent state of Armenia, more and more Armenian tourists are coming to visit Israel. Born in Jerusalem, Mr. Hagopian graduated from the Hotel and Catering Institute of Cyprus, then flew halfway around the world to San Francisco in order to study cooking at the California Culinary Academy. Today he is the food and beverage manager and executive chef at the Old City's Armenian Convent, where he cooks traditional and not-so-traditional Armenian dishes for between 130 and 150 priests, students in the seminary, and visitors and pilgrims. "Slowly, slowly, I have been learning from the old cooks," he said. "Although I miss all the restaurants in California, I like this place. If something happens to you here, other people share your sorrow with you. Even though everyone says it's more dangerous here, I feel safer."

This recipe is one of Mr. Hagopian's specialties, his version of an Armenian delicacy I first tasted in Jerusalem in the early 1970s and one I have been cooking for the past thirty years. It is one of those make-ahead dishes that tastes even better the next day, when the flavors have had a chance to meld, and is delicious served cold as an appetizer or as a vegetable side dish.

Old Jerusalem's rooftops

8 large tomatoes (about 4 pounds)

12 baby eggplants

12 large cloves garlic, quartered

4 tablespoons olive oil, plus additional as needed

1 large onion, sliced in thin rings

2 tablespoons tomato paste

1 green bell pepper, sliced in thick rings

1 cup cold water

1 tablespoon sugar

Salt and freshly ground pepper to taste

Juice of 1/2 lemon

2 tablespoons chopped fresh parsley

1. Plunge 6 of the tomatoes in boiling water for several minutes. Remove with a slotted spoon, cool slightly, and peel. Then seed and dice. Set aside.

2. Make 4 1-inch-deep slits in the middle of each of the eggplants. Stuff each pocket with a quarter clove of garlic.

3. In a large ovenproof skillet with a cover, heat 3 tablespoons of the oil. Brown the eggplants on all sides until golden, adding more oil as necessary. Remove from the skillet, drain on paper towels, and set aside.

4. In the same pan, heat the remaining 1 tablespoon of oil. Add the onions and sauté until translucent, about 5 to 7 minutes.

5. Add the chopped tomatoes and sauté with the onions for a few minutes. Add the tomato paste, green bell pepper, water, sugar, and salt and pepper to taste. Bring to a boil and add the eggplants. Reduce the heat, cover, and simmer slowly for 40 minutes or until the eggplants are tender. If the sauce is too thin, remove the eggplants and reduce the sauce by boiling over high heat until thickened. Return the eggplants to the pot. Taste and adjust the seasonings.

6. Preheat the oven to 375 degrees. Slice the remaining 2 tomatoes and arrange the slices on top of the eggplants. Bake, uncovered, for 15 minutes, until the tomato slices are slightly browned.

7. Just before serving, sprinkle the lemon juice and the parsley over the top.

Vegetables and
Vegetarian Dishes

Dona Flor's Vegetarian Eggplant Moussaka

This recipe, adapted from one of Israel's leading catering companies, is an excellent example of how varied ethnic recipes have made their way into "Jewish" cooking. The Greek moussaka, usually made with meat and a creamy béchamel sauce, is a "no-no" in kosher cooking, but this vegetarian version is a particularly popular dish in the land of abundant eggplants. There are many versions of moussaka in Israel—those with meat and no cream sauce (see page 333), those with cream sauce and no meat, and, for eaters who do not observe the dietary laws, those with both meat and cream. Although Dona Flor Caterers uses fresh tomatoes year-round, I use only fresh tomatoes for this dish during the summer. Because moussaka is a great dish for all seasons, I have given the choice of using either fresh or canned tomatoes.

YIELD: ABOUT 10 SERVINGS

4 pounds eggplant (about 4 large)

4 tablespoons salt

1/2 cup extra virgin olive oil (about)

2 large onions, chopped (about 2 cups)

4 garlic cloves, minced

Salt and freshly ground black pepper to taste

2 pounds fresh tomatoes, peeled, seeded, and chopped or 28-ounce can plum tomatoes, chopped

1 cup dry red wine

2 tablespoons tomato paste

1/4 cup finely chopped fresh parsley

4 tablespoons bread crumbs

4 tablespoons butter

6 tablespoons flour

3 cups milk

1/2 teaspoon nutmeg

A few grinds of fresh pepper

2 large egg yolks, lightly beaten

3 ounces goat cheese

1. Wash and dry the eggplants and remove the stems. Cut the eggplant into 1/2-inch-thick rounds. Sprinkle with salt and leave for an hour in a strainer. Then rinse the slices with water, squeeze them gently to remove any liquid, and pat them dry.

2. Heat a skillet with a thin film of olive oil. Brown the eggplant slices lightly in the oil, a few minutes on each side, adding more oil as needed. Drain eggplant on paper towels.

3. Sauté onions in a few tablespoons of olive oil until transparent. Add the garlic and season to taste with salt and pepper.

4. Stir tomatoes and their liquid into the onions. Continue cooking gently for 5 minutes.

5. Mix the wine with the tomato paste. Add to the onions and tomatoes and simmer over low heat, uncovered, for about 20 minutes or until the sauce has thickened. Add some of the chopped parsley and season to taste. You should have about 4 cups of sauce.

6. Preheat the oven to 350 degrees and grease a 9-by-13-inch baking dish with olive oil. Sprinkle the bread crumbs over the bottom.

7. Arrange a layer of eggplant in the dish, then spoon half the tomato sauce on top. Add another layer of eggplant and the remaining tomato sauce. Top with the remaining eggplant rounds.

8. Melt the butter over low heat in a saucepan and stir in the flour with a wooden spoon. Stirring constantly, cook for 1 or 2 minutes, being careful not to brown. Gradually add the milk. Bring slowly to a boil and simmer for 5 minutes, stirring all the time, until the sauce is smooth and creamy.

9. Remove the white sauce from the heat and season to taste with nutmeg, salt, and pepper. Put the egg yolks in a bowl, crumble in the goat cheese with your fingers, and fold into the white sauce. Pour the sauce over the eggplant and bake for about 1 hour.

Trudging home with groceries for dinner

Roasted Pepper

Pashtida

A version of this roasted-pepper pie appeared on the cover of Nira Rousso's 1994 cookbook *100 Pashtidot shel Nira Rousso* (100 Casserole Dishes from Nira Rousso). A *pashtida,* the name of which comes from the Polish word *pashtet* and means "layers of," is a one-pot dish that can range from a casserole to a kugel to a layered moussaka.

YIELD: 8 TO 10 SERVINGS

10 red, yellow, and green bell peppers

1 teaspoon salt, or to taste

A few grinds of pepper

6 ounces Swiss Emmenthaler cheese, sliced

3 tablespoons unsalted butter

3 tablespoons unbleached all-purpose flour

1 cup milk

2 large eggs, lightly beaten

1. The night before you plan to prepare the dish, preheat the oven to 450 degrees. (If you need to make the dish quickly, follow the directions in step 2 after roasting the peppers.) Place the peppers horizontally, not touching, on a jelly-roll pan or other baking sheet with sides. Roast for about 25 to 30 minutes until soft. During roasting, turn each pepper a couple of times to ensure even cooking. When the peppers are soft, turn off the oven and let them sit overnight. This is important, because you want the skins to be very dry.

2. In the morning take the peppers out and carefully peel off the skin from each pepper. The skins will come off easily, and much of the extra liquid from the peppers will drain into the pan. (If you cannot leave them overnight, when the peppers are finished roasting, remove them to a plastic bag, seal the bag, and let the peppers cool for at least 10 minutes. Peel the skin from each pepper. You must then carefully squeeze out any excess water and dab them dry with a paper towel.) Remove the seeds carefully, keeping the peppers in 1 or 2 pieces.

3. Lay half the peppers open, insides up, in the bottom of a 9-inch glass pie plate, arranging them to vary color and overlapping to completely cover the pie plate. Sprinkle with the salt and pepper.

4. Layer the cheese slices over the peppers in the pie plate. Set aside.

5. Preheat the oven to 350 degrees.

6. Heat the butter in a small frying pan, stir in the flour, and cook for several minutes until slightly colored, stirring occasionally to form a roux. Slowly add the milk to the roux and stir to heat through, then remove a half cup, cool slightly, and mix with the eggs. Gradually add the egg mixture to the roux, stirring constantly until the sauce is thick and smooth. Season with additional salt and pepper

to taste. Spoon the sauce over the cheese. Encase the top of the pie with the remaining roasted peppers, overlapping to cover completely.

7. Bake in the oven for 40 minutes. Remove and cool slightly. Drain off any excess fluid that has accumulated. Place a serving plate over the pie plate and carefully flip the pie, turning it out onto the platter. Serve warm, sliced into wedges.

NOTE   You can also layer the cheese with 6 ounces of sliced smoked salmon or 12 ounces of sautéed mushrooms.

· · NIRA ROUSSO AND THE EMERGENCE OF ISRAELI CUISINE · · ·

For several years I had been corresponding with Nira Rousso, the author of eleven cookbooks and a food columnist for *Ha'aretz,* Israel's only morning newspaper—but we had never met. She kept inviting me to visit her in her "little paradise" outside of Tel Aviv. When, on a trip to Israel in 1993, I told an army general friend that I was invited for dinner at Nira Rousso's house, he was visibly impressed. "Nira Rousso! I read everything that she writes. You are going to have dinner prepared by her?" A few short years ago, hardly a single Israeli, much less a general, would have been impressed at the idea of going to a national food writer's home. Things certainly have changed!

Nira Rousso, I soon learned, is at the center of an exciting culinary combustion. Unlike so many Israelis who dwell in apartments, Nira and her American husband, Louis, live in a white stucco, single-family home in Ramat Hashavim, a suburb of Tel Aviv. As we stepped through the gate to their home, the fragrance of jasmine filled the air. Guava, apple, Chinese lychee, kumquat, mango, and all manner of citrus trees grew in the garden. Of course, the Roussos also cultivate the native olives, figs, grapes, and pomegranates. The Roussos' one rooster, two guinea fowls, three dogs, four cats, and one partridge strutted and squawked nearby.

Inside the house, with its sunken living room and Italian tiled kitchen, the music of Stan Getz was playing. Bright blue Hebron glass objects were sparkling on the windowsill. Nira was busy cooking dinner for us in a kitchen filled with jars of grains and herbs picked from her garden. At the same time, she was finishing a *tarte tatin* for her daughters Ruth and Dania, both of whom were in the army at the time.

Flowers from the garden were in the center of the dinner table, with two pitchers of refreshing lemonade—one flavored with rose geranium and mint, and a second colored pink with a splash of homemade plum *coulis.* The menu for dinner was a sampler of the latest innovative Israeli food, including an edible fan made from Moroccan *cigare* wrappers and chicken, marinated in balsamic vinegar and olives and then baked with fennel, garlic, and currants (see page 290). Often the inspiration for Nira's recipes—like the stunning pepper *pashtida* (casserole-pie), seen on this page, that she prepared, using grilled peppers as the casing instead of a flour crust—comes from her travels. "This constantly working channel in my head is always tuned to food ideas," she said. "For me, though, the art is to adapt what I learn from abroad and to cook from what I have in my country."

During dinner, Nira talked at length about Israeli cooking. "Years ago, a visit to a New York supermarket was a cultural experience for me," she said. "Now we can get all those exotic ingredients in our own markets. Our food is not just Mediterranean. It is a mixture of eastern European, Moroccan, Hungarian...it's all there. When I was a child I lived in an apartment house in Ramat Gan [a suburb of Tel Aviv]. In that one building there were thirty cuisines represented. That is what Israeli food is."

Kibbutz Ma'ayan Baruch's Zucchini *Pashtida*

On a visit to friends at Kibbutz Ma'ayan Baruch in Upper Galilee, we tasted this delicious *pashtida* with zucchini and fresh herbs. It is very reminiscent of a Sephardic *frittada*.

YIELD: ABOUT 8 SERVINGS

3 medium onions, chopped (about 2 cups)

6 tablespoons vegetable oil

4 small zucchini (about 1 1/2 pounds)

1 teaspoon salt

1/2 cup water

3 large eggs, lightly beaten

1 1/2 cups all-purpose flour

1 teaspoon baking powder

Salt and freshly ground pepper to taste

4 tablespoons mixed fresh garden herbs like dill, oregano, mint, basil, and chives

1. Preheat the oven to 350 degrees and grease a 6-cup casserole.

2. Sauté the onions in 2 tablespoons of the oil in a small frying pan until they are soft and starting to turn golden. Remove and set aside.

3. Grate the zucchini; sprinkle with 1 teaspoon of salt and place in a strainer set over a bowl for a half hour. Then press to remove the liquid from the zucchini.

4. Transfer the zucchini to a mixing bowl. Add the onions and stir well. Add 3 more tablespoons oil, the water, and eggs and beat so that the ingredients do not separate. Mix the flour, baking powder, salt and pepper to taste, and fresh herbs together in another bowl. Fold these ingredients into the egg mixture until well incorporated.

5. Spoon the mixture into the casserole dish. Flatten with a spatula and brush with the remaining tablespoon oil. Bake for 50 minutes or until golden and set.

NOTE   For a crunchier texture, you can substitute 1/2 cup of semolina for 1/2 cup of the flour.

Mushroom Roulade

When I lived in Israel in the 1970s, one of my great pleasures was to hunt wild mushrooms in the Judean Hills around Jerusalem after the rains. Edible mushrooms were first discovered in Palestine resting on the substrate of unusable straw that remained after the cotton harvest. Today there are one thousand natural varieties of mushrooms growing in Israel, including two hundred edible strains. A new taste for mushrooms came with the immigrants from the former Soviet Union. These immigrants call the search for wild mushrooms the "third hunt," after animal hunting and fishing. Today, gourmet fungi like portobello and forest mushrooms are being cultivated in the north.

Mushroom roulade is a typical Israeli appetizer and sometimes main course. This Romanian version comes from my friend Colette Avital, a member of Knesset.

YIELD: 8 SERVINGS AS A FIRST COURSE OR SIDE DISH

2 cups milk

2½ tablespoons unsalted butter

6 tablespoons flour

4 large eggs, separated

½ teaspoon salt

¼ teaspoon freshly ground pepper

7 tablespoons grated Parmesan cheese

1 onion, diced

1 pound fresh mushrooms, wild or commercially grown

1 cup sour cream

¼ cup snipped fresh dill

1. Heat 1 cup of the milk and ½ tablespoon of the butter in a medium saucepan. Sprinkle 4 tablespoons of the flour in the other cup of milk. Stir until the flour is dissolved, then slowly stir this mixture into the hot milk. When the sauce thickens and separates from the sides of the pan, remove from the heat and let cool. Gradually stir in the egg yolks, mixing well, and add the salt, pepper, and 4 tablespoons of the Parmesan cheese.

2. Beat the egg whites until stiff and fold into the batter.

3. Preheat the oven to 350 degrees and grease and flour a jelly-roll pan lined with aluminum foil. Pour the batter into the pan, spreading evenly with a spatula, and bake for about 40 minutes or until golden.

4. If you want to refrigerate the baked dough overnight, flip the pan over onto a towel, then roll the dough up while still warm, cover in plastic wrap, and chill.

5. To make the filling, dice the onion and mushrooms and sauté them in the remaining 2 tablespoons of butter. Add the remaining 2 tablespoons of flour and all but 1 tablespoon of the sour cream, the dill, salt and pepper to taste, and 2 tablespoons of the Parmesan cheese.

6. Spread the mushroom mixture over the dough. Then roll up the roulade lengthwise, trim the edges, and smear the top with the remaining tablespoon of sour cream. Sprinkle on the remaining tablespoon of Parmesan cheese. Transfer to the jelly-roll pan and heat in a 350-degree oven for a few minutes before serving.

Marhooda— A Moroccan Potato *Pashtida*

Stories abound of the arrival of the potato in Jerusalem. Some believe that the German emperor Frederick, when he came to Jerusalem in the mid-nineteenth century, dined with the sisters at the German orphanage for girls and, in return, asked them what they would like him to send from Germany. All they wanted were potatoes—and potatoes they received! The emperor supposedly made a gift of two barrels of potatoes to the orphanage, and the tuber has been cultivated in Israel ever since.

Although the above story may have some truth to it, there were probably many groups who brought and planted potatoes in the nineteenth century and possibly earlier. The descendant of the first Romanian pioneer to Rosh Pina told me this potato legend, handed down in his family: "'Let's grow potatoes,' suggested one pioneer. Someone else, also coming from the colder central European climate, added, 'How can you grow potatoes in a place like this?' Despite the conditions, the farmers planted potatoes. When the tubers did not appear, they decided to resow the land and plant something new. But when the farmers started to dig, they found, to their surprise, potatoes growing beneath the ground."

One moving story about the potato came to me from food columnist Nira Rousso. Once Nira received a letter from an elderly man asking for a recipe for *mandeburchinik,* which he said was a potato bread, slightly heavier than a kugel. Also called *potatonik* (see my *Jewish Cooking in America*) and *bulbavnik,* it was the symbol of Galicia (the corner of Poland and the Ukraine that was part of the Austro-Hungarian Empire) cuisine before World War II. "He wrote that he wanted to re-create the flavor of his childhood kitchen, which was wiped out in one day by the Nazis," she told me. "I published the request because the letter was charming and I was touched by it." To her surprise, accounts of pre-Holocaust memories piled into her office. One man poignantly wrote that *potatonik* was baking in the oven when the Gestapo came into his house and took his mother away.

The following potato *marhooda,* a Moroccan kugel with potatoes or other vegetables and eggs, is similar to *potatonik,* but without the yeast. It comes from Argentinian-born Naomi Silberman Sisso, who is married to Shmuel Sisso, the former mayor of Kiryat Yam. Like many women married to Moroccan men, Naomi has adopted the cuisine of her husband's family. This potato dish, popular with both Jewish and Arab Moroccans, can be served at Passover as well as holidays throughout the year. It is a favorite of Naomi's four children.

5 large potatoes, peeled (about 3 pounds)	2 tablespoons fresh chopped parsley
6 large eggs	1/2 teaspoon turmeric
2 teaspoons salt	6 cloves garlic, mashed
A few grinds of pepper	1 onion, grated
1 teaspoon cumin	

1. Preheat the oven to 350 degrees and grease a 9-by-13-inch baking pan.

2. Place potatoes in a saucepan in water to cover. Bring the water to a boil and simmer, uncovered, about 20 minutes or until the potatoes are soft. Drain and mash the potatoes.

3. Beat the eggs until frothy. Add the salt, pepper, cumin, parsley, turmeric, garlic, and onion. Fold in the potatoes and mix well.

4. Spread in the baking pan and bake in the oven for about 50 minutes or until the top is golden and crusty and the potatoes spring away from the sides of the pan. Cool slightly before cutting.

Grandson of the first immigrant to Rosh Pina

Vegetables and
Vegetarian Dishes

The story of Judah Maccabee and his brothers overpowering the fierce Syrian army so appealed to the nationalism of the early Zionists that they turned Hanukkah, traditionally a minor religious holiday, into a patriotic festival. In the ancient world, Hanukkah was as much a celebration of the olive and its juice as it was of the miracle of the oil. "In Israel it is obvious that Hanukkah is connected with olive oil," said David Eitam, director of the Olive Oil Industry Museum in Haifa. "It celebrates the famous miracle in 164 B.C.E., when Judah Maccabee and his brothers found a drop of oil in the Temple of Jerusalem after it had been devastated by the Syrians. It lasted not one but eight days, and it was assuredly olive oil,

since the olive tree has been common in Israel since the time of Adam and Eve." To this day, traditional Jews light Hanukkah menorahs with olive oil instead of candles, as a reminder of the olive oil used in the Temple in Jerusalem.

More and more, Israelis celebrate not only the miracle of the oil but also its seasonal harvest. With it, they cook symbolic fried dishes, making Israel the international center of latkes, or *levivot,* the generic term in Hebrew for all manner of vegetable or flour pancakes.

A boy lighting Hanukkah candles in the dining room of a Youth Aliyah village

Apple-Potato Latkes

Latke, a Yiddish term used today in Israel by the very old immigrants from eastern Europe and new immigrants from the United States and the former Soviet Union, describes a particular type of grated or mashed potato pancake. (See my *Jewish Holiday Kitchen* and *Jewish Cooking in America.*) Most Israelis, when referring to latkes, use the term *levivot.* Potato latkes, which probably originated in late-eighteenth-century Eastern Europe or Germany, reflect the Ashkenazi tradition in Israel. Efrat Rabinovitch, whose husband, Itamar, was the ambassador of Israel to the United States, makes her latkes with this unusual combination of apple and potatoes, a recipe that was handed down to her from her mother, who was born in Poland.

YIELD: 10 3-INCH PANCAKES

1 pound russet potatoes, peeled

1 full-flavored apple such as Granny Smith or Fuji, peeled

1 large egg, lightly beaten

¼ cup all-purpose flour (about)

1 teaspoon salt

A few grinds of pepper

Vegetable or peanut oil for frying

Confectioners' sugar for sprinkling (optional)

1. Grate the potatoes and the apple into a mixing bowl, working quickly to avoid discoloration. You can also use a food processor fitted with a grating blade. Squeeze out and drain any accumulated liquid. Quickly add the egg, flour, salt, and pepper and mix thoroughly.

2. Heat about ½ inch of oil in a large skillet over medium-high heat.

3. Drop the batter in dollops of 3 tablespoons each, flattening each pancake with a spatula.

4. Cook about 3 to 4 minutes until the first side is brown, then flip the pancakes and cook until the second side is brown. Drain on paper towels and continue with the rest of the batter.

5. Serve as is or sprinkled with confectioners' sugar.

Aharoni's Pan-Sephardic Leek Latkes (*Keftes de Prassas*)

Chef Israel Aharoni's updated version of this typical Sephardic leek patty is much more flavorful than the original Balkan leek fritter, traditionally served at both Hanukkah and Passover.

6 leeks (about 2 pounds)

1 teaspoon salt, plus to taste

2 tablespoons extra virgin olive oil, plus ¼ cup for frying

1 large onion, diced

6 cloves garlic, diced

4 shallots, diced

⅓ cup pine nuts

½ bunch fresh cilantro, chopped (about 1 cup)

2 large eggs, lightly beaten

⅓ cup grated Kashkeval or Parmesan cheese

A few grinds of pepper

½ cup bread crumbs or matzoh meal, plus ⅓ cup for coating

1. Slice the leeks lengthwise and wash well to remove the grit. Bring a large pot of water to a boil. Add the salt and leeks and simmer for 5 minutes. Remove and cool.

2. Dice the white and some of the green of the leeks into small pieces, about ½ inch thick. Drain well, pressing the leeks in a dish towel to dry and remove any excess water.

3. Heat 2 tablespoons of the oil in a frying pan and add the onions, garlic, and shallots. Sauté until soft, about 5 minutes.

4. Preheat the oven to 350 degrees. Scatter the pine nuts on a baking sheet and toast in the oven for a few minutes, until evenly browned.

5. Place the leeks, onions, garlic, shallots, pine nuts, cilantro, eggs, and cheese in a mixing bowl and blend well, adding salt and pepper to taste. Add about ½ cup bread crumbs, or enough to bind the ingredients together.

6. Take about ¼ cup of the leek mixture and form a patty 2 inches in diameter. (For cocktail-size patties, use 1 heaping teaspoon of mixture. This will make a latke about ¾ inch in diameter.) Coat each patty with bread crumbs and repeat until all the batter is used up.

7. Coat a nonstick frying pan evenly with some of the remaining olive oil and fry the patties a few at a time, for 2 to 3 minutes on each side. Drain on paper towels.

Mushroom, Pecan, and Wild Rice *Levivot* Topped with Smoked Salmon and Pickled Ginger

"The first time I ever heard of a full Hanukkah meal was in the United States," said Hava Volman, an Israeli caterer living in Brooklyn. "In Israel we ate latkes all year round and also at Hanukkah." Vegetable fritters like Hava's very inventive mushroom-pecan-wild-rice levivot topped with smoked salmon and pickled ginger would not have been possible even five years ago, because until recently gourmet products like wild rice and pickled ginger were nonexistent in Israel.

YIELD: ABOUT 10 LATKES

3 tablespoons extra virgin olive oil

10 ounces white mushrooms

1 teaspoon fresh thyme

Salt and freshly ground pepper to taste

1/2 cup cooked wild rice

1/2 cup toasted chopped pecans

1 tablespoon sour cream

1 large egg, beaten

3 tablespoons matzoh meal

3 tablespoons snipped fresh dill

3/4 teaspoon grated lemon zest

1 teaspoon ground cardamom

1/2 teaspoon ground nutmeg

Smoked salmon for garnish

Pickled ginger for garnish

1. Heat 2 tablespoons of oil in a nonstick frying pan, add the mushrooms, and sauté for 5 minutes or until soft. Add the thyme and salt and pepper to taste. Place in a food processor fitted with a steel blade and pulse just until the mushrooms are chopped.

2. Transfer the mushrooms to a mixing bowl. Add the wild rice, pecans, sour cream, egg, matzoh meal, dill, lemon zest, cardamom, and nutmeg and mix well.

3. Coat a nonstick frying pan with the remaining tablespoon of oil and heat. Take heaping tablespoons of the latke batter and drop into the hot pan, flattening each slightly with a spatula, and fry for a few minutes on each side. Drain on paper towels. Repeat with the remaining batter. Garnish with strips of smoked salmon and pickled ginger, and serve.

Vegetables and Vegetarian Dishes

Corn-Scallion Latkes with Chipotle Cream

"Ascalon [*sic*] is mentioned by Strabo [the Greek geographer and historian] as famous for its onions, and it enjoys at this day a reputation for the same root, which is considered by the neighboring peasants as a delicious article of food."

This quote comes from the diary of Lady Hester Lucy Stanhope, a British woman who lived in the Sinai Desert and traveled throughout Palestine in the nineteenth century. Scallions, like all modern onions, were originally a form of Egyptian onion, and were brought by the Crusaders from the Holy Land to Europe.

Sweet corn, on the other hand, is a newcomer to Israel. When I lived in Jerusalem, the ears were huge, had to be boiled for an hour, and were still tough like cattle corn. In fact, Israeli corn was raised primarily to feed chickens. Today, one still encounters merchants in marketplaces squatting and roasting this tasteless corn over charcoal braziers, and vendors hawking it at the beaches.

So it is no wonder that caterer Hava Volman, who moved to Brooklyn from Israel as an adult, was thrilled with the sweet corn she found in the United States. In this latke recipe, she marries the familiar scallion of her childhood with ingredients from Brooklyn's Asian and Hispanic markets, and the fresh American corn.

Fresh and ground spices at a shop on Levinsky Street in Tel Aviv

YIELD: 20 LATKES

1 cup corn kernels (cut from 2 or more ears blanched fresh corn)

1/2 medium onion, grated (about 1/2 cup)

2 scallions, chopped

1/3 cup finely chopped red bell pepper

1 tablespoon grated ginger

1 clove garlic, chopped

1 teaspoon snipped fresh dill

1/2 teaspoon chopped fresh cilantro, or to taste

1 teaspoon ground cumin

1 teaspoon salt, or to taste

A few grinds of pepper

1/2 cup matzoh meal

1/2 teaspoon baking powder

2 large eggs, separated

5 tablespoons canola or other frying oil

1. Put the corn in a mixing bowl along with the onion, scallions, red pepper, ginger, garlic, dill, cilantro, cumin, salt, pepper, matzoh meal, baking powder, and egg yolks. Mix well.

2. Beat the egg whites until stiff and fold into the corn batter.

3. Heat the oil in a heavy frying pan. Carefully spoon heaping tablespoons of the corn batter into the pan and fry, a few at a time, for about 2 minutes on each side. Drain on paper towels. Serve unadorned or topped with a dollop of Chipotle Cream (see following recipe).

Chipotle Cream

YIELD: 1 CUP CHIPOTLE CREAM

1 cup sour cream

1 chipotle or jalapeño pepper

1 tablespoon lime juice

Salt and freshly ground pepper to taste

Place all the ingredients in a food processor fitted with a steel blade and puree.

Bavly's Vegetable Patties with Eggplant, Zucchini, Carrots, and Potatoes

When I lived in Jerusalem, one of my favorite lunch spots was a vegetarian restaurant called Bavly's. I loved its myriad of eggplant salads, interesting vegetable side dishes, and fried vegetable patties, which were better than any I have tasted elsewhere. In those days, Lebanese-born Bavly—I never knew his first name—also ran the eating concession at the Israel Museum cafeteria. Although Bavly's is long gone, I have been trying to get the recipe for these vegetable fritters for years. With the help of a former cook at the restaurant, I finally tracked down the ingredient list. A little experimenting did the rest. These are the best!

YIELD: 20 PATTIES

6 zucchini (about 1 1/2 pounds)

1 large eggplant, peeled (about 1 pound)

2 tablespoons salt, or to taste

1 medium onion

1 medium potato, peeled

1 large carrot, peeled

2 large eggs, lightly beaten

1/2 cup flour or matzoh meal

2 tablespoons chopped fresh parsley

1 tablespoon chopped fresh mint or 1 teaspoon dried mint

A few grinds of pepper

Vegetable oil for frying

1. By hand or using a food processor fitted with the grating blade, grate the zucchini and eggplant. Place both in a strainer over a bowl, sprinkle liberally with the salt, and drain for a half hour. Wash off the salt with cold water and squeeze vegetables well to remove the remaining liquid. Dry them carefully with a paper towel and place them in a large mixing bowl.

2. Grate the onion, potato, and carrot and add them to the zucchini and eggplant. Squeeze very well to remove any excess water, and drain. Add the eggs, flour or matzoh meal, parsley, mint, and pepper and mix well.

3. Heat a thin layer of oil in a large skillet. When the oil is sizzling, take about 1 heaping tablespoon of filling and form it into a small patty in the palm of your hand, squeezing out excess liquid. Fry the pancakes, several at a time, for a few minutes on each side. Continue to form and cook the patties until the batter is used up. Drain on paper towels and serve.

Cumin-Flavored Spinach Fritters

"Israeli food is a little Oriental and a little Russian," said Dahlia Cohen, chef-owner of Dahlia's Restaurant in Amirim, a vegetarian moshav outside Safed where my family stayed during one of our trips to Israel. The moshav sits in a beautiful biblical setting replete with pomegranate, lemon, and fig trees in the front garden and a splendid view of the mountains and the Sea of Galilee. Mrs. Cohen, of Polish background, cooks mostly Mediterranean meals at her bed-and-breakfast lodge. A typical menu starts with lemonade sweetened with grape sugar and spiked with mint. Instead of butter to top her bread, Cohen uses olive oil with *za'atar*. Her oil comes from the moshav's olives, which are pressed at the home of an Arab neighbor. The meal, served family-style, also included vegetarian moussaka, a number of salads, homemade bread, blintzes, and the following delicious spinach fritters with cumin.

YIELD: 8 TO 10 FRITTERS

1 pound fresh spinach

2 large eggs

1/4 cup chopped scallions

1/2 teaspoon ground cumin, or to taste

A dash hot pepper flakes, or to taste

1 teaspoon salt, or to taste

A few grinds of pepper

About 1/3 cup matzoh meal

Vegetable oil for frying

1. Wash the spinach thoroughly and cook just in the water clinging to the leaves, over medium heat, for 5 minutes. Drain well, pressing to squeeze out the excess moisture, and chop.

2. Beat the eggs and mix with the spinach and scallions. Stir in the cumin, pepper flakes, salt, pepper, and just enough matzoh meal to hold the fritters together.

3. Heat about 2 inches of oil to 375 degrees or until it starts to shimmer. With your hands shape the batter into ping-pong-size balls and carefully drop them into the hot oil a few at a time. Do not crowd the pan. Brown a few minutes on all sides until crisp.

4. Drain well on paper towels. Repeat with the remaining batter. Serve hot or at room temperature.

Yotvata Potato-Mushroom Casserole

In 1919 a group of German immigrants, all members of the Blau-Weiss Zionist youth group, formed Yotvata, a settlement in the Arava Desert about forty-five minutes north of Eilat. In the Old Testament, Yotvata, meaning "a land of brooks and water," was one of the way stations of the Israelites in their forty-year journey from Egypt to the land of Canaan. There, travelers drank the sweet water from a well near the date palms in a land of mostly brackish water. Until today the same spot has been an oasis for hot, thirsty wanderers on their journey through the Rift Valley, which extends from Yemen to Jerusalem. The idealistic immigrants who settled there decided, because of the well water and despite the heat of the desert, to raise cows for milk, and they have been serving it cold to travelers for more than fifty years.

As the settlement turned into Kibbutz Yotvata, the savvy leaders decided to bring their dairy products to Tel Aviv and opened Yotvata B'Ir, "Yotvata in the City," a popular milk bar and restaurant, which is sandwiched in between McDonald's and Burger King and across from the popular *tayelet,* the bustling boardwalk near the Mediterranean seashore.

Upon request, members of the kibbutz gave me the recipe for the following potato casserole with mushrooms, which is also popular at Yotvata B'Ir. The restaurant is a favorite with young Israelis and visiting Americans like my daughter Daniela, who brought me there.

A stroll on Tel Aviv's seashore after dinner at nearby Yotvata restaurant

4 medium potatoes (about 1 1/2 pounds), peeled

2 tablespoons butter

1 large onion, diced (about 1 1/2 cups)

2 cups sliced fresh mushrooms

6 large eggs

1 cup ricotta cheese

1/2 cup milk

1 tablespoon chopped fresh parsley

1 teaspoon salt, or to taste

1/2 teaspoon white pepper

3/4 cup shredded Gouda or other hard cheese, firmly packed

4 tablespoons chopped green olives

2 teaspoons *za'atar*, or to taste

1. Put the potatoes in a saucepan with cold water to cover. Bring to a boil and simmer about 20 minutes or until soft. Remove from the heat, drain, and mash.

2. Melt 1 tablespoon of the butter in a frying pan and sauté the onion until golden. Add the mushrooms and continue to sauté for a few minutes until most of the liquid is absorbed. Let cool to room temperature.

3. Preheat the oven to 350 degrees and grease a 9-by-13-inch or equivalent ovenproof pan.

4. Beat the eggs well in a mixing bowl. Add the potatoes, onions, mushrooms, ricotta cheese, milk, parsley, salt, pepper, 1/2 cup of the grated cheese, the green olives, and *za'atar*.

5. Pour the mixture into the greased pan. Sprinkle with the remaining cheese and dot with the remaining tablespoon of butter. Bake on the middle shelf of the oven for about 45 minutes, or until golden brown.

Spanakopita— Greek Phyllo Cake Stuffed with Spinach, Feta, and Broccoli

I first tasted a flat, layered version of this spanakopita when I visited the Greek Orthodox bishop of Jerusalem with Mayor Teddy Kollek. For a party I prefer this cake-like presentation shaped in a Bundt pan, as it is very easy to prepare and more dramatic. The broccoli adds a bit of tang to the spinach. This is a popular recipe in my household.

YIELD: 10 SERVINGS

2 tablespoons olive oil

1 large onion, diced (1 1/2 cups)

5 scallions, white and green parts, finely chopped (1/2 cup)

10 ounces feta cheese, crumbled (about 1 1/2 cups)

6 ounces large-curd cottage cheese, drained (about 1/2 cup)

4 large eggs, beaten

2 10-ounce packages frozen chopped spinach, thawed and drained

10-ounce package frozen chopped broccoli, thawed and drained

1/3 cup chopped fresh dill

1/3 cup chopped fresh parsley

1 teaspoon salt

Freshly ground pepper to taste

6 tablespoons unsalted butter, melted

12 sheets phyllo dough

1. Preheat the oven to 350 degrees.

2. Heat the oil in a large skillet, over a medium flame, and add the onions and scallions. Sauté until the onions are golden, about 5 to 7 minutes. Remove from the heat and let cool.

3. Put the feta, cottage cheese, eggs, drained spinach and broccoli, dill, parsley, salt, and pepper in a large mixing bowl. Add the cooled onion and scallions and mix well. Set aside.

4. Using a pastry brush, coat the bottom and sides of a 9-inch Bundt pan with some of the melted butter. Layer the bottom and sides of the pan with 9 pieces of the phyllo, arranging them lengthwise, brushing each leaf with melted butter and overlapping the layers. The dough will hang over the sides and into the opening in the center of the pan.

5. Spoon in the vegetable-cheese filling and fold the overhanging phyllo leaves in to enclose the filling, brushing more melted butter over each leaf, tucking the leaves in at the center. Top with the 3 remaining phyllo leaves, enclosing the entire spanakopita, and brush with butter.

6. Bake for 1 1/4 hours or until golden and puffy. Remove from the oven and cool for about 15 minutes. Carefully run a knife around the spanakopita to remove, place a serving plate over the mold, flip, and serve. You can prepare this spanakopita several hours or even a day in advance. Reheat just before serving.

I love artichokes, especially *akouba*, the wild prickly variety found along the roadside and brought to markets by Arab women who gather them from the fields. Simply sautéed in garlic and olive oil, they are delicious. I also love this garlicky rendition of the famous Jewish dish *carciofi alla giudia*, artichokes Jewish-style. Although this dish was created in the Jewish ghetto of Rome, I first tasted it in Israel. Recently, I tried to make the dish a bit healthier by cutting down on the oil. It is easier to prepare using globe artichokes rather than the tiny seasonal ones, which unfortunately are rarely available anyway. Here is my version, which can be made in the morning, reheated hours later, and savored by eating with your fingers.

Carciofi Alla Giudia—
Artichokes Jewish-Style

YIELD: 4 SERVINGS

4 globe artichokes or 8 tiny ones

Juice of 1 lemon

1/3 cup extra virgin olive oil

1 cup chopped fresh Italian parsley

1/2 cup fresh basil or mint leaves, chopped

1 teaspoon salt, or to taste

1/4 teaspoon fresh ground pepper, or to taste

5 cloves garlic, minced

1/2 cup bread crumbs or matzoh meal

Olive oil for frying

1. Trim the artichokes by cutting the tip of each leaf. Drop them into a large pot of boiling water. Squeeze the lemon juice over and simmer, covered, for about 30 minutes or until the leaves are tender. Drain and place on a plate.

2. To make the filling, mix the olive oil, parsley, basil or mint leaves, salt, pepper, garlic, and bread crumbs or matzoh meal in a small bowl.

3. Using a quarter of the filling per globe artichoke or an eighth per tiny artichoke, gently pull the leaves back and tuck about 1/2 teaspoon of the filling behind each leaf. Place the filled artichokes in a bowl and cover until ready to heat.

4. A little before serving, drizzle a thin film of olive oil over the bottom of a large nonstick frying pan and set the artichokes in the pan on their sides. Heat the artichokes, covered, turning to cook on all sides for just a few minutes.

Le Tsriff's Free-Form Mediterranean Vegetable and Herb Pie

Timing, good ideas, and hard work often create successful restaurants. Jerusalem's Le Tsriff (The Shack) has been a hit since it opened its doors in 1977. "Before I ever thought of going into the restaurant business, I made good pies," said Michal Cohen, one of the owners. "One day, my husband came home and I didn't have anything to make for dinner. I took what was in the refrigerator and made a kind of pie with mushrooms. Everybody loved it. When we decided to start a restaurant in this café, we were looking for an original idea." Her then-husband Yossi suggested they open a pie restaurant—and that's what they did.

The menu at the original Le Tsriff, located in an old Arab house with figs and olive trees growing in the courtyard, included sixteen kinds of savory and sweet pies: Moroccan chicken with almonds and prunes, steak and kidney pies, Mediterranean vegetable pie, and, of course, apple pie, all at reasonable prices.

To go with the pies, the owners of Le Tsriff opted for something new—lettuce salads. At first, customers, unaccustomed to fresh lettuce, did not know what to do with a Salade Niçoise or a Caesar salad with creamy garlic dressings and vinaigrettes. "Israelis, used to a kibbutz salad of cut-up cucumbers, tomatoes, onions, and peppers, or Moroccan cooked vegetable salads, would ask us where the salads were when they saw only lettuce," said Michal. Now the lettuce salads are popular accompaniments to Le Tsriff's many dishes. Through the years, Le Tsriff and its sister restaurant, in the YMCA building across from the King David Hotel, have changed slightly, but the pies from main course to dessert are still hits.

In the summer, this Mediterranean pie is a great recipe for leftover grilled vegetables. Although what follows is Le Tsriff's master recipe, which I watched them make, you can dig into your refrigerator and create your own, layering it with whatever cheese or vegetable leftovers you find. Just partially cook the vegetables beforehand, roasting, grilling, or sautéing according to your taste.

1 sheet commercial puff pastry

1 tablespoon olive oil

1 teaspoon olive tapenade

1/2 clove garlic, minced

6 slices grilled eggplant, 4–5 inches in diameter

8 slices grilled zucchini, 2 inches in diameter

1 roasted red bell pepper, peeled and cut in strips

1 cup shredded mozzarella

1 tablespoon pesto

6 black olives, pitted and diced

5 sun-dried tomatoes

5 fresh basil leaves, chopped

2 tablespoons water

1 egg

1. Preheat the oven to 375 degrees and grease a cookie sheet.

2. Roll the puff pastry out into a 12-inch round and transfer to the cookie sheet. Brush it with olive oil, then spread on the tapenade and sprinkle the garlic over it.

3. Leaving a 2-inch border, make layers of the eggplant, zucchini, roasted pepper, and mozzarella; then spread the pesto over the vegetables. Sprinkle the olives, sun-dried tomatoes, and basil on top. Fold the 2-inch border of dough toward the center, leaving the center open and pleating and brushing each fold with water to seal. Beat the egg with any remaining water and brush the border of dough with this egg wash.

4. Bake in the oven for 25 to 30 minutes, or until the crust is golden. Serve hot or at room temperature.

Pesto

To make pesto, pulse the following ingredients in a food processor equipped with a steel blade until slightly crunchy: 2 cups fresh basil, 1/2 cup walnuts or pine nuts, 2 cloves garlic, salt and pepper to taste, and 1/3 cup olive oil.

Vegetables and
Vegetarian Dishes

Khubeiza Quiche

My grandmother Hannah Bukshester was born in Rosh Pina. When she was twelve years old, her mother died. Since she and her seven siblings did not want to go to an orphanage, she had to learn to cook. Arabs taught her how to pick roots, leaves, and weeds to have enough food for everyone. You'd give her a rose and she could see the jam already.

−Zachi Bukshester, chef

In times of scarcity Jews in Rosh Pina and elsewhere learned, as Mrs. Bukshester did, to use the wild greens growing along the roads. In Israel one of those greens, called *khubeiza* in Arabic and *halamit* in Hebrew, is the leaf of the wild mallow plant that looks like a geranium leaf and tastes somewhat like spinach. Its name comes from *khubz,* the Arabic word for bread, showing how important it was and is as a springtime food. During and after the War of Independence, for example, when food was in short supply, people scavenged the countryside gathering the wild plant, using it in soups, as a cooked vegetable, and even raw as a snack for children. There is a now-famous story about how during a cease-fire Jewish women would rush out to pick *khubeiza* on one side of the dividing line, with Arab women doing the same on the other.

This quiche, which I tasted at my old friend Liz Magnes's house in Jaffa, is made in March and April before the *khubeiza* flowers into a beautiful purple bloom. When Liz lived in Jerusalem, she picked the greens that grew around her house. Later, when she lived in Jaffa, she bought them in the nearby outdoor market. After many experiments, I have substituted spinach or Swiss chard leaves combined with asparagus to approximate the flavor and texture of the original *khubeiza.* This quiche is delicious.

YIELD: 6 SERVINGS

CRUST

1 1/3 cups unbleached all-purpose flour

1/4 cup (1/2 stick) unsalted butter

1/4 cup vegetable shortening

Dash salt

4 tablespoons ice water

FILLING

3 tablespoons olive oil

6 scallions, cut into 1/2-inch pieces (about 2/3 cup)

1 1/2 cups fresh asparagus, preferably thin, trimmed and cut into 1-inch pieces

1 1/2 cups fresh spinach or Swiss chard leaves, torn into small pieces

3 tablespoons unbleached all-purpose flour

1 cup heavy cream or milk

2 large eggs, lightly beaten

1 1/2 teaspoons salt

1/4 teaspoon freshly ground pepper

1. To make the crust, put the flour, butter, vegetable shortening, and salt in the bowl of a food processor fitted with a steel blade. Pulse until you have a crumbly consistency. Gradually add the ice water and continue pulsing until a ball of dough forms. (You can also put all the ingredients in a mixing bowl and combine them with the tips of your fingers.) Remove the dough, cover in plastic wrap, and refrigerate for 30 minutes.

2. Preheat the oven to 350 degrees.

3. Roll the dough out to an 11-inch circle. Place it in an ungreased 9-inch pie pan. Prick the bottom of the crust with a fork. Bake the dough on the middle shelf of the preheated oven for 15 minutes. The crust will be slightly undercooked.

4. To make the filling, heat the olive oil in a large skillet. Add the scallions and sauté over low heat for a few minutes, until soft. Then add the asparagus and the spinach and sauté over high heat, stirring until the spinach is soft and the asparagus is slightly cooked but still has some crunch.

5. Reduce the heat to medium low. Put the flour in a small bowl and add a few tablespoons of the heavy cream or milk, stirring to make a smooth paste. Spoon into the frying pan and stir. Then pour on the remaining cream or milk and continue stirring until you have a thick consistency, about 5 minutes. Remove from the heat.

6. Let cool, then stir in the 2 beaten eggs and sprinkle with salt and pepper. Fill the partially cooked pie shell and continue cooking on the middle rack of the oven for 45 to 50 minutes or until the top is firm and golden brown.

Liz and Rafi Magnes with their children in the garden of their former home overlooking Jerusalem's Old City

Zena Harman, now in her mid-eighties, came to Palestine from England in 1940 and experienced the exciting, difficult years before the creation of the state of Israel. A retired UN high commissioner for refugees, she was also a member of Knesset and the widow of the late Abraham Harman, who was president of the Hebrew University of Jerusalem and Israeli ambassador to the United States.

Mrs. Harman remembers: "When we arrived, the situation was worsening, and it was becoming more and more difficult to store foods. Food was rationed because convoys were unable to get through to Jerusalem. We were allowed one egg every two weeks, and one-quarter pound meat, one tomato, half a carrot, one cucumber, two onions, one green pepper, and a few string beans per week. Bread, flour, and sugar were also rationed with cards. Once in a while we had some frozen fish. Relatives from abroad tried to get food for us, but Europe was also at war. In 1947 Abe's brother came from England and brought powdered eggs for us. It was such a treasure, but he couldn't get it through to us in Jerusalem. Somehow we managed to get a pilot in a Piper plane to send us the eggs and cigarettes, which we shared with friends. By 1946 I had two babies and little to feed them, only a small quantity of milk. The biggest problem was diapers, since we were allowed only a half bottle of water per day. The most moving thing I remember was that neighbors contributed water to wash them, a glass each of the meager amount allocated per person.

"During the siege of Jerusalem in early 1948, we lived on the top floor of a house with eight apartments and balconies. Early on, the gas and electricity were cut off, so we used any source of fuel available, even lubricating oil, on our Primus stoves [one-burner kerosene stoves on three legs]. Then we gathered twigs and built fires on the balcony, with bombs and *katushas* hurling in the distance. We lived in the corridors and shared whatever food supplies we had—tinned foods like sardines, chipped beef, vegetables, and a small supply of rice.

"For drinking water, the priority went to baby bottles, but nothing was thrown away. The water remaining after we used it was for the toilets. The water, which had been stored in wells for emergency, was delivered by a donkey cart, and we had to go collect it. Some were killed while queuing for water.

"During the siege we even managed to have a seder. I remember we went upstairs to our apartment. The window was near where we were sitting. *Katushas* were falling all the time. All of us lost friends. The miracle was that we who survived emerged from it without starving, even the children. I remember that this period had an atmosphere of comradeship and sharing without any petty quarreling. It was an experience I will never forget. But if the situation had not changed, a major tragedy would have been inevitable."

I have shared many meals with Mrs. Harman over the past thirty years. This is one of her favorite dishes—she served it during the 1940s, when she could rarely get all of the ingredients, and she still serves it today. In those days, whatever apple she could lay her hands on would do. Today, there is a huge variety of apples in Israel, so Mrs. Harman chooses Granny Smiths, which are good for cooking. It is very important to taste the dish before serving in order to adjust the sweet-and-sour flavors.

Zena Harman's Sweet-and-Sour Red Cabbage

YIELD: 8 SERVINGS

2 tablespoons vegetable oil

1 large onion, chopped (about 1 1/4 cups)

1 head red cabbage, shredded (about 3 pounds)

1/2 teaspoon salt, or to taste

1 large Granny Smith apple, grated

1/3 cup white or cider vinegar

4 tablespoons light-brown sugar, or to taste

1 teaspoon caraway seeds

1. Heat the vegetable oil in a pot and sauté the onions until soft. Add the cabbage and salt, and cover. Steam over medium heat for 10 minutes.

2. Remove the cover and add the shredded apple.

3. In a small bowl, mix the vinegar and sugar together and pour over the cabbage. Sprinkle with the caraway seeds, mix, and simmer, covered, stirring occasionally, for about 30 minutes or until the cabbage is soft, adding water if needed. Adjust the seasonings to taste.

Couscous, Pasta, and Rice Dishes

In the 1876 *Baedeker Guide to Jerusalem,* an entry on the city's so-called "corn-market" describes its "large heaps of grain and baskets of seed in every direction." These grains and seeds probably included the bulgur, lentils, semolina, rice, and barley still prevalent in Israeli cooking today.

Rice is perhaps the most popular grain among Israel's different ethnic inhabitants. Like many women, the late Naima Levy was a great rice traditionalist, having immigrated in 1950 to Noga, a Kurdish moshav, from Armya, Kurdistan, where her husband's family had cultivated rice for generations. She was always

Above: In summer, a great place for grains to dry

chosen to prepare special rice dishes for weddings or other occasions. What made her rice distinguished was simple: she always cooked it in rich homemade chicken stock, brought to a boil and then simmered ever so slowly. "All the grains of her rice separated from each other," recalled Tsion Levy, her son. "No one else's was like my mother's."

As painstaking as Naima was throughout the year, at Passover she was even more careful, sorting through the rice at least seven times to remove any forbidden grains that might have mixed in during harvesting or storage. Like many Middle Eastern women, Naima often found herself cooking for large extended families, and so she would sort through fifteen or more kilograms of rice before the holiday. This ceremony is performed at Passover by women throughout the Middle East, and is solely their domain; some, due to failing vision, call on daughters and granddaughters to help them sort through the rice, but this is still, as it has always been, a woman's job.

Bulgur (cracked wheat) is probably the most common grain in Israel next to rice, and has been for centuries. Similar in texture to kasha, the buckwheat groats that were a staple for Russian Jews in their homeland, bulgur became a viable substitute in Palestine during the nineteenth century, when the early Russian pioneers struggled through times of scarcity. The grain was often prepared, as was kasha, with sautéed onions and fresh or dried mushrooms.

This chapter includes many of my favorite grain dishes from Israel's various cultural traditions: couscous from Libya, Tunisia, and Morocco; a modern Israeli vegetarian "meatloaf" made with kasha; Jerusalem peppery noodle kugel; *barsch,* a Sabbath dish from Uzbekistan with rice, cilantro, and spices; the delicious Lebanese *mujeddra,* a dish with lentils, onions, and bulgur; and, of course, several modern Israeli pasta dishes.

One way of bearing sacks of grain

Rice and Lentil
Levivot (Latkes)

Australian-born chef Celia Regev came to live in Israel in 1967 at the age of eighteen. Since then Celia, whose husband is in the foreign service, has also lived in England, Italy, the United States, and France, where she studied at Le Cordon Bleu and École Lenotre. When she returned to Israel, she and a friend opened Reviva and Celia, a coffee shop in Herzliyya that served light fare and pastries.

A careful classical chef, Celia devours cookbooks, then tastes and tests her way through cultures. At Hanukkah she was inspired to create the following rice and lentil *levivot,* which she serves with *labneh* (strained yogurt) and a confit of onions. This is a great dish for leftover rice and lentils.

YIELD: ABOUT 20 *LEVIVOT*

½ cup *labneh* (see page 30)

½ teaspoon ground coriander

1 teaspoon salt, or to taste

A few grinds of pepper

3 tablespoons extra virgin olive oil

1 medium onion, diced (about 1 cup)

2 large eggs

½ cup plain yogurt

1 cup cooked lentils (½ cup uncooked)

1 cup rice, cooked (any kind will do)

¼ teaspoon ground cumin

4 tablespoons finely chopped fresh cilantro

⅓ cup unbleached all-purpose flour

Peanut or canola oil for frying

1. Place the *labneh* in a small bowl. Sprinkle with ¼ teaspoon of the coriander and salt and pepper to taste.

2. Heat the olive oil in a nonstick frying pan and sauté the onions until translucent. Remove from the heat.

3. Break the eggs into a medium bowl and beat lightly. Add the yogurt, lentils, rice, cumin, ¼ teaspoon of the coriander, salt and pepper to taste, 3 tablespoons of the cilantro, and flour, stirring well after each addition. Fold in the cooked onions.

4. Heat a large nonstick frying pan with a film of oil. Drop a few heaping tablespoons of the lentil-rice batter into the pan, flatten slightly with the back of a spoon, and fry for a few minutes on each side. Drain on paper towels and repeat with the remaining batter. Serve with a dollop of the *labneh,* topped with a confit of onions (see following recipe) and a sprinkle of the remaining cilantro.

Confit of Onions

This onion confit is a lovely complement to the above *levivot* or most any savory fritter. It should be prepared ahead of time, since the patties are best hot and fresh from the pan.

YIELD: 1 CUP ONION CONFIT

¼ cup extra virgin olive oil

3 large Spanish onions, sliced in rings

2 teaspoons pomegranate concentrate (optional)*

1. Heat the oil in a nonstick frying pan and add the onions. Reduce the heat to low and cook very slowly, adding a little water if necessary, until the onions become a nice golden brown. This may take as long as 30 minutes. The slower you cook the onions, the more flavor your confit will have.

2. Remove the onions to a bowl and, if you like, stir in the pomegranate syrup.

*Available in Middle Eastern grocery stores

Couscous, Pasta, and Rice Dishes

Mujeddra—
A Pottage of Lentils, Bulgur, and Onions

I first tasted this simple dish of lentils, large kernels of bulgur, and crisply sautéed onions at the home of Fathima Zeidan Salah in Salama, a Bedouin village in the Galilee (see page 94). Fathima's version of *mujeddra,* using bulgur instead of the rice used most often today, is clearly a very old village dish, predating the arrival of rice in Palestine.

Mujeddra, like many other dishes I encountered in rural Arab villages of the north, is seasonal, traditionally eaten after the first rain comes in the fall and throughout the winter, when people rely on stored provisions. When I asked Mrs. Salah, through an interpreter, if I could take notes for Americans who need to see written recipes, she laughed, glancing at her teenage daughters, who seemed more interested in hearing about life in the city than in watching their mother cook. "I understand," she said in Arabic. "Our next generation will also need cookbooks."

YIELD: 6 TO 8 SERVINGS

1 cup brown lentils

2 teaspoons salt, or to taste

2 large onions

4 tablespoons olive or vegetable oil

1 cup coarse (#3) bulgur

¼ teaspoon freshly ground pepper, or to taste

1. Place the lentils in a saucepan with 2 cups of water or enough to cover by several inches, and bring to a boil. Add 1 teaspoon of salt, lower the heat, and simmer, covered, for about 20 minutes, or until the lentils are cooked but not mushy. Check the water level occasionally and add more water, ¼ cup at a time as needed, so the lentils do not burn.

2. While the lentils are cooking, slice the onions in thin half-moons. Heat 2 tablespoons of the oil in a frying pan over a low flame, add the onions, and cook, covered, for 20 minutes. Remove the cover, increase the flame to high, and fry the onions until they are crisp and almost black in color. Drain and set aside.

3. Bring 2½ cups of water to a boil in a saucepan.

4. In the frying pan, heat the remaining 2 tablespoons of oil. Add the bulgur and sauté the grains until slightly browned, stirring occasionally. Turn off the heat and carefully add the boiling water and the remaining teaspoon salt. The water will continue to boil as it hits the hot pan. Let the bulgur sit for about 15 minutes or until all the water is absorbed.

5. Put the lentils and bulgur in a serving bowl and mix. Add additional salt to taste, and ¼ teaspoon pepper, or to taste. Sprinkle the onions on top and serve.

NOTE You can substitute 2 cups of cooked rice or *frika* (see page 227) for the bulgur. Serve as is or with 1 cup plain yogurt seasoned with 1 clove crushed garlic, 1 teaspoon of lemon juice, and, if you like, a sprinkling of dried mint.

Many travelers to Palestine in the nineteenth century describe the experience of a harvest where, at mealtime, grains of green parched wheat (called "parched corn" in the Bible), not yet dried and hardened, were roasted outdoors in a pan or on an iron plate and then rubbed together between the palms and eaten plain, just as they were in biblical times. Called *cale* in Hebrew and *frika* in Arabic, this toasted green wheat grain can be found commercially from Egypt and Turkey and is available in Middle Eastern grocery stores. The most unforgettable taste comes from the home-parched wheat I have tasted in Galilee kitchens. Often prepared like bulgur, it is served in Egypt as a stuffing in pigeons, and in Israel it is often mixed with rice. Today chefs like caterer Hava Volman are discovering this grain. I love the smoky flavor and nutty texture of the *frika* with the more intense flavor of the dried limes in this dish, which Hava shared with me.

Parched Wheat Pilaf Infused with Persian Dried Limes and Potato Crust

And ye shall eat neither bread, nor parched corn, nor fresh ears, until this selfsame day, until ye have brought the offering of your God; it is a statute for ever throughout your generations in all your dwellings.

—Leviticus 23:14

And she sat beside the reapers; and they reached her parched corn, and she did eat and was satisfied and left thereof.

—Ruth 2:14

YIELD: 6 SERVINGS

1 medium onion, chopped

5 cloves garlic, minced

4 celery stalks, diced

2 carrots, peeled and diced

2 tablespoons olive oil

1 teaspoon celery seed

1 teaspoon dried thyme

$1/2$ teaspoon ground coriander

$1/2$ teaspoon paprika

1 teaspoon salt, or to taste

$1/4$ teaspoon freshly ground pepper, or to taste

3 cups water

3 Persian dried limes, pierced

1 cup *frika* (parched wheat)

2 tablespoons vegetable oil

2 potatoes, peeled and sliced in $1/8$-inch-thick rounds

$1/2$ cup chopped fresh mint leaves

1. Sauté the onions, garlic, celery, and carrots in the olive oil until the onions are translucent. Add the spices, water, and dried limes. Simmer, uncovered, about 15 minutes, until the liquid is reduced by half. Let cool for a few hours or until the stock is infused with flavor. Strain into a saucepan and bring to a boil.

2. Put the *frika* in a mixing bowl. Pour the boiling stock over it, cover with plastic wrap, and leave to infuse for 30 minutes. Strain off any excess liquid.

3. Heat the vegetable oil in a large nonstick frying pan. Scatter the potatoes over the bottom and sauté them until they are lightly browned. Add the *frika*, cover very tightly with aluminum foil, and let cook on very low heat for 25 minutes or until the *frika* is al dente. Invert the pan onto a platter, garnish with the mint leaves, and serve.

Couscous, Pasta, and Rice Dishes

227

Maklubeh— Turned-Over Rice Casserole with Cauliflower and Meat

I first tasted *maklubeh* in the early 1970s on a trip to the home of an Arab colleague in the village of Silwan. *Maklubeh*, meaning "upside-down" or "turned over," is a typical Palestinian dish made with a layer of diced mutton or chicken browned in *semen* (clarified butter) or ghee in a saucepan, a layer of sliced and fried eggplant or cauliflower, and a layer of saffron-colored rice. The whole dish is turned upside down on a large platter and served sprinkled with pine nuts. There are many incarnations of this dish, varying from village to village, sometimes from family to family. Although eggplant is the most common vegetable used, I prefer this combination of cauliflower and slivered carrots with lamb or chicken.

YIELD: 6 TO 8 SERVINGS

2 cups basmati rice

4 tablespoons cooking oil

2 onions, diced (about 2 cups)

1 pound lamb shoulder, or boneless chicken breasts, cut in 1-inch cubes

Salt and freshly ground pepper to taste

1¼ teaspoons ground cumin

¾ teaspoon ground allspice

½ head cauliflower, cut into flowerets

3 cloves garlic, crushed

4 carrots, peeled and cut in slivers

Pinch of saffron

3 cups beef broth, chicken broth, or water

¼ cup toasted pine nuts

1. Soak the rice in tepid salted water for an hour, then drain.

2. Meanwhile, heat 2 tablespoons of oil in a flameproof casserole and sauté the onions until translucent.

3. Season the lamb or chicken with at least 2 teaspoons of salt and ½ teaspoon of pepper and add to the onions. Continue cooking until all sides of the meat are seared and the onions are golden. Add 1 teaspoon of the cumin, the allspice, and enough water to cover the lamb, if you are using it; then bring to a gentle boil, lower the heat, and simmer, uncovered, for 20 minutes. If using chicken, simply cook for a few minutes, then turn off the heat and continue with step 4.

4. In a separate frying pan, lightly brown the cauliflower in the remaining 2 tablespoons of oil. Season with a teaspoon of salt, a few grinds of fresh pepper, and the remaining ¼ teaspoon cumin and set aside.

5. Sprinkle salt into a nonstick 6-cup casserole, add the garlic, and then add the lamb or chicken and onions. Top with the cauliflower, carrots, and rice.

6. Dissolve the saffron in 3 cups of water, chicken broth, or beef broth, or a combination. Add enough of this broth to the casserole to cover the rice. Bring to a boil, cover tightly, reduce heat, and simmer for a half hour or until the rice is cooked and all the liquid absorbed. The rice should be moist.

7. To unmold the *maklubeh,* place a towel around the sides of the casserole. Run a knife around the inside, place a platter on top, flip, and carefully unmold. Serve sprinkled with toasted pine nuts. If your *maklubeh* doesn't form a mold, no matter—simply spoon the rice onto a platter and top with the lamb or chicken pieces and the vegetables.

Uzbeki *Barsch*— Holiday *Pilau* with Cilantro, Parsley, Mint, and Dill

The first time I was introduced to *barsch,* it was hanging in a cloth sack over a sink in an Uzbeki apartment in Holon. An ancient Sabbath dish from Uzbekistan, this rice *pilau,* often made with diced meat, cilantro, parsley, mint, and dill, is prepared before the Sabbath begins. Then, hung in a cloth container, it is steamed in water before serving to preserve the rice's texture. Margalit Shemesh, a third-generation Israeli from Samarkand now living in Holon, showed me her "Israeli" version of the dish, with diced or ground beef rather than the traditional lamb, cooked in a casserole rather than steamed.

YIELD: 6 TO 8 SERVINGS

2 tablespoons vegetable oil

1 onion, diced

1/2 pound ground or chopped beef, liver, or lamb

1 teaspoon salt, or to taste

1/2 teaspoon pepper, or to taste

1/8 teaspoon saffron strands

1 1/2 cups basmati rice

3 cups water

1 cup chopped fresh cilantro

1 cup chopped fresh parsley

1/2 cup chopped fresh mint

1/2 cup snipped fresh dill

Bukharan food readied for the Sabbath in Holon

1. Heat the oil in a large frying pan with a lid. Add the onions and sauté until translucent. Add the meat and stir constantly, breaking up the lumps. Season with salt, pepper, and saffron. Cook slowly, covered, for 10 minutes, stirring occasionally.

2. While the onions and meat are cooking, rinse the rice in water, drain, and repeat until the water is no longer cloudy. Bukharan cooks rinse their rice 3 times.

3. Pour 2 cups of the water into the meat and bring to a boil. Add ¾ cup each of the cilantro and the parsley, ¼ cup each of the mint and the dill. Simmer, covered, about 10 minutes.

4. Add the rice to the onions and meat. Press down so that the water covers the *barsch* by an inch, adding the remaining cup of water if necessary. Bring to a boil, cover, and lower the heat. Simmer until the water is absorbed, about 20 minutes. Cover with a towel until ready to serve. Just before serving, sprinkle with the remaining cilantro, parsley, mint, and dill.

NOTE I sometimes make a meatless version of this dish, cooking the onion for a shorter time before adding the rice.

Israeli *Pilav* with Pine Nuts and Currants

Similar to American Rice-A-Roni, which was created in San Francisco by Middle Eastern immigrants in the 1950s, this rice with crushed noodles was known in Syria as early as the fifteenth century. Mentioned in a Damascus cookbook, the recipe read only, "Brown the noodles in the oven and cook them with rice." According to food historian Charles Perry of the *Los Angeles Times,* dyeing rice grains with saffron or pomegranate juice and sprinkling them on a pilaf for contrast is an age-old custom. Jews from Lebanon and Syria, who have used vermicelli or angel-hair pasta for centuries, have been particularly adept at mixing the two textures of noodles and rice. I particularly like this very typical Israeli rice recipe, with sautéed onions, pine nuts, and currants or raisins sprinkled over the pasta and rice.

YIELD: 4 TO 6 SERVINGS

2½ ounces uncooked dry vermicelli or other thin spaghetti, crumbled (about 1 cup)

4 tablespoons vegetable oil

2 cups long-grain rice

4 cups water or chicken broth

1 teaspoon salt, or to taste

1 large onion, diced

¼ cup pine nuts or blanched almonds

¼ cup currants or raisins

1. Crumble the pasta strands into pieces about 2 inches long. In a medium saucepan, heat 2 tablespoons of the oil and brown the pasta strands until golden, stirring constantly.

2. Add the rice and stir-fry for a few more minutes. Then add the water or broth and salt to the pasta and rice. Bring to a boil, cover, and simmer for about 20 minutes, or until the rice is cooked.

3. Heat the remaining 2 tablespoons of oil in a small frying pan and sauté the onion slowly until golden, stirring occasionally. Then add the pine nuts and currants or raisins to toast them lightly.

4. Turn the rice and noodles onto a platter and fluff with a fork. Taste and add more salt if needed. Serve sprinkled with the onions, nuts, and the currants or raisins.

NOTE For an Arab version of this dish from the Galilee, you can replace the pasta with *frika* (see page 227) and add a teaspoon each of nutmeg and cinnamon. For an Iraqi variation, you can sauté a diced onion either before you brown the pasta or with it, add a dollop of tomato paste to the chicken broth or water, and sprinkle at the end with toasted pine nuts and currants or raisins.

Couscous, Pasta, and Rice Dishes

Desert Bulgur Patties from the Black Hebrews of Dimona

In the early 1970s, a group of about a thousand black Hebrews immigrated to Israel from the Chicago area via Liberia, where they lived for three and a half years. On a visit to Be'er Sheeva', we came across the compound of this "Hebrew Israelite Community" in the nearby city of Dimona. An American woman in a long, tie-dyed African dress greeted us with the word *shalom* and escorted us to their vegan restaurant, Taam Haki-yeem (Taste of Life). On the way she explained that the black Hebrews, followers of the Old Testament, lived in ancient Israel until the destruction of the Second Temple in 70 C.E. They then went to Africa before they were brought to the United States as slaves.

The members of the community, today citizens of Israel, are strict vegetarians. Our guide cited Genesis 1:29: " 'Behold, I have given you every herb yielding seed, which is upon the face of all the earth, and every tree, in which is the fruit of a tree yielding seed—to you it shall be for food.' " Then she added, "We try to live without meat, hate, and *pelephones*," referring to the omnipresent Israeli cell phones.

We sat down at one of the eight tables in the makeshift restaurant and ordered strong ginger punch. The waiter informed us that Coca-Cola is not served because the community does not allow processed food of any kind, including sugar and white flour. In addition, they are true vegans, excluding eggs and all dairy products from their diet. He advised our drinking the punch before our meal, explaining that the black Hebrews do not drink and eat at the same time. Since we were visiting on their once-a-week saltless day, which they believe to be good for the system, there was no salt in any of the dishes. We chose fried tofu, fried cauliflower, bulgur patties, homemade whole-wheat spaghetti with fresh tomato sauce, and deep-fried *kalabene,* a vegetarian whole-wheat flour and water mixture that tastes somewhat like fried chicken.

What started as a small restaurant for those living in their compound has become a larger vegan enterprise. Two other black Hebrew vegan restaurants, each called L'chaim (To Life), have opened in Arad and Tel Aviv. Under the label "Nature's Gate," the black Hebrews produce their own pasta, tofu, and other soybean products, including a soy ice cream. These bulgur patties, based loosely on their recipe, have become a regular fixture in my household, in which some of the younger members are vegetarians.

3 cups water

1 teaspoon salt, or to taste

1¹/₂ cups medium (#2) bulgur

1 small onion, finely chopped

2 garlic cloves, finely chopped

1 large green bell pepper, finely chopped

2 tablespoons paprika

2 tablespoons tamari or soy sauce

¹/₄ cup whole-wheat flour

1¹/₂ tablespoons ground sage or 3 tablespoons fresh sage, finely chopped

Salt to taste

Vegetable oil for frying

1. Bring the water and salt to a boil in a medium pot. Slowly stir in the bulgur, reduce the heat to low, cover, and simmer until the bulgur has absorbed all of the water, about 15 to 20 minutes. Cool.

2. Transfer the cooked bulgur to a large mixing bowl. Add the onion, garlic, bell pepper, paprika, tamari or soy sauce, flour, sage, and salt to taste and mix well.

3. Shape about ¹/₃ cup of the bulgur mixture into a patty and flatten it slightly with the palm of your hand. Repeat with the remaining bulgur.

4. Heat enough oil to coat the bottom of a large nonstick skillet. Fry the patties for a few minutes on each side until crusty and golden, and drain on paper towels.

Kasha Meatloaf

Kibbutz life turned Mordechai and Rachel Welt into pioneers of Israel's vegetarian movement. "I was a volunteer on a kibbutz, working with chickens," said Mordechai. "Every day I saw that people handling animals forgot that they were dealing with living creatures. It challenged me. I asked myself, When I am not working here, can I see myself eating chicken soup?" He could not. The experience changed his life.

Born in Queens, New York, Mordechai and Rachel met as teens and later married, and moved to Israel in the 1970s. Ten years later they took over the American Israeli natural food store in Jerusalem, the first shop in Israel to offer home-baked whole-wheat challah, as well as homemade granola and fresh-ground natural peanut butter. Rachel taught natural food cooking and nutrition classes and worked as a chef in a vegetarian restaurant.

Beans and grains market

Today the Welts are independent distributors of traditional Chinese herbal formulas and natural personal care products. They work with all segments of Israeli society, from the secular to the ultra-orthodox—Jew, Christian, and Arab alike. The Welts live with their seven children in Neve Daniel, a Modern Orthodox settlement in Gush Etzion, where Mordechai devotes his mornings to studying the Torah. They find that their vegetarian lifestyle harmonizes naturally with their Jewish values.

In their kitchen, the Welts substitute tofu for turkey, protein-rich lentils for chicken, and kasha for ground beef in the following "meatloaf." This kasha loaf with an Asian flavor substitutes carrot for the hard-boiled egg traditionally included in a meatloaf.

3/4 cup whole kasha (buckwheat groats)

1 cup water

1 teaspoon salt, or to taste

1 tablespoon Asian sesame oil

2 cups diced onions (about 1 large onion) or scallions

2 stalks celery, diced

2 teaspoons minced fresh ginger

2 1/2 teaspoons minced fresh garlic

3/4 cup coarsely grated carrots, plus 1 whole, peeled carrot

2 tablespoons miso (bean paste)

5 fresh basil leaves, chopped, or 1 teaspoon dried basil

1 tablespoon fresh thyme

1/2 cup chopped fresh parsley

1/2 teaspoon dried oregano

1 cup lightly toasted almonds, coarsely chopped

8 large lettuce leaves or green cabbage leaves

1. Stir-fry the kasha in a nonstick frying pan for a few minutes, until lightly browned.

2. Bring 1 cup of water to a boil in a medium saucepan. Add the kasha and salt and simmer, covered, about 15 minutes or until all the water is absorbed.

3. Meanwhile, heat the sesame oil in a frying pan. Lightly stir-fry the onions or scallions, celery, ginger, garlic, and the grated carrots. Add the miso, basil, thyme, parsley, and oregano and mix well. Stir in the cooked kasha and the almonds. If the mixture is very dry, add some more water. Adjust the seasonings if necessary, adding salt to taste.

4. Preheat the oven to 350 degrees and grease a 9-by-5-inch loaf pan. Steam the lettuce or cabbage leaves briefly and line the pan with them. Spoon the kasha filling into the pan, pressing the whole carrot in lengthwise, and cover with foil. Place the pan in a larger baking dish filled up halfway with water. Bake in the oven for 30 minutes or until the kasha loaf is firm and the carrot is soft. Turn out onto a platter. Slice and serve as you would a meatloaf.

Kasha Porridge
with Pumpkin

In 1987, during a trip to Moscow, I met Inna and Igor Uspensky, who were well-known refuseniks trying to immigrate to Israel. Both biologists, they were not able to work in their profession for many years. Eventually, they, like over a million other Russians, left for Israel. "After ten years of not working in our field, we are like hungry people," said Inna during our reunion in their apartment in Jerusalem. "When we retire we'll cook. But for now, we are trying to digest biology. We have a new life and a new world here."

For dinner in Moscow, the Uspenskys often ate this porridge of kasha with pumpkin. Today, in Jerusalem, it is a reminder of what life was like in the former Soviet Union, where kasha, an everyday staple when meat and other products were scarce, would make a typical dinner meal.

YIELD: 4 TO 6 SERVINGS

½ cup medium kasha

3½ cups water

Salt to taste

1½ pounds pumpkin or other winter squash, peeled and cut into 1-inch cubes

1½ cups milk

2 tablespoons unsalted butter

Sugar or honey to taste

1. Stir-fry the kasha in a nonstick frying pan until slightly browned.

2. Bring 3 cups of the water to a boil in a heavy 3-quart saucepan. Add the kasha and salt and bring to a boil again over medium heat, stirring with a wooden spoon. Turn the heat to very low, cover tightly, and simmer for 25 to 30 minutes or until tender.

3. Meanwhile, put the pumpkin or squash in another heavy saucepan, add the remaining ½ cup water, and bring to a boil. Lower the heat and simmer, covered, for 30 minutes or until the pumpkin is tender. Put through a potato ricer or meat grinder, or simply chop to the texture of chunky applesauce.

4. Add the pumpkin or squash to the kasha, along with the milk and salt to taste. Mix well and bring to a boil. Lower the heat and cook slowly for 5 to 7 minutes more.

5. Serve in heated bowls, topping each serving with 1 teaspoon butter and, if you wish, sugar or honey to taste.

Couscous

Several years ago at Dr. Shakshuka, a restaurant in Jaffa, I became transfixed watching elderly Libyan women, each seated inside a stone arch, sifting semolina pellets to make couscous. First they would take a kilo or so of coarse semolina, moisten it with a little water, and, with their hands, carefully separate the grains. Next, they raked the fingers of their right hands through the semolina in sweeping, circular motions, creating the tiny balls of dough known as couscous. The granules were rubbed against the weave of a fine basket to shape them, and, when completed, they were dried. They were then put several times through a wood-handled sieve to obtain granules of uniform size. Finally, as they received an order from the kitchen, the women would steam the couscous twice in a special pot similar to a double boiler, the bottom of which was filled with different kinds of hearty meat and vegetable stews.

A woman sifting parched wheat

Today, with the availability of pre-steamed "instant" couscous, this careful preparation is becoming an anachronism. But there is a middle ground; I greatly prefer the loose couscous, usually sold in bulk at health food stores and upscale grocery stores, to the "instant" variety. If you do not have a *couscousier,* use a regular stockpot with a vegetable steamer. If the holes are too big, just line the steamer with cheesecloth to prevent the couscous grains from falling through. Set the steamer into your pot, cover, and cook.

YIELD: 4 TO 6 SERVINGS

1 pound couscous (about 2³/₄ cups)	2¹/₂–3 cups water or chicken broth
1 teaspoon salt, or to taste	3 tablespoons vegetable oil

1. Place the couscous in a bowl, sprinkle with the salt, and cover with the water or chicken broth. Let sit for about 30 minutes or until the liquid is absorbed.

2. Drizzle the oil over the grains and gently rub them with your fingers to get rid of the lumps. Let sit for at least another 15 minutes.

3. Steam the couscous over a soupy stew, using a *couscousier* or a cheesecloth-lined vegetable steamer and stockpot, for about 15 minutes, starting your timer when you see the steam rise through the couscous. Then pour a cup of hot water over the couscous, separate the grains with your fingers, and steam for 15 minutes more. (If you are short on time, you can merely sprinkle the couscous with water and place it in a microwave for a minute or 2, always separating the grains with your fingers before serving.)

Libyan Couscous with Chickpea, Squash, Zucchini, and Eggplant

Massuda Machluf's colorful vegetable stew with couscous can be made ahead and reheated just before serving. Coming from a traditional couscous culture, Mrs. Machluf carefully sifts the couscous twice a week, sitting on a stool in her kitchen, patiently rubbing the semolina through a sieve with her fingers. Her old-fashioned method takes hours, but don't let the recipe scare you. Using a *couscousier* or vegetable steamer, it is so easy! Since Libya is geographically between Morocco and Yemen, you can serve this dish with either the Yemenite *z'hug* (see page 139) or the Moroccan *harissa* (see page 72).

YIELD: AT LEAST 12 SERVINGS

1 cup dried chickpeas

5 tablespoons olive oil

3 medium onions, roughly chopped

4 carrots, peeled and cut into 2-inch chunks

1 butternut, acorn, or other bright orange squash (about 2 pounds), peeled and cut into 2-inch chunks

2 zucchini, cut into 1-inch rounds

1 large eggplant (about 1 pound), cut into 1-inch chunks

2 celery stalks (with leaves), cut into 1-inch chunks

1/2 cabbage (about 1 pound), shredded

2–3 potatoes (about 1 1/2 pounds), peeled and cut into 1-inch chunks

2–3 cloves garlic, minced

1 1/2 teaspoons ground turmeric

1/2 cup plus 2 tablespoons chopped fresh cilantro

4 tablespoons snipped fresh dill

Salt and freshly ground pepper to taste

1 pound couscous

1. Soak the chickpeas in water to cover by at least 1 inch, for 8 hours or overnight. This will yield 2 cups of reconstituted chickpeas.

2. Heat 3 tablespoons of the olive oil in the bottom of a *couscousier* or stockpot. Add the onions and sauté until golden.

3. Drain the chickpeas, add to the onions in the stockpot, and cover with 4 cups of water. Bring to a boil and simmer, covered, for 1 hour.

4. Add the carrots, squash, zucchini, eggplant, celery, cabbage, and potatoes to the stockpot. Then stir in the garlic, turmeric, 1/2 cup of the cilantro, 2 tablespoons of the snipped dill, and salt and freshly ground pepper. Mix well and bring to a boil.

5. Place the couscous in a cheesecloth-lined vegetable steamer or *couscousier* insert, and with your fingers gently rub the grains to eliminate lumps. Set the insert in the *couscousier* or stockpot over the boiling vegetables. Cover, lower the

heat, and simmer for a half hour or until the vegetables are fork tender. Adjust the seasonings to taste.

6. Pour 1 cup of hot water slowly over the couscous into the pot, mixing it in with your fingers and the remaining 2 tablespoons oil as it is absorbed, again separating the grains. Continue to steam for another 15 minutes.

7. Transfer the couscous to the center of a large serving dish, and again separate the grains with your fingers to fluff it. Spoon the vegetables around the edge and sprinkle on the remaining 2 tablespoons each of cilantro and dill.

· · LOVE, LIBYA, AND *LAGHBI* · ·

The minute I walked into Massuda Machluf's three-room stucco house at Moshav Beit Shikma, south of Ashkelon, I could tell that she was the center of life in this bustling family. Outside, children and grandchildren were tending the chickens, goats, and cows. Inside, chatter and the aroma of meat and vegetable stews flavored with Oriental spices filled the air. With two of her eight children around her, Mrs. Machluf emanated a wonderful energy that filled her humble, happy home.

Now in her mid seventies, Mrs. Machluf came from Tripoli in 1951 with her husband, Mamus, and their two babies. Before the creation of Israel, about thirty-eight thousand Jews lived in Libya. Today, only about ninety remain. With other immigrants from Tripoli and Morocco, the Machlufs came to this moshav when it had no houses, no water, no food, and no electricity. In the beginning she and her husband lived in *mabarot* (makeshift tent dwellings), worked the fields with hand tools, and grew melons from seeds Mamus had smuggled from Tripoli.

In Libya Mamus had worked with dates. He would tap the date trees in the summer the way people in the United States extract sap from maple trees during the spring thaw. "If they take the syrup in the winter, the tree will die," explained Mr. Machluf in Hebrew with a strong Arab accent. "They use the sap like wine in Libya," he added. "We called it *laghbi*, a drink good for the stomach." Making *laghbi* was one of those time-honored professions passed down from father to son. In Israel during the early years, there were few date trees. So instead of "milking" the trees, Mr. Machluf took to milking cows, which he does to this day. But dates are still savored as they are eaten, with memories of life as it had been in Libya for hundreds of years.

At Rosh Hashanah, Libyans, like other Sephardic and Oriental Jews in Israel, eat at least seven different kinds of vegetables and fruits, symbolic of the hope for plenty in the new year. Seven kinds of jam served on that holiday include squash, both white and orange, quince, and candied eggplant, as well as the Machluf family's traditional fresh dates.

Couscous de Ceremonie—Moroccan Sweet Couscous with a Confit of Onions and Fruits

I first tasted a version of this Moroccan steamed couscous served with a confit of onions, raisins, nuts, and apricots at a wedding at Kibbutz Ma'ayan Baruch in the Upper Galilee. At the huge buffet outside—you never have to worry about rain in the summer in Israel—over seven hundred guests ate a typical cross-cultural menu of stuffed grape leaves; Eastern European beef brisket; Chinese chicken with bean sprouts; the inevitable eggplant salad; and Moroccan sweet couscous with kumquats, pine nuts, sautéed onions, and almonds. Because many kibbutz cooks are of French Moroccan origin, the kibbutz wedding cake has become a French *croquembouche* (a cake made of cream puffs stacked and attached with caramel, usually filled with pastry cream). In Israel the cream puffs are stuck together with honey and sesame seeds.

Like the *croquembouche,* the *couscous de ceremonie* is served on all happy occasions, including *Maimouna* (the feast at the end of Passover), celebrated in Moroccan Jewish homes. Traditionally, Moroccans prepare *Maimouna* tables filled with symbolic springtime dishes, including raw fish, fresh dates and candied fruits, and fresh buttermilk, often brought to the Jews by their Arab neighbors. In Israel this custom has changed slightly. During *Maimouna,* a number of open houses are given in largely Moroccan communities; in Jerusalem, a huge pan-Sephardic picnic, where many traditional foods are served, is set up in the park near the Knesset.

Although this recipe describes the traditional way to prepare the *couscous de ceremonie,* you can also use apricots, dried cherries, cranberries, figs, or, as they did on Kibbutz Ma'ayan Baruch, kumquats. I like to serve it as a grain accompaniment to brisket or chicken.

YIELD: 6 TO 8 SERVINGS

1 pound couscous

2 large onions, sliced in rounds

8 tablespoons vegetable oil or salted butter

1/2 cup blanched almonds

1 1/2 cups prunes, pitted

2 teaspoons of sugar plus sugar for sprinkling

Cinnamon for dusting

1/2 cup water

3/4 cup raisins

1. Prepare the couscous as described on page 237, steamed over water rather than over a stew.

2. Sauté the onions very slowly in 3 tablespoons of the oil or butter in a heavy frying pan, until they are golden. Remove from the pan and drain.

3. Heat 3 more tablespoons of the oil or butter and brown the almonds. Add the prunes and sugar. Sprinkle with cinnamon and add ½ cup of water. Sauté for a few minutes over medium heat. Add 2 tablespoons more of the oil or butter along with the raisins.

4. To serve, place the steamed couscous in a mound on a plate, surround with the sautéed onions, almonds, prunes, and raisins, and sprinkle with additional sugar and cinnamon.

Calsones—
Sephardic Cheese Ravioli

When I asked Meir Hameiri for a typical Safed dish, he did not hesitate before giving me this recipe for *calsones*. Definitely one of those "roaming" recipes, *calsones* is known as a Safed dish because the Sephardic Jews there would fill these oversized ravioli with the famous Safed cheese. But how on earth did the recipe get to Safed? It could have come from the Iberian Peninsula after the Inquisition, when many mystics and cabalists fled to the city. It could have come from Italy in the sixteenth century, when merchants were bringing books written by the famous rabbis in Safed to be printed in Livorno, shipped to Aleppo, and then carried by caravan back to Palestine. It could have come later, after the earthquakes in Syria, when more Jews from the East, like the Hameiris, moved to Safed.

Although some think that *calsones* are of Syrian origin, Syrian cookbooks cite Spain as the home of similar recipes. In Italy there are, of course, different types of *calsones,* made from pizza dough and often filled with ham and cheese, hardly a Jewish dish. *Cazoncei,* an Italian stuffed pasta shaped like a crescent, similar to tortellini or kreplach, may be a more likely source for this dish. That explains the shape, but baking the stuffed pasta with butter and cheese is probably a Jewish innovation—a casserole they could prepare before the Sabbath began.

The seemingly strange use of the leftover dough as egg noodles in the casserole can be explained simply: a Jewish cook never wastes anything. Since Israelis today

---

··· MEIR ARZONI AND THE CREATION OF SAFED CHEESE ···

In 1837, an earthquake killed half the population of the religious city of Safed. When Meir Arzoni heard about the disaster from his home in Iran, he decided that the time had come to take his family to Palestine to help resettle the holy city. After a six-month journey, they arrived, having trekked by foot to Iraq, through Syria, and then finally to Palestine. When he climbed up to Safed, he found a cave on the hillside, where he settled. Having discovered a well inside the cave, he soon supported his family by selling water to the Jews from Safed and the Arabs from the surrounding area, and eventually by raising goats to make cheese. The round hard cheese he produced, with a strong aroma and flavor, became known as Safed cheese. "Its unique quality comes from the goats, the altitude, the water they drink, and the air in Safed and the Sea of Galilee," said Meir Hameiri, the great-grandson and namesake of Meir Arzoni.

Mr. Hameiri still makes the cheese in the cave, long since converted into a hillside home next door to the Hameiri Museum, founded by the family to record the history of the city. He showed me how, today, both sheep- and goat-milk curds are brined and pressed into round baskets made with reeds from the nearby Sea of Galilee before they are dried. Although most Safed cheese is made commercially, a few artisans like the Hameiris still make the handmade variety. To keep up with competition from new boutique goat cheeses, the Hameiri family also makes Bulgarian sheep-milk feta, which is very popular today throughout Israel.

seem to prefer Bulgarian feta to Safed cheese, I have included that in this recipe, traditionally served at Shavuot. Another version of Safed *calsones* is served fried.

YIELD: 36 *CALSONES*, SERVING 8 PEOPLE

3 cups all-purpose flour

3 teaspoons salt, plus salt for seasoning

5–6 large eggs

8 ounces Bulgarian feta or Safed cheese

3 tablespoons farmer or ricotta cheese

Freshly ground pepper to taste

½ cup (1 stick) salted butter

6 cups water

Chopped fresh herbs such as parsley and dill

Plain yogurt for garnish

1. To make the dough, either mix in a food processor or toss the flour and 2 teaspoons of the salt in a bowl and form a well in the center. Break 3 of the eggs into the well and, using a fork, gradually stir the eggs into the flour to form a soft dough. Turn out and knead until smooth. On a humid day, use more flour; on a dry day, an extra egg. Cover with a damp cloth and refrigerate 2 hours.

2. To make the filling, first break up the feta or Safed cheese into a bowl, setting aside a few tablespoons for garnish. Stir the farmer or ricotta cheese, 1 egg, and salt and pepper to taste. Mix well.

3. Roll out the dough into a circle about 18 inches in diameter, as thin as possible. Then, using a cookie or ravioli cutter, cut into circles 3 inches in diameter. Spoon a heaping teaspoon of the cheese mixture into the center of each circle. Lightly beat 1 egg with a little water and brush the rims of each circle. Fold into a half-moon shape, pressing the edges together tightly to enclose the cheese.

4. If you run out of filling, cut the leftover dough into 1-by-¼-inch noodles.

5. Preheat the oven to 350 degrees and melt half the butter in a 9-by-12-inch ovenproof casserole.

6. Bring the water to a boil in a large pot. Then add 1 teaspoon of salt and drop 8 *calsones* in at a time. Boil the *calsones* for about 4 minutes, then add the egg noodles if you are using them, and continue cooking about 4 more minutes, or until the noodles are al dente and the *calsone* dough starts to wrinkle. Drain well. Cook the remaining *calsones*.

7. Layer the drained *calsones* and noodles in the casserole. Dot with the remaining butter and feta or Safed cheese and bake, covered with foil, for about 20 minutes. If you want a crispy top, remove the foil and cook for 5 more minutes. Serve as is or with chopped fresh herbs and dollops of yogurt.

NOTE You can also use wonton wrappers for the dough, but the texture of the *calsones* will be more slippery. Cut the wrappers into 3-inch squares. Spoon a heaping teaspoon of filling into the center, wet your finger, and moisten the perimeter of the wrapper. Fold the wrapper over, press to close, and proceed as above, cooking for a shorter time, about 3 to 4 minutes.

Couscous, Pasta, and Rice Dishes

Jerusalem Peppery Kugel

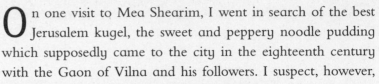

On one visit to Mea Shearim, I went in search of the best Jerusalem kugel, the sweet and peppery noodle pudding which supposedly came to the city in the eighteenth century with the Gaon of Vilna and his followers. I suspect, however, that this is one of those "wandering" Jewish dishes, as it also resembles closely an old Roman Jewish spaghetti dish with lots of pepper called *cacio e pepe*.

Stopping in a bakery packed with Chasidic Jews, I bravely asked, "Does anyone know who makes the best Jerusalem kugel?" One man spoke up quickly and told me to call his wife. She in turn said that the best that she had ever tasted came from a friend, Bluma Zegal, who is Hungarian. Mrs. Zegal told me that the secret to a great Jerusalem kugel is a perfect balance of sweetness and pepper. Here is my take on her recipe, which despite its sweetness is served as a savory dish.

Jerusalem Kugel and other Shabbat treats

YIELD: 6 TO 8 SERVINGS

6 cups water	3 large eggs, lightly beaten
2½ teaspoons salt	1 cup sugar
12 ounces capellini or other thin spaghetti	⅓ cup vegetable oil
½ teaspoon freshly ground black pepper	

1. Preheat the oven to 250 degrees.
2. Bring 6 cups of water to boil in a pot, add ½ teaspoon of the salt, and cook the capellini or spaghetti for about 5 minutes, or according to package directions, until al dente. Drain, rinse in cold water, and place in a bowl.
3. Add the pepper, remaining salt, eggs, and ⅔ cup of sugar. Mix well.
4. Heat the oil in a small saucepan and add the remaining ⅓ cup of sugar. Stirring constantly, cook over medium heat, until the sugar melts and starts to turn brown. Keep an eye on this, for once it begins to color, it darkens quickly.
5. Pour the caramelized sugar over the pasta, mixing well. Don't worry if some of the caramel hardens; it will soften later.
6. Grease a Bundt pan with vegetable oil and pour the spaghetti in. Cover with tin foil and bake overnight (as Jews would for the Sabbath), removing the foil for the last ½ hour, or for 1 hour at 350 degrees uncovered.

NOTE   For an old Sephardic Jerusalem variation, add to the cooked pasta the following ingredients: ⅔ cup of plumped raisins, 3 chopped and sautéed onions, 3 tablespoons light-brown sugar, 1 clove garlic, crushed, ½ teaspoon ground cinnamon, ¼ teaspoon ground nutmeg, ⅛ teaspoon ground allspice, ⅛ teaspoon ground cloves, and 1 teaspoon salt. Proceed as above.

Bringing in vegetable plates at Pini's in Jerusalem

Above: Shai Seltzer and his cheese in the Judean hills

Opposite: Mahane Yehudah market in Jerusalem
(garlic wards off evil spirits)

Above: The taboon at Arabe

Opposite: Margaret Tayer grilling fish
at her restaurant in Jaffe

Above: Kitchen at Rajar

Opposite: Making *kubbeh* and fried pita at Rajar

At Azura Restaurant in
Mahane Yehudah meat market

Hungarian *Shlishkes*

During the question-and-answer periods following the speeches I give around the country, I often am asked for a recipe for the Hungarian noodle called *shlishkes*. I finally tasted a modern version of this dish at the Haimishe Essen (Home Cooking) restaurant in Beit Israel, a stone's throw from Jerusalem's Mea Shearim section. This tiny restaurant, with a takeout counter offering homemade varieties of salads, herring, gefilte fish, eggplant salads, cholent, kasha *varnishkes* with mushrooms, and *shlishkes,* is located in an alley down the street from Bet Meir, the largest yeshiva in Jerusalem. When I visited there, yeshiva students at glass-topped tables would recite the blessings, which were placed under the glass, before and after their meals.

The word *shlishke* probably comes from the German word *Schulterstuck* meaning "epaulette," or "twisted knot." These noodles are traditionally made from a potato-based dough, rolled out like a snake, cut in 1-inch pieces, and twisted. Then they are boiled and served with fresh bread crumbs, browned in butter or oil, and flavored with both pepper and sugar in the Hungarian manner. Most Israelis substitute commercial fusilli, corkscrew-shaped pasta, for the homemade *shlishkes.*

YIELD: 6 TO 8 SERVINGS

12-ounce package fusilli	3 tablespoons sugar
6 tablespoons butter or vegetable oil	1 teaspoon salt
2 cups bread crumbs, made from leftover challah	1 teaspoon white pepper

1. Cook the fusilli in boiling salted water according to the directions on the package, until al dente. Drain and set aside.

2. In a frying pan heat the butter or oil over low heat and add the bread crumbs, sugar, salt, and white pepper, stirring occasionally for a few minutes, until the bread crumbs are browned. Add the cooked fusilli and mix well, adding more butter or oil if too dry.

In 1892 Edward Propper opened a noodle factory in Teplice, in what is now the Czech Republic. His son Eugen took over in 1932, running the company until the German occupation in 1939, when he and his family fled to Palestine. On the boat he met another Czech refugee in a similar business. When the two arrived in Palestine, they started an egg noodle shop in South Tel Aviv, one working the machines and the other selling the noodles. "At that time there were about thirty-six such factories in Palestine for a population of six hundred thousand Jews," said Mr. Propper's son, Gad. Eventually, three of these shops, owned by seven families from the Czech Republic, Germany, Russia, and Poland, united their sales efforts and called their company Osem (in the Yom Kippur prayer for a full harvest, the word *assam* signifies a silo). Today, Osem, partly owned by Nestlé International, is still run by the Propper family and produces, among many other grocery items, 90 percent of the pasta-based foods in Israel.

"In the early 1950s there was very little to eat in Israel," said Gad. Israel's first prime minister, David Ben-Gurion, was worried about the great influx of Sephardic and Oriental Jews who came from Middle Eastern countries, where rice and couscous were their basic foods. "Ben-Gurion asked my father if he could create a pasta product for these immigrants, since little rice and couscous was available for them in Israel at that time," said Gad. "So he made an extruded wheat pasta shaped like rice and another shaped like couscous." Both became staples for a whole generation of Israelis, who dubbed these products *orez Ben-Gurion* (Ben-Gurion's rice). Today, the round Ben-Gurion pasta, now called "Israeli couscous" and *mughrabiya*, from the Mughrab in Arab countries, is one of the favorite ingredients of superstar chefs throughout the world.

Israeli Couscous with Seasonal Vegetables

I love the texture of the so-called "Israeli couscous." My favorite way to prepare it is with pecans and stir-fried winter vegetables like Brussels sprouts, yellow winter squash, cabbage, and Swiss chard. I also recommend serving it with asparagus, tiny pearl onions, and peas in the spring, diced yellow squash and zucchini in the summer, or beans and wild mushrooms in the fall. This is one of those wonderful pasta dishes with which you can use your own imagination. If you can't find Israeli couscous, which is available in Middle Eastern markets and many supermarkets, orzo pasta or arborio rice are nice substitutes.

YIELD: 4 TO 6 SERVINGS

4 tablespoons vegetable oil

2 medium onions, diced

8 ounces Israeli couscous (about 2 cups)

3 cups water

Salt and freshly ground pepper to taste

2 tablespoons chopped fresh parsley

$^1/_2$ red cabbage, shredded

1 cup shredded Brussels sprouts

1 cup diced Swiss chard

1 cup diced winter squash (like butternut, acorn, or Hubbard)

$^1/_4$ cup chopped pecans, toasted

1. In a frying pan, heat 2 tablespoons of the vegetable oil and sauté the onions until soft. Remove half and set aside. Add the couscous to the onions in the frying pan and stir until browned.

2. Bring water to a boil in a saucepan with a cover. Add the couscous, salt and pepper to taste, and parsley. Cover and simmer for 8 to 10 minutes, stirring occasionally.

3. Meanwhile, heat the remaining 2 tablespoons of oil in the skillet and add the reserved onions, the cabbage, Brussels sprouts, Swiss chard, squash, and pecans. Stir-fry until the vegetables are soft.

4. To serve, drain the couscous, place it in the center of a shallow bowl, and surround with the vegetables.

Hana Lustigova Greenfield will never forget the Rosh Hashanah of 1945, after she was liberated, in April, from the Bergen-Belsen concentration camp. "Like many survivors, I went back to Czechoslovakia with the hope of finding my family," she said.

Mrs. Greenfield, who has lived in Tel Aviv since the end of the war, told how she returned to Kolin, a town about fifty kilometers from Prague, where her family had lived for generations. There she found her sister Irena and her rabbi, who had lost everyone in his family. "The rabbi was trying to resurrect the synagogue and to prepare it for Rosh Hashanah," she said. "He gave us a white sheet to sew a *kittel* (a special robe worn during the High Holidays by the ultra-Orthodox) and a hat for Rosh Hashanah." Before the service the rabbi told the sisters to cut up an apple as the new fruit of the season and dip it in honey for a sweet life. "I'll never forget his words," said Mrs. Greenfield, who is in her mid-seventies. " 'As bitter as was our past life, we should have a sweet future,' he told us."

Before World War II, the Jews of Czechoslovakia numbered 380,000; only 8 percent survived the Holocaust. Some immigrated to Palestine, while others went to any country that would allow them in. "We considered ourselves a Jewish community, well assimilated into the Czech way of life, with a thousand-year history," said Mrs. Greenfield. "We were proud of Franz Kafka and Max Brod, who were both Czech and Jewish."

At fifteen, Mrs. Greenfield was sent to Terezienstadt, where she worked in the kitchen, in a privileged position, until she caught typhoid. She was later sent to Auschwitz, where her mother perished. Her father died during a mass murder in a Polish camp in 1942.

"Once when I was ladling out watered-down soup, an old man begged me for some vegetables from the bottom of the pot," she recalled. "When I looked up I recognized my own grandfather." She gave him an extra potato but kept her head bowed so he would not recognize her and be humiliated. Later that day she brought her grandfather two potatoes, which he peeled with his penknife and they shared. The next day, using that same knife, he committed suicide.

Mrs. Greenfield relates these and other tales from this defining period of her life in her book, *Fragments of Memory* (1992). Today she divides her time between Tel Aviv and Prague, where she runs a program funded by the proceeds of her book to teach Czech youth tolerance and to educate them about the Holocaust. "Some of these children do not know what a Jew is," she said. "After all, it has been fifty years since the Jews were deported."

Like many survivors, Mrs. Greenfield, the mother of three Israel-born children and the grandmother of nine, is an optimist—and at no time more so than on Rosh Hashanah, the Jewish New Year. "There were always a lot of apples in Czechoslovakia, even in our own gardens," said Mrs. Greenfield. "When I cook at Rosh Hashanah I do not just dip the apples in honey as the rabbi taught me. I use them in cooking as a symbol of hope for the future I was given and for the future of our children."

Czech Apple-Noodle Kugel

Because Mrs. Greenfield was a young girl when the war began, she learned this recipe from the family's maid, Anka. "After the war, when I returned to Kolin, Anka brought me back to life, cooking and caring for me," recalled Mrs. Greenfield. "Years later, when I married and had children in Israel, I wrote to ask her for the recipes for the wonderful food I had in my memory, like this apple kugel."

YIELD: 8 TO 10 SERVINGS

- 1/4 cup raisins
- 1/4 cup orange or apricot liqueur
- 8 ounces egg noodles
- 1/4 cup (1/2 stick) unsalted butter or pareve margarine
- 2 pounds Granny Smith or other flavorful apples (about 6), cored, peeled, and grated
- 1/2 cup light-brown sugar
- 3/4 cup apricot jam
- 1/2 cup roughly chopped walnuts (optional)
- 1 teaspoon salt
- 4 large eggs

1. Put the raisins in a small bowl with the orange or apricot liqueur. Let sit for about 30 minutes while you prepare the kugel, until the raisins are plumped.

2. Preheat the oven to 350 degrees. Grease a 9-by-12-inch baking pan.

3. Cook the noodles according to the package directions and drain.

4. Meanwhile, heat the butter or margarine in a frying pan. Add the apples, brown sugar, and jam. Sauté until the apples are soft. Remove from the pan, reserving a few tablespoons of the liquid.

5. Place the noodles in a large bowl with the apples, walnuts, salt, raisins, and any liqueur not absorbed. In a separate bowl beat the eggs well; mix with the noodles, then pour into the prepared pan. Brush the top with the reserved liquid from the apples.

6. Place on the middle rack of the oven and bake for 35 minutes or until golden.

Goat Cheese and Sun-dried Tomato Lasagne

Although there is evidence that pasta has existed in the eastern Mediterranean for ages, Israelis were not particularly adept at making pasta dishes until Beth Elon showed them the way. When her *Big Book of Pasta* came out in Hebrew in 1996, it was a best-seller. Beth, a literary agent and wife of the Israeli writer Amos Elon, divides her time between Jerusalem and a farmhouse the Elons own in a Tuscan hill town not far from Florence.

"When I started cooking in Italy I discovered that Israeli produce was exactly like Italian, but Israeli food wasn't really Mediterranean," said Beth. "So I set out to make our tastes more Mediterranean. When I began writing about Italian food and pasta, not many people here even used olive oil. I knew that everyone loved pasta, but most Israelis simply ate it smeared with ketchup. So I began there."

I especially like Beth's take on lasagne; she uses goat cheese and sun-dried tomatoes, which she dries herself in Italy in July and August and brings back to Israel. Any goat cheese will do, as long as it is fairly creamy and melts well. I have added pesto, which has recently become popular in Israel.

Goat cheese has become a specialty of Israel

YIELD: ABOUT 12 SERVINGS

3 tablespoons butter

1 large onion, finely chopped (about 2 cups)

3 cloves garlic, minced

4 tablespoons all-purpose flour

1 cup vegetable broth

1 cup heavy cream

1 1/2 cups milk

12 ounces feta or other goat cheese, crumbled

Salt and freshly ground pepper to taste

1/2 teaspoon ground nutmeg

1 pound lasagne noodles

1 cup sun-dried tomatoes

1 pound ricotta cheese

1/2 cup pesto (see page 217)

1/4 cup grated Parmesan cheese

1. To make the sauce, melt the butter in a heavy saucepan over medium-low heat. Add the onions and garlic and sauté until the onions are translucent, about 5 minutes. Mix the flour with a little of the vegetable broth and stir into a paste, removing any lumps. Slowly whisk the paste into the onion mixture along with the remaining vegetable broth and simmer for a minute or 2, whisking constantly, until the sauce thickens. Add the cream and milk and continue to stir often until the sauce has thickened further, about 5 minutes. Stir in the goat cheese and season, if needed, with salt. Add lots of pepper and the nutmeg.

2. Cook the lasagne according to the package instructions. Drain and set aside in cool water.

3. Preheat the oven to 350 degrees and grease a 9-by-13-inch baking dish. Soak the sun-dried tomatoes in boiling water for a few minutes, then drain and chop them.

4. Spread a few tablespoons of the sauce across the bottom of the baking dish and cover with 5 strips of the lasagne, slightly overlapping each piece of pasta. Spoon half of the ricotta cheese over the pasta.

5. Cover with 5 more strips of the lasagne. Spread half of the remaining sauce on top and sprinkle with half the sun-dried tomatoes and the pesto. Now make a layer of 5 more strips of lasagne, cover with the remaining ricotta cheese, a final layer of the remaining 5 lasagne leaves and cover with the remaining sun-dried tomatoes and the remaining sauce. Sprinkle the Parmesan cheese on top.

6. Bake the lasagne for 25 minutes or until the top is crisp and bubbly. Allow to rest for a few minutes before serving.

Dan Eilat's Three-cheese Pasta *Pashtida* with Spinach

I like the balance of the spinach, cheese, and pasta in this *pashtida,* one of the dozens of dishes served at the elaborate breakfast buffet at the Dan Eilat, a fantastical coast hotel designed by Adam Tihany.

YIELD: 8 SERVINGS

8 ounces dry penne, rigatoni, or fusilli pasta

1 tablespoon butter

1 large onion, diced

2 cloves garlic, minced

1 pound fresh spinach or 10-ounce package frozen spinach, thawed and drained

4 large eggs, beaten

1/2 cup crumbled feta cheese

1 cup ricotta cheese

1/4 cup plus 2 tablespoons grated Parmesan cheese

1/2 cup chopped fresh chives

1 teaspoon salt, or to taste

1/4 teaspoon ground nutmeg

Freshly ground pepper to taste

1. Preheat oven to 350 degrees and lightly grease a 9-by-12-inch baking dish.

2. Cook the pasta in boiling salted water according to package directions.

3. Heat the butter in a small skillet, add the onions and garlic, and sauté until the onions are translucent. Cool and set aside.

4. If you are using fresh spinach, bring 1/4 cup of water to a boil. Add the spinach, cover, and simmer for 3 minutes. Drain.

5. Place the eggs, feta and ricotta cheeses, 1/4 cup of the Parmesan cheese, chives, salt, nutmeg, and pepper to taste in a large mixing bowl. Add the cooked drained pasta, spinach, and sautéed onions and garlic and mix well. Pour into the prepared baking dish and sprinkle with the remaining 2 tablespoons of Parmesan cheese.

6. Bake, covered with foil, for 30 minutes. Remove the foil and bake for 5 to 10 minutes more or until the top is golden brown.

Sesame Noodles

Usually when I think of sesame noodles, I think of Thai or other Far Eastern dishes made with peanut butter. I first tasted this uniquely flavored fusion recipe in Israel; it is prepared with tahina instead of peanut butter.

YIELD: 4 TO 6 SERVINGS

¼ cup tahina

3 tablespoons brewed black tea

1 tablespoon hot chili oil

3 tablespoons soy sauce

2 tablespoons minced fresh ginger

1 tablespoon minced fresh garlic

1 tablespoon red-wine vinegar

1 tablespoon sugar

8 ounces spaghetti, preferably whole-wheat

1. Mix the tahina, tea, hot chili oil, soy sauce, ginger, garlic, vinegar, and sugar in a mixing bowl.

2. Cook the pasta according to the directions on the package and drain. Stir in the tahina sauce and serve lukewarm with stir-fried vegetables.

Fish

My favorite Israeli fish story comes from Shalom Kadosh, the chef at Jerusalem's Sheraton Plaza Hotel. He told me that after he prepared a meal for the late King Hussein in Jerusalem, the king was so taken with the sea bream which had been served that when he returned to his palace in Amman he called Kadosh to ask where the chef had procured the fish. It had, of course, been farm-raised in the Red Sea, alongside the popular *burri* (gray mullet), *musht* (St. Peter's fish, also known as *Tilapia galilea*), salmon, red drum, trout, and carp.

Above: Boat filled with fish coming into dock

In 1938, immigrants from Yugoslavia established the first kibbutz fish farm at Nir David, after Jewish pioneers had drained the swamps of the Huleh Valley in the Galilee. There, using brackish water, they created carp ponds for the freshwater fish with which they were familiar and which were the sine qua non for their gefilte fish. Baked, fried, steamed, and broiled, carp was nutritious and filling for the new immigrants. Canned, it was a profitable export. In fact, gefilte fish was regarded as so important that even the North African Jewish immigrants, who were well practiced in their own traditional fish recipes, were taught in cooking classes how to prepare it. "At the community center they wanted to teach me how to make gefilte fish," recalled Hannah Zrihen, an immigrant from Morocco now living in Ma'alot. "I didn't want to eat it or to learn how to make it. First of all, I don't like sweetness in fish, and second of all, they serve it with horseradish!"

For Ashkenazic Jews, however, gefilte fish represented a time-honored tradition for a festive Friday-night or holiday meal. "I remember as a boy going to the local fish market on Mamilla Street, where they had a tiled pool, and you used to point at the carp you wanted," recalled David Harman, who grew up in Jerusalem in the 1950s. "The guy would take the carp out with a net, clop it on the head with a piece of wood, and wrap it up, and I would take it home to my grandmother. I had to cut it open and clean it, then grind it in a hand grinder for her gefilte fish."

At one time, carp alone filled the fish ponds in Upper Galilee, but mullet and tilapia were added later. After the 1967 war, with a sense of confidence that came from safer borders, Israeli farmers started trout farms on border kibbutzim. These farms used the rushing waters of the Dan and Banias Rivers, which flow from Mount Hermon to the Sea of Galilee. Now, with the popularity of new flavors in Israeli cooking, fish like striped bass and Washington State salmon are farmed in the north as well, with additional ponds or cages in the Red Sea, and some in the Mediterranean for sea bream and red drum. Today there are about fifty-five fish farms throughout the country, including in the Negev Desert.

Israel's infatuation with fish begins with the Book of Genesis, where God blesses humans by urging them to "be fruitful and multiply" like the fish. Since biblical times, the fish has come to symbolize fertility and immortality. The Book of Nehemiah recounts that "There dwelt men of Tyre also therein, who brought in fish, and all manner of ware, and sold on the Sabbath unto the children of Judah, and in Jerusalem" (13:16). In fact, it seems that so much sea fish was sold in Jerusalem during that period that one gate to the city was called the "Fish Gate." During the Roman period, fresh fish for the Sabbath was in such demand that the Romans imposed a high tax on the fishermen in the Sea of Galilee.

Because of its biblical importance, kashrut-permissible fish with fins and scales

When they came ashore, they saw a charcoal fire there with fish laid on it, and some bread. Jesus said, "Bring some of the fish you have caught." Simon Peter went on board and hauled the net to land; it was full of big fish, a hundred and fifty-three in all; and yet, many as they were, the net was not torn.

—John 21:9–11

On a recent trip to the Sea of Galilee, I visited Capernaum, where Jesus is said to have preached and healed. There, I talked with Father Pedro Bon, a Franciscan priest who is one of the custodians of *terra santa*. He said that for the fishermen in Capernaum, little has changed since the time of Jesus and the miracle of the loaves and fishes. As a result of some pollution and ecological neglect, they may catch fewer St. Peter's fish—named after the sea creature from whose mouth Peter took a piece of money in obedience to Jesus' injunction—but the waters near Capernaum still yield many other species.

"Since Jesus was an observant Jew, he went to the synagogue here every Saturday and prayed to heal people," said Father Pedro Bon, who showed us around the compound, leading us to the ancient olive oil press and flour mill. "We know from the scriptures that Jesus ate fish. Although I am not a cook, I imagine he ate his grilled, and probably sprinkled with *za'atar* and olive oil."

Fish mosaic at Capernaum

The Foods of
Israel Today

have always been critical to meals on the Jewish Sabbath and on other Jewish holidays, as well as all kinds of fish on Fridays for Catholics. Jews from Morocco serve a fish head for good luck at Rosh Hashanah and *Maimouna,* the holiday celebrating the spring; they practice this tradition in Israel today. The numerical correspondents to the letters in *dag,* the word for "fish" in Hebrew, add up to the number seven—a hint as to the importance of fish on the Sabbath, the seventh day of the week. In Greek, the word for Christ is *Ichthus,* which also means fish.

Because of the kashrut prohibition against eating shellfish, Jewish fishermen have often discarded the shrimp and other crustaceans scooped up in their nets along the Mediterranean coast of Israel. Today, however, in nonkosher seafood restaurants throughout the country, these shellfish, and other sea fish like mackerel, sardines, and red mullet, are grilled, fried, and sometimes cured as *escabeche* or seviche.

Innovative ideas for cooking and preserving fish have been brought to Israel by immigrants and Israelis who have traveled abroad. Years ago, Chicago-born Yehuda Avni, owner of the dude ranch Vered Hagalil overlooking the Sea of Galilee, started smoking fish over carob wood, a method he had learned in the United States. Jacob Avishai, then of Kibbutz Dan, observed him and now serves avocado wood–smoked trout and salmon with rosemary and bay leaves at his rustic outdoor restaurant, Dag a la Dan, nestled under wild willow, mulberry, and fig trees above the Dan River, one of the main tributaries of the Jordan River in Upper Galilee. "The Western world decided that meat is not so healthy, so they went to fish," he told me. The exciting new dishes served throughout Israel today reflect this modern trend.

Fish

Grilled Fish with Fresh Herbs and Garlic

I've traveled all over the world, and the tastiest fish is still in Akko," said Christo Triandafilides, the owner of Abu Christo restaurant on the harbor in the old city of Akko (called Acre in English). We were sitting at a table there, with a view of medieval ruins and fishing nets drying in the sun. "The best fish is grilled simply, with salt, pepper, and oregano or a sprinkle of *za'atar*," added Mr. Triandafilides, a Greek Orthodox Christian who came to Palestine in 1945, fleeing his native Izmir after the Turkish takeover.

Jako Allaloof, born to a Jewish fishing family also in Izmir, has the same opinion about fish. His restaurant, hardly a tourist mecca, is located on a tiny side street in the Turkish market near the harbor in Haifa. It is the type of place where people go to eat fresh and cheap. With no set menu, the fish served depends on what phone calls Jako gets each day telling him what the fishermen catch. They bring in whole loads of fish and dump them on the ceramic floor of the kitchen. Cradling his cell phone in his hand, Jako told me, "No matter what fish they catch, the trick is to grill them quickly."

The following is a master recipe, with lessons gleaned from many fish mavens throughout Israel. The technique is more or less the same, with varying amounts of *za'atar*, oregano, or mixed herbs, but it is always simple. In Israel, fish is most often grilled over olive or avocado wood, sometimes over olive pits. The Bedouins in the south have taught Israelis the unusual method of dipping a few pages of newspaper in olive oil, then in water, and wrapping the fish in the paper to steam over an open fire. They also often bake the fish with *za'atar* and lemon juice, wrapped in unbaked pita dough, or even coarse salt. Tilapia, trout, grouper, bluefish, salmon, carp, mullet, halibut, or tuna, as whole gutted fish or fillets, are all good. When grilling fish, figure a one-pound fish per person. If you prefer to use a larger fish, portion it once it is cooked—the fillets will slide right off the bone.

Grilling fish under the wild fig at Dag a la Dan in upper Galilee

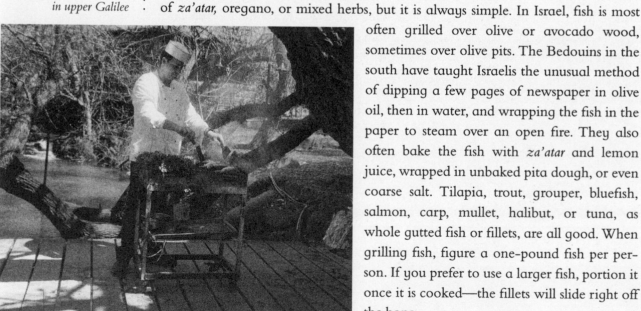

4 whole fish, about 1 pound each (or 1 4-
  to 5-pound fish), cleaned and gutted,
  with heads and tails removed

1 teaspoon salt

½ teaspoon freshly ground pepper, or to
  taste

2 cloves garlic, mashed

1 cup chopped mixed fresh herbs, such as
  thyme, tarragon, basil, sage, cilantro,
  oregano, and chives

Juice of 2 lemons

2 tablespoons extra virgin olive oil, plus
  additional for rubbing

Large sprigs of fresh oregano, basil,
  rosemary, or thyme

1. Cut each fish in half lengthwise and open up like a book. Season with the salt and pepper and spread the garlic and the chopped herbs on the flesh. Squeeze the lemon juice over the fish and drizzle on the 2 tablespoons olive oil. Close the fish and skewer them along the open sides to seal in the flavorings. Lightly brush the fish skins with more olive oil to prevent them from sticking to the herb sprigs during grilling.

2. Heat the grill to medium-high. Scatter the sprigs of fresh herbs on the grill. Place the fish on top of the herbs and grill for about 7 to 8 minutes. Using 2 spatulas, carefully flip each fish over and grill for 4 to 5 minutes more. You may need to use a cookie sheet to help slide the fish off the grill. Sprinkle on additional lemon juice and olive oil according to taste.

NOTE   You can substitute 1 tablespoon of *za'atar* (see page 62) for the mixed herbs sprinkled in the cavity. You can also grill 1 fillet skin side down, or bake the fish in a 450-degree oven for about 25 minutes, surrounded by 2 diced tomatoes, 1 diced onion, and 2 cups of white wine or water.

Grilled Grouper Patties

The entrance to Margaret Tayar's fish restaurant

What first struck me about Margaret Tayar was her amazing laugh. The chef holds forth in her tiny, four-table restaurant, with the Tel Aviv waterfront to the right, the clock tower of Jaffa to the left, and the noise of the *muezzin* in the background. Margaret, whose parents came in 1950 from Georgia in the former Soviet Union, opened this kosher fish restaurant more than twenty years ago, just before her daughter was born.

A self-taught cook, Margaret left Israel only once to sample Paris and London fare. She missed Israeli food so much that she lost three kilos during the trip. "Once I went to a fancy restaurant. The colors were pretty, but the sardines had no taste," she said, laughing. "The food in this country is the best in the world."

Whether the French would agree with her is debatable, but Gault Millau gave her restaurant the highest rating in Israel. Local ingredients abound: olive oil from a Druse village in the Galilee, where the olives are picked from the top of the tree just for her, and piles of jars of pickled lemons, olives, and eggplants. Margaret works in her tiny kitchen with only a portable stove, and she is so secretive a cook that she works alone from 8 to 11 each day before her assistants arrive. Her salads fill your mouth with flavor—beets, roasted peppers, squash, carrots, and several kinds of eggplant.

One of the dishes I especially like is her *lokus* (grouper) patties. Since Margaret keeps her recipes to herself, this is my best approximation. Although I use a food processor to chop the fish, Margaret and many other Israeli cooks use an old-fashioned meat grinder. If you like, you can substitute sea bass for the grouper. The patties also can be prepared a day in advance before grilling.

YIELD: 8 PATTIES, SERVING 4 PEOPLE

1 pound fresh grouper fillets	1 teaspoon salt, or to taste
1 medium onion, quartered	½ teaspoon freshly ground pepper, or to taste
½ cup fresh chopped parsley	
¼ cup fresh chopped cilantro	1 medium tomato, peeled, seeded, and diced
1 large egg, lightly beaten	

1. Using a meat grinder or food processor equipped with a steel blade, coarsely chop the fish with the onion, parsley, and cilantro. Transfer to a bowl and mix in the egg, salt, and pepper.

2. Form the fish mixture into 8 patties, each the size of a small hamburger, about 3½ inches in diameter. Place the patties on a plate, cover with aluminum foil, and refrigerate for at least 15 minutes or overnight.

3. Heat a grill to medium-high and brush with olive oil. Grill the patties on each side for about 3 minutes. You can also broil these, brushing the patties with olive oil. Serve garnished with the diced tomato.

Baked Stuffed Sea Bream with Cilantro

My friend Liz Magnes and I once set out from Eilat in a tiny motorboat to visit a sea bream farm in the middle of the Red Sea. Looking back at the outline of the city, flanked by tourist hotels, we could see Saudi Arabia in the distance, with Jordan and Egypt on either side. The boat took us to an old navy ship, where Oded Goldan, a marine biologist casually dressed in jeans and sneakers, greeted us. He showed us the fish cages where young sea bream, called *denise* and *chipura,* are cultivated. Considered worldwide to be the most delicious fish of the Mediterranean, the mature sea bream are efficiently exported to Europe, New York, and Boston. According to Goldan, one advantage of breeding the fish in the Red Sea rather than in the Mediterranean is the purity of the water, with temperatures ranging from 21 to 25 degrees Celsius. At 15 to 30 degrees, the more variable Mediterranean often becomes a haven for parasites.

Jihad Babai, the son of many generations of Jaffa fishermen, prepared this version of sea bream with fresh herbs when I visited his restaurant, Sea Foam, on the seashore of Jaffa. You can substitute grouper or salmon fillets for the sea bream.

Jihad Babai and his wife, Huda, overlooking the sea

YIELD: 6 TO 8 SERVINGS

1 cup chopped fresh cilantro

½ cup fresh basil leaves

¼ cup dry white wine

2 tablespoons unsalted butter

2 tablespoons extra virgin olive oil

2 cloves garlic

¼ cup fresh lemon juice

1 teaspoon salt, or to taste

½ teaspoon freshly ground pepper, or to taste

2 pounds sea bream fillet

¼ cup fine cracker crumbs, like Ritz

1½ teaspoons sweet paprika

1. Preheat the oven to 375 degrees.

2. Put the cilantro, basil, wine, butter, oil, garlic, and lemon juice in a food processor fitted with a steel blade and pulse briefly until chopped. Add the salt and pepper and pulse once more.

3. Wash and dry the fish and spread the herb mixture over it. Sprinkle the cracker crumbs and the paprika on top.

4. Place the fish in a baking dish and bake, uncovered, for about 20 minutes or until the fish flakes when pierced with a fork.

Fish

Life on a kibbutz in the twenties was very far from luxurious. To begin with, there was very little to eat, and what was available tasted dreadful. The staples of our diet were sour cereals, unrefined oil (which we bought from the Arabs in goatskin bags, making it as bitter as death), a few vegetables from the kibbutz's own precious vegetable patch, canned bully beef that came from British military supplies left over from the war, and an incredible dish made up of herring preserved in tomato sauce, which, ironically enough, was known as "fresh" (I suppose from the misleading "fresh herring" printed on the label). We ate "fresh herring" every morning for breakfast! When my turn came to work in the kitchen, to everyone's astonishment I was delighted. Now I could really do something about the frightful food....

The herring—eliminated for breakfast but now served in the middle of the day—also presented a problem. Not everyone had a knife, fork and spoon; mostly each person had one utensil, either a knife, a fork or a spoon. The girls who worked in the kitchen used to wash the herring and cut it into small pieces, but they didn't peel off the skin, so that when the herring was brought to the table, everyone had to peel his own. And since there was nothing on which one could wipe one's hands, they were wiped on our work clothes. When I came to work in the kitchen, I decided to peel the herring. The other girls complained. "You'll see, she'll get them used to that, too." But I had an answer for this as well. "What would you have done in your own home? How would you have served herring at your own family table? This is your home! They are your family!"

—Golda Meir, *My Life* (1975)

Golda Meir was not the only one who tried to make the best of the area's scarce resources. In his autobiography, *Living Bridges*, Alexander M. Dushkin tells the story of how his wife, Julia, an American nutritionist living in Palestine, and her friend Henrietta Szold—the founder, in 1912, of Hadassah, the Women's Zionist Organization—tried to help feed a group of *halutzim* who were building the road from Tiberias to Safed. The men were suffering from mouth diseases caused by their poor diet, which consisted mostly of the same herring and canned bully beef. The two women tried to change their eating habits; one day, Mrs. Dushkin served them porridge instead of the daily herring for supper. The men refused to eat. Calling her by the only Hebrew approximation of her name, they said, "*Haverah Yehudit* [Comrade Judith], we are big strong men who have been eating herring all our lives, and we are none the worse for it."

Herring Salad

This recipe, similar to one in the *Hadassah Israel Cooks*, comes from the late Gladys Sabel, a woman I was privileged to know when I lived in Jerusalem. After immigrating to Israel from the United Kingdom in 1948, Mrs. Sabel wanted to use the skills for coping with food shortages that she had learned in war-torn England. She went to small villages outside Jerusalem to teach women from North Africa how to cook with dried eggs and powdered milk. (For more on Mrs. Sabel, see page 284.) At home she made this lovely herring and apple salad, which she served to break the fast on Yom Kippur.

YIELD: ABOUT 2 CUPS, SERVING 6 TO 8

12-ounce jar of pickled herring

4 tablespoons tomato paste

2 tablespoons sugar, or to taste

4 tablespoons white vinegar

2 teaspoons vegetable oil

½ medium Granny Smith or other tart apple, unpeeled and diced in ½-inch cubes

½ cup diced Bermuda onion

¼ cup diced dill pickles

1. Drain the herring, discarding the onions, and cut into ½-inch chunks.

2. Put the herring pieces in a mixing bowl and add the tomato paste, sugar, vinegar, and oil. Stir to mix. Fold in the apple, onion, and pickles.

3. Cover the salad and let sit a day or 2 in the refrigerator. Serve as an appetizer with challah or rye bread.

A nurse introducing new foods to a child

Leo Contini's *Polpettone di Tonno* (Tuna Loaf)

Leo Contini, a scientist turned sculptor, lives in the seaport city of Jaffa. "This crazy Zionism brought me to Israel," he told me when I visited his home, an old Arab house. A member of the Italian Contini family made famous in the film *Garden of the Finzi-Continis,* Mr. Contini loves to cook. *Polpettone di tonno* is a typically Jewish Italian dish: the word *polpetta* describes an oval meatball, and the suffix *-one* means large. This *polpettone* is therefore a large tuna roll.

YIELD: 10 APPETIZER SERVINGS

- 2 6-ounce cans of tuna in oil
- 2 large eggs, lightly beaten
- 3/4 cup bread crumbs, plus more for rolling
- 2 tablespoons chopped chives, plus additional for garnish
- 2 tablespoons snipped fresh dill, plus additional for garnish
- 2 teaspoons salt
- 1/2 teaspoon freshly ground pepper, or to taste
- 1 teaspoon capers for garnish

1. Put the tuna, with its oil, in a mixing bowl with the eggs, 1/2 cup of the bread crumbs, chives, dill, 1 teaspoon of the salt, and the pepper. Mash well and mix with a fork.

2. Turn the tuna onto a work surface on which you have sprinkled some bread crumbs. Carefully mold the tuna into a sausage approximately 10 inches by 2 1/2 inches. Wrap the roll in cheesecloth.

3. Bring about 4 inches of water to a boil in a saucepan large enough to hold the tuna sausage. Add the remaining teaspoon of salt to the water, carefully slip in the *polpettone,* and simmer, covered, for about 30 minutes. Gently remove the *polpettone* with 2 spatulas. Drain and cool on a plate. Cover it with another heavier plate to weight it down, then refrigerate for several hours or overnight. Remove the cheesecloth and serve sliced with a dollop of the following Caper-Lemon Mayonnaise and sprinkled with additional chives, dill, and capers.

Caper-Lemon Mayonnaise with Fresh Herbs

This mayonnaise can also be used with other fish recipes or as a salad dressing.

YIELD: ABOUT 1 CUP

2 egg yolks

2 teaspoons Dijon mustard

Juice of 1 large lemon

1 cup extra virgin olive oil

1 tablespoon fresh chopped dill

1 tablespoon fresh chopped chives

2 tablespoons capers, rinsed and dried

1 teaspoon salt, or to taste

1/4 teaspoon freshly ground pepper, or to taste

1. In a food processor or blender, pulse or whip the egg yolks, mustard, and lemon juice.

2. Gradually add the oil in a thin, steady stream, processing until thick. At the last minute, add the dill, chives, and capers and pulse. Add salt and pepper, adjusting the seasonings to taste.

Recent Russian immigrants have brought a new taste for smoked fish—and caviar.

Caldo di Pesce—Bosnian Codfish Stew with Tomatoes, Leeks, and Peppers

For hundreds of years under the Turkish occupation, Jews in the Balkan states lived in isolated enclaves. Until World War II, their food customs remained more or less the same. "Because we lived an insular existence and spoke Ladino [Judaic Spanish] with each other but Serbian outside, we stayed the same as when we left Spain," said Bina Benzion Kaplan, a Bosnian poet who came to Israel in 1949. "When I visited Spain, something seemed familiar to me with the food. It was the method of cutting salad in large chunks and the aroma from fish stews so similar to the ones I grew up with. Now, what was once a religious heritage for us in Bosnia is a cultural heritage in Israel."

Mrs. Kaplan makes the *caldo di pesce,* this delicate fish stew made with cod, leeks, peppers, and tomatoes, in her home in Kiryat Ono, a suburb of Tel Aviv. Sometimes the fish is served whole on a platter, with the vegetable broth on the side, and sometimes the fish is cut up and served like a bouillabaisse in the broth. You can also substitute haddock for the cod.

YIELD: 6 TO 8 SERVINGS

1 large onion, diced

2 leeks, diced

6 tablespoons olive oil

4 large tomatoes, peeled, seeded, and chopped

1 green bell pepper, seeded and chopped

4 tablespoons chopped fresh parsley

1 bay leaf

2 tablespoons fresh or 1 tablespoon dried marjoram

1 teaspoon salt or to taste

A few grinds of freshly ground pepper to taste

Juice of 1 lemon, or to taste

1 cup water, vegetable broth, or white wine

2 pounds cod fillets, skinned

1/4 cup green olives, pitted

1. Sauté the onions and the leeks in the oil in a heavy casserole until the onions are translucent.

2. Add the tomatoes, green peppers, parsley, bay leaf, marjoram, salt and pepper to taste, lemon juice, and water, vegetable broth, or white wine. Bring the mixture to a boil, reduce heat, and simmer, covered, for about 15 minutes.

3. Add the fish and the olives and continue to simmer, covered, about 15 minutes or until the fish flakes when cut with a fork. Adjust seasonings to taste, remove the bay leaf, and serve in soup bowls, including a piece or 2 of fish in each serving.

Khreimi— Libyan Friday-Night Fish with Peppers and Tomato

*K*hreimi, the spicy Libyan Friday-night fish, has become a popular dish among Israel's many cultures and regions. When I visited Massuda Machluf (see page 239) at her home in Beit Shikma, she showed me the secret to the dish—a spice mixture called *pilpel shuma* (garlic pepper) that she makes each summer and uses throughout the year. In August she buys hot peppers and dries them on a nylon cloth outside in the sun, or strings them and dries them on a line. Then she grinds them in her mortar and pestle with garlic, *nigella* (black caraway seeds), and cumin. This fish goes stunningly with Moroccan *Pan de Casa,* on pages 118–19.

YIELD: 6 TO 8 SERVINGS

2–3 teaspoons crushed, dried hot red peppers or pepper flakes

1 tablespoon garlic

1 teaspoon *nigella*

1 teaspoon ground cumin

1 teaspoon salt

1/2 teaspoon freshly ground black pepper

2 tablespoons tomato paste

1 1/2 cups water

1/3 cup extra virgin olive oil

2 pounds tuna, grouper, gray mullet, carp, or whiting, cut in steaks or filleted

1. Grind the peppers, garlic, *nigella,* cumin, salt, and pepper together in a spice grinder or with a mortar and pestle. Mix with the tomato paste and water.

2. Heat the oil in a frying pan that has a cover. When it is very hot, stir in the tomato paste mixture.

3. Bring to a boil and carefully slip in the fish. Reduce the heat and simmer, covered, about 5 to 7 minutes or until the fish flakes when pierced with a fork, and turn it onto its other side for another 5 to 7 minutes. Tuna will require less cooking time.

4. Using 2 spatulas, gently remove the fish from the sauce. Boil the sauce down for about 5 minutes, to reduce by half, and adjust the seasonings. Cut the fish in pieces, cover with the sauce, and serve, either at room temperature or reheated just before serving.

Moroccan White Fish
with Red Peppers,
Cilantro, and Fava Beans

Elana Levy-Zrihen had a dream. She wanted to package and sell the spices she used every day in her Yemenite and Moroccan cooking. Step Wertheimer, one of Israel's leading industrialists, also had a dream. He wanted to encourage business in developing towns like Ma'alot—where Elana lives—so that Jews, Christians, and Moslems could work together. So he agreed to help her start her business, which she now calls Spices by Elana.

When I visited her factory at the Tefen Industrial Park in the Lower Galilee, I saw young Druse, Christian, and Moslem Arabs working hand-in-hand with Jewish youth, feeding colorful spice combinations into decorative bottles to be packaged and shipped abroad.

Usually, lunch at the factory is a kind of potluck, with Elana serving pita bread and hummus and the staff bringing additional side dishes from home. But during my visit Elana prepared her Yemenite chicken soup, as well as two of her mother-in-law's Moroccan fish recipes, all using her prepared spice mixtures.

Elana, who comes from a Yemenite background in Tel Aviv, moved to the north during her military service. Her assignment was to teach Moroccan immigrants how to read. One student was Hannah Zrihen (see page 162), who introduced Elana to her son, and they later married. Like many traditional mothers, the elder Mrs. Zrihen does not understand her daughter-in-law's ambition outside the home. "Every morning I pray that God will save Israel and my daughter-in-law," she said. "She works so hard."

Because hers is a "mixed" Israeli marriage, Elana has learned many new cooking techniques and recipes from Mrs. Zrihen, including several of her *"dagim shel shabbat,"* marvelous Sabbath fish dishes. I have tasted variations on the Friday-night Moroccan fish dish, using fava beans or chickpeas, in many homes throughout Israel. In the United States, it is sometimes prepared with lima beans. Most cooks rub the fish with lemon juice, which not only flavors it but also cures it, as in a seviche. This technique was necessary in the days when there was no refrigeration; today, it just is used to season the flesh. This dish, best made a day in advance and served at room temperature, is a great first course at a Friday-night Sabbath dinner, or for company anytime. I also make it in the summer as a main course with a salad.

1/4 cup extra virgin olive oil

8 cloves garlic, diced

2 red bell peppers, diced

1 green bell pepper, diced

1 teaspoon pepper flakes, or to taste

1 teaspoon ground turmeric

2 tablespoons paprika

1 teaspoon salt, or to taste

1/2 teaspoon freshly ground pepper, or to taste

4 cups water

4 tablespoons lemon juice, or to taste

1 bunch fresh cilantro, chopped (about 1 packed cup)

2 cups fresh fava or lima beans

2 fillets of shad, sea bass, whiting, rockfish, tilapia, or orange roughy (about 3 pounds)

1. Heat a heavy skillet that has a cover and pour in the oil. When hot, add the garlic and diced peppers and stir-fry for a few minutes. Add the pepper flakes, turmeric, paprika, salt, and pepper, and stir again. Add the water, lemon juice, and all but 2 tablespoons of the cilantro; bring to a boil, reduce heat, and simmer, uncovered, for about 15 minutes.

2. Add the beans, stir, and slip the fish into the pan. Make sure the liquid almost covers the fish, adding more water if necessary. Cover and simmer for 10 to 15 minutes, or until the fish flakes when pierced with a fork.

3. Gently remove the fish to a plate and, using a slotted spoon, remove the fava beans and the peppers to another plate. Bring the sauce to a boil and simmer, uncovered, for about 20 minutes or until most of the liquid is evaporated. Adjust the seasonings to taste.

4. Cut the fish into 6 to 8 pieces and return them to the reduced sauce, along with the beans and peppers, to heat through. Serve covered with the sauce and sprinkle the remaining cilantro on top. This dish can be served at room temperature, or it can be set aside and reheated.

NOTE You can also use dried fava beans or chickpeas, in which case you should prepare them ahead: first soak them overnight, then simmer them in water to cover for about an hour or until they are cooked.

Fish

Moroccan Baked Rockfish with Preserved Lemon, Cilantro, Tomatoes, and Olives

This is another Moroccan Friday-night fish that I adore. If you do not have the preserved lemons on hand, use the quick method on page 180 to cure fresh ones.

YIELD: 6 TO 8 SERVINGS

1 whole 3-pound rockfish, snapper, or other meaty white fish, gutted

3 cloves garlic, crushed

1 teaspoon salt

1/2 teaspoon freshly ground pepper

3 preserved lemons, diced (see pages 179 and 180)

3 tomatoes, diced

1/2 cup chopped fresh parsley or cilantro

1/2 cup Moroccan green olives, pitted

Pinch of saffron

1. Preheat the oven to 350 degrees.

2. Rub the fish with the garlic and sprinkle the salt and pepper all over. Place in a baking pan.

3. Surround the fish with the preserved lemons, tomatoes, parsley or cilantro, and olives.

4. Dissolve the saffron in a tablespoon or so of water and sprinkle it over the fish.

5. Bake for 20 minutes or until the fish flakes when pierced with a fork.

Two men fishing on the Sea of Galilee

These flavorful fish balls, perhaps the precursor of the Ashkenazic gefilte fish, originated in medieval Spain. They can be served for any Friday-night meal but are often reserved for Rosh Hashanah and Passover.

Boulettes de Poissons— Moroccan Fish Balls

YIELD: 40 BALLS, SERVING ABOUT 10 PEOPLE

3 pounds whiting, cod, haddock, or whitefish fillets

2 tablespoons chopped fresh parsley

1 small onion, diced

8 cloves garlic, crushed

1 large egg, lightly beaten

2 teaspoons cumin

1/4 teaspoon mace

1/4 cup vegetable oil

2 large tomatoes, peeled and diced

2 carrots, peeled and cut into tiny rounds

1 orange or red bell pepper, diced in 1/2-inch pieces

2 teaspoons hot paprika

2 heaping tablespoons chopped fresh cilantro

1 teaspoon salt

1 cup water

1. Chop the fish with the parsley and the onion, using a grinder or a food processor fitted with a steel blade.

2. Add 4 cloves of the garlic, egg, cumin, and mace to the fish, mixing well with your hands. Refrigerate for an hour or so.

3. Heat the oil in a nonstick frying pan with a cover and add the tomatoes and the remaining garlic. Cook for a few minutes, then mash the tomatoes with a fork.

4. Add to the pan the carrots, peppers, paprika, and cilantro. Sprinkle on the salt, add the water, and simmer, covered, for about 15 minutes, adding more water if the mixture becomes too dry.

5. Mold the chilled fish mixture into balls the size of walnuts and place in the sauce, adding more water if needed, just to cover the fish. Cook for 25 minutes, stirring occasionally. Serve the fish balls immediately, covered with the sauce, or refrigerate and serve later at room temperature.

Siniya—
Baked Tahina-Fish

St. Peter's fish, served deep-fried, grilled, or baked with a tahina sauce, is a standard dish at kibbutz restaurants overlooking the Sea of Galilee. The classic preparation throughout Israel and the Middle East is to bake the fish whole and then fillet it. You can prepare the tahina sauce as directed below or cook the fish separately and serve with the tahina and cooked onions on the side. Although tilapia is the fish most often used in Israel, flounder, sole, trout, or snapper fillets are good substitutes.

YIELD: 6 TO 8 SERVINGS

2 pounds tilapia, flounder, sole, trout, or snapper fillets

1 teaspoon salt

1/2 teaspoon freshly ground pepper

1/4 cup extra virgin olive oil

2 medium onions, sliced into rounds

2 cloves garlic, crushed

1/2 cup tahina

2 tablespoons lemon juice, or to taste

1/2 cup water

1/4 cup chopped fresh parsley

1/2 tomato, peeled, seeded, and diced

1. Preheat the oven to 350 degrees. Place the fish in a 9-by-12-inch ovenproof baking pan. Season it with the salt and pepper and drizzle on a little olive oil. Bake for 10 minutes or until the fish flakes easily when pierced with a fork.

2. Sauté the onions in a pan in the remaining oil, until golden.

3. Place the garlic, tahina, lemon juice, and water in a mixing bowl. Mix well with a spoon and sprinkle on additional salt and pepper to taste.

4. Scatter the onions on top of the fish and cover with the tahina sauce. Return to the oven for about 10 more minutes or until the sauce is thick and bubbling.

5. Before serving, sprinkle the parsley and diced tomato on top.

Avi Steinitz, chef at the kosher Dan Hotel in Eilat, is at once an innovator, a traditionalist, and a purist. "Today you have enough ingredients to cook kosher cleverly," he said. "I use mostly fresh fish, fruit, and herbs. In the last ten years in Israel we have new lettuces, ginger, and lemongrass, mostly grown in the Sharon Valley." He plays with old tastes and new themes in some unusual dishes, like this salmon trout stuffed with Eastern European root vegetables. It can be served on a bed of kasha *varnishkes,* mashed potatoes, squash puree, or polenta and with a lemon or Hollandaise sauce.

Avi Steinitz's Salmon Trout with Root Vegetables

YIELD: 12 SERVINGS

2 tablespoons butter

2 tablespoons peanut oil

3 tablespoons olive oil

1/4 pound celery root, peeled and julienned (about 1 1/4 cups)

1/2 pound rutabaga, peeled and julienned (about 1 3/4 cups)

1 medium carrot, peeled and julienned (about 1/2 cup)

1-inch piece horseradish root, peeled and grated coarsely lengthwise (about 2 tablespoons)

Salt and freshly ground pepper to taste

2 teaspoons sugar

2 tablespoons chopped fresh parsley

2 tablespoons chopped fresh chives

6 8-inch salmon trout or other trout fillets (about 2 1/2 pounds total), cut in half lengthwise

Juice of 1 lemon

1. Heat the butter, peanut oil, and 2 tablespoons of the olive oil in a large skillet. Add the celery root, rutabaga, carrot, and horseradish root and sauté over medium-high heat until just cooked, about 7 to 9 minutes. Season to taste with salt and pepper, add the sugar, and sprinkle with parsley and chives. Set aside to cool.

2. Sprinkle the fish fillets with additional salt and pepper. Divide the vegetables into 12 equal portions, about 1/4 cup each, and roll a piece of fish around each. Secure with a toothpick or a small metal skewer. Drizzle the lemon juice and the remaining tablespoon of olive oil over the fish.

3. Transfer each bundle carefully into a bamboo vegetable steamer and steam for 4 minutes, or wrap in aluminum foil and bake in a preheated 375-degree oven for 5 minutes or until the fish is cooked.

4. Serve surrounded with any leftover filling, kasha *varnishkes* (buckwheat groats and bowtie noodles), mashed potatoes, or polenta.

Fish

The Real Thing— *Ima* Sharansky's Gefilte Fish

Ima Sharansky used her hands and a face full of animation to describe to me her recipe for gefilte fish, which means "filled fish." Hers is the real thing, the kind I tasted at a cooking school in Vilnius, Lithuania, in 1987, with the patties stuffed back into the whole fish skin.

The stuffed head was the prize portion in Mrs. Sharansky's family. In the Ukraine she would buy river fish like carp, *sazam* (buffel), and *sudak* (valley pike). "In every place we had rivers, with fish fresh and alive," she said. "I used to call fish I bought in the market sleeping fish. In the Ukraine I had to clean the fresh fish myself. It was hard work. Here in Israel I buy naked, empty fish from the supermarket." When I tried this adaptation of her gefilte fish, I was surprised at how soft and flavorful it was, much tastier than the poached fish balls that I usually make.

· · · IMA SHARANSKY · · ·
A RUSSIAN *BALABUSTA*

I visited *Ima* (Mother) Sharansky, the mother of Natan Sharansky, former prisoner of conscience (see page 72), at her son's home in Jerusalem's Old Katamon. As I walked into the house on a tree-lined lane, the fragrance of ripe figs from the tree right outside the front door filled the air. Her twelve-year-old granddaughter, Raquela, wearing the long, modest dress of religious Jews, ushered me in and immediately offered me a glass of cold apple juice. I had the feeling that this child was used to being polite to visitors in her home. A few minutes later, her grandmother walked in, a diminutive woman with the ready, winning smile and animation of her famous son.

With the help of Ludmila Chielminski Schiffman, a niece raised by Mrs. Sharansky, we were able to communicate in English about the Ukraine, the family's ordeal when her son was in solitary confinement there for eight years, and the foods she has made for him all his life.

"Very, very seldom, maybe one time in six months, if he behaved very good—but he never behaved very good—we could send him two pounds of cookies," she said. "My son Leonid made cookies, vitaminized things with nuts and white chocolate. I tried millions of times to visit Natan. I went to receptions at the government. I spent half my time writing letters to the KGB. And I wouldn't leave the Ukraine until my son left in 1986."

Born in 1908, Mrs. Sharansky was a child during the Russian Revolution. When she was five years old she left her hometown of Balta for Odessa, where she grew up and went to university. "In my apartment the door was closed, so I could cook what I wanted," she said. "Who knew what was Jewish and what was Russian?" Although dishes like challah and bagels were unknown, she prepared recipes handed down orally from her mother. She made her own cottage cheese, which she hung in a net, and after Stalin's time used a "partisan action" to sneak in the matzoh.

"My mother has the patience for many things," said her son Natan. "Since we had limited opportunities in the Ukraine and we had to make everything on our own, she worked hard into the night to cook for us."

5-pound carp

2 pounds whitefish fillet

4 large onions

1/4 cup vegetable oil

2 matzohs, or 4 slices white bread

4 medium carrots, peeled and roughly chopped

3 stalks celery, diced

2 medium beets, peeled and cut into large chunks

2 tablespoons salt, or to taste

1 teaspoon freshly ground pepper

2 bay leaves

1 teaspoon sugar

8 cups water

4 large eggs

1 teaspoon freshly ground pepper, or to taste

Red horseradish for garnish

1. Have the fishmonger slice open the stomach of the carp and carefully remove the guts and the backbone, reserving the bones and the skin in long strips. If you like, have the fishmonger grind the flesh. You should have about 2 pounds of finely ground carp, to which you should add the ground whitefish. If you choose to grind it yourself, use a manual grinder or a food processor equipped with a steel blade. If using a food processor, chop in short pulses, until finely ground but not mushy, then place in a mixing bowl.

2. Preheat the oven to 375 degrees.

3. Peel and finely dice 3 of the onions and sauté them in the oil in a frying pan. Reserve the onion skins, which are used for color, and put them in a large, wide pot or fish poacher.

4. Soak the matzoh or bread in cold water until moistened. Drain and squeeze dry.

5. Put the fish bones in the pot with the onion skins and add the remaining onion, peeled and cut into chunks, as well as the carrots, celery, beets, 1 table-spoon salt, pepper, bay leaves, and sugar. Add water and bring to a boil, then simmer while you prepare the fish. The beets will add a pleasant color and sweetness to the broth, which will later serve as a gelled sauce.

6. To the ground fish, add the sautéed onions, the matzoh, eggs, remaining tablespoon salt, and the freshly ground pepper and mix well with your hands. The fish mixture should have a tacky consistency.

7. Lay 2 large sheets of aluminum foil flat on the counter, then place the bottom half of the fish skin on top of them, scale side down. Carefully spoon the fish stuffing over the skin and fold the sides of the foil up around the sides of the fish. Cover the fish with the remaining skin and seal tightly with the foil. You can also use an aluminum poaching envelope for this. The result should resemble a whole stuffed fish, without head or tail.

8. Gently place the wrapped fish in the pot or fish poacher with the simmering

Fish

continued on next page

broth, and add water if necessary to almost cover the fish. Cover the pot or poacher and remove it to the preheated oven. Bake for 45 minutes, then open the top of the foil to expose the skin, and continue to bake for another 15 minutes. Remove from the oven and cool in the broth.

9. When the fish cools, remove it from the poacher and strain the broth. Carefully unwrap the foil from the fish, place the fish back in the broth, and refrigerate. As it chills, the liquid will become a gel. Place the fish on a platter, decorate with the cooked vegetables, and garnish with the gel and red horseradish. To serve, peel back the top layer of skin and slice, replacing the skin as you go to preserve the appearance.

Sea Bream with a Confit of Eggplant

One of my favorite food memories is the meal I was privileged to cover for the *New York Times* in celebration of the three thousand years of the city of Jerusalem, in 1996. The meal, prepared by twelve chefs, including seven three-star chefs from France, was strictly kosher. The image that remains with me is of a beautiful young *sabra,* a student at Hadassah's College of Technology, seated next to one of the doyens of French cooking, the elderly Pierre Troisgros of Troisgros in Roanne, France. They were conversing while painstakingly plucking chervil, leaf by leaf, to decorate the sea bream for the gala dinner. As chef Troisgros worked, clearly enjoying the company of this young *sabra,* he said, "This dinner is the *rencontre* of nouvelle cuisine with the Old Testament." Here is an adaptation of Troisgros's sea bream recipe from that memorable meal.

YIELD: 4 SERVINGS

6 tablespoons extra virgin olive oil (about)

1 large onion, diced

2 large tomatoes, peeled, seeded, and diced

2 teaspoons fresh thyme leaves

1 bay leaf

1 clove garlic, crushed

2 tablespoons red-wine vinegar

2 teaspoons honey

1 teaspoon salt

1/2 teaspoon freshly ground pepper

1 large eggplant (about 1 pound), peeled and cut in 1/4-inch-thick rounds

1 1/2 pounds sea bream fillets (or substitute rockfish, red snapper, tilapia, or trout), boned with skin left on one side, cut in 8 rectangular slices

1. Pour 1 tablespoon of the olive oil into a large covered saucepan, add the onions, and cook over low heat, covered, for about 10 minutes. Add the tomatoes, thyme, bay leaf, garlic, 1 tablespoon of the vinegar, honey, and another tablespoon of the oil. Simmer over medium heat, uncovered, for 15 minutes or until much of the liquid has evaporated. Discard the bay leaf and season with the salt and pepper. Puree the mixture in a food processor, then put it through a fine sieve and set aside.

2. Heat 2 more tablespoons of the oil in a large nonstick frying pan and fry the eggplant until golden brown on both sides. Repeat until all the eggplant has been browned, adding more oil, as needed, for each new batch. Season the eggplant slices with salt and pepper.

3. Add the remaining tablespoon of vinegar to the eggplant pan, increase heat and deglaze the pan, stirring to incorporate the concentrated juices. Spoon the vinegar evenly over the eggplant. Cool and set aside in the refrigerator until ready to be used. This can be done a day in advance. Before serving, bring the eggplant to room temperature or reheat.

4. Very carefully sprinkle salt and pepper on both sides of the fish fillets. In a clean nonstick pan, fry them in the remaining 2 tablespoons of oil. Gently remove them with a wide spatula.

5. For each serving, place the tomato sauce in the middle of a dinner plate, then top with several rounds of the eggplant and then 2 fish fillets. Serve warm.

Pierre Troisgros (far right) discussing the harmony of the menu for the Jerusalem 3000 dinner

Chicken, Turkey, Quail, and Duck

In Israel today there is an elderly lady who has come to be known as the "Chicken Lady of Jerusalem." Every Thursday, she gives her butcher three thousand shekels (about $750) to distribute chickens for the Sabbath to 118 needy families. Clara Hammer started this mitzvah one day when standing in line for her Sabbath chicken. Noticing that the butcher was quietly giving a plastic bag filled with leftover scraps of chicken, fat, and skin to a young girl, she asked him what he was doing. He told her that since the family was poor, with a sick father and many children, he tried to give them scraps so that they could make soup and a chicken *cholent* for the Sabbath. As soon as Mrs. Hammer heard this, she said, "You give this family two chickens and a half kilo of turkey every week. I will pay for it."

Through her butcher, she learned of other needy large families who could not afford chicken for the Sabbath. At first, only Mrs. Hammer, her three children, and her ten grandchildren shared in this mitzvah. Today, with the help of others, they reach over one hundred needy families weekly and, during the holidays, more than four hundred.

Mrs. Hammer understands what Jews have known throughout history: no matter how scarce one's resources might be, the Sabbath is the time to roast, bake, or grill permissible fowl—chicken, goose, quail, turkey, duck, and even pigeon. This festive custom dates back to the time of the Exodus, when the Jews wandering in the desert received manna in the morning and quails at night. Later, an offering in the First Temple included "a pair of turtle-doves or two young pigeons."

In Israel today, there are probably as many different chicken dishes as there are families. But when the state was first established and chicken production had not yet caught up with the influx of new immigrants, families were lucky to have a simple roast chicken for the Sabbath. At that time, with poultry a rarity, odd parts were used in what has become known as *meorav yerushalmi,* "Jerusalem mixed grill," which is actually more often fried than grilled. The parts include chicken and beef livers, hearts, and spleens, plus lots of onion and spices, particularly cumin.

Later, foie gras became a popular addition to "Jerusalem mixed grill"; curiously, force-feeding geese has always been a Jewish trade, starting among families in France, Romania, and Hungary. Today, descendants of those families are living in Israel, making the country one of the foie gras centers of the world, with France and Hungary. Many grill restaurants throughout Israel now serve foie gras cut in chunks, grilled briefly on skewers, sprinkled with salt, and often eaten in the Iraqi *aish tanoor,* but its popularity originated in a three-table restaurant in a working-class neighborhood in Tel Aviv. Its owner, Yehuda Avazi, a Kurdish Jew whose last name coincidentally means "goose," skewered unusual parts of meat, like the tail and the intestines, on the street for lack of space. Once, he had this idea to grill goose liver, so he went to Z'ev Friedman, whose Romanian family had long been raising geese for liver in Israel. "I thought he was crazy," said Friedman. The grilled goose liver was an instant success. Today, Avazi has six restaurants, and Friedman produces more than three hundred tons of goose liver per year.

Surprisingly, Israel also boasts the highest per capita consumption of turkey in the world. Moshe Dayan, Israel's minister of agriculture in the late 1950s, was responsible in large part for the increase in turkey production. Although he himself was infatuated with the large Minnesota turkey—too large for an Israeli oven, even if the cook was lucky enough to have one—he encouraged the cross-breeding of smaller turkeys in the new state so that families would be able to prepare turkey at home.

As the threat of war lessened and Israelis took to traveling, the economy improved and cooks became more daring. The first "Israeli" Friday-night innovation, deviating from the classic Jewish roast chicken, was a Jaffa orange roast chicken recipe, introduced in the 1950s. Various other roast chickens—stuffed with apples from the Czech Republic or cooked with olives and preserved lemon from the Atlas Mountains—are common in Israel today. Other exciting incarnations include *chimichurri* chicken from Argentina, Nabatean quail with date sauce, and cookbook author Nira Rousso's smashing fennel and currant chicken. My all-time favorite chicken recipe is *mousakhan,* a Palestinian dish with sumac, pine nuts, and sautéed onions.

Shipudiyah *cook making "Jerusalem mixed grill"*

Sea of Galilee Greek Oregano Chicken with Rice

At the onion-domed Greek Orthodox church next to Capernaum, you just have to slide open the gate to enter another world. The path to the church meanders past citrus orchards, a peacock or two, some guinea hens, and loads of chickens strutting through the trees and shrubs. In the distance is the Sea of Galilee, where Father Erinarchos, a Greek Orthodox priest from Macedonia, often performs baptisms. Always dressed in a black cloak from which dangles a large key to the nearby church, Father Erinarchos believes in the quiet of holy places. He began his priesthood in the convent of Artas, outside Bethlehem, then moved to the patriarchate in Jerusalem. He only recently came to the new church above the sea, where, to preserve the sanctity of the holy place, he refuses to welcome tour groups.

Like other priests I have met who cook, Father Erinarchos sometimes calls his mother for recipes. One recipe I particularly like is his oregano chicken with rice, a dish he makes from the convent's chickens, using the bones to make *avgolemono,* a Greek egg-lemon soup. He bones the breasts, seasons them simply with garlic and oregano from Macedonia, and bakes them on top of rice. When I asked how much garlic, his reply was "For me, it is never enough. Garlic is the best antibiotic."

Father Erinarchus at his Greek Orthodox Church overlooking the Sea of Galilee

YIELD: 4 SERVINGS

2 boneless and skinless chicken breasts, halved

1 teaspoon Greek oregano

3 cloves garlic, mashed

Juice of 1 lemon

Salt and freshly ground pepper to taste

4 tablespoons extra virgin olive oil

3 cups water

1 teaspoon salt

1 cup long-grain rice

1. Season both sides of the chicken breasts with oregano, garlic, lemon juice, and salt and pepper to taste.

2. Heat the oil in a frying pan and sear the chicken breasts, just a minute or 2 on each side.

3. In a casserole, bring the water to a boil. Add 1 teaspoon salt and the rice. Place the chicken breasts on top, cover, and simmer for 30 minutes. Serve with a green salad.

Chicken, Turkey, Quail, and Duck

Jaffa Orange–Ginger Chicken with Baharat

Freshly slaughtered chicken—how those feet add flavor to soup!

Jaffa oranges—practically seedless, thick-skinned, easily peelable, sweet and juicy—have captured the attention of consumers for the past century and, along with kosher wine, were the first exports from Palestine in the 1880s. Although these *shamuti* oranges still exist, they are rapidly being replaced by other varieties. Jaffa orange chicken made its way into mainstream Israeli kitchens by way of a recipe from the popular Israeli cookbook *A Taste of Tradition,* Ruth Sirkis's first cookbook in English. Mrs. Sirkis, whose parents came to Israel as Zionists from Poland, is typical of a whole generation raised during and just after the state was created, who had the opportunity to live abroad and learn the culinary traditions of other countries. She wrote *A Taste of Tradition* upon her return from California, where her husband was studying in the 1970s. She often served chicken with orange sauce when entertaining in the States. My version uses the eastern Mediterranean spice combination of *baharat,* meaning "pepper," which varies from cook to cook but often includes paprika, chili, cumin, coriander, cinnamon, black pepper, allspice, nutmeg, cardamom, cloves, and salt. If you can't find the mixture at a Middle Eastern market, choose from your favorites of these spices instead, making sure you include pepper.

This is a great dish, perfect for a dinner party. The beauty of it—besides the marvelous marriage of ginger and orange—is that you can do everything in advance, merely reheating just before your guests arrive.

4 whole boneless, skinless chicken breasts	4 tablespoons honey
Salt to taste	1 1/2 cups orange juice
1 tablespoon *baharat,* or to taste	1 tablespoon grated fresh ginger
1 tablespoon ground ginger, or to taste	2 teaspoons grated orange zest
4 tablespoons olive oil	2 tablespoons finely chopped crystallized ginger
1/2 cup white wine	
1/3 cup orange liqueur	2 oranges, peeled and sectioned
1 cup chicken broth	

1. Cut each chicken breast in half lengthwise. Mix together the salt, *baharat,* and ground ginger in a small bowl. Sprinkle each side of the halved chicken breasts with this spice mixture.

2. Heat the oil in a heavy frying pan with a cover and sauté the chicken gently for a few minutes on each side, just to brown the outside. Remove the chicken from the pan and set aside.

3. Add the wine, orange liqueur, chicken broth, honey, orange juice, and fresh ginger to the pan. Bring to a boil and simmer for about 15 minutes to reduce slightly, until a light syrup has formed. This can be done 1 day in advance.

4. Return the chicken to the sauce in the skillet and add the orange zest and crystallized ginger, cover, and simmer for about 5 minutes. Then turn the breasts, and continue cooking for another 5 minutes or until the chicken is cooked through. Add the orange sections and heat just until warm. Serve the chicken with the orange segments on a bed of couscous or rice, with the sauce drizzled on top.

Citrus-Roasted Chicken

In 1950, the late Gladys Sabel presented a typical Friday-evening Sabbath meal at an international cookery exhibition sponsored by the British Gas Board in London. Representing the two-year-old state of Israel, she had so little space that she had to arrange the candles and the challah on top of the refrigerator in her tiny booth. A passerby asked, "Do the Jews always place the altar on the fridge?"

At home in Israel, Mrs. Sabel won the prestigious Queen of the Kitchen competition in 1966 with the following citrus-roasted chicken (a variation of which was included in my first cookbook, *The Flavor of Jerusalem*). With my addition of garlic and fresh herbs, this effortless recipe has been a staple in my family for many years.

YIELD: 6 TO 8 SERVINGS

5-pound roasting chicken

Salt and freshly ground pepper to taste

1 whole orange, well washed

A handful of fresh herbs, such as rosemary, sage, and thyme, plus extra mixed herbs for garnish

4 cloves garlic

½ cup fresh orange juice

1 teaspoon ground ginger

4–6 tablespoons honey

½ cup white wine

1. Preheat the oven to 375 degrees.

2. Sprinkle the chicken inside and out with salt and pepper. Insert the whole orange, the herbs, and the garlic in the cavity of the chicken, truss closed, and place in a roasting pan, breast side down. Mix the orange juice and ground ginger and pour the mixture over the chicken. Roast, uncovered, for half an hour.

3. Remove the chicken from the oven, turn it over, smear the outside with the honey, and pour the wine over it. Return the chicken to the oven. After 5 minutes, baste with the juice from the roasting pan. If the breast seems to be browning too quickly, cover it with foil. Basting occasionally, roast until the drumstick moves easily, about 45 to 60 minutes more. Remove the orange, the herbs, and the garlic, and place the chicken on a serving platter. Slice the orange and scatter around the chicken and garnish with the additional herbs.

Gladys Sabel meets the Queen Mother

Czech-Style Roast Chicken Stuffed with Fruit

Every time Hana Lustigova Greenfield (see page 248) makes this chicken in Tel Aviv, it becomes a tangible memory of life in Czechoslovakia before World War II. "My grandmother would have a *shochet* come every Friday to slaughter the chickens and goose for Shabbat dinner," she recalled. The rest of the week, like most Czechs today, her grandmother ate a heavy diet of roast meat, including duck and beef, and occasionally a ham sandwich. "We would never serve other pork, but somehow the ham was okay because it was the national food," said Mrs. Greenfield. "We were also German-speaking and, until World War I, were products of the Enlightenment, which transferred itself to the table, where religious dietary laws were usurped by Enlightenment reasoning." This dish, now made in Israel with chicken and pine nuts, was traditionally prepared with duck, goose, and walnuts in Czechoslovakia.

YIELD: 8 SERVINGS

½ loaf challah or other soft white bread (about 8 ounces), cubed

2 tablespoons vegetable oil

1 medium onion, diced (about 1 cup)

6-pound roasting chicken with its liver

½ cup finely chopped mushrooms

¼ cup finely chopped fresh parsley

¼ teaspoon dried oregano

1 teaspoon salt, or to taste

A few grinds of pepper

¼ cup pine nuts, roasted, or ¼ cup chopped walnuts

1 Granny Smith or other tart apple, peeled and chopped

Juice of 3 oranges (about 1 cup)

1. Preheat the oven to 350 degrees.
2. Soak the bread briefly in lukewarm water and squeeze until dry.
3. Heat the oil in a frying pan and sauté the onions until they are soft.
4. If observing the Jewish dietary laws, broil the chicken liver to remove the blood, then dice. Otherwise, dice it raw. Add it to the onions, along with the mushrooms, parsley, oregano, salt, and pepper. Sauté until the mushrooms are just cooked, about 5 minutes. Add the bread, nuts, and apples and mix well. Let cool.
5. Stuff this filling into the cavity of the chicken; sew or truss closed. If desired, lightly sprinkle the outside of the chicken with salt.
6. Place in a roasting pan and bake in the oven for about 1½ hours or until the chicken is almost completely cooked. Pour the orange juice over the chicken and continue cooking for about another half hour or until the drumstick moves freely.

NOTE Another Israeli stuffing for Rosh Hashanah includes 1 finely chopped and sautéed onion, ½ pound each of diced dried pitted prunes and apricots, ½ cup raisins or dried cranberries, 2 peeled and diced medium apples, 1 teaspoon cinnamon, and salt and pepper to taste.

Moroccan Chicken with Olives and Lemons

I have always loved this flavorful lemony chicken dish. It is served in Morocco as one of the courses at state dinners, and Moroccan Jews in Israel also often serve it in their homes to break the fast of Yom Kippur. In Israel the saffron used in Morocco is often replaced with the less expensive turmeric. Although I prefer using preserved lemons (see pages 179 and 180) rather than fresh ones, either is acceptable. Traditionally made in a clay *tagine,* I make mine in an ovenproof frying pan or a Dutch oven.

YIELD: 6 TO 8 SERVINGS

3 cloves garlic, mashed	1/2 cup chopped fresh cilantro
Salt and freshly ground pepper to taste	4-pound chicken, cut into 8 pieces
1 teaspoon paprika	2 tablespoons olive oil
Pinch of saffron or turmeric	1 cup pitted green olives
1/2 cup chopped fresh parsley	1–2 preserved lemons, diced

1. Mix the mashed garlic with the salt and pepper, the paprika, saffron or turmeric, and half the parsley and cilantro. Rub onto the surface of the chicken and leave in the refrigerator, covered, overnight.

2. The next day, preheat the oven to 375 degrees and heat the olive oil in an ovenproof frying pan or a Dutch oven. Add the chicken, skin side down, and sauté for 5 minutes, until the skin browns.

3. Turn the chicken skin side up and sprinkle the olives over it. Transfer the pan to the oven and bake for 20 minutes. Add the lemon and continue to cook for 15 more minutes or until the chicken is done. Just before serving, sprinkle with the remaining parsley and cilantro.

Bukharan *Chelou*— Rice with Carrots and Chicken

Margalit Shemesh (see page 230) always has peeled and cut carrots in her freezer so she can make this chicken with rice for unexpected guests. It is very similar to an Iranian Rosh Hashanah recipe, which uses cinnamon and sugar instead of the turmeric and calls for a sprinkling of pine nuts and raisins, which I have added. This is also a great dish for leftover chicken.

YIELD: 6 TO 8 SERVINGS

4-pound chicken, cut in 8 pieces

Salt and freshly ground pepper to taste

2 large onions, sliced in rounds

1/4 cup vegetable oil

8 carrots, peeled and julienned

1/2 teaspoon turmeric

3 cups basmati rice

1/4 cup toasted pine nuts

1/4 cup raisins

1. Season the chicken with salt and pepper. Place in a flameproof casserole and cover with water. Bring to a boil and simmer for about 40 minutes or until the chicken is cooked.

2. Meanwhile, sauté the onions in the oil in a nonstick frying pan until they are translucent. Add the carrots, salt and pepper to taste, and turmeric, stirring well.

3. Remove the chicken from the pot with a slotted spoon and pour the cooking liquid into the pan with the vegetables. Keep the chicken in a warm oven until the rice is cooked.

4. Wash the rice with cold water 3 times, draining after each wash. Scatter the rice on top of the carrots. If necessary, add more water so that the rice is covered by 1 inch. Bring to a boil, cover, and simmer, slowly, about 20 minutes or until the rice is cooked.

5. Remove the chicken from the oven and cut the meat from the bones in bite-size pieces. Spoon the rice and vegetables onto a serving platter and scatter the pieces of chicken on top. Sprinkle with the toasted pine nuts and the raisins.

Argentinian Roast Chicken with Vegetables and *Chimichurri* Sauce

Although Naomi Sisso, wife of the former mayor of Kiryat Yam, mostly cooks North African food for her Moroccan-born husband, this is one of the few dishes from her native Argentina that she prepares for her family in Israel. It is a real winner, easy to prepare, and tastes even better the next day.

YIELD: 6 SERVINGS

1/4 cup white vinegar

1 tablespoon ground cumin

1 teaspoon sweet paprika

1/4 teaspoon hot red pepper flakes

Salt and freshly ground pepper to taste

1 head garlic, crushed

2 teaspoons chopped fresh or
 1/2 teaspoon dried oregano

1/2 cup vegetable oil

3 1/2-pound roasting chicken, cut into 8 pieces

2 large green bell peppers, diced

3 large tomatoes, sliced

5 large potatoes, each peeled and cut into 6 large chunks

1. To make the *chimichurri* sauce, put the vinegar, cumin, paprika, pepper flakes, salt and pepper, garlic, and oregano in a small bowl. Whisk in the vegetable oil. Pour the sauce over the chicken pieces, rubbing well into the skin. Cover them with plastic wrap and refrigerate overnight.

2. When ready to cook the chicken, preheat the oven to 400 degrees. Grease a large baking pan. Add the peppers and tomatoes. Place the chicken pieces on top of the vegetables, pouring half the marinade over it. Scatter the potatoes around the chicken.

3. Bake for 20 minutes, then turn the chicken pieces over and continue cooking until the chicken is crispy on top, about 30 minutes more.

This popular dish comes from the Telhani family of Isfiya, a two-hundred-year-old half-Druse, half-Greek Catholic village on Mount Carmel, close to Haifa. The first Telhanis came from Bethlehem (*Tel Hani* means "Bethlehem" in Arabic) looking for work as carpenters. "My grandfather, after whom I am named, was the *mukhtar* [leader] of the village," recalled Shibley Telhani. "Before the 1948 war, the Druse and the Greek Catholic Arabs like my family got along very well in the village. Because my grandfather was the *mukhtar*, he always had a table ready to host Jewish, Christian, Moslem, and Druse visitors from the neighboring villages and from Haifa. The family of the former president Ezer Weizmann were very close friends of our family. Whenever guests came, a feast would be prepared, including rice and lamb on big trays, *mujeddra* (see page 226), and often this popular chicken dish." Now Dr. Telhani, a professor at the University of Maryland, prepares it for his own family.

Muhammar— Chicken with Potatoes, Onions, Peppers, and Sumac

YIELD: 6 TO 8 SERVINGS

2 teaspoons salt, or to taste

1 teaspoon freshly ground pepper, or to taste

2 1/2 tablespoons ground sumac, or to taste

1/2 teaspoon cayenne pepper

1 teaspoon ground cumin

6 chicken breasts, not boned

1/2 cup extra virgin olive oil

3/4 cup diced red bell pepper

1 1/2 cups roughly chopped onions

8 medium potatoes, peeled and sliced

1. Preheat the oven to 375 degrees.

2. Mix together the salt, pepper, sumac, cayenne pepper, and cumin and rub half of this spice combination on the chicken.

3. Place the olive oil, red pepper, and remaining spices in the bowl of a food processor fitted with a steel blade. Pulse a few times, then add the onions, pulsing just until finely chopped.

4. Place the chicken breasts skin side up in a 9-by-13-inch pan. Sprinkle the potatoes liberally with salt and pepper and tuck them around the chicken breasts.

5. Spoon the onions and peppers over the potatoes and chicken. Bake in the oven for about 40 minutes.

Nira Rousso's Roast Chicken on Pita with Fennel, Garlic, and Currants

The first time I visited cookbook author Nira Rousso (see page 199), she served this dish. It was so delicious that *Food & Wine* magazine ran it as an accompanying recipe when I profiled her for the magazine.

YIELD: 6 TO 8 SERVINGS

4-pound chicken, cut into 8 pieces

1/2 cup balsamic vinegar

1/2 cup light-brown sugar

1/4 cup extra virgin olive oil

10 brine-cured green olives, pitted and crushed

3 garlic cloves, crushed, plus 2 whole heads garlic, separated into unpeeled cloves

1 teaspoon salt, or to taste

1/2 teaspoon freshly ground pepper, or to taste

1/2 cup dry white wine

1/2 cup water

4 fennel bulbs, cored and quartered lengthwise

1 tablespoon soy sauce

1/4 cup dried currants

1 large pita or 4 8-inch pitas

5 sprigs fresh oregano or parsley, cut to about 3 inches long

1. Wash the chicken well and pat dry. Place in 1 layer in a flameproof baking dish.

2. To make the marinade, put the vinegar, brown sugar, oil, olives, and crushed garlic in the bowl of a food processor fitted with a steel blade and pulse to a coarse paste.

3. Sprinkle salt and pepper over the chicken pieces and pour the marinade on top, rubbing it in well. Add the wine and water. Cover the dish with plastic wrap and refrigerate for at least 2 hours, or overnight.

4. Preheat the oven to 400 degrees.

5. Drain off most of the marinade from the chicken and reserve. Scatter the fennel and the whole (unpeeled) cloves of garlic around the chicken.

6. Roast the chicken, uncovered, on the top shelf of the oven for 20 minutes. Reduce the temperature to 375 degrees, turn the fennel, and bake for 20 to 25 minutes longer or until the chicken is cooked. Transfer the chicken pieces, fennel, and whole pieces of garlic to a serving platter, leaving the juices in the pan.

7. Add the soy sauce, currants, and the reserved marinade to the pan and cook for about 5 minutes on the top of the stove to reduce by half.

8. When ready to serve, heat the pita and place it on a large platter. Spoon on the chicken, fennel, and garlic. Pour the currant sauce over the dish, garnish with the fresh oregano or parsley, and serve.

I have seen this "overnight" chicken, a shortcut, unstuffed version of the complicated *tabyeet* on page 294, in many guises, sometimes served with rice or spaghetti. (See my *Jewish Cooking in America*.) Iraqi, Syrian, Egyptian, and Jerusalem Jews all have their own versions, depending on the ingredients available. One of the oldest Sabbath recipes of the Jewish people, it was served in Old Jerusalem, inside and outside the walls of the Old City, as a delicious hot lunch after returning from synagogue on a Saturday.

Hamim— Old Jerusalem Overnight Chicken

YIELD: 6 TO 8 SERVINGS

1 whole 4-pound chicken

Salt and freshly ground pepper to taste, plus 1 teaspoon salt

4 tablespoons vegetable oil, plus 1 teaspoon oil for spaghetti

1 pound spaghetti

1 cinnamon stick

6 cardamom pods

3 whole cloves

1 head garlic

1 teaspoon ground cumin

1. Wash and dry the chicken, season it with salt and pepper, then brown it on all sides in 3 tablespoons of the oil.

2. Cook the spaghetti in a large pot of boiling water with 1 teaspoon salt and 1 teaspoon of the oil. Boil until al dente, then drain.

3. Place the chicken in a well-greased casserole. Surround it with the spaghetti strands, the cinnamon stick, cardamom pods, cloves, garlic, cumin, additional salt, and the remaining tablespoon of vegetable oil.

4. Preheat the oven to 250 degrees and bake, covered, for 8 hours or overnight. Flip and serve.

Ethiopian *Doro Wat—* Spicy Chicken

This spicy Ethiopian chicken recipe comes from Adi Disse, the daughter of Gete Zavadia, the late chief rabbi of the Ethiopian Jews. I spent a morning watching Adi cook in her apartment in Bet Shemesh, where she lives with her husband, Abera, and eight children. A patient cook, she started at dawn to prepare the *injerra,* the spongy bread made in Ethiopia from *tef,* a nutritious grain similar to millet that cuts the spiciness of the stew. Although she uses wheat flour in Israel, she still ferments it as she did in Ethiopia, leaving the flour in water for several days before frying it. For those not familiar with the bite of Ethiopian sauces, it is best to hold back on the hot pepper, starting small with 1/2 teaspoon of hot pepper flakes and adding more to taste. On the Sabbath, Adi adds hard-boiled eggs to the meat.

YIELD: 6 TO 8 SERVINGS

4-pound chicken, skinned, cleaned, and cut into 12 pieces

1 lemon, sliced

1 tablespoon salt, or to taste

3 large Spanish onions, very finely diced

3 tablespoons vegetable oil

1 head garlic (about 15 cloves), chopped

1 dried red chili pepper with the seeds, ground, plus additional to taste (or start with 1/2 teaspoon hot red pepper flakes)

1 tablespoon ground cumin

1 teaspoon freshly ground black pepper

1 tablespoon ground ginger

1 tablespoon ground nutmeg

1 tablespoon ground coriander

1 cup water

1 teaspoon cinnamon

1 teaspoon turmeric

1 tablespoon powdered chicken bouillon

1 medium tomato, diced

1. Put the chicken in a bowl and add water to cover, the sliced lemon, and the tablespoon salt. Let sit for an hour. Although Adi buys chicken that has been kashered, she still does this step. (In Ethiopia, Adi would have put the chicken pieces in a pot of boiling water and blanched them for about 2 minutes in order to eliminate the forbidden blood in the Jewish Ethiopian way.)

2. Put the onions in a heavy casserole, sprinkle additional salt over them, and sauté for a minute or 2. Add the oil and the garlic and continue to cook until the onions are soft.

3. Add the ground chili pepper or flakes, cumin, black pepper, ginger, nutmeg, coriander, and 1/2 cup of the water. Stir and cook for a few minutes. Then add the cinnamon, turmeric, bouillon, the remaining 1/2 cup water, and the tomato. Continue to simmer, stirring occasionally, for about 15 minutes more.

4. Drain the chicken pieces and add them to the casserole. Simmer gently, uncovered, for about 45 minutes or until chicken is cooked, adding water if needed. Serve with rice and the Ethiopian Sabbath bread (see page 116).

NOTE   When I visited Adi's brother in Be'er Sheva', I learned a variation of this recipe from his Pakistani wife. The aroma of their dishes for the Shabbat meal—his *doro wat* and her Pakistani chicken—wafted through the air. He used an Ethiopian spice combination and she a Pakistani mix, both assembled at the local outdoor market. Her chicken recipe was similar to his, with slightly different spices: 1 cinnamon stick, 4 whole cloves, 1 teaspoon turmeric, 4 cups chopped fresh cilantro, 1 diced green pepper, 2 cups chopped fresh parsley, and 2 heads of garlic, chopped. To make a beef *wat,* you can use about 2 pounds of brisket, twice the amount of garlic as for chicken, and omit the lemon.

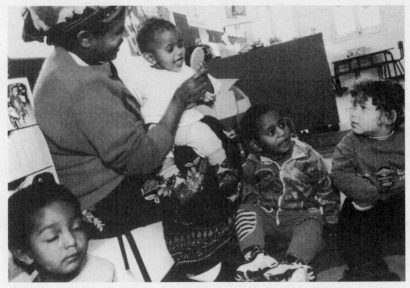

"Where's our doro wat?" ask these Ethiopian preschoolers.

Chicken, Turkey, Quail, and Duck

Tabyeet—
Iraqi Overnight-baked
Chicken with Rice

Although Jews had lived in Babylonia, now Iraq, since 1200 B.C.E., more fled there from Jerusalem when Nebuchadnezzar expelled them in 586 B.C.E. Over forty years later, when Cyrus the Great defeated the Babylonians and invited the Jews to return to Jerusalem, they were so well settled in Babylonia that many chose to stay. In fact, Jews stayed in Iraq throughout the centuries, until the creation of the state of Israel, when the great majority immigrated there. This mass exodus began in 1951, after five bombs were aimed at the Jewish community in Baghdad, killing two hundred people. Today, only about sixty or sixty-five Jews are left in Iraq. The other 125,000 or so brought to Israel a millennium-long legacy of Iraqi culture and cuisine.

Tabyeet, made in Israel today by Iraqi Jews for the Sabbath, is as ancient as the legacy of the Baghdadi Jews. Also called *tannoori,* meaning "oven chicken," or *hishwa,* meaning "the prized stuffed part," this overnight chicken dish is a cross between a galantine and the Iraqi *hamim.*

In Baghdad, this recipe was eaten at lunch after the morning Sabbath services. It comes from the family of Heskel Sofair of Kiryat Ono, who wrote it out in Arabic for his brother Meir, who in turn showed me how to make it. In secular circles in Israel today, this elaborate dish is served for parties and weddings, with the stuffed pouches of chicken skin served alongside the meat, sometimes gar-

A Yemenite boy holds a seventeen-day-old chick

nished with chickpeas. In Iraq it was cooked on Friday afternoon and set in low embers with eggs baking slowly on the pot cover, then covered tightly to be kept hot overnight. The cooked eggs, called *haminadav,* have a brown color and a unique aroma and flavor. They are eaten Saturday morning with fried eggplant, scallions, parsley, pickled mango (see page 75), and pita bread. The *tabyeet* consists of two distinct components: the broth and the *hishwa,* or stuffed meat. Except for the modern additions of tomatoes and tomato paste, this dish dates back thousands of years.

2 cups long-grain rice

1 tablespoon salt, plus salt to taste

4- to 5-pound chicken

2 large tomatoes

3 heaping tablespoons tomato paste

1 heaping teaspoon ground allspice

3/4 teaspoon ground cardamom

Freshly ground pepper to taste

12 dried rose petals (optional)

1/2 pound chuck steak, diced into 1/4-inch cubes

1/2 cup vegetable oil

4 cups water

2 onions, diced

1/8 teaspoon turmeric

1. Rinse the rice and soak in hot water to cover with the 1 tablespoon salt, for several hours or overnight.

2. Wash the chicken. Using a sharp knife, remove the wings from the body, then carefully peel the skin back from the entire chicken and reserve it. Separate the legs and thighs from the chicken and cut them each into 2 pieces each. Cut out the back of the chicken. Wash all of the pieces again.

3. Bring a pot of water to a boil. Place the tomatoes in the water for a minute or 2, then remove them to cold water. Drain, peel, seed, and dice the tomatoes.

4. To make the stuffing, drain 1 cup of the soaked rice and put it with 1 tablespoon of the tomato paste and 2 tablespoons of diced tomato in a large bowl. Add the allspice, 1/4 teaspoon of the cardamom, and salt and pepper to taste. Discard the green parts from 6 of the rose petals, if using, and crumble these into the bowl. Add the diced beef and 1 tablespoon of the oil, and mix.

5. Make 1 or several pouches out of the chicken skin by sewing up 2 sides with a needle and thread. Fill the pouches loosely with the rice stuffing and sew or use toothpicks to seal it in.

6. Bring the 4 cups of water to a boil.

7. Meanwhile, heat the remaining oil in a heavy pot and add the onions, sautéing until translucent. Add the remaining diced tomatoes, pepper to taste, and the turmeric. Stir a few minutes. Then add the chicken pieces and the stuffed pouches and sauté them in the sauce on all sides.

8. Add the boiling water, the remaining tomato paste, and the remaining 1/2 teaspoon cardamom. Simmer, covered, for 30 minutes.

9. Remove the chicken pieces and pouches and add the remaining rose petals, the remaining rice, and any leftover stuffing to the boiling broth. Cook uncovered for 10 minutes or until the liquid is absorbed, stirring occasionally so that the rice doesn't stick.

10. Preheat the oven to 400 degrees. Transfer the chicken, the stuffed pouches, and the rice to a very large casserole and bake, covered, for 30 to 40 minutes. Then reduce the oven to 250 degrees and leave for 2 to 3 hours or reduce to 150° and leave overnight. Serve with a green salad, pickles, and pickled mangoes.

Chicken, Turkey, Quail, and Duck

Today, if any one poultry recipe could be described as particularly Israeli, it would be turkey schnitzel. In Hebrew, the word for turkey is *hodoo*, which also means India. The origin is French: when the turkey was brought from Mexico to Europe in the sixteenth century, French farmers and cooks called it *coq d'Inde* or "bird of India," since in their minds the West and East Indies were one and the same.

In Israel, turkey production began after World War II, when beef was scarce and cattle expensive to maintain. European immigrants started using the cheaper and more abundant turkey to make schnitzel, which traditionally was prepared with veal. Now, families have become quite used to the idea, and frozen turkey schnitzel is one of the best-selling products in Israeli supermarkets.

One of the first restaurants to serve this favorite was the Penguin Buffet in Nahariya. Settled in 1934 by middle-class immigrants from Germany, Nahariya means "the river of God," and, indeed, a river runs right through the town. To this day, the primarily southern-German city is still considered to be the cleanest in the country, with swept streets, sparkling houses, neat gardens, and an orderly belt of grass and flowers running through the main street in front of the restaurant. Once, German was the main language of the town. Today, Russian and Hebrew are more often heard.

According to Ilan Oppenheimer, grandson of the Penguin's founders, who hailed from Offenbach, the Penguin Buffet was founded in 1940 as a glorified news kiosk-café, selling newspapers, food, and coffee. It soon became a second home for old and new German immigrants. (A huge blown-up photograph of the original kiosk, now a mural on the wall of the restaurant, attests to the Penguin's beginnings in a tin shack.) During the War of Independence, when Nahariya was under siege, the only newspaper in the city was posted on the walls of the café. One of the Penguin's specialties always has been schnitzel with potatoes and sauerkraut. Later, the menu included sausage, sauerbraten, and *pfahnkuchen* (filled doughnuts), rich cocoa, and fancy pastries. In the 1960s, the Oppenheimer family hired a band to play in the restaurant's garden. Today, inside a small mall, the Penguin still serves schnitzel and goulash soup.

Penguin Buffet's Classic Israeli Schnitzel

Almost every restaurant in Israel features turkey schnitzel on the menu. Most homemakers buy it breaded and frozen and serve it preceded by hummus, tahina, and other salads for a quick main meal. As I went from table to table throughout Israel, I found the dish to be more or less the same, prepared with spice combinations that vary depending on the ethnic background of the cook. Yemenite Jews, for example, add garlic, cumin, turmeric, cardamom, and *hawayij* (see page 140). Polish cooks often use matzoh meal. A classic schnitzel includes both butter and oil, which has been changed to just oil in Israel. Even in remote corners of Latin America, restaurants try to woo Israeli travelers by putting up signs in Hebrew saying WE HAVE SCHNITZEL.

YIELD: 6 SERVINGS

6 boneless, skinless turkey or chicken breasts, sliced thin (about 1½ pounds)

Salt and freshly ground pepper to taste

1 cup all-purpose flour

3 large eggs

2 cups fresh bread crumbs

Vegetable or soybean oil for deep frying

2 lemons, sliced in wedges

1. Place one cutlet at a time inside a large plastic bag. With a meat mallet, pound the turkey or chicken slice as thin as possible and season well with salt and pepper.

2. Spread the flour on a flat plate. Break the eggs into a pie plate and beat well. Put the bread crumbs on a third plate.

3. Pour the oil into a heavy skillet to a depth of 1 inch and heat over a medium flame until almost smoking.

4. Dip each turkey or chicken breast in flour, then in egg, and then in bread crumbs.

5. Fry the schnitzels for 2 to 3 minutes on each side, until golden brown.

6. Drain the schnitzels on a plate lined with paper towel. Serve immediately with lemon wedges.

NOTE You can also bake the breaded schnitzels in a 350-degree oven for a few minutes ahead of time. Then, just before serving, deep-fry quickly to crisp the outside.

The original Penguin Buffet in Nahariya

Chicken, Turkey, Quail, and Duck

297

Passover
Nut Stuffing

"Since my mother was American, we always had stuffed turkey for Passover," said Ruthie Sabel, a stellar home cook living in Jerusalem. "I have continued that tradition with my own family. It wasn't until we went to the States to live for a few years that I realized that she must have transferred this idea from her memories of Thanksgiving turkey." Here is Ruthie's stuffing for your Passover turkey. She suggests basting the turkey with sweet red wine.

YIELD: ENOUGH STUFFING FOR 1 MEDIUM TURKEY

1 1/2 sticks pareve margarine (3/4 cup)

1/2 cup chopped onion

1 cup chopped fresh celery stalks

1/4 cup chopped fresh parsley

2 teaspoons dried sage

1 teaspoon dried thyme

1/2 teaspoon ground cloves

1 1/2 teaspoons salt

3/4 teaspoon black pepper

3/4 teaspoon celery seeds

1/2 teaspoon nutmeg

2–2 1/2 cups matzoh meal

2 cups finely chopped pecans

1. In a large frying pan, melt the margarine. Add the onion, celery, parsley, and all of the spices. Cook for about 3 minutes over low heat.

2. Remove the pan from the heat and stir in the matzoh meal and the pecans. Mix well, and add more matzoh meal if needed, to achieve a crumbly but moist consistency. Then stuff the turkey.

Navy Schnitzel Cordon Bleu

It was Friday afternoon, time for a staff meeting in the navy base in Eilat. The staff invited me to join them for a snack of fresh tomatoes, cooked beets, avocados, pickles, *mitz* (the popular Israeli grapefruit drink), and tea. This navy base, like others in Israel, is a rather gastronomic equalizer; the three chefs, who are Egyptian, Polish, and Moroccan, cook for five hundred soldiers with different religious and cultural beliefs and culinary tastes. On the day of my visit they had prepared a Friday-evening dinner of chicken soup and schnitzel cordon bleu, accompanied by a rice dish topped with pine nuts, raisins, and sautéed onions. Although Israelis almost always use turkey, boneless chicken breasts are a good substitute.

YIELD: 6 SERVINGS

6 turkey cutlets or tenderloins, or boneless chicken breasts

1 teaspoon salt, or to taste

$1/2$ teaspoon freshly ground pepper, or to taste

6 tablespoons good-quality French mustard

2 cups mixed diced vegetables (cucumber, pickles, carrots, and red or yellow bell pepper), and/or cooked sausage, chopped

2 large eggs, beaten

2 tablespoons water

2 cloves garlic, crushed

$1 1/2$ cups bread crumbs

$1/2$ cup toasted sesame seeds

4 tablespoons olive oil

1. Place one turkey cutlet or chicken breast inside a large plastic storage bag. With a meat tenderizer or mallet, pound out the meat to a $1/4$-inch thickness. Repeat with the remaining 5 cutlets.

2. Season each cutlet with salt and pepper and spread 1 tablespoon of mustard on top of each. Place $1/3$ cup of the diced vegetable mixture and/or sausage on 1 side of each schnitzel. Fold the breast meat over the filling and press firmly along the edges to seal, threading each closed with a few toothpicks.

3. In a bowl, whisk together the eggs, water, and garlic.

4. Mix the bread crumbs and the sesame seeds in another bowl.

5. Holding the edges sealed, dip the stuffed schnitzel in the egg mixture, then in the bread crumbs and sesame seeds.

6. Heat the oil in a large skillet. Fry the schnitzels until golden brown, about 5 to 7 minutes per side. Drain on a paper towel and serve.

Eucalyptus's Chicken-stuffed Figs, Onions, and Eggplant with Tamarind Sauce

Chef Moshe Basson spends half his time musing about the place of food in biblical history. How many chefs can be said to ponder how in antiquity sour grapes were pickled and used as lemons, or how to stuff Jerusalem sage in winter? I have followed Moshe's career for years, from a tiny makeshift restaurant in an industrial zone of Jerusalem, where a Eucalyptus tree grew right in the center, to his present location in the complex of the new Jerusalem municipality. Here, Basson's Levantine dishes utilize herbs, plants, and vegetables from the Judean Hills mentioned in both the Talmud and the Bible. He is always studying, testing, and sharing the wonders of his discoveries in what he calls his "Canaanite cuisine."

Every time I go to Israel, I visit him at his restaurant, now white stucco with clay tiles and decorated with nineteenth-century farm implements and bottles filled with pickled vegetables. It is always a show-and-tell of dishes like pickled eggplants, olives, or capers. "During the biblical period," he explained to me, "they pickled capers and the leaves with salt water. Tithes were brought to the priests at the Temple. But which part should you tithe, the fruit, root, or stem?" he mused, citing references from the Mishnah. In this, one of the most popular dishes at the restaurant, he uses tamarind, which was often used in sauces centuries ago, before the arrival of tomatoes from the West.

YIELD: 10 SERVINGS

12 medium onions	½ teaspoon white pepper
3 tablespoons olive oil	3 tablespoons tamarind concentrate
2 whole chicken breasts, skinned and boned	4 cups hot water
½ teaspoon ground cardamom	2 dried or fresh figs, diced, plus 10 fresh figs for stuffing
¼ teaspoon ground cloves	3 tablespoons light-brown sugar
1 teaspoon salt	10 small Italian eggplants

1. Dice 2 of the onions and sauté them in a large skillet in 2 tablespoons of the olive oil over medium-high heat for 5 minutes.

2. Meanwhile, using a meat grinder or a food processor fitted with a steel blade, grind or pulse the chicken until finely diced. Add the chicken, along with the cardamom, cloves, salt, and white pepper, to the onions in the pan, and continue cooking over low heat until the chicken is lightly browned. Adjust seasonings, cool, and set aside.

3. To make the sauce, mix the tamarind concentrate with the water in a large saucepan with a cover and bring to a boil. Add the 2 diced figs and the brown sugar. Reduce the heat, cover, and simmer for 5 minutes.

4. Core the remaining onions from the bottoms up, leaving the tops intact, and remove all but a few outside layers. Stuff them ¾ full with the chicken mixture and close the hole by wedging a small piece of the onion core into the base. Place the stuffed onions in the saucepan with the tamarind sauce. Cover the pot and bring to a boil. Reduce the heat and simmer for a half hour.

5. Meanwhile, in a large skillet, brown the eggplants on all sides in the remaining tablespoon olive oil. Remove from the heat and allow to cool for 5 minutes before handling. Make a slit in the side of each eggplant about 1 inch deep and 2 inches long; carefully open and scoop out the seeds, making a pocket large enough to hold about ¼ cup of the chicken mixture. Stuff the eggplants and add them to the simmering onions. Cook, covered, for a half hour more.

6. Open the whole figs from the bottoms up, as you did the onions, and remove the seeds. Stuff with about 1 tablespoon of the chicken filling or until ¾ full. Add the figs to the saucepan and simmer them in the tamarind sauce for 10 minutes. Serve one stuffed fig, eggplant, and onion to each person, with the sauce drizzled over all three.

Yeshiva boys await their rice

Palestinian *Mousakhan*— Chicken with Sumac, Onions, and Pine Nuts

I first ate *mousakhan* many years ago, and my mouth waters every time I think about it. The word *mousakhan* means "hot," coming from the root word *sakhan*. Sautéed onions are mixed with sumac, cloves, and pine nuts and baked with the chicken. Before serving, the chicken is baked on top of pita bread, drenched with olive oil. The secret to a good *mousakhan* is high-quality sumac—not the poisonous American variety, but the spice made from red berries picked fresh from fields in the Galilee, then dried and crushed. Middle Eastern markets carry them. You can also sprinkle the sumac on rice, as the Persian Jews do, or onto flatbread with sautéed onions and pine nuts to make a delicious focaccia.

YIELD: 8 SERVINGS

½ cup extra virgin olive oil

5 large onions, coarsely chopped (about 10 cups)

Salt and freshly ground pepper to taste

4 chicken breast halves

4 chicken legs with thighs

1 cup pine nuts

4 tablespoons ground sumac

1 teaspoon ground allspice

½ teaspoon ground cloves

8 small pita breads, 4 large pita breads cut in half, or 1 Oceanus oversized pita (see pages 112–13)

1. Preheat the oven to 450 degrees.

2. Heat ¼ cup of the oil in a large skillet over a low flame. Add the onions and sauté for 20 minutes, or until golden, stirring occasionally. After 5 minutes, sprinkle on salt to taste.

3. Season the chicken pieces with salt and pepper, rubbing well into the skin.

4. Transfer the onions to a 9-by-12-inch baking dish and place the chicken on top. Bake, uncovered, for 5 minutes. Reduce the heat to 375 degrees and bake for 15 minutes more.

5. Drizzle a tablespoon or so of the remaining olive oil into a frying pan. Heat the oil, then add the pine nuts. Fry over very low heat, stirring occasionally, until the pine nuts are lightly browned.

6. Mix the sumac, allspice, cloves, and pine nuts in a small bowl.

7. Remove the chicken from the oven and sprinkle on the sumac–pine nut mixture. Drizzle the remaining olive oil over the top and return the dish to the oven. Continue baking for 20 to 25 minutes more or until the chicken is cooked. Remove the chicken from the oven.

8. Preheat the broiler. Transfer each chicken piece to a round of pita bread, or place all the chicken pieces on the oversized pita. Sprinkle the onions, with a small amount of the cooking liquid from the chicken, on top and around the chicken. Place on the middle shelf of the oven and broil for 5 minutes (don't let it burn).

When Natan Sharansky (see page 72) was growing up, his *ima* ("mother," in Hebrew) baked his favorite duck dish for him. Today his mother, now also living in Israel, makes the duck for holidays, birthdays, and New Year's Eve.

Ima Sharansky's Duck Stuffed with Prunes and Apples

YIELD: 6 SERVINGS

1 large duck, about 5 pounds

1 teaspoon salt, or to taste

$1/2$ teaspoon freshly ground pepper, or to taste

$1^1/2$ pounds apples, cored and diced

$2/3$ pound pitted prunes, diced (10 ounces)

2 tablespoons sugar

2 tablespoons brandy

1. Preheat the oven to 450 degrees.
2. Clean the duck and its cavity well. Sprinkle salt and pepper inside and out.
3. Place the apples in a large bowl.
4. Add the prunes to the apples, along with the sugar and the brandy.
5. Stuff the duck cavity and its neck with the prune and apple mixture. Sew to seal in the filling. Place the duck on a rack in a baking pan and prick the skin several times with a fork.
6. Bake for 40 minutes, pricking the skin occasionally. Remove from the oven and use a turkey baster to siphon away the fat in the bottom of the pan. Return the pan to the oven and roast for 25 minutes more or until the juices run clear. When the duck is ready, remove it from the oven and take out the thread. Remove the stuffing and place it in the middle of a platter. Using poultry shears, cut the duck into 6 pieces and arrange the pieces around the stuffing.

And it came to pass at even, that the quails came up, and covered the camp.   —Exodus 16:13

And there went forth a wind from the Lord, and brought across quails from the sea, and let them fall by the camp, about a day's journey on this side, and a day's journey on the other side, round about the camp, about two cubits above the face of the earth.   —Numbers 11:31

Once, on a camel ride in the Negev near Eilat, I kept seeing covies of quail, the bird that, according to the Bible, "came from the sea" when Moses and the children of Israel were wandering in the desert at night. I later learned that the salt marshes at the Inter/Birdwatching Center in Eilat are a natural food stop for small birds like quail on their way to and from the Great Rift Valley in Africa, where they winter before flying to the Steppes in Russia for the summer. In Israel today, quails are also raised on some kibbutzim.

Quails, by all accounts the poultry of choice of wandering people, were one of the foods eaten by the Nabateans, a people of ancient Arabia who ruled the Great Rift Valley, which runs from Mozambique to Jerusalem, from 250 B.C.E. until the second century C.E. Originally semi-nomads, tending sheep and robbing travelers, they carried perfume, gold, and spices on their camel caravans to the Red Sea. The first to plant shrubs and vineyards near Be'er Sheva', they worshipped Dushara, god of the mountains and the valley. They built way stations that later became cities and protected spots, including the great city of Petra in Jordan and the lesser-known Mamshit, located in the Negev near Be'er Sheva'.

Nabatean Grilled *Slav* Quail with Date Sauce

One of the tastiest quail dishes I have ever eaten was at Mamshit National Park, the reconstructed Nabatean village in the Negev, not far from Be'er Sheva'. This "city" included for a short time a stunning restaurant that served quasi-Nabatean food. The dishes served there were made with staples like lentils and chickpeas, grape leaves, dates, wheat grains like bulgur and cracked wheat, parsley, garlic, olives, carob, lamb, *za'atar,* and the following quail with date jam, figs, and apricots—all prepared with ingredients as ancient as the land.

YIELD: 4 SERVINGS

8 quails

1 teaspoon salt, or to taste

1/2 teaspoon freshly ground pepper, or to taste

1 clove garlic

1/2 teaspoon ground cumin

1/2 teaspoon ground cardamom

8 dried figs

8 dried apricots

1/4 cup raisins

1 cup red wine

1/2 cup date syrup*

1 teaspoon cornstarch

1/4 cup cool water

1. Rub the quails with the salt, pepper, garlic, cumin, and cardamom, and let sit in a bowl, covered, while preparing the sauce.

2. Soak the figs, apricots, and raisins in the wine for a few minutes to soften them. Drain, reserving the wine.

3. Pour the wine and the date syrup into a saucepan and bring to a boil. Simmer, uncovered, for about 10 minutes, to reduce the liquid by half.

4. Dissolve the cornstarch in the water and add to the sauce. Stir to incorporate and thicken, then add the softened figs, apricots, and raisins.

5. You can cook the quails under the broiler or on a stovetop grill pan over a medium-high flame. Broil or grill the quails breast side down for 3 to 4 minutes, then brush both sides with the sauce and broil or grill on the other side another 3 to 4 minutes, or until cooked.

6. Reheat the remaining sauce and serve over the quails, allowing 2 quails, 2 figs, and 2 apricots per serving.

NOTE   You can also make this with Cornish hens or quartered chickens. Grill the hens about 7 minutes longer on each side, or the chicken pieces 10 minutes longer, until the juices run clear at the leg joints. You can also bake Cornish hens or chicken pieces for a half hour in a preheated 400-degree oven. Then cover with the sauce and cook for 10 to 20 minutes more or until done.

*You can make date syrup (see *halek,* pages 44–5) or buy it at Middle Eastern markets.

Meat Dishes

Kotleti, *Kofta*, Kebab, and *Ktzitzot*

Under the Turkish Empire and even in the modern state of Israel, kashrut-observant Jews and *hallal*-observant Moslems have always shown respect for each other's dietary laws, as Lady Montefiore observed in her diary. According to the laws of kashrut, Jews can eat only the forequarters of permissible animals (see pages 56–7). Thus, their meat buying and eating habits have

Above: Samaritan Feast of the Passover at Mount Gerizim

always been compatible with the Moslems' in Israel's cross-cultural environment. "The Mohammedans purchase at the stall of the Jewish butcher the hind part of the animal, which the Jew is forbidden to use," wrote Ludwig August Frankl in his *Nach Jerusalem* (1858). "The *cadi* [religious judge who interprets the laws of Islam], however, must give the butcher a certificate stating that he and his forefathers have always been regular and strictly orthodox Jews, and that they are direct descendants of Israel. Before slaughtering the animal, the butcher must not only offer up the usual Hebrew prayer, but, turning the animal's head towards Mecca, he must, at the same time, offer up in Arabic a Mohammedan prayer, which is called *'Bissem Alah Agbar.'* Otherwise, no Mohammedan would eat his meat."

Notwithstanding the religious restrictions, meat was once a rare commodity in Israel, a special-occasion food for rituals, holy days, and holidays. During the biblical period, roast meat was brought to the Temple in Jerusalem as an offering. Josephus describes the hundreds of thousands of lambs roasted at Passover on the hillside of Jerusalem. To this day, also at Passover, on a mountaintop near Nablus, the Samaritans roast lamb and eat it before dawn as decreed in the Book of Exodus (12:9–10).

With no means of refrigeration until late in the nineteenth century, the day a lamb was bought or slaughtered was the day it was eaten. When I visited a Bedouin village in the Negev, they slaughtered a lamb to cook for us, taking some of the blood and rubbing it on the doorposts to keep away evil spirits. This custom reflects the actions of the Israelites in Egypt during the last of the ten plagues of the Exodus; they performed the ritual so that the Angel of Death would note that the offering of the lamb had been given and pass over their homes, saving their first-born sons (Exodus 12).

During the early 1970s, when visiting Arab villages surrounding Jerusalem, we occasionally were treated to a whole roasted sheep. A large pit was dug in the ground, lined with stones, and filled with a big wood fire; when the wood had burnt out and the stones were red-hot, the sheep was lowered into the pit, which was then roofed over with earth. The sheep cooked slowly and was served with rice and yogurt. I also have eaten the meat boiled and prepared as *mansaf,* the national dish of Jordan, with rice infused with spices.

Today the most popular way of eating meat is skewered on an iron spit (called a *shipud* in Hebrew) and then grilled, often at a simple restaurant called a *shipudia*. The large steel *shipud* is used for all sorts of grilled meat, as well as for making *schwarma,* the fast-food meat of Israel. *Schwarma,* a dish that the Turks brought to Israel (the term meaning "grilled" in Turkish), is made from slices of lamb and sometimes from dark-meat turkey, marinated overnight with seasonings like cumin, hot sauce, and occasionally soy sauce. The next day, the slices are

Meat Dishes

wrapped in layers around a large *shipud* and covered with slabs of mutton fat. The meat is then roasted on the spit, producing a juicy, spicy flavor with an equal balance of fat and meat. Grill cooks shave off the meat to order, leaving it to roast in a cone shape, narrower on the bottom (closer to the fire) so that it will cook evenly. It is served in pita bread with as many as twenty kinds of salads.

Since the time of the early pioneers, Israelis have also relished the *kumsitz,* the nighttime barbecue of meat and vegetables over an open fire at the center of a circle of family and friends. Traditionally, among the Arab cultures where the *kumsitz* originated, guests would forage for their food; today, the gathering is simply an opportunity to get together and to eat good grilled meat.

When the Eastern European pioneers came to Palestine, they were accustomed to beef, not lamb, as their special-occasion meat. According to A. Abrahams, in his *Background of Unrest* (1945), before World War II, Jewish agents were importing cattle from Hungary and Romania for the Jewish market in order to supplement the local mutton and poultry. Twice a week, ships went out from Haifa harbor taking oranges, religious articles, kosher wine, and potash for fertilizer to the port of Constanza, Romania. They returned to Palestine with kosher meat, apples, timber, grains, and eggs. During the war, this trade was cut off. "The result has been that the price of meat has risen fantastically," wrote Mr. Abrahams. "There are many Jewish families that taste meat only on Sabbaths and Festivals, and frequently only by saving up for it. The meat ration allotted by the Administration remains largely theoretical. Strangely enough, there is only one kind of meat in Jewish Palestine which is fairly abundant and obtainable without coupons—pork and ham. I have seen Jewish families, anxious to provide their children with nutriment, laying their tables with pig meat for their children only, and describing it to the uninitiated child as mutton or beef."

Israelis today call pork *steak levan* ("white steak"). Wild boar, of course, have been in Israel since biblical times, living in the Huleh Valley, near the Sea of Galilee. Although neither the Jewish nor the Moslem dietary laws permit pork, it is important to remember that Christian Arabs have lived in Palestine for centuries, and that from 1917 until 1948 Palestine was under the British Mandate, during which pork would have been imported for the British soldiers. In 1936 two kibbutzim started raising pigs for Christians as well as for the non-kashrut-observant Jews. On one kibbutz, pork was bred on wooden platforms because it could not be raised directly on land owned by the Jewish National Fund.

Because of increased Jewish immigration in the 1940s, it was difficult to provide enough kosher meat for the population. With the influx of refugees during and after World War II and from Arab nations, meat rationing went into effect, with just one-fifth of a pound of frozen meat allowed per person per week. "The Israeli housewife cannot tell the butcher what cut of meat her family feels like having this week," wrote Judy Shepard and Alvin Rosenfeld in *Tickets to Israel* (1952). "She stands on line and gets the next cut and, if the tiny slice happens to be half bone or fat, that is too bad. The Israeli *pater familias* who wants to take his family out for a meat meal at a restaurant can do so only on Friday, Saturday or Sunday, and then only at the price of sacrificing half the butchershop ration for the week."

After the war, the government of Israel looked worldwide for beef to feed its ever-growing population. Kosher beef has, at various times, been imported from countries like Ethiopia, Mexico, and Argentina, which have more grazing land and more accessible water. In the early years of the state, political alliances with these and other beef-producing nations were established, and beef became more readily available. Middle Eastern immigrants, raised on lamb, soon adjusted their culinary practices accordingly. A North African brisket, for example, with olives, preserved lemons, and tomatoes, can be traced to a Moroccan lamb *tagine*. Today, succulent lamb stews with spinach, Swiss chard, split peas, and dill usually are prepared with beef.

Ground meat, too, has a prominent place in Israeli kitchens. Chopped expertly with sharp knives, as it is today at Restaurant Diana, in Nazareth, or cut with a *sikatch,* a single-bladed manual chopper used in preparing Russian dishes, it is often also pounded with a mortar and pestle into *kibbi,* a meat and bulgur casserole baked in a flat pan. Meatball preparations come from many cultures: Moroccan, with olives; Russian, with bread crumbs, eggs, and onions; and Tunisian, stuffed into artichoke hearts. Ground meat can also be made into an Argentinian empanada or a Turkish moussaka, two of the numerous other meat dishes brought to Israel from throughout the world.

Moroccan Brisket with Olives, Tomatoes, Onions, and Preserved Lemons

On a trip to Morocco with the Oldways Preservation Trust, a group of us dined at the home of an olive merchant from the town of Sefrou. Driving there from nearby Fez, we passed a Jewish cemetery. During dinner, our Moslem host told us that until the creation of the state of Israel and the independence of Morocco, half of the population of Sefrou was Jewish. Not one Jew remains.

Rosette Ilkouby Toledano, now living in Netanya, came from Sefrou in 1956. "First it was the poor that came here from Morocco," she told me during a cooking session in her apartment. "A whole boat from Sefrou sank, killing all the people. When we arrived in Israel, there was nothing. Now there is everything."

If a well-stocked freezer is the indication of a good cook, Mrs. Toledano is exactly that. Hers includes everything from peeled and frozen cloves of garlic to potato *pastelles* with onions, the Moroccan equivalent of knishes; *warka,* the Moroccan dough made from a paste of flour and water, to be thrown on a flat, hot pan and peeled off when cooked; and, of course, all kinds of Moroccan cookies for her grandchildren.

Mrs. Toledano's beef brisket recipe, which she made with lamb in Morocco, is something she prepares frequently for Friday-night dinner in Netanya, using Israeli olives instead of those from Sefrou. Like most briskets, this dish tastes better prepared a day in advance. Served with couscous or rice, it has become one of my favorite Friday-night main courses.

YIELD: 10 TO 12 SERVINGS

5- to 6-pound beef brisket

5 garlic cloves

Salt and freshly ground pepper to taste

5 tablespoons vegetable oil

4 large onions, diced (about 8 cups)

$1/2$ teaspoon turmeric

$1/2$ teaspoon ground ginger

$1/2$ teaspoon ground white pepper

2 bay leaves

1 celery stalk, diced

3 large tomatoes, diced

1 cup water

$1 1/2$ cups green Moroccan olives, pitted

2–3 preserved lemons, diced (see pages 179 and 180)

$1/4$ cup coarsely chopped fresh parsley

$1/4$ cup coarsely chopped fresh cilantro

1. Preheat the oven to 350 degrees.

2. With a knife, pierce the skin of the brisket in 5 places and insert the garlic cloves. Sprinkle with salt and pepper. Heat 2 tablespoons of the oil in a heavy skillet or roasting pan; add the meat, sear on all sides, and remove.

3. Add 2 more tablespoons of the oil to the same pan and sauté ¾ of the onions (about 6 cups) until they are limp. Add the turmeric, ginger, white pepper, bay leaves, celery, ⅓ of the diced tomatoes, and water to the pan. Stir-fry a minute or 2 and let cool.

4. Place the brisket in a baking pan and surround with the cooked vegetables. Roast, covered, in the oven for 3 hours or until a fork goes in and out of the meat easily. Remove, cool, and refrigerate, reserving the vegetables. You can prepare this a day ahead of time.

5. The tomato-onion sauce can be done a day in advance as well: heat the remaining tablespoon of oil in the frying pan; add the remaining onions and sauté until onions are translucent. Then add the remaining diced tomatoes and simmer, covered, for a few minutes. Set aside or refrigerate overnight or until ready to serve the meat.

6. When ready to serve, remove any fat that accumulated on the brisket as it cooled. Cut, against the grain, into slices about ¼ inch thick. Return the slices to the baking pan along with the reserved vegetables in which the meat was cooked in step 4.

7. Preheat the oven to 350 degrees and reheat the brisket, covered, for about a half hour.

8. Add to the tomato-onion mixture olives, preserved lemons, and 2 tablespoons each of the parsley and cilantro, and heat in a small saucepan.

9. Remove the brisket and some, or all, of the vegetables to a serving platter and serve, covered with the tomato-onion sauce and garnished with the remaining parsley and cilantro.

I visited the late Lili Sharon, wife of five-star general Arik Sharon, for coffee and cake in the stunning Mediterranean kitchen of their ranch at the gate to the Negev Desert. With its tile floor, red chairs, and blue-and-white-checked tablecloths, the kitchen inspires an appetite; on the shelves, jars of pickled olives, kumquats, and hanging strands of garlic and peppers looked inviting, as did the beautiful array of copper pans, Middle Eastern coffee urns, and Russian samovars.

Outside in the fields, geese, horses, roosters, and birds roamed; in the distance, some of the Sharons' four thousand head of sheep and cattle grazed the four-thousand-dunam (one-thousand-acre) ranch. Hidden from view were the wolves, hyenas, deer, rabbits, mongooses, and foxes that inhabit the nearby desert.

Lili and Arik, who was born on a farm, moved to the desert after the 1967 war. Today, the general often rises at the first light of day to look at the fields and the silhouette of the rolling terrain against the sunrise. "I always told my husband that he is most relaxed on the tractor or riding on his horse in the fields," Lili said. "Is it common to have a farm in Israel? My husband is not a common person." Nor is Lili Sharon, or her cooking.

General Sharon said of his wife, "When a couple or ten or fifteen people were coming to dinner and I arrived home and saw no food, I got worried. The only one that didn't was Lili. This was *her* theater of operation, and when she tried all the new things, she always succeeded."

Lili inherited her talent from her mother, a well-known Hungarian cook who went to culinary school. "My mother fell sick when I was about ten, so I had to cook for Shabbat, including making the challah. At weddings in the shtetl, nothing started before my mother arrived. She decorated and gave instructions. She knew how to do things well."

So did Lili—she never served fewer than twelve people on a Saturday. "Lots of youngsters come, friends of our sons. I feel 'myself' in the kitchen, with all the family helping me cook the meal. And I always think of my mother with all those youngsters around. Like my mother, when I cook I make love to the dish. It's never just a recipe."

Lili Sharon in her kitchen

Lili Sharon's Roast Lamb

One of the signature dishes on the Sharon sheep ranch was Lili's roast lamb, which she served with rice and a green salad. Her secret: a whole head of garlic pressed into the lamb.

YIELD: 8 TO 10 SERVINGS

5-pound shoulder of lamb

1 head of garlic, broken into cloves

1 to 2 tablespoons sweet paprika

1 teaspoon salt, or to taste

1/2 teaspoon freshly ground pepper, or to taste

5 to 6 onions, halved

4 tomatoes, halved

2 sprigs fresh rosemary

2 sprigs fresh thyme

1. Preheat the oven to 500 degrees.

2. Wash the lamb and cut with a knife deep slits into the skin. Press the individual garlic cloves into the slits.

3. Massage the lamb with the paprika and salt and pepper, and place in a roasting pan. Scatter the onions, tomatoes, rosemary, and thyme around the meat.

4. Cover tightly with aluminum foil and bake for 30 minutes. Reduce the heat to 350 degrees, remove the foil, and bake for 2 hours, basting occasionally.

5. Transfer the roast and vegetables to a serving platter. Place the pan with the juices over low heat, adding a little water if necessary. As the pan heats, scrape the drippings from the bottom with a wooden spoon. Remove the gravy from the bottom of the pan with a baster to eliminate the fat on top. Serve the lamb with its gravy, surrounded by the vegetables from the roasting pan.

NOTE   Another way to make lamb Israeli-style is to sprinkle it with *za'atar* (see page 62) and olive oil and bake it, covered with aluminum foil, in a 200-degree oven for at least 6 hours.

Moroccan Lamb *Tagine*

Rafi Cohen, learning to cook from his grandmother Aziza

Ask an Israeli which person in his life has been the best cook, and invariably a grandmother will be mentioned. But not everyone is like Rafi Cohen, the twenty-four-year-old chef at the King David Hotel in Jerusalem, whose Moroccan-born grandmother, Aziz, has been the greatest influence on his star-studded gastronomic career. A tasting menu at the hotel's La Regence Restaurant hints of the food Cohen grew up with: homemade anise bread, a vegetarian sushi made from Moroccan cured olives and pine nuts surrounded by seaweed and served resting on a spoon, and a cooked salad on a bed of roasted red peppers, anchovies, and balsamic vinegar.

Rafi began his career as an apprentice in the King David kitchen when he quit school at age thirteen, and he continued his education in France. With skills learned from some of the best chefs in the world, he still remembers the great recipes taught to him by his grandmother, such as this *tagine* made from lamb neck, a winter stew he serves at the restaurant.

YIELD: 6 SERVINGS

Olive oil	1 parsley root, peeled and chopped (optional)
3 pounds lamb neck, with the bone	
Salt and freshly ground pepper to taste	3 tomatoes, diced
1 whole head of garlic, chopped	6 cups water
2 large onions, diced	1 bay leaf
2 medium carrots, peeled and chopped	3 sprigs fresh thyme
1 leek, cleaned well and diced	1 teaspoon salt
½ head of celery root, peeled and chopped	4 tablespoons chopped fresh parsley

1. Heat the olive oil in a heavy frying pan and season the meat with salt and pepper. When the pan is hot, add the lamb and sear on all sides. Remove and set aside.

2. Heat a thin film of additional olive oil in a heavy 6-cup casserole and sauté the garlic, onions, carrots, leeks, celery root, and parsley root for about 7 minutes until the onions are translucent and the other vegetables slightly soft. Add the tomatoes and cook for 2 more minutes. Add the water and bring to a boil.

3. Place the lamb in the casserole, along with the bay leaf, thyme, 1 teaspoon of salt, and several grinds of pepper. Reduce the heat and simmer, covered, over a very low flame for about 3 hours or until the meat is very soft. Then remove the meat and set aside.

4. If the sauce is not thick, turn the heat to medium and continue cooking to reduce slightly. Remove the meat from the bones and return to the sauce. Serve garnished with chopped fresh parsley over couscous or rice.

The traditional way to cook this Libyan Sabbath stew is to start with the spinach, beet greens, or Swiss chard, sautéeing them in oil with the celery leaves. I have reversed this procedure, adding the greens toward the end to preserve their full, fresh flavor. This soupy stew goes very well over white rice and tastes as good, if not better, the next day, when the flavors have melded.

Tabikha B'salk— Libyan Spinach, Chard, or Beet Greens, with Beef and White Beans

YIELD: 6 TO 8 SERVINGS

2 cups dry white beans

6 medium onions, diced

3 tablespoons olive oil

8 cloves garlic, minced

2 pounds beef chuck, cut in 2-inch chunks

4 cups water

1/2 cup roughly chopped celery leaves

1/2 cup chopped fresh cilantro

1 1/2 teaspoons hot paprika

1 pinch saffron

2 teaspoons salt, or to taste

1 teaspoon freshly ground pepper, or to taste

2 pounds fresh spinach, Swiss chard, or beet greens, roughly chopped

1. The night before you prepare the dish, put the beans in a bowl and cover with cold water by about 2 inches. Let soak overnight. This should provide 4 cups of soaked beans.

2. The next day, sauté the diced onions along with the olive oil in a large frying pan with a cover until the onions are translucent. Add the garlic cloves and meat, and brown the meat lightly on all sides.

3. Drain the soaked beans, then rinse them with cold water and drain again. Add the beans to the meat in the pan. Add 4 cups of water or to cover, and the celery leaves, cilantro, paprika, saffron, salt, and pepper. Bring to a boil, cover, and simmer very slowly, for about an hour.

4. Remove the cover, add the spinach, Swiss chard, or beet leaves and continue to simmer, uncovered, for another 15 minutes. Adjust the seasonings and serve over rice or potatoes.

Old Jerusalem *Shoouit*— Green Bean and Veal Stew

Many of my cookbooks include a recipe for a traditional green bean and meat stew called *shoouit* ("green bean" in Hebrew) or *fassoulia* ("green bean" in Arabic). This recipe predates the arrival of the tomato from the New World. When tomatoes were introduced to the Turkish Empire, the recipe was updated to include the new and popular fruit. I especially enjoy this Jerusalem version from Pini Levy, who uses veal instead of beef or lamb.

YIELD: 8 SERVINGS

2 tablespoons vegetable oil

2 large onions, diced

4 cloves garlic, minced

2 pounds veal shoulder, cut into 2-inch cubes

2 teaspoons salt, or to taste

1 teaspoon freshly ground pepper, or to taste

3 cups water, and more as needed

1 tablespoon dried mint

1/2 teaspoon ground cinnamon

1/2 teaspoon ground cardamom

2 pounds fresh green beans

4 large fresh tomatoes, chopped, or 28-ounce can whole tomatoes, coarsely chopped

2 cups tomato puree

1/2 teaspoon *hawayij* (see page 140)

Chef Pini Levy outside his restaurant

1. Heat the oil in a Dutch oven or heavy pot over a medium heat and sauté the onions until translucent. Then add the garlic and continue sautéing a few minutes more or until the onions are golden.

2. Season the veal cubes with salt and pepper and add to the onions. Add 2 cups of the water or enough to cover; bring to a boil and skim off the foam that will accumulate.

3. Add the mint, cinnamon, and cardamom. Reduce the heat to low, cover, and simmer for 30 minutes.

4. Meanwhile, wash and snip the ends off the green beans and set aside.

5. After 30 minutes, return the meat to a boil. Add the green beans, tomatoes, tomato puree, *hawayij,* and the remaining cup water. Return to very low heat, cover, and simmer slowly for about 2 more hours, or until the water has evaporated, creating a rich sauce. Adjust the seasonings and serve.

Ragu of Veal and Sausage

The Yo'ezer Wine Bar in Jaffa, though located in a five-hundred-year-old vaulted stone cave, embodies the "new" Israel. The bar is open from 1 p.m. to 1 a.m. for tastings of Israeli, French, and Italian wines by the glass, accompanied by Israeli goat cheese. Because Shaul Evron, the owner and a former journalist, has traveled widely, drinking and eating his way through Europe, his work has been a catalyst for young chefs in Israel. "Years ago," he said, "when no one here knew what a rare piece of roast beef was, I opened a restaurant with Haim Cohen, now the chef at Keren Restaurant (see page 136). We tried new things." Today the wine bar tries new dishes too, one of the latest being a foie gras–filled *soufganiyot* for Hanukkah. The following more mainstream meat *ragu* was served at an Italian wine tasting at the restaurant.

YIELD: 6 TO 8 SERVINGS

1/4 cup olive oil

2 medium onions, diced (about 2 cups)

1 cup chopped fresh parsley

4 medium carrots, peeled and cut in 1-inch rounds (about 2 cups)

4 celery stalks, cut into 1-inch pieces (about 1 1/4 cups)

2 pounds veal shoulder, cut into 2-inch pieces

1/2 pound spicy link sausage, sliced in 2-inch rounds

2 cups dry red wine

2 tablespoons tomato paste

2 teaspoons salt, or to taste

1 teaspoon freshly ground pepper, or to taste

1. Heat the olive oil in a heavy casserole. Sauté the onions, parsley, carrots, and celery for 5 minutes, stirring occasionally. Add the veal and sausage and sauté a few minutes more.

2. Add 1 cup of the wine and reduce, simmering uncovered for about 10 minutes. Add the tomato paste, the remaining cup wine, salt, and pepper and mix well. Lower the heat, cover, and simmer for 45 minutes, stirring occasionally, adding water if needed. Serve the *ragu* hot, tossed with pasta or rice.

Lamb Stew with Split Peas, Dill, and Olives

"Considering that in the Middle East, recipes cross borders far more easily than people do, it is not surprising that Egyptian, Syrian, and Moroccan Jews all claim that the following dish had its roots in their own country," said Daniel Rogov, restaurant and wine critic for the daily *Ha'Aretz* newspaper. "Whatever its origins, the country-style dish is well known throughout Israel, and it is one I especially enjoy preparing in my own kitchen." No wonder! This lamb stew is a perfect marriage of flavors, a fabulous addition to any dinner party.

YIELD: 4 TO 6 SERVINGS

1/2 cup dried split green peas

4 tablespoons extra virgin olive oil

2 medium onions, finely chopped

3 pounds lamb shoulder or stew meat, cut into 2-inch chunks

1 teaspoon turmeric

Salt to taste

3/4 teaspoon freshly ground pepper

1 cup beef stock

3/4 cup lemon juice

1 1/2 pounds spinach, chopped

Leaves of 2 bunches celery, chopped finely

8 scallions, white parts only, finely chopped (green parts can be used for garnish)

1 cup cured green olives, pitted and halved

2 tablespoons finely chopped fresh dill, plus extra sprigs for garnish

1. Soak the split peas in water to cover for 2 hours. Drain.

2. Heat 2 tablespoons of the oil in a large flameproof casserole over moderate heat. Add the onions and sauté until translucent. Then brown the lamb with the onions. Season with the turmeric, salt, and pepper. Add the beef stock and lemon juice. Cover and simmer for 15 minutes, stirring several times.

3. Sauté the spinach, celery leaves, and scallions in the remaining 2 tablespoons oil in a heavy skillet over a very low flame. Cook for about 5 minutes or just until the vegetables begin to wilt. Add the vegetables to the meat and stir; add the olives, split peas, and the 2 tablespoons dill. Simmer gently, covered, stirring occasionally, until the meat and peas are tender, about 45 minutes. Serve hot, over rice, garnished with the remaining dill and, if you like, the green onion tops.

One beautiful but stifling July day, a friend and I attended a wedding in Ma'ghar, a Druse and Arab town of seventeen thousand in the Galilee. We were the guests of Naim Ariedi, the cousin of the groom, a poet who writes in both Arabic and Hebrew and is a known television personality. Naim told us that the celebration would include the symbolic bringing of the bride from her village of Raama to the groom's village, but that the official ceremony with the sheik had been done earlier.

When we arrived, the wedding break-fast for the groom's extended family and close friends had already begun, with the men eating in a separate room. We sat at a long table with the women, all of whom were dressed in ankle-length black dresses, with white cloth covering their heads. As each woman arrived, she kissed the other women three times on one cheek. The tables were laden with dishes of onions, cucumbers, tomatoes, lemons, pickled eggplant, and hummus. The centerpiece was raw *kibbi* with onions, made from a lamb slaughtered for the event. Throughout the hot day, we were served cold drinks as well as hot tea made from dried ginger and other roots. The famous *lavash*, the paper-thin mountain bread that Druse women stretch over a disk and bake over an open fire, was served, as was a thicker special bread flavored with anise.

After breakfast was over, several women who evidently often cooked for weddings started cooking other parts of the lamb to make *mansaf* for the feast that night. First they browned the lamb bones and stew meat. Then they added rice to a big vat with oil on the bottom, along with lemon, bay leaf, pepper, cumin, cardamom pods, dried ginger, all-spice, and broth, stirring with large wooden spoons. The slivered almonds and pine nuts for garnish had been browned in oil two days earlier.

While some women were working at the stove, the others sat cross-legged on the floor, myself included, making torpedo-shaped *kibbi* (see pages 230–1) from the raw meat that was left from breakfast. As we cooked, the women

Women eating together at a traditional Druse wedding breakfast

explained to me how things have changed in their village. They used to eat seated on the floor, all sharing from one large platter. Now, they eat from individual plates, at tables with chairs. Instead of cooking the bread over an open fire each day, they all have ovens and freezers in their homes. Now, they make the *lavash* bread once every two weeks, from flour, semolina, salt, and water, and then freeze it.

After the *kibbi* were shaped and deep-fried, we went to the house of the best man. Soon the mother and sisters of the groom arrived, each kissing the groom three times on his cheek. Then the rest of the women of the village visited, pinning two-hundred-shekel bills, American dollars, and gold pieces onto his suit and kissing him on one cheek before the wedding party set off to retrieve the bride from her village.

With a cavalcade of drivers and a cacophony of horns, the groom's wedding party arrived at the bride's home, about twenty minutes away by car; years ago this procession would have been on horseback. As soon as the women of the groom's village arrived at the home, the bride's mother put three gold bracelets around her daughter's wrist. The bride, dressed in a rented modern white wedding gown, was escorted by her two brothers to the car where the groom was seated. The women ululated ceremoniously, their voices resonant in the hot afternoon air, and everyone drove back to the groom's village for the reception.

As the bride walked upstairs to her new home, she pasted a cloth heart with fresh dough on it onto the wall to symbolize the wish for a problem-free life and a house full of love. Cold drinks were once again served, this time with nectarines, grapes, and candy. Soon the groom removed his bride's veil to look at her, and the two sat down before the entire party, which now had increased to about three hundred people. They all proceeded toward the food, eating and dancing throughout the night—women with women, men with men.

Kibbi—
Bulgur and Beef
Casserole

Kibbi, the national "meatloaf" of Lebanon, also popular in Israel, is served in an everyday form as a baked layered casserole of lamb, onions, and bulgur, traditionally pounded together with a large stone mortar and pestle. According to an adage of the region from the Book of Proverbs, known among both Arab and Jewish communities, even if a fool were mixed with wheat and pounded into a batch of *kibbi,* his foolishness would not depart from him. I make *kibbi* for my family with ground turkey, using a food processor to blend together the bulgur, onions, and meat. To my surprise, I found it to be an almost effortless preparation, one you can prepare in the morning and bake in the evening.

YIELD: 6 TO 8 SERVINGS

1 1/2 large onions, roughly diced (about 2 cups)

3 tablespoons vegetable oil

1/4 cup pine nuts or coarsely ground almonds

1 1/2 pounds ground lamb, beef, or turkey

2 teaspoons salt, or to taste

3/4 teaspoon freshly ground pepper, or to taste

1/2 teaspoon cayenne pepper, or to taste

1/4 teaspoon allspice

1/2 teaspoon cinnamon

1/4 teaspoon nutmeg

1 teaspoon lemon juice

1 1/2 cups medium (#2) bulgur

1. Sauté 1 1/2 cups of the onions in 2 tablespoons of the oil until golden. Cool and remove from the pan.

2. Add the remaining tablespoon of oil to the frying pan, quickly brown the pine nuts or almonds, and set aside.

3. Place half the meat and the sautéed onions in a food processor fitted with a steel blade and pulse to soften the meat, but do not pulverize it. Remove to a bowl, add 1 teaspoon of the salt, 1/2 teaspoon of the pepper, cayenne pepper, allspice, cinnamon, nutmeg, lemon juice, and all but 2 tablespoons of the pine nuts or almonds. Knead well with your hands until smooth, adding a little cold water if too dry.

4. Place the bulgur in a bowl and cover with cold water. Leave for a few minutes and squeeze with your fingers until it is soaked and soft, adding additional cold water if necessary. Drain well, place with the remaining chopped onion in the food processor, and pulse. Then add the remaining meat, 1 more teaspoon of salt, the remaining 1/4 teaspoon of pepper, and pulse until smooth. Spoon half of this mixture into a greased 8-by-8-inch or 9-by-9-inch baking pan and flatten it.

5. Spoon the meat and pine nut mixture into the center, smoothing it over the first layer, then cover with the remaining bulgur-meat combination, smoothing again with the spoon. Cut diagonally, about halfway down in the pan, into diamond shapes about 3 inches wide. Place the remaining pine nuts on the top in the center, then brush with vegetable oil and refrigerate for several hours.

6. Preheat the oven to 350 degrees and bake on the middle rack for about 30 minutes. Serve as is with a fresh green salad, or as the Druse and Lebanese do, with plain yogurt on the side.

A campfire with camels and stew

Chief of Staff *Cholent* (Hebronite *Hamim*)

According to the Ten Commandments, "On the seventh day thou shalt rest," which means that no cooking can be done on the Sabbath. This tradition is the reason Israel is truly the center of the world for *cholent,* an overnight stew. Almost all Jewish families have brought their own unique versions—with Hungarian smoked goose breast, Brazilian black beans, Moroccan rice, Bukharan turkey giblets and raisin-stuffed cucumbers, or Polish barley and meat. A dish that has experienced a rebirth even among secular Israelis in the last few years, *cholent* is often served as a centerpiece main course for parties, usually blending several traditions in one exciting creation.

Eons ago, needing a dish that could be kept warm for the Sabbath, Jewish cooks came up with an overnight stew, the ingredients for which varied depending on where they lived. The stew was tightly sealed, often with a paste-like dough, and cooked before the Sabbath began, then left overnight in the embers to warm until the next day. During World War II, before Israelis had proper ovens, the *cholent* often was simmered over the small flame of a kerosene stove, the lid covered with two heavy bricks.

The word *cholent* comes from the French *chaud,* meaning "warm," and *lent,* meaning "slow." In Israel, it is also called *hamim,* Hebrew for "warm." Like outdoor grilling, preparing *cholent* seems to have become the Israeli man's domain. It is served on every Israeli army base on Saturday, even in small military units on their own at lookout posts throughout the country, since the army, which officially observes the dietary laws, must serve a traditional Sabbath meal.

This Hebronite *hamim* recipe was given to me by Amnon Lipkin Shachak, a former Israeli army chief of staff. He combines the Ashkenazic basic beans and barley with Sephardic sausages and the long-cooking eggs in their shells called *huevos haminadav* to make an innovative Sabbath dish from Hebron, the city from which part of his family hails. According to him, the recipe changes each time he

A soldier buying the ingredients for his family's dinner

makes it, depending on what he can find in the cupboard. This version requires *kishke* (a traditional delicacy made of flour and fat stuffed into sausage casing, today obtainable from Jewish specialty stores) and the robust and highly aromatic eastern Mediterranean spice combination of *baharat* (see page 282).

YIELD: 10 TO 12 SERVINGS

1½ cups white or red kidney beans

1½ cups chickpeas

2 large onions, chopped

2 tablespoons vegetable oil

½ cup light-brown sugar

¼ cup water

4-pound beef brisket, with fat

1 cup long-grain rice

1 teaspoon salt

Freshly ground pepper to taste

1 cup parched wheat (*frika*), bulgur, or barley

4–5 beef soup bones

1 pound *kishke*

1 pound pearl onions

5 medium potatoes, peeled and halved

6 large eggs in the shell

2 tablespoons *baharat,* or to taste

4–5 teaspoons beef soup powder or 4 beef bouillon cubes

1. On Thursday night, soak the white or red beans and chickpeas in cold water to cover.

2. On Friday morning, in a large heavy pot, sauté the onions in the vegetable oil until translucent. Then add the brown sugar and the water and carefully caramelize the onions over very low heat. Turn off the heat until the remaining ingredients are prepared.

3. Drain the beans and scatter them on top of the onions.

4. Cut the fat from the brisket, dice the fat, and set it aside. Rinse the rice in cold water and then drain; repeat twice more. Season the rice with ½ teaspoon salt and a few grinds of black pepper and dot with about 4 tablespoons of cubed beef fat. Place the rice in the center of a sheet of cheesecloth and enclose it loosely, so that the rice can expand. Tie with a thin strip of cheesecloth or twine and set aside.

5. Season the *frika,* bulgur, or barley with ½ teaspoon salt and a few grinds of black pepper, dot with about 4 tablespoons of cubed beef fat, and put it in another piece of cheesecloth. Tie it up loosely.

6. Add the beef bones to the onions in the pot. Set the brisket on top, then the 2 bags of grains, the *kishke,* pearl onions, potatoes, and eggs. Sprinkle with additional salt to taste, pepper, *baharat,* and soup powder. Add water to cover, cover the pot, and bring to a boil. Then transfer to a preheated 200-degree oven to cook overnight or put the pot on a *blech* (a heated asbestos pad which many Jewish cooks use to keep Sabbath dishes warm) over low heat and leave until ready to serve.

Tunisian Couscous with Beef, Chicken, and Chickpeas

I remember so vividly the day I watched the late Suzy Sce-mama prepare this dish in her home in Jerusalem. Her husband, Andre, the *Le Monde* correspondent in Israel at the time, was one of my favorite journalists. Whenever there was a municipal function, Andre would ask me in French, "Who isn't here?" That told him more about the politics of the moment than the list of those dignitaries who *were* present.

Although I have tasted many versions of couscous, I still prefer this one—with Suzy's Tunisian *boulettes* surrounding the stew (see page 326). Don't let this recipe scare you. It is a great make-ahead dish for a party. Get a two-day head start by soaking the dry chickpeas overnight before you make the dish. Letting the stew sit for one day only enhances the flavors and makes your job so much easier the day of your party—all you'll have to do is reheat the stew and steam the couscous.

YIELD: AT LEAST 12 SERVINGS

2 cups dry chickpeas

4 tablespoons olive oil

1 large onion, roughly chopped

1 large tomato, cut in quarters

½ medium cabbage (about 1 pound), cut in quarters

2 parsnips, peeled and cut into 1-inch chunks

1 turnip, peeled and cut into 1-inch chunks

3 stalks celery, cut into 1-inch chunks

2 teaspoons ground cumin

3 teaspoons salt, or to taste

1 teaspoon freshly ground pepper, or to taste

2 pounds beef chuck or other stewing beef, cut into 2-inch cubes

2 tablespoons tomato paste

4½ cups couscous (not instant)

6 carrots, peeled and cut into 1-inch chunks

2 3-pound chickens, each cut into 6 pieces

3 medium zucchini, cut into 1-inch chunks

1. Place the chickpeas in a bowl with water to cover by 2 inches. Let sit overnight, then drain.

2. To make the stew, heat 2 tablespoons of the oil in the bottom of a *couscousier* or a stockpot in which a vegetable steamer will fit. Add the onion and sauté until translucent. Add the tomato, cabbage, parsnips, turnip, celery, cumin, 1 teaspoon of the salt, and the pepper. Stir-fry for 10 minutes. Add the stew meat, tomato paste, and chickpeas, pour in 10 cups of warm water or enough to cover, and bring to a boil, skimming the foam off as it rises to the surface. Lower the heat and cook, covered, for 30 minutes or until the meat is almost tender and the chickpeas are almost cooked through. Fish out a small number of chickpeas and reserve them for garnish. Remove and set aside 1 cup of the liquid.

3. Meanwhile, place the couscous in a bowl with the remaining 2 teaspoons of salt. Add 2½ cups hot water and let sit until the water is absorbed. Then drizzle on the remaining 2 tablespoons of oil. Gently rub the grains with your fingers to get rid of the lumps. Let sit for a half hour.

4. Add the carrots and chicken to the stew.

5. Place the couscous in a cheesecloth-lined vegetable steamer or *couscousier* insert, again using your fingers to gently rub the grains. Set in the *couscousier* or stockpot, cover, and simmer for 15 minutes. Remove the couscous and add the zucchini to the pot. Pour the reserved cup of the liquid from the stew over the couscous, quickly mixing it in with your fingers as it is absorbed, again separating the grains. Reset over the pot and continue simmering slowly for another 15 minutes or until the chicken is cooked and the couscous steamed. Adjust the seasonings to taste.

6. To serve, spread the couscous over the bottom of a large platter. Spoon the stew over the couscous, reserving the chicken pieces for the top. Spoon enough stewing liquid over the top to saturate the couscous. Sprinkle on the reserved chickpeas. If you are feeling ambitious, or for a traditional Tunisian banquet, serve this stew with the following meatballs, the Tunisian Squash Salad on page 180, the *harissa* on page 72, and the eggplant salad on page 177.

Tunisian *Boulettes*— Meatballs Pressed into Artichoke Hearts and Peppers

In Tunisian Jewish homes, women make *boulettes* for the Sabbath on Thursday. Although I have tasted many other renditions of these meatballs since Suzy Scemama made this dish for me many years ago, her version of ground meat pressed into artichoke hearts and peppers still stands out. I have found that today many cooks in Israel substitute turmeric for the saffron. I prefer the saffron. You can make these meatballs a day in advance.

YIELD: 25 MEATBALLS

½ large Spanish onion, finely grated (about 1 cup)

¼ cup chopped fresh parsley

½ teaspoon salt, or to taste

¾ pound ground beef or lamb

2 slices white bread, slightly stale

Dash saffron

2 large eggs

6-ounce can tomato paste

¼ teaspoon pepper, or to taste

¾ teaspoon cumin

¼ teaspoon cinnamon

12 artichoke bottoms*

1 green bell pepper, cut into 1-inch square pieces

Flour for dredging

Vegetable oil for frying

1. Toss the grated onion, the parsley, and salt together in a bowl. Let sit for 15 minutes to bring out the juices. Drain well and return to the bowl, then add the meat.

2. Meanwhile, cover the bread slices with water in another bowl and set aside for a few minutes. Then squeeze out the water and fold the bread into the onion and meat mixture.

3. Dissolve the saffron in 1 teaspoon of water and add to the meat.

4. Stir in 1 of the eggs, 3 tablespoons of the tomato paste, the black pepper, cumin, and cinnamon. Mix well with a spoon or, better yet, with your hands. Shape about 2 tablespoons of meat into a meatball, pressing the meat into an artichoke bottom or a green pepper piece.

5. Beat the remaining egg in a small bowl with 1 more tablespoon of tomato paste. Sprinkle the flour into another bowl. Dip the meatballs into the egg mixture, then into the flour.

6. Heat ½ inch of oil in a large skillet. Fry the meatballs until they are brown on all sides. Drain on paper towels. After all the meatballs are cooked, place them in a large, wide pot. Stir the remaining tomato paste into 1 cup of water to dissolve it. Add this to the meatballs, plus enough water to almost cover them. Cover and bring to a boil. Reduce the heat and allow to simmer slowly for 20 minutes. Either serve as is or arrange around the Tunisian Couscous on pages 324–5.

*I prefer frozen artichoke bottoms to canned, especially those available in Middle Eastern markets, which are intended for this type of recipe. They hold together much better.

One of the delights of cooking in Israel today is the multitude of pan-ethnic spice combinations found in the open marketplaces: the *ras el hanout,* meaning "top of the spices," used in this recipe is a mixture of many Moroccan spices found in both Morocco and Israel. If you cannot find it, substitute ½ teaspoon each of ginger and cumin.

This meatball dish came to Israel from the Atlas Mountains in Morocco. In the winter, when fresh vegetables were scarce, the Moroccan Jews would serve meat grilled on an open fire or meatballs, often sauced with canned tomatoes and with preserved olives as an accompaniment. According to Jerusalemite Yaffa Friedman, whose family hails from Morocco, the dish was turned into a delicacy in two ways: either large pitted olives were served stuffed with tiny meatballs or the meat-stuffed olive was dipped in beaten egg and then bread crumbs, and deep-fried in oil. "Either way you'd have to be crazy to spend the time to fill each olive," added this modern homemaker. So this is her take on the recipe. I sometimes serve it as a sauce with spaghetti.

YIELD: ABOUT 20 MEATBALLS

1 cup pitted Moroccan green olives

1 pound ground beef, lamb, chicken, or turkey

1 medium onion, chopped

1 large egg

2 tablespoons matzoh meal or bread crumbs

1 teaspoon salt, or to taste

¼ teaspoon freshly ground pepper, or to taste

1 teaspoon *ras el hanout,* or ½ teaspoon ground ginger and ½ teaspoon ground cumin

2 tablespoons chopped fresh parsley

1 cup water

1 28-ounce can crushed tomatoes

1 teaspoon crushed garlic

½ teaspoon crushed chili peppers

½ teaspoon cinnamon

½ teaspoon ginger

½ teaspoon cardamom

1. Rinse the olives in water, then drain.

2. Mix the meat, onions, egg, matzoh meal or bread crumbs, salt, pepper, *ras el hanout,* and parsley in a bowl. Form into balls about the size of walnuts.

3. Put the water, tomatoes, garlic, and chili peppers in a saucepan and bring to a boil. Add the meatballs, cinnamon, ginger, cardamom, and olives. Simmer, uncovered, for about 20 minutes.

Meat Dishes

327

Pini's Old Jerusalem *Ktzitzot* (Meatballs) with Swiss Chard and Beef

Pini Levy grew up in the Old Jerusalem neighborhood of Nahlaot, where recipes were passed on by word of mouth in the open courtyards between houses. In the Middle Eastern mix of his neighborhood, Iraqi, Yemenite, and Kurdish cooks learned recipes from each other, which Pini re-creates from his memory and from the lessons gleaned from his father, who was a butcher in the municipal slaughterhouse. Pini's laboratory is his unassuming restaurant, Pini Bahatzer (Pini's Courtyard), which is decorated with bottles of pickles, rosemary in olive oil, cured olives, dried herbs, and old cooking utensils found on his many trips to the Sinai and Turkey. (See page 165 for more on Pini.)

I watched Pini prepare his mother's recipe for a Syrian stew with Swiss chard, also called "Arabic spinach." The trick to the success of this stew is to press out all the water from the Swiss chard.

Meatball vendor in Old Jerusalem

The Foods of
Israel Today

328

MEATBALLS

½ teaspoon salt

Leaves from 2¼ pounds Swiss chard (reserve stalks for sauce)

1 large onion

1 pound ground beef or lamb

3 cups slightly dry bread crumbs (made from a whole day-old baguette)

1 large egg

½ teaspoon ground cardamom

½ teaspoon freshly ground black pepper

1 teaspoon salt

½ cup vegetable oil for frying (¼ cup per batch)

SAUCE

4 stalks celery, diced

White stalks from the Swiss chard, cut into ½-inch pieces

8 cloves garlic, crushed

Juice of 1 lemon

1 teaspoon turmeric

½ teaspoon ground cardamom

2 cups chicken broth

1 tablespoon *hawayij* or ½ tablespoon cumin

Salt and freshly ground pepper to taste

1. Fill a 6-quart pot with 4 quarts of water; bring to a boil and add the salt. Submerge the Swiss chard leaves in the water. Cook for 1½–2 minutes. Drain well, pressing out all the water. Then dry in paper towels. Chop finely or pulse in a food processor until chopped but not pureed. Wrap again in a paper towel and squeeze out any remaining moisture.

2. Grate the onion and press out all the water in a paper towel.

3. Place the ground meat, the Swiss chard leaves, and the onion in a large mixing bowl. Add the bread crumbs, egg, cardamom, pepper, and salt and knead together thoroughly. Form about 2 tablespoons of the meat into an oval-shaped patty. Repeat with the rest.

4. Heat ¼ cup of oil in a frying pan. Add half the meatballs and brown, stirring occasionally and turning with a wooden spoon, for about 5 minutes. Drain on a plate covered with paper towels. Repeat with the remaining patties, adding oil as needed.

5. To make the sauce, place diced celery in a heavy casserole with the Swiss chard stalks, garlic, lemon juice, turmeric, cardamom, chicken broth, *hawayij* or cumin, and salt and pepper to taste. Adjust the seasonings, slip the meatballs into the sauce, and add enough boiling water to cover. Bring to a boil and simmer, covered, about 20 minutes. Serve with rice.

Meat Dishes

Russian *Kotleti* (Ground-meat Cutlets)

Call them *kotleti*, *ktzitzot*, *caclefin*, or *hockfleish*—I remember fondly these Eastern European ground-meat patties from many meals at the home of Rosa Goldberg in Caesarea. One of the grandes dames of Israel today, Rosa, now in her nineties, is still a terrific orchestrator of food events in her house. How often I used to seek refuge there from my busy life in Jerusalem.

Born in Riga, Latvia, in the beginning of the twentieth century, Rosa moved with her family to Manchester, England, after the Russian Revolution. She and her late husband, Alexander Goldberg, former president of the Technion, migrated to the newly created state of Israel in 1948. With the monies she earned on a book called *Altneuland*, showing how Theodor Herzl's dream had been turned into a reality, the Goldbergs built a small home in Caesarea overlooking the ancient Roman aqueduct. There, they had marvelous gatherings each Sabbath, at Passover, and throughout the year, at a time when there were only a handful of houses in the town. My favorite was the yearly *Tu Bishvat* party, where children planted saplings for the new year of the trees. Today, the trees that were planted tower above the property. On the patio, a huge table always overflowed with potluck dishes brought by the visitors. "I asked them to bring the best thing they could make," recalled Rosa. "There were lots of salads, meats, fish, and some minced meatballs." For the past few years, a new immigrant from St. Petersburg has been making for Rosa these *kotleti,* similar to the meatballs with which Rosa grew up.

YIELD: ABOUT 12 MEATBALLS

1 pound ground beef, veal, or turkey

2 slices white bread crusts, soaked in water and drained well

1 medium onion, grated (about ½ cup)

2 cloves garlic, mashed

1 large egg

2 tablespoons chopped fresh parsley

2 tablespoons snipped fresh dill

Salt and freshly ground pepper to taste

3 tablespoons bread crumbs for dredging

¼ cup vegetable oil for frying

1. Using your hands, mix the meat, bread crusts, onion, garlic, egg, parsley, dill, and salt and pepper in a bowl. The mixture should not be too dense.

2. Before forming the patties, wet your hands in cold water. Take about 2 tablespoons of the mixture and mold into an oval, then roll the meatball in bread crumbs. Repeat with the rest of the meat.

3. Heat the oil in a pan large enough to hold the meatballs without crowding. Fry the meatballs for a few minutes on each side, until well browned. Drain on a paper towel and serve as is, with a slice of lemon or with tomato sauce.

Saniah B'tahina—Baked Ground Meat, Eggplant, Tomato, and Potato with Tahina

Giving me advice on what to do in and around Jerusalem, a friend instructed me simply to go to the restaurant next to the mosque in Abu Ghosh and order the baked meat with tahina. Until the modern era, this Arab town was the last caravan stop from Jaffa on the way to Jerusalem, about six miles away. This dish, baked in a tray (*saniah* means "tray" in Arabic), was one of the first dishes taught to a young girl learning to cook. It was well worth the cooking lesson, and my trip out to Abu Ghosh.

YIELD: 12 PIECES, SERVING AT LEAST 6 PEOPLE

1 pound ground lamb or beef

2 tablespoons chopped fresh parsley

1 large onion, finely chopped

1/2 teaspoon ground cumin

1/2 teaspoon ground cinnamon

Salt and freshly ground pepper to taste

1 large potato, sliced in 1/8-inch-thick rounds

2 large tomatoes, sliced in 1/8-inch-thick rounds

1 large eggplant (about 1 pound), sliced in 1/8-inch-thick rounds

1 clove garlic, finely chopped

1 cup tahina

1 cup water

2 tablespoons cider vinegar or red-wine vinegar

1 tablespoon olive oil

Handful of pine nuts

1. Preheat the oven to 350 degrees. Put the meat, parsley, onions, cumin, cinnamon, and salt and pepper in a bowl. Mix well with your hands.

2. Spoon the meat into a greased 9-by-12-inch baking dish and flatten. Then make a layer of the potato slices on top, followed by the tomatoes and eggplant, sprinkling each layer with salt and pepper.

3. Mix together the garlic, tahina, water, and vinegar, and pour this sauce over the meat and vegetables. Bake, uncovered, for 30 minutes.

4. Meanwhile, heat the oil in a skillet, and add the pine nuts. Stir constantly until golden brown. Sprinkle the nuts over the hot casserole. Cut into 3-inch squares and serve with a salad.

Meat Dishes

Nazareth Lamb Kebab

When Ibrahim Faraj of Restaurant Diana in Nazareth lifts up his huge knife, watch out! With what seems a single cut and a single slash, he either slices his meat into chunks or chops it so fast that it becomes ground meat for kebabs. The larger the audience, the more this impresario likes it. First he fires up his oven, burning lemon and avocado wood, and waits until the embers are white. Then, with the flourish of an accomplished showman, he sprinkles onions, parsley, salt, and black and white pepper onto the meat, and forms the ovals with an almost magical efficiency. In a country which prides itself on its grilled meat, his recipe wins, hands down.

YIELD: 15 KEBABS, SERVING 4 TO 6 PEOPLE

1 pound ground lamb	1 onion, cut into 2-inch pieces
1 onion, finely diced (about 1 cup)	1 large tomato, cut into 2-inch pieces
1 cup finely diced fresh parsley	5 pita breads
Salt and freshly ground pepper to taste	Tomato halves, green bell peppers, and
Freshly ground white pepper to taste	parsley for garnish (optional)

1. Put the meat, diced onions, parsley, and salt and peppers on a wooden board or in a bowl. Knead with both hands until well mixed.

2. Divide the meat into 15 pieces and mold these into ovals.

3. Thread 3 of the meat ovals onto a thin meat skewer, each separated by an onion and a tomato.

4. Set the skewers on a grill over white embers. Also place an Iraqi pita or other type of pita on the grill. Watch the meat carefully and turn after a few minutes to grill on the other side.

5. Serve on a platter with the pita, and, if you like, with tomato halves, peppers, and parsley in the center.

Skewering meat for kebab

This popular Israeli moussaka omits the traditional béchamel sauce, making it permissible for those observing the dietary laws.

Israeli Beef Moussaka

YIELD: 8 SERVINGS

4 medium eggplants (about 4 pounds)

1 tablespoon olive oil, plus additional for brushing

1 large onion, chopped

4 garlic cloves, chopped

1 pound ground beef

3 tablespoons chopped fresh parsley

1 1/2 teaspoons ground cumin

1/4 cup dry red wine

2 large eggs, beaten well

2 tablespoons all-purpose flour

6-ounce can tomato paste

1 1/2 cups water

1 teaspoon oregano

1 teaspoon paprika

1 teaspoon sugar

Salt and pepper to taste

14-ounce can crushed tomatoes

1. Preheat the oven to 450 degrees.

2. Peel the eggplant, slice in 1/4-inch-thick rounds, and pat dry with paper towels. Brush both sides of the slices with oil and place them on a baking sheet. Bake the eggplant in the oven for 20 minutes, turning the slices over after 10 minutes. Remove from the oven and allow to cool. Lower the oven to 375 degrees.

3. Heat the remaining 1 tablespoon of the oil in a skillet. Add the onions, garlic, and meat and brown for 10 to 15 minutes, stirring frequently to break up the lumps of meat and cook them evenly. Then add the chopped parsley, 1/2 teaspoon of cumin, and wine to the meat mixture and cook, uncovered, 5 minutes longer. Set aside.

4. In a small bowl, mix together the eggs, flour, tomato paste, and water until a moderately thick sauce has formed. Add the remaining cumin, the oregano, paprika, sugar, and salt and pepper. Set aside.

5. Layer 1/3 of the sauce in a 9-by-12-inch baking dish. Top with half the eggplant slices, all the meat mixture, and another 1/3 of the sauce. Then layer the remaining eggplant slices on top, followed by the crushed tomatoes with their juice, and top with the remaining sauce.

6. Bake, covered, for 40 minutes. Remove the cover and bake 20 minutes more.

Meat Dishes

Mimulaim or Cusa Mashy—Syrian Stuffed Vegetables with Meat

Throughout Israel, stuffing vegetables is one of the most common ways of stretching meat, and everyone from a Middle Eastern background has his or her own version. Years ago, tiny Cohen's Restaurant in Jerusalem was renowned throughout the country for its Syrian preparations. If you left the ordering to Aleppo-born Moussa Cohen, he would—depending on his mood—give you a meal of eggplant stuffed with meat and rice, carrots stuffed with rice and mint leaves, or stuffed onions, peppers, squash, and tomatoes, with prunes or figs stuffed with nuts and poached in pomegranate sauce for dessert (see my *Jewish Holiday Kitchen*). Although Cohen's is long gone, this recipe is derived from my memory of Moussa Cohen's vegetables, flavored with the tamarind he remembered from his childhood, a centuries-old sauce legacy from Syria. He added tomato to the sauce, which probably will replace the tamarind flavor in future generations. This is a recipe that tastes better prepared a day ahead of time.

YIELD: 6 TO 8 SERVINGS

VEGETABLES

- 12 whole vegetables—medium tomatoes, onions, bell peppers, baby eggplants, and/or zucchini
- 1 pound ground beef or lamb
- 1/2 cup diced onion
- 1/2 cup short-grain rice
- 1/4 cup pine nuts
- 1/2 teaspoon ground cumin
- 1/2 teaspoon ground allspice
- 1 teaspoon ground cinnamon
- 1 teaspoon salt, or to taste
- 1/2 teaspoon freshly ground pepper, or to taste
- 1/2 tomato, diced (about 1/2 cup)
- Vegetable oil for frying

SAUCE

- 6-ounce can tomato paste
- 5 cups water
- 2 tablespoons tamarind concentrate (available at Middle Eastern stores)
- 1 tablespoon sugar
- 1 teaspoon cinnamon
- Salt and freshly ground pepper to taste

1. Wash the whole vegetables. Cut off the tops of the onions, tomatoes, and peppers, and hollow out the insides, leaving enough of the tomatoes and several onion layers for sturdy shells. (To make the onion easier to hollow, microwave it for about 2 minutes to soften, then carefully remove the inner rings.) Using a vegetable or apple corer, tunnel out the insides of the zucchini and the eggplant, leaving a shell about ⅛ inch thick. Dice the pulp of the vegetables and save it to add to the sauce.

2. Put the ground beef or lamb, the diced onion, rice, pine nuts, cumin, allspice, cinnamon, salt, pepper, and diced tomato in a mixing bowl. Mix well with your fingers. Stuff the hollowed vegetables about three-quarters full with the meat filling. (The rice will expand when cooked, so be sure not to overstuff the vegetables.)

3. Heat a frying pan and add a film of vegetable oil. Brown the stuffed vegetables on all sides and then place them close together in a large heavy casserole.

4. Preheat the oven to 350 degrees.

5. To make the sauce, mix the tomato paste, water, tamarind, sugar, cinnamon, and salt and pepper; if you like, add the diced vegetable pulp. Pour the sauce over the stuffed vegetables. Add additional water, if needed, almost to cover. Bring to a boil on top of the stove. Cover, put in the oven, and bake for 1 hour. Remove the top and continue cooking for another 15 minutes. Using tongs, gently remove each vegetable from the pan. If preparing a day in advance, refrigerate; the next day, remove any fat that has formed, reheat, and serve with the sauce.

Youth Aliyah boy preparing
vegetables on a kibbutz

Mafroom—
Libyan Potatoes Stuffed with Meat and Spices

A few years ago, Daniel Lagziel, his wife, Hannah, and his daughter, Karen, whose nickname is Noona, opened a restaurant on Moshav Netua, right next to the Lebanese border. They called it Noona Baavir ("Noona up in the air"), because the family thought they were crazy to have a restaurant right next to the dangerous border. Hannah said, "I always made what I wanted according to my gastronomic mood of the day—it was not always easy so close to the border." Nor was life there. "Once," said Noona, "a *katousha* rocket destroyed our whole house, but it didn't destroy us." The restaurant, located in a converted chicken coop, with flowers planted in old tires, has since closed.

The Oriental Jewish menu served at this simple restaurant was a reflection of Daniel's Libyan and Hannah's Moroccan backgrounds, as well as of the pan-Sephardic tastes of the new Israeli cooking. The following Libyan *mafroom,* which means "ground" in Arabic, was a specialty.

YIELD: 12 *MAFROOM,* SERVING 6 TO 8 PEOPLE

2 pounds baking potatoes (about 6)

2 teaspoons salt, or to taste

3½ cups chopped mixed fresh herbs like parsley, cilantro, celery leaves, dill, and mint

1 cup ground lamb or beef

2 large eggs

3 scallions, diced

4 cloves garlic, minced

½ teaspoon ground ginger

½ teaspoon cinnamon

½ teaspoon freshly ground white pepper

½ teaspoon cumin

1 cup whole-wheat flour

1½ teaspoons paprika

1 cup bread crumbs or matzoh meal

Vegetable oil for frying

1 onion, diced (about 1 cup)

4 tomatoes, peeled and pureed

1 tablespoon light-brown sugar or honey

1 teaspoon turmeric

1 teaspoon freshly ground pepper, or to taste

1. Peel the potatoes and cut each in half lengthwise. Then carefully cut each half lengthwise down the center, leaving a half inch at the bottom, making sure not to sever the potato. Place the potatoes in a bowl with cold water to cover and a teaspoon of the salt.

2. Put the parsley, cilantro, celery leaves, dill, mint, meat, 1 more teaspoon of salt, 1 egg, the scallions, garlic, ginger, cinnamon, white pepper, and cumin in a bowl and mix well.

3. Open 1 of the potato halves carefully, like a clam. Insert about 3 tablespoons of the meat filling in the center and close. Repeat with the rest of the potatoes and meat.

4. Set out 3 wide soup bowls side by side. Fill 1 with the flour. In the second, beat the remaining egg with ½ teaspoon of the paprika. Fill the third with the bread crumbs or matzoh meal. Dip each stuffed potato in the flour, then in the egg, and then roll in the bread crumbs or matzoh meal.

5. Heat about 3 inches of oil in a heavy pot or wok to 375 degrees. Deep-fry a few of the *mafroom* at a time just to brown, turning after a few minutes, and drain on a paper towel. Repeat with the remaining potatoes.

6. Place the onions, tomatoes, brown sugar or honey, the remaining paprika, turmeric, and salt and pepper in a shallow flameproof casserole. Bring to a boil on top of the stove. Add the *mafroom* and simmer, covered, over low heat, for about 30 minutes or until the potatoes are cooked through.

Sam the Argentine Baker's *Pastel de Carne*—Argentinian Meat Pie

Some people are larger than life, and Sam Weinberg was one of them. I first met him in the late 1970s, when he wanted someone to collaborate with him on a history of bread. Born in Bessarabia, he immigrated to Argentina, where he became a Jewish *gaucho*, a farmer, and then a reporter. Studying in an agricultural school and then a cooking school, he learned to bake, and practiced the craft fervently in his later years. In the late 1950s, Sam came to Washington, D.C., where he baked up a storm for about ten years before retiring in Ashdod. The customers at his bakery, including the late President John F. Kennedy and Arthur Goldberg, all called him "Sam the Argentine Baker." A longtime Zionist who reported on and fought in Israel's War of Independence, Sam helped young boys in jails in Jerusalem by teaching them baking, the trade that gave him so much joy throughout his life.

Like many of his devotees, I loved his empanadas. Because he was very protective of his recipes, this recipe is only my best interpretation, but it works beautifully. Whereas Sam would have made his own dough, my version calls for prepared puff pastry, which was suggested to me by Naomi Sisso, who also came to Israel from Argentina. The pastry is so good and simple that I always use it.

YIELD: 10 TO 12 SERVINGS

2 tablespoons vegetable oil

10 scallions, diced (both green and white parts)

1½ pounds ground beef

2 tablespoons sweet paprika, or to taste

1 teaspoon hot paprika

1 teaspoon salt, or to taste

¼ teaspoon freshly ground pepper, or to taste

2 tablespoons ground cumin

1 tablespoon sugar

4 cloves garlic, crushed

¾ cup raisins

1 cup green olives, pitted and halved

5 hard-boiled eggs, diced

2 sheets prepared puff pastry

1 egg, beaten

1. Preheat the oven to 350 degrees and grease a 9-by-12-inch rectangular baking pan.

2. Heat the oil in a frying pan and sauté the scallions. When they are soft, add the ground beef and stir, breaking up the meat as it cooks. Add both paprikas, salt, pepper, cumin, sugar, and garlic; continue to stir-fry.

3. When the meat is cooked, stir in the raisins, olives, and hard-boiled eggs.

4. Roll 1 sheet of pastry out as thin as possible, to a rectangle about 9 by 12 inches. Place in the baking pan. Spoon the meat filling on top, flattening it out evenly. Roll out the second sheet of puff pastry and cover the meat with it.

5. Brush the beaten egg on top of the upper crust. Bake for 40 minutes or until golden. Cool slightly, cut in squares, and serve.

NOTE   You can also use this recipe for empanadas hors d'oeuvres. You will need 4 pastry sheets, each rolled out thin and cut into circles 4 inches in diameter. Put a tablespoon of filling slightly to 1 side of each circle, moisten the edges with cold water using your finger, fold the dough over to a semicircle, and crimp the edges with a fork. Brush with the egg wash and bake in the 350-degree oven for 25 minutes or until golden. You can also form and freeze them, bringing them out to bake for company whenever they are needed. Yield: about 60 empanadas.

Chremslach—

Mashed Potatoes

Stuffed with Meat

I have tasted this old-fashioned Jewish dish in Vilnius, Tel Aviv, and Buenos Aires. Traditionally served at Hanukkah and Passover, it was always popular with any teenagers around when I tested the recipe! Sometimes I substitute sweet potatoes for the baking potatoes.

YIELD: 12 *CHREMSLACH*, SERVING 6 PEOPLE

2 pounds baking potatoes

2 tablespoons grated onion

3/4 cup ground beef, liver, or turkey

2 tablespoons vegetable oil, plus extra oil for frying

Salt and freshly ground pepper to taste

2 large eggs, lightly beaten

1/4 cup matzoh meal (about)

1 teaspoon salt, or to taste

1/2 teaspoon freshly ground pepper, or to taste

1. Peel the potatoes, cut them into even chunks, and put them into a pot of cold, salted water. Bring the water to a boil and simmer until the potatoes are soft, about 15 minutes.

2. While the potatoes are cooking, sauté the onion and meat in the 2 tablespoons of oil, stirring to break up any lumps until the meat is cooked. Season with salt and pepper and let cool.

3. When the potatoes are cooked, drain them and let them cool slightly. Then mash and mix with the eggs, matzoh meal, salt, and pepper. Mold the mashed potatoes into a pliable dough, adding additional matzoh meal if necessary. Separate into 12 equal pieces on a board dusted with matzoh meal.

4. Place a heaping tablespoon of the meat filling into 1 portion of the potato dough. After dusting your hands with matzoh meal, enclose the meat carefully in the dough, forming a round about the size of a golf ball. Repeat with the rest of the meat and dough, placing the balls on a plate or baking sheet. Refrigerate for several hours or overnight.

5. Pour about 2 inches of vegetable oil into a wok or skillet and heat to 375 degrees. Deep-fry about 5 *chremslach* at a time, a few minutes on each side, turning carefully with a slotted spoon and cooking until golden. Drain well and serve immediately.

Chicken-stuffed Figs, Onions, and Eggplant with
Tamarind Sauce, page 300, and other stuffed
vegetables in the kitchen at Eucalyptus

Above: A specialist in *mimulaem* (stuffed vegetables) on Ibn Guirol Street in Tel Aviv

Opposite: Kurdish woman making *kubbeh*

Above: Shop at Levinsky Market, Tel Aviv

Opposite: Making Libyan *shakshuka*, page 27, at the Tripolitana Doktor Shakshuka Restaurant in old Jaffa.

Above: Chocolate cake at the American Colony

Opposite: Making juices from fresh citrus

Herb tea

Desserts

I sraelis dearly love their cake and coffee, and given the scarcity of ingredients and resources in the early years of the state, they always have exercised delightful ingenuity in creating desserts. When few people had the luxury of a home oven, they concocted sweets like a *knacknick* (salami) of cocoa, crushed vanilla wafers, wine, and nuts rolled together, refrigerated, and then cut into slices. A Passover cake made from layers of matzoh dipped in wine and slathered with chocolate and halvah (ground-sesame-seed candy) and chopped nuts reminded new immigrants of the Hungarian and Turkish layered desserts of their childhoods. During *zena,* the austerity period in the late 1940s and early 1950s, cooks often substituted peanuts for the more costly walnuts and almonds in their tortes, with powdered eggs replacing fresh eggs in delicacies like cream puffs.

In the late nineteenth century, traditional cakes often were brought to a com-

Above: A cooking class at the Alice Seligsberg High School in the late 1940s

munal oven. "A public oven is built not far from the Synagogue," wrote Hannah Barnett Trager, an English visitor to Palestine. "It is very large, and each family sends cakes in its own tins to be baked in it. Generally about half a dozen tins are carried by each boy. Nothing I have seen before can be compared with the many kinds of delicious cakes and stuffed monkeys [English-Jewish almond pastries] that are seen here. My mouth waters even when I think of the delicious strudels filled with sesames and plenty of raisins and *shiros!*" In those days, the oven meant more than a place to bake cakes. "There is probably not a thing that has happened in Jerusalem during the last two months that is not discussed around the public oven while people are waiting for their cake tins; and, as everyone wants to talk rather than to listen, the noise is like the buzz in a factory," wrote Mrs. Trager.

Then came the *wunderpot,* also called the *wunderkucher.* Nobody seems to know the exact origin of this German covered Bundt pan created in the 1920s, but it was a miraculous solution for home bakers with no oven and no steady supply of fuel or reliable electricity, because the cake could be baked over a propane burner. The batter would be poured into the Bundt pan, covered with a metal lid with holes around the sides, and put on a plate which covered the *p'tiliah* (propane burner), so as not to burn the bottom of the cake. "We would even make yeast doughs in our *wunderpot,*" recalled Dalia Carmel, who grew up in Jerusalem. "Because of the cross-ventilation in our apartment and the fragility of the *wunderpot,* my mother made me stop running and keep the doors closed when a cake was baking. Sometimes I felt like the *wunderpot* was a live person that you couldn't disturb." Today, although almost a vanished species in Israel, *wunderpots* are occasionally used in rural villages elsewhere.

Some immigrants did not know the art of cake baking until they came to Israel. I remember one Yemenite cook who told me that before she arrived in the late 1940s on Operation Magic Carpet, she never had tasted a cake in her life. As part of her assimilation process, she was taught by British-born women the benefits of using cheese and eggs in cooking, and in cooking classes for new immigrants she learned to bake cheesecakes and apple tortes. Now, she told me with surprise, nutrition experts tell her that these treats are detrimental to her diet, and they ask her instead for the "healthy" fruit desserts that she used to eat in Yemen!

To others, like many North African immigrants, cake baking is a holy act. "For these women, who raised their children through times of famine (World War II and the 1948 War of Independence), having enough food to eat is indeed a sign of divine favor," wrote Professor Susan Starr Sered in "Food and Holiness: Cooking as a Sacred Act Among Middle-Eastern Jewish Women" (*Anthropological Quarterly,* July 1988). "It is significant that the women use food to thank God for granting a petition. For example, they distribute cookies or cakes to all of the pilgrims at holy tombs when a prayer has been answered as a result of pilgrimage to that tomb. In providing food for others, the women are, in a way, imitating God."

For them, as well as for women of the local Arab communities, a dessert like a plain cookie, which does not require any skill to make, is not a dessert worthy of guests. So we have the unusual *ka'ak b'adjwah,* a Syrian circular butter cookie filled with dates; *galettes sucrées,* a Moroccan biscotti-like cookie with dried apricots and nuts; and other Middle Eastern cookies in many incarnations, beautifully executed with great dexterity and pride.

Many traditional desserts, which are reminders of life in the Diaspora, are also seasonal celebrations of the natural cycle of the Jewish year. Czech apple cake, served at Rosh Hashanah, is symbolic of the new fruit of the fall harvest; a Polish cheesecake made at Shavoot, the "dairy" holiday, is prepared during the season of the most abundant milk and cheese production in the land of Israel; the Galicianer chocolate torte for Passover celebrates the barley harvest and the exodus of the Jews from Egypt; and the fruit-filled hamantaschen and other pastries use up the flour at Purim before Passover. For many families who hail from Europe, these desserts, now prepared in Israel, are also reminders of the lives left behind because of the Holocaust.

Eretz Israel Cake with Orange, Dates, and Marzipan

Israeli chef Celia Regev created this orange cake to incorporate all the ingredients she loves from her adopted land. You can substitute store-bought marzipan, although Celia makes her own from almonds, sugar, and egg whites. Marzipan was used in the Middle East as early as the fifth century C.E. Always a delicacy of the Jews, it was also, according to Moslem tradition, a particular favorite of the prophet Mohammed.

YIELD: 8 TO 10 SERVINGS

3/4 cup sugar

1/2 cup marzipan (see recipe below, or use store-bought)

Grated zest of 2 oranges

4 large eggs

1 3/4 cups all-purpose flour

1/2 cup pitted dates, chopped

1/3 cup candied citrus peel, chopped

1 teaspoon baking powder

1/4 teaspoon salt

3/4 cup orange juice

3/4 cup (1 1/2 sticks) unsalted butter, melted

Desserts

continued on next page   343

Celia Regev, one of Israel's preeminent pastry chefs

Eretz Israel Cake with Orange, Dates, and Marzipan
continued from previous page

1. Preheat the oven to 350 degrees and grease a 9-inch springform pan. Line the bottom of the pan with parchment paper cut into a circle.

2. Place the sugar, marzipan, and orange zest in the bowl of an electric mixer fitted with a paddle; beat to break up the marzipan until it is the texture of sand.

3. Replace the paddle with the whisk and add the eggs to the marzipan mixture. Whisk until light, fluffy, and pale yellow in color.

4. Take 2 tablespoons of the flour and sprinkle over the dates and candied citrus peel in a small bowl. This flour coating prevents them from sinking to the bottom of the batter.

5. Sift the remaining flour, the baking powder, and salt into a medium bowl.

6. Replace the whisk with the paddle and add the sifted dry ingredients, orange juice, and melted butter to the marzipan-egg mixture. Mix on low speed until the dry ingredients are just incorporated. Don't overmix—the batter should be soft and creamy. Fold in the dates and citrus peel.

7. Pour the batter into the springform mold, tap the mold a couple of times against the counter to remove the air bubbles, and bake on the middle rack of the oven for 40 minutes.

Homemade marzipan

YIELD: 1 1/2 CUPS MARZIPAN

1 cup finely ground almonds or almond
    flour

1/2 egg white (about 1 1/2 tablespoons)

1/2 cup sugar

Place the almonds and sugar in a food processor equipped with a steel blade and process, adding just enough egg white to bind the sugar and the almonds together.

NOTE Celia suggests adding a little cognac, rum, orange-blossom water, orange peel, cinnamon, coriander, or whatever flavor you like to the marzipan before processing. If it is too soft, add a bit more ground almonds or almond flour.

When a friend heard that I was writing this book, he told me that I had to include the coconut cake from Jako's Restaurant, in Haifa (see pages 258–9). Searching through guidebooks, I couldn't find any mention of the restaurant, but I located the number in the phone book and called the owner, Yaakov "Jako" Allaloof, who said he would meet me. The son of a fisherman in Izmir, Jako came to Israel in 1949 and opened the restaurant in the early 1970s.

Although his grilled fish is famous throughout the country, I was also in search of his family recipe for *tishpishti,* which is one of the few desserts served at the restaurant. In Turkish, *tez* means "quick," and *pisht* means "done." The Jews of Turkey created an onomatopoeic word, *tishpishti,* for a quickly cooked cake. Usually made with semolina and ground walnuts, Jako's Israeli adaptation includes coconut.

Jako's *Tishpishti*— Turkish Coconut Semolina Cake

YIELD: 12 SERVINGS

CAKE

3 large eggs

¼ cup vegetable oil

½ cup sugar

1 teaspoon vanilla

1½ cups smead (finest-grade semolina, not semolina flour)

1 cup all-purpose flour

½ teaspoon salt

1½ teaspoons baking powder

1 cup sour cream

1¼ cups shredded unsweetened coconut

SUGAR SYRUP

1½ cups sugar

2 cups water

1. Preheat the oven to 350 degrees.

2. Break the eggs into a large bowl and add the oil, sugar, and vanilla. Mix well.

3. Mix the smead, flour, salt, and baking powder together in a separate bowl. Add the dry ingredients gradually to the egg mixture, alternating with the sour cream and 1 cup of the coconut.

4. Pour into an ungreased 9-by-13-inch pan and bake for 30 to 35 minutes, until golden or until a toothpick inserted in the center comes out clean.

5. While the cake is baking, make the sugar syrup. Mix the sugar and water together in a heavy saucepan. Bring to a boil, then lower the heat and simmer the syrup, uncovered, for 1 hour or until it is reduced to ⅓ of its volume.

6. When the cake is done, remove it from the oven and let cool for 10 minutes. Cut into 3-inch squares in the pan and pour the syrup over the cake. Recut the squares and allow to sit, covered with a clean dish towel, for 1 hour.

7. Sprinkle the remaining ¼ cup of coconut on top before serving.

Desserts

345

Elisabeth's *Gerbeaud Szelet—* Chocolate Slices

This recipe, now served at Michael Andrew's Belgian restaurant in Jerusalem, was a Sunday-evening specialty of Sandra Rosenfeld's family in Mexico City. "My mother used to make this large chocolate cake that she cut into squares. Every Sunday was a feast. I'd spend the mornings watching her cook. But when my grandmother was alive, the best for us children were the weekends, because we could take several pieces of her cake home."

YIELD: ABOUT 30 SLICES

CAKE

1 cup (2 sticks) unsalted butter	1/2 cup lukewarm milk
2 large egg yolks	3 1/2 cups all-purpose flour
1 tablespoon sugar	Dash of salt
1/2 package dry yeast	1 1/2 cups raspberry jam
2 tablespoons warm water	1 cup sugar
2 tablespoons sour cream	1 1/4 cups ground walnuts

CHOCOLATE GLAZE

8 ounces bittersweet chocolate	1/2 cup sugar
1/2 cup water	2 tablespoons unsalted butter

1. To make the cake, place the butter, egg yolks, and 1 tablespoon sugar in an electric mixer with a paddle and beat until smooth.

2. Dissolve the yeast in the water in a small mixing bowl. Add the sour cream and milk, mix well, and stir into the butter mixture.

3. Gradually add the flour and salt and continue to mix until smooth.

4. Divide the dough into 3 equal portions, wrap in plastic, and place in the refrigerator for a few hours or overnight.

5. When you are ready to bake the cake, preheat the oven to 375 degrees and grease and flour a cookie sheet.

6. On a heavily floured board, roll out each piece of dough to a rectangle approximately 9 by 15 inches. Place 1 layer of dough on the cookie sheet and spread half the jam on top, leaving a 1/2-inch border. Sprinkle half the sugar and half the nuts over the surface.

7. Repeat with the second piece of dough and the remaining jam, sugar, and nuts; cover with the remaining dough and pinch the edges together all around to seal.

8. Prick the surface all over with a fork. Bake for 25 minutes. Remove from the oven and allow the cake to cool for a few minutes. Gently, using 2 spatulas, transfer it from the baking sheet to a serving platter and allow to cool completely.

9. To make the chocolate glaze, put the chocolate and the water in a small saucepan and cook over medium heat, stirring continuously, until the chocolate melts. Add the sugar, stirring until it dissolves. Remove the pan from the heat and stir in the butter.

10. Let the chocolate glaze cool slightly, then spread it with a spatula over the top and sides of the cooled cake. Allow the glaze to set. Cut the cake into 1½-by-3-inch rectangles.

· · · A BAKING LEGACY, FROM YUGOSLAVIA TO MEXICO TO ISRAEL · · ·

Jerusalem pastry chef Sandra Rosenfeld Katz thinks some people are just born to bake. Her grandmother, Elisabeth Rosenfeld, was a famous baker before World War II in Subotica, Yugoslavia. Then came the concentration camps during the war and communism after the war. Finally, Mrs. Rosenfeld brought her family to Mexico City, where she taught baking and ran a restaurant, with desserts her forte. (See my *Jewish Holiday Baker.*)

After moving to Israel from Mexico in 1996, Sandra worked as a researcher at the Israel Museum in Jerusalem, selling her grandmother's *linzertorte* on the side, and it was there that Andrew Jacobs, a restaurateur from London, first tasted it. He immediately offered to sell it in the restaurant he was opening. When Andrew's partner, Israeli-born chef Michael Katz, heard about the cake, he told Andrew to hire Sandra as pastry chef. "Although my profession was in museums, I had always wanted to bake," said Sandra. "It is my roots. I thought, 'I am working with the Dead Sea Scrolls, which are four thousand years old. This idea is young, an adventure. Let's try it.'"

Two months later, Michael asked her out. Six weeks later they were engaged, and soon they celebrated their Mexican-Israeli wedding on Mount Zion. "My goal is to rescue my grandmother's recipes," she told me as we sampled the Central European *gerbeaud szelet* that her grandmother learned in Subotica and taught in Mexico City, and which Sandra is now keeping alive on the other side of the world in Jerusalem.

Baklava

Today baklava comes in infinite variations: some with a honey syrup, others with a sugar syrup, and some, as I prefer it, with a combination of the two; some with pistachio, almonds, or walnuts, or a combination of all three nuts. As far as I can tell from many interviews, perusal of cookbooks, and much experimentation, there are few hard and fast baklava rules. Who uses what is not defined by regional borders but rather by familial practice.

After the baklava is baked, a sweet hot syrup is poured over it, infused with cardamom, ginger, or cinnamon, or sometimes orange-blossom or rose water, which is traditionally made by distilling the fragrant petals and exposing the jars in the sun. The only absolute rule is long, slow baking to dry out those leaves.

I haven't included a recipe for making the dough as the Nasser family does, as it is a particularly laborious art which takes years of practice to perfect. Commercial rectangular phyllo dough is available frozen in most supermarkets. I also have suggested baking the baklava in a rectangular dish rather than in rounds, as this is simpler and more efficient for less-practiced cooks.

YIELD: 24 SERVINGS

2 sticks (1 cup) unsalted butter, melted, or 1 cup vegetable oil

4 cups of pistachios, walnuts, or almonds, shelled and finely chopped but not ground

1 teaspoon ground cinnamon

1/2 teaspoon ground ginger

1 pound phyllo dough

2 cups sugar

1 1/2 cups water

1 cinnamon stick

2 whole cloves

Juice of 1/2 lemon

1/2 cup honey

A few drops of rose water (optional)

1. Preheat the oven to 350 degrees and brush the bottom of a 9-by-13-inch glass baking dish with some of the melted butter or oil.

2. Put the nuts in a small bowl and rake through them with your fingers in case there are any stones or pieces of shell that should be discarded. Sprinkle the cinnamon and ginger over the nuts.

3. Keep your phyllo covered with a damp cloth while you are preparing the baklava. Remove 1 sheet of phyllo dough from the stack and place it in the pan. Brush the surface with butter or oil. Layer another sheet on top and brush this as well. Repeat 7 more times until 9 sheets of phyllo dough have been stacked in the dish, each brushed with butter or oil. (You can also brush after every third sheet if you want to cut down on butter or oil.) Sprinkle the nuts and spices evenly over the top sheet. Then cover with 9 more pieces of phyllo dough, brushing each sheet with butter or oil as you did before.

4. Using a very sharp, heavy knife, cut diagonally across the dish and down through the layers. Repeat, making a crosshatch of 2-inch diamond shapes.

5. Bake for 15 minutes, then lower the heat to 250 degrees and continue cooking for about 1 hour and 15 minutes or until the leaves are crisp and golden. Remove from the oven.

6. Put the sugar, water, cinnamon stick, cloves, lemon juice, and honey in a small saucepan. Bring to a boil, reduce heat, and simmer gently for about 8 minutes. Add a few drops of rose water if you like, and pour half of the hot syrup over the baked baklava. When the syrup has soaked into the nuts and phyllo, pour on the remaining syrup. Let stand uncovered for several hours or overnight. Before serving, drain off any extra syrup that has not been absorbed.

NOTE For a slightly more textured pastry, you can also layer 6 sheets of phyllo, then half of the nuts, another 6 sheets, the rest of the nuts, and the final 6 sheets. Also, if you have a few sheets of leftover phyllo, you can make triangular treats with chocolate chips, leftover jam, or grated apples.

· · · A BAKLAVA BAKERY IN THE GALILEE · · ·

One of the legacies of the four-hundred-year Turkish occupation of Palestine is baklava, the phyllo dough dessert bathed in a sweet syrup. Although the Turks may have brought baklava to Palestine during the sixteenth century, sweets made with layered dough were prepared as early as the eleventh century. According to *Los Angeles Times* food sleuth Charles Perry, baklava may have been the first layered pastry baked in an oven, and the practice of making the layers of dough paper-thin was probably an innovation of the royal kitchens at the Topkapi Sarayi, in the century or so after the Ottoman conquest of Constantinople.

One of the best places to find baklava in Israel is a tiny two-story bakery in Raine, a mixed Christian and Moslem Arab town of fifteen thousand on the outskirts of Nazareth. For the last four generations, the Hamahayan family has been rolling out the dough by hand. "My ancestors learned how to make baklava from the Turks before the British," said Radi Ichsen Nasser, a third-generation baker. "Recently, a group of Turks came to visit and we showed them how we make our baklava. They learned from us because in Turkey today things are different. During Turkish times, my grandfather baked the dough in a wood-burning clay oven and sold the sweets from a small wagon. About fifty years ago he started to bake it in a gas oven." Today, Mr. Nasser's wife, his six sons, and his three daughters all make the baklava, which they sell throughout Israel from Metulla to Eilat.

When I visited Raine, I watched the family make the dough, first mixing flour and water in a huge bowl, then pulling off medium-sized balls and stacking them eighteen high, sprinkling on cornstarch so they wouldn't stick together. Then, with a rolling pin, they gently rolled out each round. When the dough became too large for the pin, they switched to a long pole, gently and firmly rolling the phyllo until paper thin. Then they cut out a circle template about two inches larger than the perimeter of the dough, placed nine rounds of the dough on top, and sprinkled pistachio nuts over it (son Afik already having carefully sorted through the nuts to remove any hard stones). Another nine layers of phyllo were then carefully placed on top. The baklava was baked in big commercial ovens for two and a half hours or, as Afik said, "until the dough dries out . . . the key to a good baklava."

In Moslem communities of Israel, baklava is served at all special occasions, but most importantly during the month of Ramadan, after dinner as a sweet with tea. Jews from Middle Eastern countries traditionally serve it bathed in oil, not butter, at *brit milah* (circumcision ceremony) as well as at other special occasions.

Kinaffeh—Cheese-filled Phyllo Pastry Bathed in Sugar Syrup

The Foods of
Israel Today

350

One of the jewels of Middle Eastern desserts, *kinaffeh* is made from a crumbly dough that is filled with fresh sheep's curd cheese and served heated with a sweet syrup and pistachio nuts. Many years ago, this popular pastry taught me the power of food as an icebreaker. I was accompanying my husband, Allan, to Nablus, where he was interviewing the then mayor for a legal book on the military occupation of the West Bank. Their heated political discussion lasted for almost two hours, when I finally became hungry and slightly bored. I interrupted to ask the mayor if it was true that the best *kinaffeh* in the Middle East was served in Nablus. Surprised by this culinary question, he looked at his watch and said, "The best *kinaffeh* in the Middle East is served at my house. Would you like to come for lunch?" We accepted his invitation and had a magnificent meal of a variety of *mezze*—including hummus, *baba ghanouj,* and stuffed vegetables—with *kinaffeh* served on a large round tray for dessert. As the day progressed, the political discussion became much less heated, and when we left, we embraced our hosts, having broken down many human barriers.

Today, when I want very good Israeli *kinaffeh,* I head for Adnan Ja'far's bakery inside Jerusalem's Damascus Gate. Mr. Ja'far's grandfather started the business by selling his *kinaffeh* from trays on the street. In 1942, he opened a shop where people could eat slices of *kinaffeh* while seated at tables. The Ja'far family now has three shops in Jerusalem, as well as shops in nearby Beit Hanina and Ramallah, and they even send *kinaffeh* weekly via overnight mail to Samadi Sweets Café in Baileys Crossroads, Virginia.

Kinaffeh dough resembles shredded wheat. At Ja'far it is made from a batter of flour, oil, and water, which is crumbled and then extruded through perforated slits onto a warmed sheet of metal, forming a fine pasta that is oven-dried on the sheet. A large round tray covered with orange food coloring and sugar is heated, and the pieces of dough are scattered on top and drizzled with clarified butter. The tray is then put on top of a gas grill and heated further. When the dough is warm, the sheep's cheese, and sometimes nuts, is sprinkled on top. As the cheese melts, another layer of dough is scattered over it and baked. To serve, the entire concoction is flipped, covered with a sweet syrup, and sprinkled with pistachio nuts.

What follows is a version of *kinaffeh* that easily can be made at home, using the Greek shredded phyllo dough called *kataifi,* known in the Middle East as *kinaffeh* dough. (Do not confuse this Greek *kataifi* dough with the Arab pancakes, called *kataif,* found on page 38.)

3 tablespoons plus 2 teaspoons ghee or
unsalted butter

5 cups *kataifi* dough (8 ounces), available
in Middle Eastern markets

A few drops of red and yellow food
coloring

2 tablespoons sliced blanched almonds

2 tablespoons pine nuts

1 3/4 cups ricotta cheese or any unsalted
curd cheese, drained

2 tablespoons chopped pistachio nuts

SUGAR SYRUP

2 cups sugar

1 cup water

Juice of 1/2 lemon

1. Preheat the oven to 350 degrees.

2. Put 3 tablespoons of the ghee or butter in a bowl and melt in a microwave
or in a saucepan on the stove.

3. Put the dough in a large bowl and sprinkle the butter over it, working it in
and separating the strands of dough with your fingers.

4. Drizzle a drop or 2 of red and yellow food coloring on the remaining 2 teaspoons butter to make it a reddish-orange color, and coat the bottom of a 12-
inch-round pan with it, leaving a 1-inch border around the edges.

continued on next page

· · · A SWEET STOP NEAR THE CHURCH OF THE HOLY SEPULCHRE · · ·

One of my favorite early-morning stops in Jerusalem's Old City is Zalatimo's, located between the eighth and the ninth stations of the cross, beneath one of the entrances to the Church of the Holy Sepulchre. Here, upon request, the flaky, thin pastry called *m'tabak* (pronounced "*mootabak*"), stuffed with sheep's cheese and bathed in a sugar syrup, is baked and served at one of the two tables in the grotto-like space. Allegedly started by a Venetian pilgrim, the bakery has been operating in this way, making pastries fresh to order, since the time of the Crusades. The shop stayed in the same family until 1860, when Mohammed Ali Zalatimo took over. He learned to make the family specialty in Da-mascus, and when the original owners were satisfied with his prowess, they sold him the shop.

It is quite an experience to sit at the tiny table and watch the father and son, descendants of Zalatimo, make *m'tabak*, dramatically stretching and twisting a mound of dough until it is paper-thin, then rapidly enfolding the cheese before they bake it in their huge, coal-fired oven (if it is working—otherwise, they take it into a back room to cook it in a small electric oven). When it's baked, they soak it in sugar and water and sprinkle it with confectioners' sugar. *M'tabak* is best eaten hot from the oven in the shop, which is open from 7 a.m. to noon. If you are dying to make it at home, try the following recipe for *kinaffeh*—a similar, less labor-intensive treat—substituting whole sheets of phyllo, brushed with butter, for the shredded *kinaffeh* dough.

5. Sprinkle the sliced almonds and pine nuts evenly over the greased area of the pan. Carefully top with 3 cups of the *kataifi* dough and press down with your fingers, evening out the dough.

6. Top with the cheese, leaving a ½-inch border around the edges to keep it from melting onto the pan. Then cover with the remaining *kataifi* dough and press down to flatten.

7. Bake for 20 to 25 minutes or until brown at the edges.

8. Meanwhile, make the sugar syrup. Bring the sugar and water to a slow boil, add the lemon juice, and stir constantly for about 15 minutes.

9. Remove the *kinaffeh* from the oven and flip onto a plate, colored side up. Drizzle the sugar syrup over it, then sprinkle on the chopped pistachio nuts. Cut into diamond shapes and serve.

Kinaffeh *in the making at Ja'far's*

Having read the autobiography of Ruby Daniel, a Cochin Jew from South India, I went in search of her at Kibbutz Naot Mordechai in the Upper Galilee. I found her, now in her late eighties, seated in her kitchen, cutting up apples to make jam.

She has lived for fifty years on the kibbutz. "When I came in 1949 there were not even huts," she said. "Only tents. The whole place was mud." Today, with lychee, cotton, and mangoes growing in this semidesert climate, the Galilee seems the right part of Israel for this immigration of Indians. But it was not so easy back then, when they had to live in very primitive and even dangerous conditions.

Ruby showed me the Malabee dictionary that was given to her by her mother. "Although I brought this with me to Israel, I never looked at it for years," she said. Later, when conditions allowed more time for leisure, she started to record the details of her past—songs, poems, and recipes. She showed me a Cochin cookbook. "The author wanted me to give him recipes," she said, "but I never wrote them down." But she did know by heart the ingredients for this spice cake, a dessert traditionally prepared for weddings and one she frequently bakes for her friends and family.

Although ghee (clarified butter) is commonly used in India, melted butter works just fine. I especially like the cardamom flavor in this tea cake.

YIELD: 6 TO 8 SERVINGS

3 large eggs

2/3 cup sugar

1/2 cup (1 stick) unsalted butter or pareve margarine, melted

1/4 teaspoon ground cloves

1/2 teaspoon cardamom

1/2 teaspoon nutmeg

1/2 teaspoon cinnamon

Dash salt

2/3 cup semolina flour

3/4 cup almonds, roughly chopped

3/4 cup unsalted cashew nuts, roughly chopped

2/3 cup golden Sultana raisins

1. Preheat the oven to 350 degrees. Grease a 9-by-5-inch loaf pan, line with parchment paper, and grease the parchment paper.

2. Put the eggs and sugar in the bowl of an electric mixer fitted with a whisk. Beat on high speed until pale yellow in color. Add the melted butter, cloves, cardamom, nutmeg, cinnamon, and salt; continue to mix until fully incorporated. Stir in the flour. The batter will be stiff.

3. Fold in the almonds, cashews, and raisins.

4. Spoon the dough evenly into the prepared pan. Bake on the middle shelf of the oven for 60 minutes or until the top is mahogany in color. Cool for a few minutes in the pan, then turn out onto a plate.

Desserts

353

The American Colony and Its Chocolate Cake

This excerpt was written years before I first tasted the chocolate cake that is a specialty of the American Colony Hotel in Jerusalem. The Colony was started by Horatio Spafford, a wealthy Christian lawyer from Chicago, and his wife, Anna, after a shipwreck in England in 1873 killed their four young daughters. The Spaffords decided to move to Jerusalem in 1881 with their young daughter Bertha, and were eventually joined by others, many of whom were Swedish-Americans. The commune called itself the American Colony and eventually ran a hostel, and later a hotel.

Adjusting to food in Jerusalem was difficult for the American Colony. "The native cooks were taught to prepare American dishes (to the extent that this was possible using local foodstuffs)," wrote Ruth Kark in *Communal Societies* (1995). "For the Swedes, accustomed to dry rye bread, meat, butter, potatoes, and fish, it was difficult to get used to wheat bread, porridge, rice, hot wheat, vegetable stew with relish, and the local goat milk and sesame oil. On festive occasions, sandwiches, tea, scones, cakes, ice cream, and lemonade were served. Later on, the Swedes' background in agriculture enabled them to improve their diet by raising potatoes, cows, hogs, and chickens."

When I sat with Valentine Vester of the American Colony family beneath the limestone arches in the charming, lushly planted courtyard of the former pasha's palace, she told me that she had recently learned that their famous chocolate cake, made from leftover bread crumbs, was of Swedish origin. Here is my version of this chocolate cake, which my husband, Allan, and I served at our wedding twenty-six years ago.

YIELD: 8 TO 10 SERVINGS

CAKE

- 8 large eggs, separated
- 1 cup (2 sticks) unsalted butter, at room temperature
- 1 cup sugar
- 2 teaspoons baking powder
- 1/2 cup unsweetened imported cocoa
- Dash of salt
- 1 1/4 cups finely ground almonds
- 1/2 cup fine bread crumbs

FILLING AND FROSTING

- 1/2 cup (1 stick) unsalted butter, softened
- 1 1/2 cups confectioners' sugar
- 1/4 cup unsweetened cocoa
- 2 tablespoons rum
- 2 teaspoons vanilla
- 1/4 cup slivered almonds for decoration

Christmas was at hand [and] I was determined to make a plum pudding.... Constantine found in the market all that was wanting for it except currants, and these our Jewish baker had got, brought from abroad by some of his friends. There were raisins from the other side of Jordan; flour from Samaria wheat; the spice bazaar produced very good and fragrant nutmegs, and cinnamon, and cloves, and allspice, and others whose English names I don't know, brought by the Mecca pilgrims from Arabia; citron, and lemon, and orange from Jaffa, preserved by my Jewess Sarah; sugar from the West Indies; and part of the tail of a fat sheep pastured on Judean hills. These were some of the ingredients that went to make up my very interesting pudding.... No less curious were the fruits for our dessert. Oranges and sugar came from Jaffa; apples and walnuts from Damascus; sweet lemons from one of the sheltered valleys of Judah; figs from Bethlehem; dates from Sinai; and almonds from Bethany and Gaza.

—Elizabeth Anne Finn,
A Home in the Holy Land (1882)

1. Preheat the oven to 375 degrees. Line a 9-by-13-inch or 2 8-inch round cake pans with aluminum foil, greasing the bottom and sides.

2. Put the egg yolks, butter, sugar, baking powder, cocoa, and salt in the bowl of a food processor equipped with a steel blade; process until smooth. Add the almonds and bread crumbs and pulse just to combine.

3. In the bowl of an electric mixer fitted with a whisk, beat the egg whites until stiff peaks form. Fold into the chocolate mixture. Pour the batter into the pan and spread it evenly with a spatula. Bake for 25 minutes or until a knife inserted in the center of the cake comes out clean. Cool the cake for about 15 minutes in the pan (or pans). Then carefully remove from the pan, and peel off the foil.

4. To make the filling and frosting, blend the butter, confectioners' sugar, cocoa, rum, and vanilla in a food processor fitted with a steel blade until smooth.

5. For the 9-by-13 cake, using a sharp knife, cut the cake crosswise into 3 equal layers and place 1 layer on a plate. With a spatula, spread ⅓ of the chocolate cream on the top and sides of the first layer. Then cover with the second layer. Spread the chocolate cream on top again, then add the third layer. Cover the top and sides with the remaining chocolate cream. Simply use each round cake as a layer, frosting between them as well as over the top and sides.

6. Toast the slivered almonds in a toaster oven or hot frying pan for a few minutes. Cool and sprinkle on top of the cake as a decoration.

The American Colony at Sunday dinner at the turn of the century

Desserts

355

When I asked a friend for directions to Bubby Irma Charles's home in the Jewish Quarter of Jerusalem's Old City, she said I didn't need any. "Ask anyone," she said. "Everybody knows her." The first person I stopped was a yeshiva student from Kansas City, who led me through a warren of narrow streets to a reconstructed town house not far from the Western Wall, the only segment remaining of the Temple built by Herod. The excavations in the Jewish Quarter have unearthed about twenty-two layers of history, including remnants of the cities of David and Solomon, the Maccabees, Herod, Hadrian, Constantine, the Mamelukes, and the British. On top of these ruins, many of which are preserved for the public to see, new stone-arched homes like the Charleses' carefully have been built.

Before I arrived at the Charleses', the Sabbath candles already had been lit. After the blessing was said over the wine, symbolic of all fruit in ancient Israel grown from the vine, the children were blessed by their grandfather. Then everyone filed silently into the kitchen to ritually wash their hands and returned to the table to say the blessings over the Sabbath bread, symbolizing all food that grows from the earth. Portions of the bread were passed to the guests, and everyone said, "*Shabbat Shalom*."

Before dinner was served, Irma's grandson-in-law, an Orthodox rabbi, discussed the Torah portion of the week. He talked about the fourth commandment: "Six days shalt thou labor, but the seventh is the Sabbath so keep it holy." Then he mused, "If cooking is so joyful, then why should you have to stop it for the Sabbath?" His answer: refraining from cooking for one day, as well as from other delights in life, makes us enjoy them all the more the rest of the week.

The Charleses, who came to their Orthodoxy as adults, love the fervor of the Sabbath preparations and the joy of opening their home to so many people. The author of two cookbooks, including *Adventures in Bubby Irma's Kitchen*, Bubby Irma works with her husband, Natie, in preparing for the Sabbath meal: he bakes the richly fragrant challah coated with a variety of seeds, and she prepares the rest of the meal, including her justly famous *babka*, which rises high over the sides of an angel-food cake pan.

The Foods of
Israel Today

Phyllis Richman, a food writer and novelist and Bubby Irma's niece, grew up eating this *babka* throughout her childhood at every family occasion. Bubby Irma makes it for a meat meal with water, pareve tofu sour cream, and pareve margarine, and with milk, regular sour cream, and butter for a dairy meal.

YIELD: 10 TO 12 SERVINGS

1 envelope or 1 scant tablespoon dry yeast

1/4 cup warm water

3/4 cup plus 1 teaspoon sugar

4 1/2 cups unbleached all-purpose flour

1 cup (2 sticks) unsalted butter or pareve margarine, melted

4 large eggs, separated

1 teaspoon vanilla

1/2 cup milk or water

1/2 cup sour or pareve tofu sour cream

3/4 cup raisins

3/4 cup chopped walnuts

1/2 cup shredded coconut

2 teaspoons cinnamon

3/4 cup apricot or raspberry jam

1. Mix the yeast, water, and 1 teaspoon of sugar in a small bowl and let stand for 5 minutes.

2. Put the flour in a large bowl or bowl of an electric mixer and make a well in the center. Add the dissolved yeast, melted butter or margarine, egg yolks, 1/4 cup of the sugar, vanilla, milk or water, and sour cream. Mix until a smooth dough is formed. Cover and refrigerate for 2 hours or overnight.

3. When you are ready to bake the *babka,* roll the dough out on a floured surface to a 30-by-24-inch rectangle. The thinner the dough, the better the *babka*.

4. Place the egg whites in a mixing bowl and beat with the remaining 1/2 cup sugar into a meringue, until stiff peaks form. Spread the meringue over the dough, leaving a 1-inch edge. Sprinkle the meringue generously with the raisins, walnuts, and coconut. Dust with the cinnamon and dot with spoonfuls of the jam.

5. Roll the dough into a large jelly roll, starting from 1 long side and gently rolling up, pinching the seam closed.

6. Cut the roll into 6 equal pieces and place these, cut side up, side by side in the bottom of a well-greased angel-food cake or tube pan with a removable bottom. Cover with a damp cloth and allow to rise for 1 hour.

7. Preheat the oven to 400 degrees. Bake for 10 minutes, then lower the oven to 350 degrees and bake for an additional 35 to 40 minutes.

NOTE   You can substitute chocolate chips for the raisins.

Apricot Meringue Kuchen

A few years ago on a trip to Israel, we stayed at Moshav Beit Hillel in the Upper Galilee. Our tiny cabin was set right in the middle of a lush apricot orchard. The host-farmer explained to us that at one time a variety of apricots were grown on his moshav, but now they are more uniform for the local and European markets. Because it was the height of the short growing season, his wife served us a lovely summertime meringue-topped apricot kuchen for tea. In the following recipe, you can substitute or combine the apricots with peaches, blueberries, or Italian prunes. Meringue-topped fruit cakes are very common in Israel, a cultural contribution from Eastern and Central Europe. In the United States, where we try to make things easier, similar recipes do not call for separating the eggs but instead for merely putting the whole eggs into the dough batter, then sprinkling the top with sugar and cinnamon. I like both versions.

YIELD: 1 CAKE, SERVING 8 TO 10 PEOPLE

½ cup (1 stick) unsalted butter, softened and cut into 1-inch pieces

¾ cup sugar

Dash of salt

2 large eggs, separated

Grated zest of ½ lemon

1 tablespoon lemon juice

1 cup unbleached all-purpose flour

1 teaspoon baking powder

4 tablespoons apricot jam

1½ pounds fresh apricots

1. Preheat the oven to 350 degrees.

2. Put the butter, ½ cup of the sugar, salt, egg yolks, and lemon rind and juice in the bowl of a food processor fitted with a steel blade. Blend until smooth.

3. Put the flour and baking powder in a small bowl and mix with your fingers. Slowly add them to the other mixture, pulsing each time just until the ingredients are incorporated. Refrigerate the dough an hour or so, until firm. Then turn out the dough and, flouring your fingers if necessary, press it into the bottom and sides of a greased springform pan or a 9-inch pie pan with a removable bottom. Flute the sides. Smear the top with the apricot jam.

4. Wash the apricots, cut them in half, and remove the pits. Press the apricots skin side down into the dough.

5. Place the cake pan on a cookie sheet and bake on the middle rack of the oven for 40 minutes.

6. Meanwhile, beat the egg whites until frothy, then add the remaining ¼ cup sugar and beat until the whites form stiff peaks.

7. Remove the kuchen from the oven and spoon the egg white mixture evenly over the apricots, spreading with the back of the spoon. Lower the oven to 325 degrees and bake for about 10 minutes or until the top of the cake is golden.

When I worked on a kibbutz in 1970, our daily late-afternoon ritual was the enjoyment of cake, coffee, and conversation at a member's home. In those days meals were served in the communal dining room, and only cakes were prepared at home—in a *wunderpot* (see page 342), set over a burner. The ingredients for making cakes were free for members at the kibbutz store. Alas, the leisurely tea or coffee hour after the siesta has rapidly become a once-a-week occurrence, usually indulged in only on Shabbat. "Today, even on the kibbutz, cakes are more often than not store-bought," said Hava Raveh, a member of Kibbutz Dafna, who shared the recipe for this quick kibbutz cake filled with apples from the nearby Golan Heights.

Quick Kibbutz Apple Cake

YIELD: 8 TO 10 SERVINGS

1 cup fine semolina flour

1 cup unbleached all-purpose flour

1 cup sugar

1/2 teaspoon baking powder

1/8 teaspoon salt

1/2 cup (1 stick) unsalted butter or pareve margarine

6 full-flavored apples (about 3 pounds), unpeeled, cored, and grated coarsely

1 teaspoon cinnamon

1/2 cup chopped walnuts or pecans

1. Preheat the oven to 350 degrees and grease a 9-inch round springform pan.

2. Put the semolina and all-purpose flours, sugar, baking powder, and salt in a medium bowl.

3. Melt the butter, then drizzle a third of it over the dry ingredients and gently mix with your fingers. Spoon half the batter into the greased pan, carefully leveling the top.

4. Scatter the grated apples on top and sprinkle the cinnamon and nuts over the surface. Spoon on the remaining flour mixture, smoothing the top with a spatula, and drizzle the remaining melted butter over the cake.

5. Bake in the oven for 45 minutes. Cool in the pan and remove before cutting.

Cake time on the kibbutz

Desserts

359

Rosh Hashanah Apple Torte

Although this apple torte from Hana Lustigova Greenfield (see pages 248 and 285) is often called Apple Cake Eden, if there were any apples in the Garden of Eden, they were tiny, unlike the ones grown today. Despite popular belief, apples, although mentioned in old scriptures, were not specifically noted in the Bible. For many years before the establishment of the state, most apples came from Damascus and Romania, because farmers did not believe they could grow in Palestine's climate. In 1858 James Turner Barclay, an American missionary, wrote in his *City of the Great King,* "It is a matter equally of surprise and regret that the apple seems to be almost insusceptible of acclimation to this region."

Later settlers imported apples, and they were a rare treat. "For us, getting these *tapuach zahav,* 'golden apples,' from abroad was more special than the *tapuach kesev,* the orange which grew in Israel," recalled Kena Shoval, who was raised in Tel Aviv in the 1940s. Interestingly, for Jews living in Eastern Europe at the time, the oranges, shipped all the way from Palestine, were the treasure.

Today, Israel has many varieties of apples from the Golan Heights and the Upper Galilee, including Granny Smith, Grand, Jonathan, Golden Delicious, Starking, Orleans, Fuji, and Gala. A grated apple filling, rather than the chopped apples used in American apple pies and crisps, is typical of Central and Eastern European cakes. So is the sweeter dough that this recipe yields. It is a perfect cake for ushering in the New Year, the seasonal debut of apple desserts in my family.

YIELD: 8 TO 10 SERVINGS

2 cups unbleached all-purpose flour

1/2 teaspoon baking powder

1/4 teaspoon salt

1 large egg

3/4 cup (1 1/2 sticks) unsalted butter or margarine, cut into small pieces

1 cup sugar

Grated zest of 1 lemon

6 medium (about 3 pounds) Granny Smith or other flavorful apples, peeled and cored

1/2 teaspoon cinnamon

1. Put the flour, baking powder, salt, egg, butter or margarine, ¾ cup of the sugar, and the lemon zest in the bowl of a food processor fitted with a steel blade. Process until a soft dough is formed. Remove and roll the dough in flour, then cover with plastic wrap and refrigerate for about 20 minutes.

2. Meanwhile, coarsely grate the apples in a food processor fitted with a grating blade or use the large holes of a hand grater. Toss with the remaining ¼ cup sugar and set aside in a colander to drain for 30 minutes. Add the cinnamon.

3. Preheat the oven to 450 degrees.

4. Take ⅔ of the dough and with floured fingertips, press it lightly into the bottom and 2 inches up the sides of a 9-inch springform pan.

5. Spoon the apple mixture evenly into the dough shell.

6. Roll out the remaining dough to a 9-inch circle, about ⅛ inch thick, and place on top of the apples, crimping the edges of the dough together to seal them. Make a few holes in the top of the cake with the tines of a fork.

7. Bake on the middle rack of the oven for 15 minutes. Reduce the heat to 350 degrees and bake for 30 minutes more or until golden brown.

Sabbath morning in Jerusalem

The story of the Strauss Dairy of Nahariya, the largest private producer of milk products in the country, is the story of the evolution of milk in Israel. In the dairy museum, adjacent to the factory, a diorama traces the voyage of businessman Richard Strauss and his wife, Hilde, from Ulm, Germany. When they came to Palestine, the two built a barn and raised cattle, selling the milk, cream, and homemade cheese from their front porch. During strawberry season the pairing of strawberries and Strauss cream was an instant hit, especially with British soldiers and the large population of German Jews, who whipped the cream and called it *schlag.*

"In Israel, fresh milk products always dominated," said Mickey Strauss, son of the founders and current chairman of the board of the company. "In North Africa, Jews gave milk to their children but didn't give them fresh cheese. We soon learned that Israelis in general don't like strong-smelling cheeses." The Strauss Dairy set the standard in Israel, producing fresh soft white cheeses, yogurt, cottage cheese, *leben,* and sour cream. As taste buds developed, the Strausses introduced stronger-flavored cheeses like Camembert and Limburger. Hilde Strauss found an old, battered, wooden ice cream maker, starting the tradition of dairy desserts for which Strauss is famous today. With it she often served this *linzertorte,* a recipe she brought from Germany, filled with jam made from strawberries growing around Nahariya.

A woman's job, milking the cows

Linzertorte

YIELD: 8 TO 10 SERVINGS

1 1/4 sticks unsalted butter, cut into 1-inch pieces

1 cup sugar

1 large egg

1 tablespoon cognac

1 3/4 cups finely ground almonds

1 3/4 cups unbleached all-purpose flour

1/4 teaspoon salt

1 teaspoon unsweetened cocoa (optional)

1 teaspoon grated lemon zest

1/4 teaspoon cloves

1/2 teaspoon nutmeg

1/2 teaspoon cinnamon

1 1/2 cups strawberry jam

Confectioners' sugar for dusting

1. Put the butter and the sugar in the bowl of a food processor fitted with a steel blade and blend to a cream. Add the egg, cognac, almonds, flour, salt, cocoa, lemon zest, cloves, nutmeg, and cinnamon and process until a ball of dough is formed. If the dough is too sticky, add a bit more flour. Remove, wrap in plastic, and refrigerate for 30 minutes.

2. Preheat the oven to 350 degrees and grease a 10-inch springform pan.

3. Divide the dough into 2 pieces, 1 larger than the other. Lightly dust your fingers with flour, then press the larger piece of dough into the bottom of the pan and 1 1/2 inches up the sides.

4. Spread the jam evenly over the dough.

5. On a heavily floured pastry board, roll out the remaining dough and cut into long, 1-inch-wide strips, about 1/4-inch thick. Place the strips in a criss-cross pattern over the jam and crimp the edges to make an attractive crust.

6. Bake on the middle rack of the oven for 40 minutes. Remove from the oven, let sit a few minutes, and remove the sides from the pan. Before serving, dust with confectioners' sugar.

NOTE   You can also make individual cookies by rolling the dough, then cutting it into 24 2-inch rounds with holes in the center, and another 24 whole 2-inch rounds. Bake all the rounds in a 350-degree oven for about 12 minutes and let cool. Place about 1 teaspoon of jam on top of each solid round, then top with a round with a hole. Sprinkle with confectioners' sugar. Yield: about 2 dozen cookies.

Lili Sharon's Sour Cream Strudel Filled with Apricot Jam and Pecans

This melt-in-your mouth *ooga,* or shortcut strudel, is Lili Sharon's signature dessert (see page 312 for more on Lili). "When people come to visit us on the ranch, I time when they leave Tel Aviv or Jerusalem," said Lili. "Then I start assembling the cake. By the time they arrive it is hot from the oven. If people are coming and I have ten other cakes but not this one, they are disappointed," she said, sprinkling her famous strudel with confectioners' sugar. And as her husband, the famed General Arik Sharon, bit into a piece of the cake, he remarked, "My wife is beautiful, clever, soft, and gentle. She is my best friend, and she has made our house a home. I can beautifully describe the taste of the food made by Lili, but how to do it only Lili knows."

YIELD: 2 STRUDELS, 12 SLICES EACH

CRUST

2 cups unbleached all-purpose flour	1 teaspoon baking powder
Dash of salt	1 cup sour cream
^{3}/$_4$ cup (1^1/$_2$ sticks) unsalted butter	1 large egg yolk

FILLING

1^1/$_2$ cups good-quality apricot jam	1 cup ground pecans
^{1}/$_4$ cup sugar	^{1}/$_2$ cup shredded unsweetened coconut
Grated zest of 1 lemon	Confectioners' sugar for garnish

1. Place the flour, salt, butter, and baking powder in the bowl of a food processor fitted with a steel blade. Pulse until crumbly in texture.

2. Add the sour cream and the egg yolk and continue to pulse until smooth. Flouring your hands, gather up the dough from the food processor, pat it into a ball, cover with plastic wrap, and refrigerate for at least 2 hours, or up to a week.

3. When ready to bake the dough, preheat the oven to 350 degrees. Remove the dough from the refrigerator and divide it into 2 equal pieces. Sprinkling flour on your hands and working on a floured pastry cloth or a clean pillowcase, roll out 1 piece of dough to a 10-by-14-inch rectangle.

4. Leaving a 1-inch border on all sides, smear half the apricot jam over the dough. Sprinkle on 2 tablespoons of the sugar, half the grated lemon zest, ^{1}/$_2$ cup of the pecans, and ^{1}/$_4$ cup of the coconut. Carefully roll up the strudel, starting from 1 long side. With the seam side down, fold the ends under. Using the tip of a knife, make a ^{1}/$_2$-inch puncture every 2 inches on the top of the roll. Repeat the filling and rolling process with the second piece of dough. (At this point, you can freeze the strudels, unbaked. Carefully wrap them with plastic wrap, and gently

place on a flat, even surface in the freezer—until it freezes, the strudel is flexible. Defrost for 2 hours before baking.)

5. When ready to bake, place the strudels on a greased cookie sheet.

6. Bake on the middle rack of the preheated oven for 35 minutes or until the crust is golden and firm. Let sit a few minutes and cut into 2-inch slices. Sprinkle with confectioners' sugar.

NOTE   If you like, you can substitute pureed dates for the apricot jam. Another version, which I tasted at Margaret Tayer's restaurant in Jaffa, was made from quinces cooked for a long time over low heat, then mixed with ground walnuts, lemon zest, sugar, and coconut.

German immigrants, despite the hardships in Palestine in the late 1930s, could not give up their *Jause,* their afternoon coffee break; so they opened a number of European bourgeois cafés. They also entertained each other at home. "Around six o'clock in the late afternoon, my mother would get slightly depressed because the flat was getting dark with strict electricity rationing during World War II. She would take me out for a walk," said Naomi Harris Rosenblatt, author of *Wrestling with the Angels,* who grew up in Haifa. "We would walk in such a way that we would catch the eye of one of our German neighbors who was leaning over the balcony or sitting at a table with a coffee cart. They would right away say, 'Mrs. Harris, why don't you come up for coffee.' After the necessary protestations, we would go up right away, yearning for that rich coffee and to taste their wonderful chocolate tortes and minuscule sausage sandwiches. I enjoyed it so much because in my home, that of Scottish and Canadian Jews, we drank endless cups of tea accompanied by dry ginger biscuits.

"The conversation always inevitably revolved around the same subject, whether it was with Mrs. Ambach or Frau Doktor Mattsdorf. 'How did you get out in time?' my mother would ask. Mrs. Ambach would tell us how she had to leave her elderly mother, who ended up in Terezienstadt. And my mother would respond in the same way: 'Frau Ambach, there was nothing you could have done at the time—your mother must have been happy that you were able to get away.' We all always ended up in tears."

This is the cheesecake that the late Zelda Schnur, who was my mother-in-law's best friend from Zamość, Poland, served every time I visited her in Netanya. Whenever my husband eats this dessert, he is right back in his mother's kitchen.

Zelda Schnur's Polish-Israeli Cheesecake

CRUST

1 1/2 cups cookie crumbs, from vanilla wafers or graham crackers (about 4 ounces of cookies)

1/2 cup sugar

8 tablespoons unsalted butter, melted

1/4 teaspoon cinnamon

CAKE

20 ounces cream cheese

3 large eggs, separated

1 1/4 cups sugar

Juice and grated zest of 1 lemon

2 teaspoons vanilla

1/2 cup unbleached all-purpose flour

1 cup sour cream

1. Preheat the oven to 350 degrees.

2. To prepare the crust, put the crumbs, sugar, melted butter, and cinnamon in the bowl of a food processor with a steel blade. Process until fine crumbs are formed.

3. Press the crumb mixture into the bottom and 2 1/2 inches up the sides of a 10-inch springform pan. Set aside.

4. To make the filling, put the cream cheese, egg yolks, 3/4 cup of the sugar, lemon juice and zest, and 1 teaspoon of the vanilla in the bowl of the food processor and puree. Then add the flour and pulse until well blended.

5. In the bowl of an electric mixer, beat the egg whites with 1/4 cup more of the sugar, until stiff peaks are formed.

6. Carefully fold the cream cheese mixture into the egg whites until just incorporated. Pour into the crumb-lined pan.

7. Bake on the lower rack of the oven for 60 minutes.

8. Meanwhile, mix the sour cream, the remaining 1/4 cup sugar, and the remaining 1 teaspoon of vanilla in a small bowl until well blended.

9. Remove the cake from the oven and allow it to sit for 10 minutes. Pour the sour cream mixture over the cake. Return to the oven and bake for 10 minutes more or until a toothpick comes out clean.

10. Cool slightly and remove from the pan. Chill for at least 2 to 3 hours before serving.

Desserts

Halvah Cheesecake— A Recipe Recalled

Throughout the forty-plus years he's lived in his apartment in Haifa's Carmel, Jacob Lishansky has been holding open houses every Saturday afternoon, cooking up a storm for all his friends. The apartment is filled with decades' worth of labeled pickled vegetables, exotic liqueurs made from fig, eggplant, pomegranate, and myrtle, and many varieties of jam, including tomato. The windowsill in his tiny kitchen houses small pots of thyme, basil, and rosemary, stacks of garden herbs drying, and cherry liqueur fermenting.

Mr. Lishansky was born on a cattle farm in Metulla in 1912, in the northernmost part of Israel. "My father would bring me pita with halvah as a treat," he told me during one of his cooking sessions. "From the Arabs, my mother learned how to make cheese and cook halvah in tins." In a letter from his late sister, Mr. Lishansky found a recipe for the following halvah cheesecake, which his mother made for him as a child from the confection made from ground sesame seeds in a base of honey or other sweet syrup. This is a recipe for halvah enthusiasts.

YIELD: 10 TO 12 SERVINGS

CRUST

½ cup ground blanched walnuts

⅓ cup sugar

½ cup (1 stick) unsalted butter

1 cup all purpose flour

FILLING

5 large eggs, separated, at room temperature

¾ cup sugar

1½ pounds ricotta or farmer cheese

¾ cup sour cream

½ cup dried apricots or pistachio nuts

¼ teaspoon cream of tartar

12 ounces plain halvah, crumbled (about 1½ cups)

1. To make the crust, grind the nuts with 1 tablespoon of the sugar in a food processor fitted with a steel blade. Cut up the butter and add the pieces, with the remaining sugar and the flour, to the processor. Pulse until a ball of dough is formed.

2. Wrap the dough in plastic and refrigerate for 30 minutes.

3. Preheat the oven to 350 degrees. Press the dough into the bottom and against the sides of a greased 10-inch springform pan. Bake the crust on the middle rack of the oven for 15 minutes or until golden in color.

4. Remove the crust from the oven and let cool. Leave the oven on.

5. To make the filling, put the egg yolks and the sugar in the bowl of an electric mixer. Using the whisk attachment, beat on high speed for 2 minutes or until the eggs are pale yellow.

6. Add the ricotta or farmer cheese and sour cream and beat until smooth. Add the apricots or nuts and incorporate fully.

7. In a separate bowl of the electric mixer, beat the egg whites with the cream of tartar until stiff but not dry. Stir ⅓ into the cheese mixture, then fold in the rest. Fold in 1 cup of the halvah.

8. Pour the batter into the crust, return to the middle rack of the oven, and bake for about an hour or until a toothpick comes out clean when inserted into the middle.

9. Sprinkle the remaining crumbled halvah over the cheesecake. Return to the oven and bake for 7 to 10 minutes or until melted. Cool and serve.

Pick your flavor of halvah.

Aunt Fanny's Passover Chocolate Mousse Cake

This chocolate mousse cake comes from Fanny Mayer, a Polish Holocaust survivor who rebuilt her life in Tel Aviv after World War II. Fanny's variation of the famous Prince Albert Torte, named in honor of Queen Victoria's husband, is great for Passover and throughout the year.

YIELD: 12 SERVINGS

8 ounces bittersweet chocolate, plus an ounce or so of chocolate for shaving

1 cup (2 sticks) unsalted butter or pareve margarine

2 teaspoons strong coffee, or 1 teaspoon instant coffee powder and 1 teaspoon water

3 tablespoons kosher-for-Passover brandy or cherry liqueur

6 large eggs, separated

1 cup sugar

2 tablespoons matzoh cake meal, plus additional for sprinkling

1. Melt the chocolate and the butter or margarine in the top of a double boiler. Add the coffee and brandy or liqueur. Remove from the heat and pour into a mixing bowl.

2. Add the egg yolks 1 at a time, beating well after each addition.

3. In the bowl of an electric mixer, beat the egg whites, gradually adding the sugar and continuing to beat until the whites are stiff but not dry.

4. Fold the beaten egg whites into the chocolate batter. Remove 1½ cups of this batter and refrigerate. Fold the 2 tablespoons matzoh cake meal into the remaining batter.

5. Preheat the oven to 350 degrees; grease a 9-inch springform pan, and sprinkle additional matzoh cake meal over the bottom and sides. Pour the batter into the pan and bake for 30 minutes. Cool completely, then spread the reserved refrigerated chocolate batter over the top and decorate with chocolate shavings.

··· WHEN YOU WALK BY ELITE'S CHOCOLATE FACTORY THE AROMA IS FREE ···

For many Israelis, the aroma coming from the Elite Industries Ltd. Chocolate factory in Ramat Gan evoked such raptures growing up that it inspired the lyrics of a popular song in the 1970s: "Big chocolate, small chocolate, expensive chocolate, cheap chocolate, chocolate with nuts...but the aroma, when you pass the factory, is for free!"

Like many of Israel's businesses, Elite was started by an immigrant family. "In 1932, everybody saw Hitler coming," said Abe M. Fromcenko, whose family owned a candy factory in the Crimea. After his father opened Elite's chocolate factory in Tel Aviv in 1934, they began exporting chocolate and chewing gum. "In 1940, a man from Iraq came over with dates and asked us to make chocolate-covered date candies for the king," said Mr. Fromcenko. "He also told us that King Farouk loved our chewing gum." Later, Elite opened a Jewish-Arab chocolate factory in Beirut, which closed after the creation of Israel. The Fromcenkos still hope that with peace, another factory may open in Beirut.

oduce Dalia enjoys this sweeter, more sophisticated halvah Passover layer cake, an example of a dessert created during the austerity period when eggs were scarce and few people had ovens. It is also reminiscent of her grandmother's *oblaten,* a torte made with very thin cookies. Make this the day you plan to serve it or it will become soggy.

Matzoh Halvah Chocolate Cake

YIELD: 8 TO 10 SERVINGS

4 ounces bittersweet chocolate

4 ounces halvah

2½ cups heavy cream

2–3 tablespoons brandy

1½ cups sweet or semisweet red wine

8 whole plain matzohs

2 tablespoons roughly chopped pistachio nuts or walnuts

1. Melt the chocolate in a pan over low heat. Crumble the halvah and add it to the chocolate with 1 cup of the cream, stirring until smooth. Stir in the brandy and let cool.

2. Whip the remaining cream.

3. Pour the wine into a shallow bowl, dunk each matzoh on both sides, and set them aside.

4. Place a sheet of wine-coated matzoh on a serving plate. Generously spread some of the halvah and chocolate mixture on it, spread on a layer of whipped cream, and place another matzoh on top. Again spread with the filling and whipped cream until all the matzoh are used up. Spread the remaining whipped cream over the top matzoh and frost the sides. Refrigerate for a few hours.

5. Just before serving, sprinkle with chopped nuts.

When I was growing up in Jerusalem, we used to take sandwiches to school. When there was nothing in the house on Sunday— no sausage, no chicken, no cheese—my mother would give me leftover challah, with butter and a piece of halvah on it. Let me tell you, that was the best. That day I loved my mama a lot. There were days when other kids would have sandwiches with halvah so we would exchange, ah, the halvah sandwiches!

—Dalia Carmel, cookbook collector

Rationing out those monthly eggs during zena

Easter *Ka'ak* with *Adjwah* Dates

We made many different kinds of cookies before Easter," said Therese Ashy, who grew up in the Greek Catholic community in Haifa. "All the neighborhood helped make them for holidays, weddings, and funerals. Before Good Friday we usually put the music of the Good Friday prayer on, and we enjoyed listening to it while baking." One of the cookie recipes often made in the Greek Catholic community was sweet *ka'ak,* cookies stuffed with dates. The crown-shaped butter cookie which encases the dates is said to resemble Jesus' crown of thorns. The thorns are made with a *malkat* (pronounced *"ma-lat"*), a tool similar to a strawberry pincher. Mrs. Ashy also adds *mahlep* (ground cherry-pit centers), plus orange-flower and rose water to the dough for flavor. The orange flower is not only used as a flavoring extract, but a little of it in water is supposedly good for a stomachache.

This same dough and date filling are used to make *m'amoul,* which means "stuffed." *M'amoul* are traditionally made in wooden molds which, after being filled with the dough encasing nuts or dates, are slapped onto the table, so that the emerging cookie is shaped into a lovely design. I adore the crunchy texture of the semolina in these cookies. Bakers adept at molding cookies with semolina are respected in the Arab community of Israel, since it takes much more dexterity to use semolina than flour.

Greek Orthodox Archimandrite Kelladion takes a pause from his Easter cooking.

YIELD: ABOUT 2½ DOZEN COOKIES

1 pound pitted dates, mashed

½ teaspoon ground cinnamon

¼ teaspoon ground nutmeg

1 cup (2 sticks) unsalted butter, at room temperature, plus butter for your hands

½ cup warm water

½ teaspoon yeast

½ teaspoon sugar

2 cups smead (finest-grade semolina)

1 cup unbleached all-purpose flour

Dash of salt

Pinch *mahlep* (ground cherry-pit centers)

¼ teaspoon orange-flower water and/or rose water

Confectioners' sugar for dusting

1. Put the dates in a bowl and sprinkle the cinnamon and nutmeg over them. Blend well with a fork or with your hands. Grease your hands with a bit of butter and roll out a handful of the date filling into a string as thin as your pinky and about 12 inches long. Repeat with the rest of the dates.

2. Pour the water into a glass bowl. Sprinkle on the yeast and sugar, stir, and let stand until it bubbles.

3. Place the smead, flour, salt, *mahlep,* and butter in the bowl of a food processor fitted with a steel blade. Add the yeast mixture with the orange-flower water or rose water and process until a smooth and pliable dough is formed. If you feel the dough is too sticky to handle, add flour; if it doesn't seem sticky enough, add water.

4. Dusting your hands with flour, take a handful of dough and roll it with both hands to form a string as thick as your index finger. Place the dough on the table, and using your 3 center fingers, flatten the dough so that it is about ⅛ inch thick and 12 inches long. Then press 1 of the date strings into the center of the length of dough, and enclose by pinching the long edges together so that the dates are encased. With your palms, roll carefully to smooth the covering of dough; the diameter of the roll should be about ½ inch. If it is still too thick, keep rolling until the snake becomes thinner, dusting your hands with flour as needed. Repeat with the remaining dough and date filling. You will make about 10 strings.

5. Preheat the oven to 350 degrees.

6. Using a dull knife, cut the dough strings into 4½-inch-long pieces and twist each into a circle, pinching the ends closed. Then, if you like, pinch the top and the sides to form "thorns."

7. Place the cookies on an ungreased cookie sheet about 1 inch apart, and bake in the oven for 15 minutes, or until golden. Be careful not to overbake. Remove from the oven, let cool slightly, and sprinkle with confectioners' sugar.

One of my beloved Jerusalem pastimes is to wander through the Old City with no agenda other than to peek into courtyards and kitchens. I love to let the aromas guide my stroll through the narrow streets. Just off some of the rocky paths are whole stone worlds with beautiful archways and extraordinary inner courtyards filled with fragrant flowers and greenery. The Greek Orthodox patriarchate contains one of the most interesting of these sanctuaries, with large cypress, orange, and lemon trees.

On a recent visit, I met Archimandrite Kelladion, who has been cooking for all the priests and bishops, as well as for the boys in the Greek Orthodox school, for the past forty years. Originally from Corfu, the black-cloaked archimandrite and his helpers cook Greek and Middle Eastern food for about one hundred people twice a day in the large kitchen. The morning I was visiting, they had made about two hundred *koftes* (meat patties) that were to be served with rice for lunch. Except on Christmas, Easter, the Feast of the Patriarch, and November 30th (the Feast of St. Andreos), the priests and the students carry

The Ceremony of the Holy Fire at the Church of the Holy Sepulchre

trays of food from the refectory to their quarters, where they eat alone. On the few feast days, everyone eats together. Desserts for these special days include baklava and *kinaffeh*, ordered from nearby Ja'afer (see pages 350–2), except on November 30th, when the cook makes *loukomades*, doughnuts dipped in honey. On Easter, after seven weeks of a strictly observed Lent, during which they abstain from eating meat, fish, eggs, butter, milk, and cheese, the archimandrite prepares a roasted Pascal lamb and makes *kourambiedes*, rich Greek butter cookies, for dessert.

The first time that I tasted *kourambiedes* was at a reception at the Greek patriarchate one Easter many years ago, after I had the honor of attending the kindling of the Holy Fire in the Church of the Holy Sepulchre. Thousands of pilgrims had assembled, all holding white tapered candles, commemorating the light which sprang up at the resurrection of Jesus. Amidst the ringing of bells, singing, and clapping, the then patriarch, dressed in white satin and wearing a gold crown, blessed the people as he wove his way through the crowd. After he entered the Holy Tomb where Jesus was buried, he lit a candle which a parish priest brought to the altar. As the people saw the light, they chanted louder in appreciation and held up thousands of candles. The patriarch, taking off his cloak, entered the Holy of Holies, while the other patriarchs waited in another room. After a few minutes, he emerged, borne aloft on the shoulders of the crowd, holding a flaming torch and followed by people struggling to light their candles from it. While the Greeks received the fire on one side of the tomb, the Copts, Syrians, and Ethiopians, the minor holders of rights from the Church of the Holy Sepulchre, lit theirs on the other side, and the Armenian patriarch hastened with his candle from the tomb up to the ambulatory. It was amazing to see the entire church in one great blaze of light, and filled with song.

Kourambiedes— Greek Butter Cookies

Traditionally made with *semen* (clarified butter) and a strong brandy strained through ash oak, this is truly one of the great butter cookies. In Israel today, most people substitute Indian ghee bought in the Old City for the clarified butter. I simply use softened butter.

YIELD: ABOUT 4 DOZEN COOKIES

½ pound unsalted butter, at room temperature (2 sticks)

8 tablespoons confectioners' sugar, plus sugar for dusting

1 large egg

Zest of 1 lemon

2 tablespoons grappa or other brandy

1 tablespoon vanilla

½ teaspoon ground cinnamon

½ teaspoon baking powder

Dash of salt

1 cup finely chopped, blanched almonds

2 cups all-purpose flour (about)

1. Using a food processor equipped with a steel blade, cream the butter and the confectioners' sugar.

2. Add the egg, lemon juice, grappa or brandy, and vanilla and continue to process until blended.

3. Gradually add the cinnamon, baking powder, salt, chopped almonds, and enough of the flour to produce a dough that is firm but not dry.

4. Chill the dough in the refrigerator ½ hour.

5. Preheat the oven to 350 degrees and grease 2 cookie sheets.

6. Take 2 teaspoons of dough and roll it by hand into a torpedo shape, 1½ inches long by 1 inch wide at the center. Continue forming the rest of the dough and place the cookies 1½ inches apart on the greased cookie sheets. Bake 2 sheets at a time for 20 to 25 minutes, or until slightly firm but still white.

7. Remove from the oven, cool slightly, then roll the cookies in confectioners' sugar. Store in an airtight container.

Kurabiye— Wedding Butter Cookie

Although I have tasted this pan–Middle Eastern melt-in-your-mouth butter cookie on many occasions, it was most beautifully presented at a Druse wedding that I attended in the Galilee (see page 319). In the Druse tradition, the bride's attendants served platters of the perfectly circular butter cookies decorated with nuts to all of the women guests, who were sitting in one room. Later, the bride fed her husband a cookie crowned with a single pistachio meant to represent her tiara, symbolizing her purity. Most Middle Eastern countries have a version of *kurabiye,* which means "cookie," also called *ghouribi* (see my *Jewish Holiday Kitchen*). Similar to shortbread, it is usually made with flour, sugar, and butter. Although traditionally made by hand, it is so much easier—and works beautifully—with a mixer or a food processor. Don't overwork, and don't overbake. Otherwise, the cookies will be hard.

YIELD: ABOUT 3 DOZEN COOKIES

1 cup (2 sticks) unsalted butter, at room temperature

¾ cup confectioners' sugar, plus additional for dusting

1 teaspoon vanilla

Dash of salt

3 cups unbleached all-purpose flour

½ cup whole blanched almonds, shelled pistachio nuts, or pecan halves

1. Preheat the oven to 325 degrees.
2. Put the butter, sugar, and vanilla in the bowl of a food processor fitted with a steel blade and blend to a cream. Add the salt and the flour, then process just until well blended. You can also mix all the ingredients in the bowl of an electric mixer.
3. Dust your hands with flour, then take about a tablespoon of batter in the palm of 1 hand. Mold into a ball the size of a walnut, about ¾ inch thick. You may have to use both hands to make a perfect ball. Repeat until all the batter is used up, placing the balls on greased cookie sheets about ½ inch apart.
4. Gently make an indentation with your finger in the center of each ball and press in an almond, pistachio, or pecan.
5. Bake the cookies in the oven for 12 to 15 minutes or until slightly firm but still white. Remove from the oven, cool slightly, and transfer the cookies to a plate.
6. Using a sieve, dust with confectioners' sugar. Store in an airtight container.

Hamantaschen— Purim Cookies

My love affair with hamantaschen began in my childhood home, where I was accustomed to my mother's fillings. When I lived in Jerusalem, the world of hamantaschen fillings opened up to me, as did the *shalah manot,* the gift baskets stuffed with fruits and cookies, traditionally made in order to use up the year's flour before the beginning of Passover.

YIELD: ABOUT 40 COOKIES

DOUGH

1 1/4 cups (2 1/2 sticks) unsalted butter or pareve margarine

1/2 cup sugar

1 large egg

1/2 teaspoon vanilla

1 tablespoon orange juice

2 1/2–3 cups unbleached all-purpose flour

1 teaspoon baking powder

1/2 teaspoon salt

FILLING

1 cup walnuts

3/4 cup sugar

1/2 teaspoon vanilla

1/2 lemon, quartered and seeded

1/2 orange, quartered and seeded

1 tablespoon rum

2 figs, roughly diced

1/2 teaspoon ground cinnamon

1/2 cup orange marmalade or apricot jam

1. To make the dough, cream the butter or margarine with the sugar. Add the egg, vanilla, and orange juice and continue to cream until smooth. A food processor is great for this.

2. Add the 2 1/2 cups flour, baking powder, and salt. Mix or process until a ball of dough is formed, adding flour as needed. Chill for 2 to 3 hours or overnight.

3. Meanwhile, to make the filling, place all of the filling ingredients in a food processor and pulse until chopped but not pureed. You should have approximately 2 cups. Set aside until the dough is chilled.

4. Preheat the oven to 375 degrees and grease a cookie sheet.

5. Roll 1/4 of the dough out on a lightly floured board to a thickness of 1/8 inch. Cut into 3-inch circles. Place 1 teaspoon of filling in the center of each circle. To shape the hamantaschen, first brush water around the rim of the circle with your finger. Pull the edges of the dough up to form a triangle around the filling and pinch the 3 corners together, leaving a small triangular opening in the center. Transfer to the cookie sheet and bake in the oven for 10 to 15 minutes or until the tops are golden.

NOTE With any leftover dough, you can use Nutella or chocolate chips as a filling.

Desserts

377

The King David's Chocolate-covered Coconut Macaroons

The Foods of
Israel Today

378

Six years before Edna Ferber wrote her memoir, the Federmann brothers started running the venerable King David Hotel in Jerusalem. Twenty years earlier, Schmuel Federmann had arrived in Palestine, a concentration camp survivor. "The day we got to Haifa port after two and a half years in a camp, we received an orange and a small bar of Cadbury chocolate," recalled Mr. Federmann. "Then we were put into a British camp at 'Atlit for eleven days to find out if there were any spies among us. After we were released, the British left us and said 'Good luck.'"

Sam joined his brother Yekutiel, who had opened a restaurant in Haifa that was frequented by the British naval officers running the port. After the war, the Federmann brothers took over a closed twenty-one-room hotel in north Tel Aviv. "Because of our connection with the Zionist movement," he said, "people like Nahum Goldmann, Rabbi Abba Hillel Silver, and Arturo Toscanini stayed there. With its wonderful view, inviting terrace, and the coffee, kuchen, and apple strudel with *schlag* that we served in the afternoon, it became a meeting place for the *yekkes* (German Jews)."

In 1953, the Federmanns opened Israel's first superhotel, with 121 rooms, now the Dan Tel Aviv Hotel. "People thought we were off our rockers, but it worked. We followed our European tradition and had mostly French kosher food." Today the hotel chain, with ten hotels throughout the country, steers clear of "French kosher food," to reflect the cuisine of the country.

It was to the terrace of the King David Hotel, overlooking the Old City of Jerusalem, that I often would go for afternoon tea when I lived in Israel. Somehow I passed over the strudel and *schlag* for the following chocolate-covered coconut macaroons, which to this day make me remember those glorious afternoons. They are great for Passover as well. Please, King David, put them back on the menu!

3¹/₂ cups unsweetened shredded coconut

¹/₄ cup all-purpose flour (or matzoh cake meal for Passover)

1¹/₄ cups sugar

2 large eggs

1 egg white

4 ounces imported bittersweet chocolate

¹/₄ cup water

1. Preheat the oven to 325 degrees and cover 2 baking sheets with parchment paper.

2. Mix the coconut, flour or matzoh cake meal, and 1 cup of the sugar together in a bowl. Add the eggs and egg white and mix with your fingers until well blended.

3. Gently shape about 2 tablespoons of the dough into a pyramid and set on the baking sheet. Repeat with the remaining dough, leaving about 2 inches between the cookies. Bake for about 25 minutes, or until golden on top. Cool completely.

4. In a saucepan, melt the chocolate with the water and remaining ¹/₄ cup sugar. Bring to a boil, then simmer slowly for a few minutes until the mixture starts to thicken. Let the chocolate cool slightly.

5. Hold a macaroon with 2 fingers and dip half the cookie in the chocolate, so that it is half black and half white. Dry for a few moments tilted over a dish, then place on waxed paper. Repeat with the rest of the cookies. Cool completely.

A great place for tea—the terrace of the King David Hotel

Desserts

Anise Holiday Cookies

Many people associate anise, which grows wild in Israel and is the flavoring in *arrack,* the local liqueur made from grapes, with the Middle East. But not Teddy Kollek, born in Prague and raised in Vienna. Once, after midnight mass on Christmas Eve in Bethlehem, we were invited to a reception held at the Franciscan Church of St. Catherine, just near the manger in which Jesus is thought to have been born. A sister offered Teddy an anise-flavored cookie which she had made for the occasion. After eating the cookie, the mayor remarked to me that it reminded him of the anise cookies he ate as a boy in Vienna.

YIELD: ABOUT 4 DOZEN COOKIES

1/4 cup vegetable oil	1/2 teaspoon baking soda
1/2 cup (1 stick) unsalted butter	1 teaspoon baking powder
1 cup sugar	Dash of salt
1 teaspoon vanilla	1 tablespoon anise seeds
2 cups all-purpose flour	1 1/2–2 tablespoons cold water

1. Preheat the oven to 350 degrees and grease a cookie sheet.

2. Put the oil, butter, sugar, and vanilla in the bowl of a food processor equipped with a steel blade. Process until creamed. Add flour, baking soda, baking powder, salt, and anise seeds. Continue to process until a ball is formed, adding cold water as needed so that the dough is soft but not sticky.

3. Refrigerate the dough for at least a half hour. Then roll it out on a floured surface to a circle 1/8 inch thick, sprinkling on more flour if too soft. Cut into circles, diamonds, or ovals about 2 inches in diameter. Bake on the cookie sheet, with about an inch between the cookies, for 12 to 15 minutes, or until slightly golden.

Sefrou Apricot
Galettes Sucrées

Call them *galettes sucrées, mandelbrot,* or *biscotti*—I love these Moroccan cookies, made by Rosette Toledano of Netanya, who, as her daughter says, "puts her heart in her cooking."

YIELD: ABOUT 30 COOKIES

4 large eggs

3/4 cup sugar

1/2 cup vegetable oil

3 cups unbleached all-purpose flour

2 teaspoons baking powder

1/2 teaspoon salt

1/2 teaspoon cinnamon

1/2 cup chopped almonds

1/2 cup chopped walnuts

1/2 cup chopped dried apricots

1/2 cup chopped pitted dates

1 tablespoon sesame seeds

1. Preheat the oven to 350 degrees and grease a cookie sheet.

2. In the bowl of an electric mixer, beat 3 of the eggs with the sugar. Add the oil, flour, baking powder, salt, and cinnamon, then fold in the chopped nuts and fruit.

3. Turn the dough out onto a floured board. Divide the dough into 2 pieces and form each piece into a roll about 14 inches long and 1 1/2 to 2 inches wide. Place the rolls on the cookie sheet, leaving an inch between them.

4. Beat the remaining egg and brush it over the dough. Sprinkle with sesame seeds.

5. Bake for 20 minutes on the middle rack. Let the rolls cool for 5 minutes. Using a serrated knife, slice each roll into 3/4-inch pieces. Place the slices, cut side up, on the cookie sheet and return them to the oven for 15 more minutes, or until the cookies are golden brown.

NOTE I sometimes substitute chocolate chips for the chopped dates and nuts for my chocoholic family.

Desserts

381

Viennese *Kupferlin*— Almond Crescent Cookies

For all the years I have known Tamar Kollek, her signature dish has been *kupferlin*. This stirrup-shaped almond butter cookie, which she learned to make in her native Vienna, was always served when guests came to the Kolleks' apartment in Jerusalem. The difference between her cookies in the early years in Israel and her mother's in Vienna was the use of the cheaper margarine instead of butter. I prefer the flavor of butter.

YIELD: 5 DOZEN COOKIES

1 cup (2 sticks) unsalted butter or pareve margarine, softened

1/2 cup sugar, plus additional for sprinkling

1/2 cup very finely ground unblanched almonds

2 cups unbleached all-purpose flour

Dash of salt

1. Preheat the oven to 250 degrees.
2. Put the butter or margarine and the sugar into a large mixing bowl. Add the almonds and then the flour and salt, using your fingers to mix the ingredients together until you have a soft dough. (You can also make the dough in a food processor fitted with a steel blade: first blend the butter and sugar to a cream, then pulse as you add the dry ingredients, taking care not to overmix.)
3. Take a piece of dough the size of a plum and roll it into a 2-inch-long tube. Repeat with the rest of the dough. Shape each piece into a crescent and press the ends flat.
4. Place the cookies, close to each other but not touching, on ungreased cookie sheets. Bake them for 40 minutes or until they are firm to the touch. The cookies should be white in color, not even slightly golden. Remove them from the oven, let them stand for a few minutes, and, while they are still warm, sprinkle them with additional sugar.

For years I have been in pursuit of a good recipe for those amazing potato dumplings filled with fruit and finished off with butter, ground nuts, and a sprinkling of sugar. Since they have been raised to a high art in central Europe, I asked Melanie Abramovici, originally from Bacău, Romania, and now living in Tel Aviv, to share her version with me. Often served in the summer as the main course for a dairy meal, these are a great substitute at Hanukkah for the traditional latkes or *soufganiyot*. At Passover, use matzoh cake meal instead of the flour and, if plums or apricots are out of season, use a thick jam instead of the fresh fruit.

Zwetschgen Knoedel— Dumplings Stuffed with Plums

YIELD: 12 *KNOEDEL*, SERVING 6

1 pound baking potatoes (about 2 large), peeled	2 cups all-purpose flour or matzoh cake meal (about)
1 large egg yolk	12 Italian plums, or apricots
1 teaspoon salt	Grated zest of 1 lemon
3 tablespoons plus $1/2$ cup sugar, plus additional sugar for dusting	1 teaspoon cinnamon
6 tablespoons ($3/4$ stick) unsalted butter or pareve margarine, melted	$1/2$ cup ground walnuts

1. Boil the potatoes, drain well, and mash through a ricer.

2. Mix the potatoes with the egg yolk, salt, 3 tablespoons of the sugar, and 2 tablespoons of the melted butter. Gradually add the flour and knead with your hands, working in enough flour to make a dough that is soft but not too sticky. Refrigerate for 1 hour or overnight.

3. Meanwhile, halve the apricots or plums and discard the pits; place a teaspoon of sugar and some lemon zest inside each piece, and close. Repeat with all the fruit.

4. Remove the potato dough from the refrigerator and roll into a thick sausage shape. Then cut into 12 equal pieces. Roll each piece into a flat circle about 3 inches in diameter. Place an apricot or plum in the center of the dough, and pull the sides up and over, forming a ball enclosing the fruit.

5. Bring a large pot of water to a boil. Carefully insert 6 of the dumplings and simmer, uncovered, for about 7 minutes. Drain well and repeat with the remaining 6 dumplings.

6. Heat the remaining butter in a frying pan; sprinkle with the cinnamon, remaining $1/4$ cup sugar, and the ground walnuts. Place the *knoedel* in the pan and turn to coat with the nuts on all sides. Serve warm, dusted with additional sugar, allowing 2 per person.

My grandmother was born in Odessa, Russia, and always talked about the fact that as a child she wasn't a great Jew, but a real Russian. She said she became passionate about Judaism, a fervent Zionist, and lover of Israel by living in Palestine in the early 1900s. She was tough, too, in her battle jacket. She liked the concept of the *halutz*, building a country and living sparsely. For a while she ran a boarding house and restaurant. She was always cooking and boiling and baking. Most of all, I liked the *zwetschgen knoedel* that we ate at Passover.

—Mona Riklis Ackerman

Desserts

Soufganiyot—
Israeli Hanukkah
Jelly Doughnuts

Every baker in Israel worth his dough makes these jelly doughnuts for Hanukkah. *Soufganiya,* the modern Israeli word for a doughnut stuffed with jam, also called *ponchik* in Russian, comes from the Greek *sufgan* ("puffed," "fried," and "spongy") and from the Hebrew *sofiget* ("water") and *sofeg* ("to blot"). It is typical of new Israeli words that they are sometimes inspired by the Arabic, by the Hebrew, or by other languages, and sometimes just invented; but they are all deeply discussed by the Academy of the Hebrew Language before being incorporated into the lexicon.

In the beginning, a *soufganiya* consisted of two rounds of dough sandwiching some jam, but the jam always fell out during the frying. Today, with new injectors on the market, balls of dough can be deep-fried first and then injected with jam before being rolled in sugar. This is a much easier and quicker way of preparing the doughnuts, and no jam escapes during cooking. This recipe is adapted from that of Bulgarian-born Sophie Ashkenazi, one of Tel Aviv's leading caterers. It is perhaps the only distinctly Israeli holiday dish.

YIELD: ABOUT 24 DOUGHNUTS

1 package dry yeast	Pinch of salt
3 tablespoons sugar	Grated zest of 1 lemon
1/4 cup lukewarm water	3 1/2 tablespoons butter, at room temperature
3 1/2 cups unbleached all-purpose flour (about)	Vegetable oil for deep-frying
1/2 cup lukewarm milk	Apricot jam, about 1/2 cup
1 large egg	Confectioners' or granulated sugar for rolling
1 large egg yolk	

1. Dissolve the yeast and 1 tablespoon of the sugar in the water. Let sit for 10 minutes.

2. Put the flour in the bowl of a food processor equipped with a steel blade. Add the dissolved yeast, milk, whole egg, yolk, salt, lemon zest, and the remaining 2 tablespoons sugar. Process until blended. Add the butter and process until the dough becomes sticky yet elastic.

3. Remove the dough to a bowl, cover, and let rise in a warm place for at least an hour. If you want to prepare it ahead, as I often do, place the dough in the refrigerator overnight, then let it warm to room temperature before rolling and cutting.

4. Dust a pastry board with flour. Roll the dough out to a ½-inch thickness. Using the top of a glass, cut into rounds about 2 inches in diameter and roll these into balls. Cover and let rise 30 minutes more.

5. Pour 2 inches of oil into a heavy pot and heat to 375 degrees.

6. Drop the doughnuts into the oil, 4 or 5 at a time. Cook about 3 minutes on each side, turning when brown. Drain on paper towels. Using an injector (available at cooking stores), insert a teaspoon of jam into each doughnut. You can also use a turkey baster, first softening the jam in a food processor. Simply push a knife halfway into the doughnut to cut a slit, then put the turkey baster into the slit and squeeze out the jam. Roll the *soufganiyot* in confectioners' or granulated sugar and serve immediately.

While visiting the Sea of Galilee with a group of three-star chefs from France—a tough group to please in any country—we happily stumbled on the House, a Chinese-Thai restaurant located in Tiberias. Lisbeth Gross, the Dutch-born owner, told us that she and her Israeli husband, Tzach, first opened a kosher Chinese restaurant in this villa. Then, after an influx of Thai workers arrived in Israel, they opened a second restaurant next door called the Pagoda, changing the food from Chinese to Thai. Although both restaurants use kosher ingredients and have the same staff, the House is open only on Saturday, the one day of rest for the observant, and a busy restaurant day for nonobservant Israelis; the strictly kosher Pagoda is open every day but Saturday.

"In the beginning Israel had no fresh bean sprouts, ginger, or lemongrass," said Lisbeth. "So my husband went to Thailand to learn about spices and vegetables, and then we started growing our own. Because we don't need milk products in Thai or Chinese cooking, it makes having kosher restaurants much easier."

Asian products are increasingly sought after since the first Asians who came to Israel—the "boat people" who fled from Vietnam and were rescued by the Israelis—and Israelis who traveled to the Far East sought out cooks and waiters from Thailand and the Philippines. At the Carmel market in Tel Aviv, two grocery stores are devoted entirely to Chinese products, some produced in China with Hebrew lettering. Other Asian stores are springing up throughout the country.

T hese fritters, served at the Pagoda restaurant, make excellent use of the bananas and dates grown locally. Bananas were brought to Palestine from India in the seventh century C.E., possibly earlier. Of course, those first Israeli bananas were much tinier than the ones grown today.

Banana and Date Fritters with Sesame Seeds

YIELD: 24 FRITTERS

2 cups ice water

2 cups plus 3 tablespoons cake or pastry flour

1 cup sesame seeds

4 large, ripe bananas

8 dates, pitted

Vegetable oil for deep-frying

Vanilla ice cream

Confectioners' sugar

1. Mix together the water and flour in a large bowl, stirring until a medium-thick batter is formed. Place sesame seeds in a shallow bowl.

2. Cut each banana into 4 equal pieces. Dip the bananas quickly into the batter, then roll in the sesame seeds. Do the same with the dates, keeping them whole.

3. Heat the oil in a deep fryer or wok to 375 degrees. Deep-fry the fruits until the sesame seeds are browned. Drain on a paper towel.

4. Serve hot, with vanilla ice cream and a sprinkling of confectioners' sugar.

NOTE   Though these fritters are very sweet as is, they are also delicious with maple syrup drizzled on top.

Jaffa Orange Delight

The oranges grow to the size of an ostrich egg and have thick skins. In season the pulp is sweet, juicy, tender, and contains few seeds. Not even California or Florida, having the advantage of the most skilled horticulturists, can dispute with Jaffa for primacy in the orange growing world. Everything about the city smells of oranges. Visiting these orange groves, one finds himself in a sea of golden globes which form the most beautiful contrast with the green leaves that surround them. This spectacle is especially memorable when seen in a full-moon night.

—Benjamin Gordon,
New Judea (1919)

The Foods of
Israel Today

388

Oranges were probably brought to Palestine from Southeast Asia as early as the seventh or eighth century. From the 1850s onward, the citrus orchards slowly expanded; in 1948, when the Israeli state was established, citrus-growing had become the largest fruit industry in Israel; Jaffa's *shamuti*-type orange, with its thick, easily peeled skin and sweet flavor, was considered by many to be the best in the world. The orchards' scent was so strong that it was perceptible to approaching ships miles from land.

Kena Shoval, wife of the former ambassador of Israel to the United States, Zalman Shoval, sometimes served this orange dessert at her luncheons. You can use any type of flavorful orange in this recipe.

YIELD: 6 SERVINGS

6 Jaffa, or other flavorful oranges

2 1/2 cups water

2 cups sugar

1/4 cup orange brandy liqueur (like the Israeli brand Hallelujah)

6 sprigs of fresh mint

1. With a sharp knife, remove the rind and pith of 4 oranges. Cut the peel into very narrow strips, about 1/8 inch wide. Put them in a saucepan of boiling water and boil for 2 minutes. Drain and wash with cold water, then drain again.

2. Peel the remaining 2 oranges and remove the pith. Leave all 6 oranges whole.

3. Mix the water and sugar in a saucepan. Bring to a boil, then slip in the 6 peeled oranges. Cover with a plate so they won't float, lower the heat, and simmer slowly for 1 hour.

4. Remove the pot of oranges from the heat and let cool. Fish the fruit out of the syrup and drain, then refrigerate. Add the strips of rind to the syrup, bring to a boil, and cook to reduce the syrup by half. Remove from the heat and add the orange liqueur.

5. When the oranges are completely cold, slice them in thin rounds. Serve with the syrup and strips of the peel on top. Decorate with fresh mint leaves.

Grading oranges during the Ottoman Empire

"This isn't the best ice cream in Israel, it's the best ice cream in the world," said Yulia Rottenberg, founder of Glida Beer Sheva. "I've tried them all. Häagen Dazs, French ice cream— I should know."

Who ever thought of Be'er Sheva as the ice cream capital of the world? And who would have expected that such innovative ice cream, made from ingredients such as avocado, candied chestnuts, carrots, and Malaga wine, could be produced in this desert city? Mrs. Rottenberg, now in her late eighties, has presided over Glida Beer Sheva for almost fifty years, constantly creating such unusual treats. "Once I was making halvah," she said. "I thought I would turn it into ice cream with chunks of walnuts." Today, professors from the nearby Ben-Gurion University bring over exotic varieties of fruits, like the bright-purple African *petayia*, with which she was experimenting the day I visited. "When I speak with most people about crazy fruits like the *petayia* or the black *sapote*, a relative of the persimmon that grows wild in Mexico and Guatemala, they say, 'Who needs these strange fruits?'" said Yossi Mizrachi, a professor at Ben-Gurion. "But not Yulia. Her eyes light up. When I gave her black *sapote* to taste, she went wild."

Mrs. Rottenberg, a Holocaust survivor from Poland, did not always eat ice cream. "During the war I dreamt about cakes," she said. "I loved to cook before." Faced with the reality of rebuilding her life, she learned how to make ice cream, which she continued to do in Poland from 1946 to 1950. In 1950, when she decided to leave for Israel, she sold her company to the Polish government. In Israel, because of asthma, she moved to the dry desert climate of Be'er Sheva, where she opened her ice cream shop. Today her daughter and grandchildren run four branches of Glida Beer Sheva throughout the country.

Ever since her husband passed away, Mrs. Rottenberg has spent more time at her shop. "Here I have people to talk to," she said. "Otherwise I would be alone." And what is the first thing this octogenarian does when she walks into her shop? She rolls up her sleeves and starts making ice cream.

Desserts

Halvah Parfait

Like many young Israelis, Zachi Bukshester came out of his army service in the Sinai confused about his future. He knew that he didn't want a regular job, but being a chef was not a distinguished career in those days. Despite parental opposition, he went to the Tadmor Cooking School of Hotel Management, in Herzliyya. Eventually he opened a restaurant and became famous for many dishes, especially his halvah parfait, made from the ground-sesame-seed candy. He said, "Although halvah is Turkish, a parfait is mostly French and Western. In Israel these things can meet."

YIELD: 8 SERVINGS

½ cup water

½ cup sugar

1 cup heavy cream

8 ounces halvah

5 large egg yolks

¼ cup kirschwasser

¼ cup amaretto liqueur (like Bartenura)

1. Bring the water and sugar to a boil in a saucepan. Continue to boil for 2 minutes.

2. Whip the heavy cream until stiff. Cover and refrigerate.

3. Crumble the halvah into the bowl of an electric mixer. Using the whisk attachment, gradually blend in half the sugar water on low speed. Do not over-mix—you want to retain some texture.

4. Whisk the egg yolks in a stainless-steel bowl. Place the bowl over a pot of simmering water and whisk in the remaining sugar water.

5. When the yolks are pale and frothy, remove the bowl from the water and add the yolk mixture to the halvah, mixing on low speed. Gradually increase the speed to high and beat a few more minutes, until the halvah mixture is slightly frothy.

6. Add the kirschwasser and amaretto to the halvah. Beat for another minute.

7. Fold in the whipped cream. Pour into a 4-cup container, cover tightly, and freeze for several hours or overnight. Serve spooned into parfait cups, as is or drizzled with a little amaretto, kirsch, or the brandy of your choice.

NOTE You can also toast 1 cup of roughly chopped walnuts, then fold half into the parfait and sprinkle the other half on top.

W hen I lived on Kibbutz Yifaat in 1970, I wrote in my journal at the end of a day of harvesting pears, hoping to
capture the satisfaction I felt at being a part of the process:
"There is an art to picking a pear. It must not be too small or too
green. One holds it from the base and gently lifts it up so that the fruit snaps from
the stem, not harming the skin. The pear is then gently placed in the basket. The
procedure continues over and over again until the basket is
filled up. . . . Why is pear picking so enjoyable? A feeling of
accomplishment. Confronted by a huge tree covered with
pears, the pear picker sees a job completed when all the pears
are in his basket. For girls who want to reduce there is nothing
better than stretching for a pear out of reach. For linguists, pear
picking is a time to exercise your language ability. Volunteers
picking next to you might speak German or French or Italian
or Spanish. One volunteer was the son of a German Jew and a
Chinese Jew brought up in Israel! Another was a Czech refugee
who spoke not one language in common with me."

*Young women picking
fruit at a kibbutz*

Gilles Bajolle, pastry chef of Taillevent, one of Paris's
Michelin three-star restaurants, was equally taken with Israel's pears. When he
came to Jerusalem searching for ideas for the dinner celebrating the city's three
thousandth anniversary, he decided to make this poached pear sorbet, using pears
and honey from Kibbutz Yad Mordechai.

YIELD: 6 SERVINGS

¼ vanilla bean

6 Bosc pears (about 2 pounds), peeled,
cored, and quartered

⅓ cup water

¼ cup sugar

Zest of 1 lemon

½ bay leaf

1 teaspoon honey

1 whole clove

¼ teaspoon fresh grated ginger

1. Rub the outside of the vanilla bean 3 times against the fine holes of a
grater. Put the grated vanilla along with the bean in a saucepan with the pears,
water, sugar, lemon zest, bay leaf, honey, clove, and ginger. Simmer, covered,
about 10 to 15 minutes or until the pears are soft.

2. Remove the vanilla bean, clove, and bay leaf; puree the pear and liquid in a
food processor. Pour the puree into an ice cream maker and follow the manufac-
turers' directions. You can also put it in a bowl in the freezer; when puree is almost
frozen, process again to break the crystals, then return to the freezer. Serve garnished with fresh fruit.

Marble Bavarian Cream

In the 1970s, Masswadeh Restaurant in East Jerusalem made a layered black-and-white version of Bavarian cream with almonds and dark chocolate. This is the closest I can come to re-creating the wonderful dessert made with gelatin, egg yolks, and heavy cream. I especially liked, and still like, the crunchiness of the nuts paired with the silky texture of the Bavarian cream.

YIELD: 12 SERVINGS

6 ounces bittersweet chocolate

1/2 cup almonds, unshelled

2 cups milk

4 large egg yolks

1/2 cup sugar

2 packages unflavored gelatin

1/2 cup warm water

1 teaspoon vanilla

1/2 teaspoon almond extract

1 cup heavy cream

1. Grease a 9-inch square glass cake pan or a 6-cup glass circular mold.

2. Put the bittersweet chocolate in the top of a double boiler and melt over simmering water. You can also put the chocolate in a bowl, cover it with plastic wrap, and microwave it for 30 seconds or until melted. Cool to room temperature.

3. Drop the almonds into boiling water and let boil for 1 to 2 minutes to blanch them. Cool to a temperature comfortable enough for you to dip your fingers into the water, then squeeze the nuts with your fingers to remove the shells. Dry the almonds, then roughly chop them and set aside.

4. Heat the milk in the microwave or in a saucepan on the stove just to boiling. In a separate bowl, beat the egg yolks and the sugar until light and lemon-colored. Gradually beat the hot milk into the eggs.

5. Dissolve the gelatin in the water and stir well.

6. Stir the gelatin and the vanilla into the egg mixture and divide between 2 bowls. Using a whisk, stir the bittersweet chocolate into 1 bowl and cool to room temperature. Add the almond extract to the second bowl, mixing well.

7. Whip the cream in a mixer. Fold half the cream into the chocolate and half into the white mixture. Then fold the almonds into the white mixture.

8. Pour the chocolate mixture into the bottom of the mold and refrigerate for about 10 minutes. Then pour the white mixture on top, swirling the cream around with a knife, making figure eights through the mold. Refrigerate until firm. Either serve from the glass bowl or, if using the square container, cut into 12 squares and serve.

Apricot Bavarian Cream

Maya Bailey (see page 135) prepares this delightful version of Bavarian cream with the apricots that grow in Israel in midsummer. When apricots are not in season, Maya switches to peeled mango, and serves it with a chocolate mint sauce. Plums, peaches, and nectarines are also good substitutes. She serves Apricot Bavarian Cream surrounded with wild mulberries, called "white strawberries" in Israel.

YIELD: 8 SERVINGS

5 large egg yolks

1 cup sugar

2 pounds fresh apricots

1 envelope unflavored gelatin

¼ cup orange brandy liqueur (like Hallelujah)

1 cup heavy cream

1. Put the egg yolks and the sugar in the top of a double boiler and heat over simmering water, stirring constantly.

2. Pour 3 quarts of water into a second pot and bring to a boil. Add the apricots and simmer for just a few minutes, uncovered, until they are slightly soft. Drain, cool, and remove the pits. Pulse the fruit until chunky in a food processor fitted with a steel blade.

3. Sprinkle the gelatin into a mixing bowl and add the orange brandy. Mix with a spoon until the gelatin softens.

4. Whip the cream and fold into the gelatin. Add the egg mixture, then fold in the apricots. Transfer to a serving dish, cover with plastic wrap, and refrigerate until serving.

Only those sick with a fever were entitled to such delicacies as lemons. When Golda had a high fever, the young man in charge of the mail brought back some lemon and ice for lemonade. [Golda said,] "I have eaten many wonderful things in my life, but none which could compare with the exquisite taste of that lemonade." The ice was as rare as the lemon. Ice was available mainly in hospitals. Lemon was so rare that the kibbutz was scandalized when a young woman was discovered washing her hair with lemon. All citrus fruit was scarce, and kibbutzniks considered it a great gift when Golda visited Shana in Tel Aviv and lugged back a bag of oranges for everybody.   —Ralph G. Martin, *Golda* (1975)

The universal hospitable gesture is an offer of something to drink. It is even more the case in Israel, where drinks and their symbolism vary from culture to culture. Sitting in a café in Tel Aviv, you might sip wine or iced coffee. At the home of a Bedouin in the Negev, you will be offered first bitter coffee, then sweet tea spiked with mint. A Russian immigrant might offer a shot of vodka or strong tea with sugar served in a glass, and the average modern Israeli also will offer you Coca-Cola or *mitz,* a sweetened fruit drink.

My favorite pastime when I lived in Jerusalem was sitting at a café that we called "the Rails," inside Jaffa Gate at the entrance to the *souk.* We would sip *arrack,* the anise-flavored liqueur, while watching the procession of Jews, Christians, and Moslems hurrying by. In winter I often chose *sahlab,* a thick white drink made from the orchid flower, and in summer *pepitada,* a refreshing drink of melon seeds that Jews use to break the fast of Yom Kippur. *Tahn,* a cold yogurt drink thinned with water, is probably one of the oldest drinks known to mankind, and was also a specialty at the Rails.

Coffee in Israel ranges from the instant Nescafé, which Israelis call "*nes*" (meaning "miracle" in Hebrew), to *botz* coffee made from a mudlike powder and hot water, to the exquisitely sweet Turkish coffee, flavored with a pinch of *hel* cardamom. The Turkish coffee, made from beans freshly roasted in a long-handled iron pan and ground in a wooden mortar, is always mixed with water and brought to a boil twice, sweetened, and then ceremoniously poured from a *finjan.* Tradition dictates that the man who does the pounding must also be musical, because he should make a drum-like tune as he grinds the beans.

Whereas making Turkish coffee is traditionally man's work, among the new Jewish immigrants from Ethiopia making coffee is a woman's domain. I witnessed their coffee ceremony: the woman of the family buys raw coffee beans, which she washes, dries, and then roasts in a frying pan, stirring with a spoon until they are cooked. After the man grinds the coffee, she brings water to a boil and brews it carefully, the rich aroma surrounding her and her guests.

The Foods of
Israel Today

A Few Suggested Menus

Vegetarian Buffet

Libyan Couscous with Chickpea, Squash, Zucchini, and Eggplant Stew

Milhouliya or Swiss Chard with Fava Beans

Roasted Pepper *Pashtida*

Asparagus with Jaffa Orange and Ginger Vinaigrette

Sliced fresh fruit

Kourambiedes cookies

Meat Buffet

Syrian Stuffed Vegetables with Tamarind-Tomato Sauce

Israeli Couscous with Seasonal Vegetables

Lamb Stew with Split Peas, Dill, and Olives or Moroccan Lamb Stew

Eretz Israel Cake with Orange, Dates, and Marzipan

Modern Israeli Menu

Hummus

Pomegranate

Taboulleh

Pita Bread

Penguin Buffet's Classic Israeli (Turkey) Schnitzel or Falafel

Old City Eggplant with Tomato Sauce

Jaffa Orange Delight

Israeli Breakfast Buffet

Aboulafia's Sunny-Side-Up Za'atar Pita Pizza

Shakshuka

Herring Salad

Turkish Salad—Kibbutz Vegetable Salad

Moroccan Eggplant Salad with Pickled Lemon

Labneh with Za'atar

Fresh fruit salad

Viennese *Kupferlin*—Almond Crescent Cookies

Easter *Ka'ak* with *Adjwah* (Dates)

Pan-Sephardic Israeli Menu

Moroccan Pan de Casa (Shabbat Bread)
Libyan *Khreimi*
Tunisian Couscous with Beef, Chicken, and Chickpeas
Tunisian Boulettes
Moroccan *Matbucha*

Concia—Marinated, Fried Zucchini
Rachama's Eggplant Salad with Tomato
Moroccan Eggplant Salad with Pickled Lemon
Sefrou Apricot *Galettes Sucrées*

Israeli Arab Dinner Menu

Baba Ghanouj
Old City Tahina Salad with Flat Italian Parsley and Onions
Hummus

Palestinian *Mousakhan*
Taboulleh
Kinaffeh

Israeli Arab Breakfast Menu

Hummus
Old City Tahina Salad with Flat Italian Parsley and Onions

Taboulleh
Kataif with Sugar Syrup

Israeli Sabbath Breakfast

Huevos Haminadavos

Burekas with three fillings

Israeli Dinner Buffet

Hummus
Falafel
Jaffa Orange Chicken
Cancra (Zucchini Salad)

Israeli Carrot Salad
Israeli Couscous
King David's Coconut Cookies
Fruit Salad

A Note on Israeli Wine

Grapes have been a fruit of Israel since the time of Noah, and, because of the strict dietary laws, Jews have always produced their own wine.

Kosher wine must conform to Jewish laws such as no harvesting on the Sabbath and having only observant Jews working in production from start to finish. For stringent kosher reasons, kosher wines are *mivushal,* boiled. In the old days *mivushal* meant the wine was literally cooked in big vats and cooled for days. Today flash pasteurization exposes wine to heat for just a few seconds, thus not affecting the taste negatively. When the kiddush is said over the "fruit of the vine," the blessing literally describes the fresh-squeezed grape drink from the ancient land of Israel. During the four hundred years of the Ottoman Empire, when the Moslem culture (which forbids alcohol) dominated Israel, there were few wine grapes there. A ceremonial wine was made from table grapes rather than wine grapes, and was therefore sweeter. The growth of the wine industry thereafter follows the history of the Jewish settlement of Israel, with its greatest improvement in the last few years. What follows is a listing of what are considered the best current wines, according to Israeli wine specialist Daniel Rogov:

Barkan Cabernet Sauvignon 1997, Merlot 1998 Special Reserve Series
Binyamina Cabernet
Carmel Mizrachi Cabernet Sauvignon and Merlot, 1976, '79, '85, '88
Golan Winery's kosher Red Katzrin—unquestionably the best wine produced in
    Israel. Their Cabernet Sauvignon, Chardonnay, Merlot, Gewürtztraminer, and
    Sauvignon Blanc are also fine.
Golan's Har Hermon Adom
Tishby Sauvignon Blanc and Cabernet

Several boutique wineries are also making excellent wines:

Eli Ben Zaken Castel's Cabernet Sauvignon and Chardonnay (not kosher)
Ya'ir Margalit Cabernet Sauvignon and Merlot (not kosher)

Others worth trying include Tzora, Soreq, Saslove, Gustavo, and Jo and Kfira.

Guide to Good Eating in Israel

What follows is a list of Israeli restaurants, bakeries, and markets mentioned in this book, to guide you when you are traveling in Israel and want to eat well. Certain establishments are open by reservation only, and I've provided phone numbers where they are needed or available.

Jerusalem

Abu Shukri Restaurant, 63 Al Wad Rd., Old City, 200 m from Damascus Gate
  (tel. 02-271538)
Adnan Ja'far's Bakery, inside Jerusalem's Damascus Gate (tel. 02-62833582)
American Colony Hotel, 1 Nablus Rd. (tel. 02-6279777)
Angelo's Restaurant, 9 Horkanos St. (tel. 02-6236095)
Arcadia Restaurant, off 10 Agrippas St. (tel. 02-6249138)
Armenian Tavern, 79 Armenian Orthodox Patriarchate Rd., Old City
  (tel. 02-6273854)
Brizel's Bakery, 68 Mea Shearim St.
Eucalyptus Restaurant, 4 Safra Sq. (next to City Hall complex) (tel. 02-6244331)
Fink's Bar and Restaurant, 13 King George St. (tel. 02-6234523)
Haimishe Essen Restaurant, Beit Israel
La Regence Restaurant, King David Hotel, 23 King David St. (tel. 02-6208791)
Le Tsriff Restaurant, 5 Horkanos St. (tel. 02-6255488)
Lendner's Bakery, 10 Beit Israel
Mahane Yehudah (Jewish market), Jaffa Road near King George St.
Michael Andrew Restaurant, 12 Emile Botta St. (in Confederation House)
  (tel. 02-6240090)
Pini Bahatzer (Pini's Courtyard) Restaurant, 31 Yaffa St., Nahlat Shiva Quarter
Shalom Falafel, 19 Bezalel St., on the corner of Even Sapir St.
Cow on the Roof, Sheraton Plaza Hotel, 47 King George St. (tel. 02-6298666)
Shlomo Zadok's Falafel, Bukharan Quarter
Zalatimo's Bakery, Old City Jerusalem, between 8th and 9th Stations of the Cross

Tel Aviv/Jaffa

Abouelafia Bakery, 6 Mifratz Shlomo St., Jaffa (tel. 03-6814335)
Burekas Penzo, Levinsky St., Tel Aviv
Dr. Shakshuka Restaurant, 3 Beit Eshel, Jaffa (tel. 03-6822842)
Margaret Tayer Restaurant, 5 Ha'aliya Hashniya, near the clock tower, Jaffa
  (tel. 03-6824741)

399

Keren Restaurant, 12 Eilat St., at Auerbach St., Tel Aviv (tel. 03-5181358)

Yotvata B'Ir Restaurant, 78 Herberz Samuel St., off the *tayelet,* Tel Aviv (03-5107984)

Other Areas

Abu Christo Restaurant, Crusader Port, Akko (tel. 04-9910065)

Dalia's Restaurant, Acre-Safed Rd., Amirim (tel. 06-989349)

Dag a la Dan, off Route 99 east of Kiryat Schmoneh, Upper Galilee

Dan Eilat Hotel, Promenade, North Beach, Eilat (tel. 07-6362222)

Dona Flor (caterer), 22 Hagalim Blvd., Herzliyya (tel. 09-509669)

Ein Camonim (cheese farm and restaurant), Farod Ami'ad Rd., Upper Galilee (tel. 06-989680)

Glida Beer Sheva (ice cream shop), 50 Hadassah St., Be'er Sheva' (tel. 07-277072)

Hallelujah Restaurant, Eilat (tel. 07-375752)

The House Restaurant, northern exit to town, opposite the Lido, Tiberias (tel. 06-725513)

Jako Restaurant, 12 Hadekalim St., Turkish market, Haifa (tel. 04-668813)

Ja'uni Restaurant, 30 David Shub St., Rosh Pina (tel. 06-6931881)

Khamuz Family Restaurant, by reservation only, Rajar (tel. 05-2440054)

Lehem Erez Bakery and Restaurant, 13 Maskit St., Herzliyya

Mabroum Sweets, Rehov Paul VI, Nazareth (tel. 06-60214)

Mansur Family Guest Restaurant, Daliat el Carmel Rd., Isfouiya (tel. 04-390108)

Missada Bulgarit Grill Restaurant, K.K. le Israel St., Be'er Sheva' (tel. 238504)

Neot Kedumim (biblical landscape reserve and restaurant), on Route 443 near Mod-i'in and the Ben Shemen Forest (tel. 08-977-0777), www.neot-kedumim.org.il

Ocean, 7 Rehov Shenkar, Building 3, Herzliyya Petuach (tel. 09-957-2270)

Penguin Buffet, 31 Hagaaton Blvd., Nahariya (tel. 04-928855)

Pina B'Rosh Restaurant and Bed and Breakfast, in Old Rosh Pina, by reservation only (tel. 06-937028)

Raine Baklava Bakery, Raine

Restaurant Diana, 114 Paulus the Sixth Rd., Nazareth (tel. 06-572919)

Reviva and Celia Cafe, 1 Hameyasdim St., Herzliyya

Spices by Elana, Tefen Industrial Park, Lower Galilee (tel. 04-9872303)

Vered Hagalil (dude ranch), Rehov Korazim between Rosh Pina and Tiberias (tel. 06-935785)

Zeidan Salah Family Restaurant, Salim, Lower Galilee, by reservation only (tel. 06-984613)

A Note on Ingredients

Many of the ingredients used in the recipes in this book are available at supermarkets. If you have a local Middle Eastern grocery, try that for harder-to-find items, or you can mail-order them through the following companies:

Kalustyan (212) 685-3451, www.kalustyans.com
Soofer Foods (800) 852-4050, www.sadaf.com (individual mail order by internet only) (Kosher)

Glossary of Terms

Key

(A)	=	Arabic	(I)	=	Italian
(AR)	=	Armenian	(L)	=	Ladino
(E)	=	Ethiopian	(M)	=	Moroccan
(F)	=	French	(P)	=	Polish
(G)	=	Greek	(R)	=	Russian
(H)	=	Hebrew	(T)	=	Tunisian
(HU)	=	Hungarian	(Y)	=	Yiddish

aghvania: Tomato. (H)

aish: Another word for bread. (A)

aisha: Life. (A)

aish tanur: Large pocketless pita. (A)

albondigas: Meatballs, or chicken balls (sometimes called *bundigas*). (L)

aliya: Wave of immigration to Israel. (H)

amba: Pickle sauce. (A)

Ashkenazim: Central and Eastern European, including Yiddish-speaking Jews and their descendants. (H)

assam: Silo; in the Yom Kippur prayer this signifies the hope for a year with a full silo. (H)

baba: Father. (A)

baharat: Eastern Mediterranean spice combination (A)

bamiya: Okra. (H)

barsch: A Sabbath rice dish from Uzbekistan. (R)

bejma: Tunisian Sabbath bread. (T)

borscht: A soup having fermented or fresh red beet juice as the foundation, with sour cream or sour milk added when the soup is served. (R)

bulema: Rosette of phyllo filled with spinach. (A)

burekas: A triangular and sometimes round pastry filled with spinach; spinach and cheese; eggplant; or meat; of Turkish origin. (H)

burri: Gray mullet. (H)

cadi: Religious judge who interprets the laws of Islam. (A)

calsones: Sephardic cheese ravioli. (L)

chametz: Any food, drink, and other products made from wheat, barley, rye, oats, corn, or pulses, which by coming into contact with a liquid for more than eighteen minutes either rise or ferment. (H)

cholent: Sabbath stew of slow-baked meat, potatoes, and beans. (Y)

cigare: Long, thin, filled appetizer. (F)

couscousier: Pot that allows couscous to be steamed slowly over water in basket. (F)

dabo: Ethiopian sabbath bread. (E)

dag: Fish. (H)

dibs: A honey-like date syrup. (A)

falafel: Vegetable and chickpea mixture formed into balls and fried. (A)

fallahin: Farmers, peasants. (A)

fassoulia: A stew of green beans and meat. (A)

fettush: Arabic caesar salad. (A)

fleishig: Made of, prepared with, or used for meat or meat products. (Y)

fongelom: Vegetable fritters (Cochin).

frika: A toasted, immature green wheat grain. (A)

gefilte fish: A mixture of chopped fish flesh, bread crumbs or matzoh meal, eggs, and seasonings, stuffed into a fish skin, or shaped into balls or oval, and simmered in a fish stock, stewed or baked. (Y)

gisher: Yemenite coffee. (A)

halal: Food that is permissible under the Moslem dietary laws. (A)

halutz: Pioneer. (H)

halvah: Ground-sesame-seed candy. (H + A)

hamantaschen: Triangular-shaped Purim cookie filled with prunes, poppy seeds, nuts, or chocolate chips. (Y)

hamim: Moroccan long-simmering Sabbath stew (literally means "warm"), similar to *cholent,* made with meat, potatoes, chickpeas, vegetables, rice, etc. (H)

harissa: Hot sauce. (A)

haroset: Paste-like mixture of fruit, nuts, cinnamon, and wine eaten during the Passover seder and symbolic of the mortar the Israelites used in building during the Egyptian slavery. (H)

hawayij: Yemenite spice combination. (Y)

hilbe: Yemenite fenugreek sauce. (Y)

huevos haminados: Long-cooked eggs served by Sephardic Jews on the Sabbath and other holidays. (H)

hummus: Spread made with chickpeas and garlic. (A)

ima: Mother. (H)

injerra: Bread eaten daily by Ethiopians. (E)

Israeli couscous: Round wheat pasta shaped like couscous.

jerisheh: Finest-grade crushed wheat. (A)

ka'ak: Pretzel-like rings. (A)

kasha: Buckwheat groats, a staple for many Russian Jews. (R)

kasher: Fit, following Jewish dietary laws. (H)

kashrut: Dietary laws. (H)

ketubah: Written Jewish marriage contract. (H)

khiyar: Cucumber. (A)

khreimi: Spicy Libyan fish with tomatoes. (A)

khubeiza: Wild greens that taste something like spinach; abundant in the Israeli countryside, they were commonly eaten during times of rationing, when food was scarce (*halamit* in Hebrew). (A)

khubz: Bread. (A)

kibbi: Bulgur and beef casserole. (A)

kibbutz: Agricultural settlement. (H)

kishk: Gruel made from dried sour milk and bulgur. (A)

kishouim: Light-green squash grown in Israel. (A)

kofta: Sephardic meatball or fried patty, generally. (H)

kotleti: Meatballs. (R)

ktzitzot: Meatballs. (H)

kubannah: Yemenite overnight bread for the Sabbath.

kubbeh: Iraqi torpedo-shaped meat-filled fritters. (from the Kurdish)

kugel: Baked sweet or savory pudding or casserole made of noodles, potatoes, bread, or vegetables and often served on the Sabbath or for festivals. (Y)

kumsitz: Nighttime outdoor barbecue of meat and vegetables; an important Israeli social event. (H)

kusa: Zucchini. (A)

labneh: Yogurt that's been strained in order to convert it into a type of cheese. (A)

latke: Pancake usually made from grated raw potatoes and eaten at Hanukkah. (Y)

lavash: Paper-thin bread prepared by Druse women. (A)

leben: Yogurt. (A)

lehem: Bread from the earth, blessed before each meal by observant Jews. (H)

levivot: Israeli latkes, or vegetable patties, eaten throughout the year. (H)

ma'abarot: Makeshift dwellings. (H)

maimouna: Moroccan Passover feast. (M)

mallah: Arabic precursor to phyllo. (A)

malouach: Yemenite pancakes. (H)

manna: The bread-like substance God bestowed upon the Israelites during their time of hunger. (H)

marhooda: A Moroccan kugel with potatoes and sometimes vegetables and eggs. (M)

marmouna: Spicy vegetable salad. (M)

matbucha: Cooked tomato salad. (M)

melach: Salt. (H)

melihah: Salt-curing or "koshering" of meat. (H)

meorav yerushalmi: "Jerusalem mixed grill"; the odd parts of poultry fried together and often served at the *shipudiyah* in a pita. (H)

mezze: Appetizers and salads served family-style before a meal in Israel and throughout the Middle East. (A)

milhama: War. (H)

milchig: Made of, or derived from, milk or dairy products. (Y)

milhouliya: Wild green, somewhat like Swiss chard. (A)

mousakhan: Palestinian chicken with sumac. (A)

moussaka: Layered casserole commonly made with eggplant, ground meat, and béchamel sauce. (G)

mu'azzin: Announcer of the hour of prayer. (A)

mufti: A Muslim person capable of giving Islamic legal opinion. (A)

muhammar: Chicken and potato dish. (A)

mujeddra: Lentil stew with rice or bulgur and fried onions. (A)

mukhtar: Village mayor. (A)

murrar: A bitter herb. (A)

musht: St. Peter's fish, also known as tilapia. (H)

pareve: Made without milk, meat, or their derivatives. (Y)

pashtida: Literally "layers of"; describes any type of casserole or pie. (H)

pastel: Turnover filled with meat, vegetables, or cheese. (L + M)

phyllo: Paper-thin dough. (G)

pilau: Rice dish. (Turkish from Persian *polo*)

polpetta: Meatball. (I)

potatonik: Heavy potato bread. (P)

rashad: Wild greens from the mustard family. (A)

sabra: Jew born in Israel; also a prickly pear. (H)

saniah: Tray. (A)

schochet: Person officially licensed by rabbinic authority as a slaughterer for food in accordance with Jewish dietary laws. (H)

schwarma: Meat grilled on a rotisserie. (A)

seder: Home or community service and ceremonial dinner on the eve of Passover, commemorating the Exodus from Egypt. (H)

semen: Clarified butter. (A)

shekel: Israeli unit of currency. (H)

shipud: Iron spit on which *schwarma* is grilled (the restaurant where this is served is often called a *shipudiyah*). (H)

shlishke: Twisted noodle traditionally made from a potato-based dough. (Hungarian from the German)

shipudiyah: Grill restaurant. (H)

sikatch: One-blade manual grinder for meat or fish. (R)

sinaya: Tahina-fish. (A)

soufganiyot: Doughnuts served in Israel at Hanukkah. (H)

spanakopita: Greek spinach and phyllo-dough pie. (g)

steak levan: Literally "white steak," used by Israelis to refer to pork. (H)

sukkah: The canopy or hut built outdoors by Jews during the festival of Sukkot. (H)

Sukkot: Thanksgiving festival, originating as an autumn harvest festival, with eating out of doors, in a *sukkah*. (H)

solet chitim: From the Book of Exodus, gruel used as an offering on the altar at the Temple in the Wilderness. (H)

taboulleh: A light bulgur salad. (A)

tabunah: Outdoor oven (*taboon* in Hebrew). (A)

tabyeet: Iraqi overnight chicken; also called *hishwa* ("prized stuffed part") or *tannoori* ("oven chicken"). (A)

tahina: Sesame paste. (A)

tahinli: Sesame bread. (AR)

tartator: Sauce with tahina and lemon. (A)

tavlanim: Popular Israeli spice combination. (H)

teff: Fermented bread starter. (E)

tipat shalav: Drop of milk. (H)

tonno: Tuna. (I)

tzatziki: Armenian cucumber salad. (G)

varnishkes: Noodles, often square or shaped like a bowtie. (Y)

wat: Spicy Ethiopian meat dish. (E)

yalanchi sarna: Stuffed grape leaves. (AR)

za'atar: Popular Middle Eastern spice combination; includes oregano and wild thyme. (A)

zena: Food rationing during the time of austerity. (H)

z'hug: Yemenite hot sauce. (A)

Bibliography

Here is a list of books and articles that were exceptionally helpful in researching this book. (Works cited at the end of each quotation and in the text are, for the most part, not included here.)

Abdalla, Michael. "Bulgur—An Important Wheat Product in the Cuisine of Contemporary Assyrians in the Middle East." Oxford Symposium on Food & Cookery.

Agnon, S. Y. *Betrothed*. New York: Schocken Books, 1966.

Aharoni, Israel. *The Melting Pot: Cooking of Ethnic Groups in Israel*. Tel Aviv: Yedioth Ahronoth Books and Chemed Books, 1998.

Alpert, Carl. *Palestine Between Two Wars*. Washington, D.C.: Zionist Organization of America, 1944.

Antzky, Sherry. *Eating in Jerusalem*. Tel Aviv: Modan, 1992.

Banister, J. T. *A Survey of the Holy Land, Its Geography, History and Destiny*. London: Binns & Goodwin, 1853.

Bar-Adon, Dorothy Ruth (Kahn). *Spring Up, O Well*. London: J. Cape, 1936.

Baratz, Joseph. *A Village by the Jordan*. London: The Harvill Press, 1954.

Ben-Arieh, Yehoshua. *Jerusalem in the 19th Century*. New York: St. Martin's Press, 1984.

Bentwich, Helen. *If I Forget Thee*. London: Paul Elek Books, 1973.

Bentwich, Norman. *Palestine*. London: E. Benn Limited, 1946.

Benvenisti, Meron. *Crusaders in the Holy Land*. New York: Macmillan, 1972.

———. *Sacred Landscape*. Los Angeles: University of California Press, 2000.

Bernstein, Deborah S., ed. *Pioneers and Homemakers: Jewish Women in Pre-State Israel*. New York: State University of New York Press, 1992.

Beth Hillel, Rabbi David d'. *The Travels of Rabbi David d'Beth Hillel: From Jerusalem through Arab Kurdistan, part of Persia and India, 1832*. Tel Aviv: Ktav, 1973.

Bialik Institute. *Milon le-Munhe ha-mitbah Dictionary of Kitchen Terms*. Jerusalem: 1938. (In Hebrew, English, and German.)

Board, Barbara. *Newsgirl in Palestine*. London: M. Joseph, Ltd., 1937.

Cooper, John. *Eat and Be Satisfied: A Social History of Jewish Food*. London: Jason Aronson, Inc., 1993.

Cornfeld, Lilian. *How to Cook in Wartime*. Tel Aviv: W. Schussler, 1943.

Cornfeld, Lilian. *Israeli and International Cookery*. Tel Aviv: G. Cornfeld, 1978.

Davis, Moshe. *America and the Holy Land, With Eyes Toward Zion*. Westport, Conn.: Praeger, 1995.

Dayan, Ruth, and Helga Dudman. *And Perhaps . . . The Story of Ruth Dayan*. New York: Harcourt Brace Jovanovich, 1973.

Elon, Amos. *Herzl*. New York: Holt, Rinehart and Winston, 1975.

———. *The Israelis: Founders and Sons*. Holt, Rinehart and Winston, 1971.

Finn, Elizabeth Anne McCaul. *A Home in the Holy Land*. New York: Ty Crowell & Co., 1882.

Fishkoff, Sue. "Pressing Ahead." *Jerusalem Post International Edition,* December 2, 1995.

Futterer, Antonia Fraser. *Palestine Speaks*. Los Angeles, Calif.: A. F. Futterer, 1931.

Ganor, Avi, and Ron Malberg. *Taste of Israel: A Mediterranean Feast*. Tel Aviv: Galahad, 1993.

Goldberg, Ruth L. Polhemus. *I Saw Israel: An American Reports*. New York: Exposition Press, 1955.

Gruber, Ruth. *Israel Without Tears*. New York: Current Books, Inc., 1950.

Gruber, Ruth. *Raquela: A Woman of Israel*. New York: Coward, McCann & Geoghegan, 1978.

Haskell, Guy H. *From Sofia to Jaffa: The Jews of Bulgaria and Israel*. Detroit, Mich.: Wayne State University Press, 1994.

Heuberger, Georg. *The Rothschilds: A European Family*. Frankfurt am Main: Jan Thorbecke Verlag, 1994.

Herman, Zvi. *The River and the Grain*. Tel Aviv: Herzl Press, 1988.

Hrathern, Ernst. *Going Home*. Indianapolis: The Bobbs-Merrill Company, 1938.

Johnson, Sarah Barclay. *Hadji in Syria* or *Three Years in Jerusalem*. New York: Arno Press, 1977.

Jordan, Ruth. *Daughter of the Waves: Memories of Growing Up in Pre-War Palestine*. New York: Taplinger Publishing Company, 1983.

Kaufman, Sybil. *The Wonders of a Wonder Pot*. Tel Aviv: JNIV, 1973.

Keith, Marion. *Under the Grey Olives*. New York: George H. Doran Company, 1927.

Khoury, Heneine B. *Glimpses Behind the Veil*. London: Sampson, Low, Harston & Co., 1935.

Laqueur, Walter. *History of Zionism*. New York: Schocken Books, 1989.

Levin, Marlin. *Balm in Gilead: The Story of Hadassah*. New York: Schocken Books, 1973.

Light, Henry. *Travels in Egypt, Nubia, Holy Land, Mount Lebanon, and Cyprus, in the Year 1814*. London: Rodwell and Martin, 1818.

Loewe, Louis, ed. *Diaries of Sir Moses and Lady Montefiore*. London: The Jewish Historical Society of England, 1983.

Ludwig, Emil. *On Mediterranean Shores*. London: G. Allen and Y. Unwin, 1929.

Lyons Bar-David, Molly. *The Israeli Cookbook*. New York: Crown Publishers, 1964.

Magnes, Beatrice L. *Episodes: A Memoir*. Berkeley, Calif.: Judah L. Magnes Memorial Museum, 1977.

Ma'oz, Moshe, ed. *Studies on Palestine During the Ottoman Period*. Jerusalem: The Magnes Press, 1975.

Margoliouth, Moses. *A Pilgrimage to the Land of My Fathers*. London: Richard Bentley, 1850.

Marks, Copeland. *Sephardic Cooking*. New York: Donald I. Fine, Inc., 1992.

Marmorosch, A. *Old and New Places in Palestine*. Jerusalem: Self-published, 1946.

Maxwell, Donald. *The Last Crusade*. New York: John Lane Co., 1920.

Meir, Golda. *My Life*. New York: G. P. Putnam's Sons, 1975.

Melville, Herman. *Journal of a Visit to Europe and the Levant*. Westport, Conn.: Greenwood Press, 1976.

Meyer, Erna. *How to Cook in Palestine*. Tel Aviv: H. N. Z. Palestine Federation of Wizo, 1936. (In Hebrew, English, and German.)

Mikes, George. *Milk and Honey: Israel Explored*. London: A. Deutsch, 1959.

Mintz, Sidney L. *Sweetness and Power: The Place of Sugar in Modern History.* New York: Viking Books, 1985.

Montefiore, Lady Judith. *Private Journal of a Visit to Egypt and Palestine.* London: Joseph Rickerby, 1836.

Okun, Jodi, and Beth Roth, eds. *Tastefully Yours.* Kearny, Nebr.: Cookbooks by Morris Press, 1997.

Perez, Pascal. *North African Cooking.* Tel Aviv: Bayit Va-Gan Publishing Co., 1983.

Perry, Charles. "Couscous and Its Cousins." Oxford Symposium on Food & Cookery, 1989.

Perry, Charles. "Grain Cooking Tales from the Bulgur Belt." *Los Angeles Times,* January 27, 1994.

Perry, Charles. "Pitta Patter." *The Journal of Gastronomy* 1, no. 3 (winter 1985).

Perry, Charles. "Judhah and Lauzinaj: Or, What to Order in Ninth-Century Baghdad." Oxford Symposium on Food & Cookery, 1991.

Perry, Charles. "The Taste for Layered Bread among the Nomadic Turks and the Central Asian Origins of Baklava." In *Culinary Cultures of the Middle East,* edited by Sami Zubaida. London: I. B. Tauris Publishers, 1996.

Rivka, Esther. *Shock Absorption: A Survival Guide for Living in Israel.* Israel: Shock Absorption Press, 1990.

Robinson, Edward. *Biblical Researches in Palestine, Mount Sinai, and Arabia Petraea.* New York: Arno Press, 1977.

Rogers, Mary Eliza. *Domestic Life in Palestine.* London: Bell and Daldy, 1862.

Sachar, Howard. *History of Israel.* New York: Alfred A. Knopf, Inc., 1996.

St. George Antiochian Orthodox Church, ed. *Gourmet Middle Eastern Cuisine.* Flint, Mich.: C. J. Koory & Associates, 1991.

St. John, Robert. *Tongue of the Prophets: The Life Story of Eliezer Ben Yehuda.* Westport, Conn.: Greenwood Press, 1972.

Salaman, Redcliffe N. *Palestine Reclaimed: Letters from a Jewish Officer in Palestine.* London: G. Routledge & Sons, Ltd., 1920.

Schur, Nathan. *Jerusalem in Pilgrims' and Travellers' Accounts.* Jerusalem: Ariel Pub. House, 1980.

Schwartz, Oded. *In Search of Plenty: A History of Jewish Food.* London: Kyle Cathie Ltd., 1992.

Sered, Susan Starr. "Food and Holiness: Cooking as a Sacred Act Among Middle-Eastern Jewish Women." *Anthropological Quarterly* 61, no. 3 (July 1988).

Shepard, Judith, and Alvin Rosenfeld. *Ticket to Israel.* New York: Rinehart & Co., 1952.

Smith, George A. et al. *Correspondence of Palestine Tourists Comprising a Series of Letters.* New York: Arno Press, 1977.

Thalmann, Naftali. "Introducing Modern Agriculture into Nineteenth-Century Palestine: The German Templars." In *The Land that Became Israel,* edited by Ruth Kark. New Haven, Conn.: Yale University Press, 1990.

Twicken, Esther, ed. *Hadassah Israel Cooks.* Jerusalem: Hadassah-Israel, 1991.

Valero, Rina. *Delights of Jerusalem.* Tel Aviv: Nahar, 1985.

Wigoder, Devorah. *The Garden of Eden Cookbook.* San Francisco, Calif.: Harper & Row Publishers, 1988.

Wilson, Derek. *Rothschild: A Story of Wealth and Power.* London: Andre Deutsch Limited, 1988.

Wolfert, Paula. *Mediterranean Grains and Greens.* New York: Harper Collins, 1998.

Wright, Thomas. *Early Travels in Palestine.* London: H. G. Bohn, 1948.

Bibliography

Index

Index

Index

Illustration Credits

The illustrations reproduced in this book were provided with the permission and courtesy of the following individuals and organizations:

Israeli Ministry of Tourism: ii, 39, 213, 223, 270, 277, 278, 321, 374, 391
Central Zionist Archives, Jerusalem: 3
Municipality of Jerusalem: 4
Library of Congress Prints and Photographs Division: 14, 68, 126, 157, 178, 237, 254, 388
Jerusalem Foundation: 19
American Jewish Joint Distribution Committee: 22, 34, 263, 293, 371
Hadassah, The Women's Zionist Organization of America, Inc.: 24, 26, 154, 185, 204, 294, 335, 341
Dalia Vardi: 43
Dalia Carmel: 45, 47, 83, 85, 131, 181, 244, 251, 265, 332, 369
Jessica Hirsch: 46, 59, 97, 113, 139, 190, 322
Peggy Pearlstein: 49, 319
David Harman: 51
Pearl Nathan: 70, 152, 203
Bronwyn Dunne: 72, 208, 222, 234, 258, 260
Allan Gerson: 90, 142, 143, 197, 230, 280, 312, 361,
Nelli Sheffer: 95, 314
Gariwaany Hamdy: 98
Peter Anderson: 127
Rafi Magnes: 137
Tzivia and Yosef Gamlieli: 142
Ora Matalan: 145
Eve Lindenblatt: 151
Eitan Raz: 165, 359
Rafi Magnes: 219
Pamela Loval: 284
Ilan Oppenheimer: 297
Alfred Bernheim, Israel Museum: 301
Carpenter Collection, Library of Congress: 306
Randy Goldman: 308
Celia Regev: 344
Valentine Vester: 355
Dan Hotel Corporation: 379

All other illustrations are from the collection of the author.

A Note About the Author

Joan Nathan was born in Providence, Rhode Island. She graduated from the University of Michigan with a master's degree in French literature. For three years she lived in Israel, where she worked for Mayor Teddy Kollek of Jerusalem. In New York, she co-founded the Ninth Avenue Food Festival. She then went on to earn a master's in public administration from Harvard University. Ms. Nathan currently contributes articles on international ethnic food and special holiday features to the *New York Times, Food and Wine, Hadassah, Gourmet,* and the Los Angeles Times Syndicate. In addition to her several other books, she is the author of *Jewish Cooking in America,* which won both the James Beard Award and the IACP/Julia Child Cookbook of the Year Award. She is the host of the PBS national television series *Jewish Cooking in America with Joan Nathan,* based on the book. Ms. Nathan lives in Washington, D.C., with her husband, Allan Gerson, and their three children.

A Note on the Type

This book was set in a "schoolbook" version of the well-known Monotype face Bembo. The original Bembo was cut for the celebrated Venetian printer Aldus Manutius by Francesco Griffo, and first used in Pietro Cardinal Bembo's *De Aetna* of 1495. Schoolbook Bembo was introduced by Monotype in the 1930s.

Composed by North Market Street Graphics, Lancaster, Pennsylvania

Printed and bound by Quebecor Printing, Fairfield, Pennsylvania

Designed by Ralph L. Fowler